UNIVERSITY OF CAMBRIDGE

ORIENTAL PUBLICATIONS

NO. 8

FINANCIAL ADMINISTRATION UNDER THE T'ANG DYNASTY

UNIVERSITY OF CAMBRIDGE
ORIENTAL PUBLICATIONS PUBLISHED FOR THE
FACULTY OF ORIENTAL STUDIES

1 *Averroes' Commentary on Plato's Republic*, edited and translated by E. I. J. ROSENTHAL

2 *FitzGerald's 'Salaman and Absal'*, edited by A. J. ARBERRY

3 *Ihara Saikaku: The Japanese Family Storehouse*, translated and edited by G. W. SARGENT

4 *The Avestan Hymn to Mithra*, edited and translated by ILYA GERSHEVITCH

5 *The Fusūl al-Madanī of al-Fārābī*, edited and translated by D. M. DUNLOP

6 *Dun Karm, Poet of Malta*, texts chosen and translated by A. J. ARBERRY; introduction, notes and glossary by P. GRECH

7 *The Political Writings of Ogyū Sorai*, by J. R. MCEWAN

8 *Financial Administration under the T'ang Dynasty*, by D. C. TWITCHETT

9 *Neolithic Cattle-Keepers of South India: a Study of the Deccan Ashmounds*, by F. R. ALLCHIN

10 *The Japanese Enlightenment: a Study of the Writings of Fukuzawa Yukichi*, by CARMEN BLACKER

11 *Records of Han Administration*, vol. I, *Historical Assessment*, by MICHAEL LOEWE

12 *Records of Han Administration*, vol. II, *Documents*, by MICHAEL LOEWE

13 *The Language of Indrajit of Orchā: a Study of Early Braj Bhāsā Prose*, by R. S. MCGREGOR

14 *Japan's First General Election 1890*, by R. H. P. MASON

ALSO PUBLISHED FOR THE FACULTY

Archaeological Studies in Szechwan, by T.-K. CHENG

CAMBRIDGE ORIENTAL SERIES

1 *Modern Arabic Poetry: an Anthology*, by A. J. ARBERRY

2 *Essays and Studies presented to Stanley Arthur Cook*, edited by D. WINTON THOMAS

3 *Khotanese Buddhist Texts*, by H. W. BAILEY

4 *The Battles of Coxinga*, by DONALD KEENE

6 *Studies in Caucasian History*, by V. MINORSKY

FINANCIAL ADMINISTRATION UNDER THE T'ANG DYNASTY

BY

D. C. TWITCHETT

*Professor of Chinese in the
University of Cambridge*

SECOND EDITION

CAMBRIDGE

AT THE UNIVERSITY PRESS

1970

Published by the Syndics of the Cambridge University Press
Bentley House, 200 Euston Road, London, N.W.1
American Branch: 32 East 57th Street, New York, N.Y. 10022

First Edition © Cambridge University Press 1963

Second Edition © Cambridge University Press 1970

Standard Book Number: 521 07823 7

First published 1963
Second Edition 1970

First printed in Great Britain at the University Press, Cambridge
Reprinted by photolithography in Great Britain by Bookprint Limited, Crawley, Sussex

PREFACE TO THE FIRST EDITION

This book was originally written in 1953 as a doctoral dissertation for the University of Cambridge. In revising it for publication I was faced with the alternatives of either writing a completely new work or leaving it in its original form with a few additions and some alterations bringing it into line with more recent research and new documents published since its completion. Considerations of time led me to take the latter course.

The topical arrangement of chapters was dictated by the original design of the thesis, which was to have been an introduction and commentary to an integral translation of the Financial Monograph (*Shih-huo chih*) of the *Chiu T'ang-shu*. The difficulty and expense of including this translation in the present volume have forced me to publish the introductory matter alone.

In one field I have made no attempt to give a complete and systematic account of recent work. This is the study of the MSS. from Tun-huang and Turfan. The availability of microfilms of the Stein MSS. in the British Museum, and more recently the publication of the many unique MS. fragments discovered by Count Otani's expeditions, have given a new perspective on financial and land policy at the lowest levels, and these deserve separate treatment. I intend therefore to devote a second volume to this aspect of T'ang institutions.

I have deliberately confined myself to considerations of state financial policy, to the exclusion of any discussion of the economic history of the period in the broadest sense. It is quite obvious that the T'ang witnessed great changes in agricultural techniques, in the exploitation of marginal lands, and development of mineral resources, the growth of industry and trade and of the economic and social influence of merchants and artisans, a great increase in the use of money and vastly increased circulation of commodities and currency, and very extensive shifts of population. These changes were of course reflected in government financial policy, and cannot be entirely left out of the picture, but they again require separate treatment. They also present a much less tractable problem for the historian, since the institution-alised bureaucratic histories of China, to which government finance was a matter of prime importance, pay economic problems as we understand them scant attention.

Even within the broad category of state finances the available source material has serious shortcomings. The official histories were essentially court-centred works, and thus we are very well informed on the highest levels of administrative activity, which were conducted at the capital, but given little information on affairs in the provinces, where the policies dictated by the central government were actually enforced. A result of this is that whereas we can draw up an excellent picture of taxation policy which was the concern of the central authorities, we know very little about government expenditure, most of which was made in the provinces, or about the very important question of labour services which were essentially a matter for local arrangement, and in general it may be said that the material at our disposal stresses theory and general policy pronouncements rather than actual everyday practice. This of course conforms precisely with the aims of the historians writing in the bureaucratic tradition.

Much of the present work covers ground which has already been worked over by Balázs who, in his articles 'Beiträge zur Wirtschafts-geschichte der T'ang-Zeit' published in 1931–3, produced for the first time a work of western sinology dealing with economic history at a level comparable with ordinary historical standards. His work marked a major advance in the interpretation of medieval Chinese society. However, bearing in mind the immense advances which have been made during the past three decades in the study of T'ang institutions, especially by Japanese sinologists, whose early works were not con-sulted by Balázs, I feel that a new study of this very important subject is by no means superfluous.

Readers will at once recognise the debt which I owe to the labours of two generations of Japanese and Chinese scholars who have trans-formed out of all recognition the picture of medieval Chinese society currently accepted thirty years ago. If this volume does no more than introduce to the western reader some of the results of their researches, it will have fulfilled a very useful purpose.

D.C.T.

LONDON
22 October 1959

PREFACE TO THE SECOND EDITION

I have taken the opportunity in this Second Edition to correct a number of minor errors and to make some slight changes in the text and notes, but the body of the book remains substantially the same as in the First Edition.

Much has been published in this field since 1959, when the original manuscript was completed. It would have necessitated extensive re-writing to incorporate the results of this recent research into the text and notes, and rather than do this I have summarized in a Postscript the major contributions to the subject to have appeared down to 1968.

D.C.T.
Cambridge 1969

CONTENTS

APPENDIX III

APPENDIX IV

APPENDIX V

MAPS

ABBREVIATIONS

Further details about the books and journals below
are given in the Bibliography

BSOAS	*Bulletin of the School of Oriental and African Studies.*
Code	*Ku T'ang-lü shu-i.*
CTS	*Chiu T'ang-shu.*
CTW	*Ch'üan T'ang wen.*
CYYY	*Kuo-li chung-yang yen-chiu yüan Li-shih yü-yen yen-chiu so chi-k'an.*
Ennin's Diary	*Nittō guhō junrei gyōki.*
HTS	*Hsin T'ang-shu.*
MSOS	*Mitteilungen des Seminars für Orientalische Sprachen ʒu Berlin.*
PSLT	*Po-shih liu-t'ieh shih-lei-chi.*
RGG	*Ryō-no-gige.*
RSG	*Ryō-no-shūge.*
STCSKS	*Shan-t'ang chün-shu k'ao-so.*
TCTC	*Tʒu-chih t'ung-chien.*
TFYK	*Ts'e-fu yüan-kuei.*
THY	*T'ang hui-yao.*
TLT	*T'ang liu-tien.*
TPKC	*T'ai-p'ing kuang-chi.*
TPYL	*T'ai-p'ing yü-lan.*
TT	*T'ung-tien.*
TTCLC	*T'ang ta chao-ling chi.*
WHTK	*Wen-hsien t'ung-k'ao.*
WYYH	*Wen-yüan ying-hua.*
YHCHC	*Yüan-ho chün-hsien t'u-chih.*

MANUSCRIPTS RECOVERED FROM TUN-HUANG

P	Fonds Pelliot Chinois Touen-houang, Bibliothèque Nationale.
S	Stein Collection, British Museum.

LIST OF THE T'ANG EMPERORS

Kao-tsu	618–26	Te-tsung	779–805
T'ai-tsung	626–49	Shun-tsung	805
Kao-tsung	649–83	Hsien-tsung	805–20
Chung-tsung	684 (deposed)	Mu-tsung	820–4
Jui-tsung	684–90 (deposed)	Ching-tsung	824–7
Wu empress	690–705 (usurped throne,	Wen-tsung	827–40
established Chou dynasty)		Wu-tsung	840–6
Chung-tsung	705–10 (restored)	Hsüan-tsung	846–59
Jui-tsung	710–12 (restored)	I-tsung	859–73
Hsüan-tsung	712–56	Hsi-tsung	873–88
Su-tsung	756–62	Chao-tsung	888–904
Tai-tsung	762–79	Ching-tsung	904–7

PROVINCE NAMES

Some T'ang provinces were commonly known by alternative names:

Tien-te chün: Feng-chou tu-fang-yü shih.
I-ch'eng chün: Cheng-hua chieh-tu shih.
Chung-wu chün: Ch'en-hsü chieh-tu shih.
Hsüan-wu chün: Pien-sung chieh-tu shih.
Wu-ning chün: Hsü-ssu chieh-tu shih.
Huai-hsi: Ts'ai-chou chieh-tu shih.
P'ing-lu chün: Tzu-ch'ing chieh-tu shih.
Chao-i chün: Tse-lu chieh-tu shih.
Huai-chou: Ho-yang san-ch'eng chieh-tu shih.
Ch'eng-te chün: Heng-chi chieh-tu shih and Ts'ang-ching chieh-tu shih
    (Heng-chi occupied the west and Ts'ang-ching the east of the province).
I-wu chün: I-ting chieh-tu-shih.

Names of T'ang provinces are hyphenated in the text. Unhyphenated provincial names are those of modern provinces used for convenient regional descriptions.

WEIGHTS AND MEASURES

(*a*) Length

    10 *tsun* = 1 *ch'ih* (slightly less than English foot).

    5 *ch'ih* = 1 *pu* (double pace).

    10 *ch'ih* = 1 *chang*.

    1800 *ch'ih* = 1 *li* (approx. $\frac{1}{3}$ English mile).

(*b*) Area

    1 *mou* = a strip one *pu* wide by 240 *pu* long.

    100 *mou* = 1 *ch'ing*.

(*c*) Capacity

    3 *sheng* = 1 [*ta-*]*sheng* (the normal measure).

    10 [*ta-*]*sheng* = 1·[*ta-*]*tou*.

    10 [*ta-*]*tou* = 1 *hu*.

    1 *hu* = 1 *shih* (approx. $1\frac{3}{4}$ bushels).

(*d*) Weight

    3 *liang* = 1 [*ta-*]*liang* (the normal measure).

    16 [*ta-*]*liang* = 1 *chih* (approx. $1\frac{1}{2}$ English lb.).

For further details see Balázs, 'Beiträge', *MSOS*, 36 (1933), pp. 49 ff.

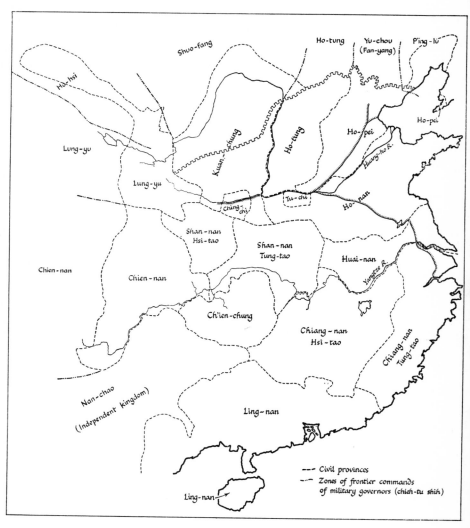

Map 1. Provincial boundaries in 742.

At this date civil provinces had no centralised administration, and the frontier governors no territorial civil jurisdiction.

Until 733 Shan-nan hsi-tao and Shan-nan tung-tao formed the single province of Shan-nan; Chiang-nan hsi-tao, Chiang-nan tung-tao and Ch'ien-chung formed the single province of Chiang-nan; the Metropolitan Districts Ching-chi and Tu-chi formed parts of Kuan-chung and Ho-nan respectively.

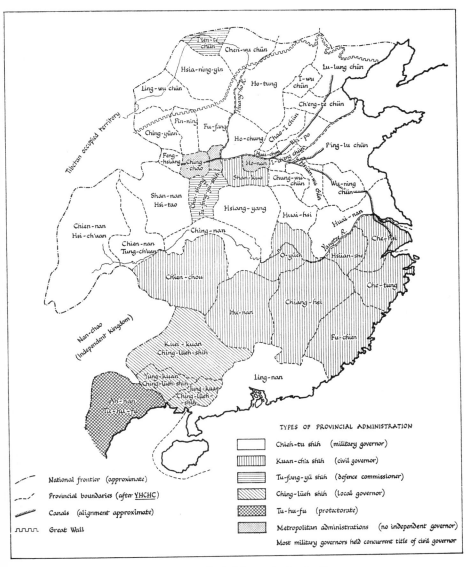

Map 2. Provincial boundaries in 810.

Some provinces were commonly known by alternative names (see note on Province-Names).

TYPES OF PROVINCIAL ADMINISTRATION

Chieh-tu shih (military governor)

Kuan-ch'a shih (civil governor)

Tu-fang-yü shih (defence commissioner)

Ching-lüeh shih (local governor)

Tu-hu-fu (protectorate)

Metropolitan administrations (no independent governor)

Most military governors held concurrent title of civil governor

--- National frontier (approximate)

--- Provincial boundaries (after YHCHC)

Canals (alignment approximate)

Great Wall

CHAPTER I

LAND TENURE

During the T'ang dynasty, and indeed until our own day, China was a predominantly agrarian society. In spite of the great expansion of trade and industry which characterised the period, the land remained the major means of production and thus the chief source of revenue. At the same time land-ownership was the key to individual power, for the land was not only the chief means of production, but also the principal means by which the labour of others could be exploited. A land-owner could obtain a strong hold over his tenants and easily reduce them to the status of dependants. Landed property was also the safest and most conservative, though by no means the most profitable, method of investing wealth. Thus there arose a continual struggle between the government, which sought to keep control over land tenure and to ensure that land remained in the hands of those over whom the tax-collector could exercise his authority on the one hand, and on the other the more prosperous and powerful elements of the people who sought to accumulate lands for their own advantage.

Traditionally,[1] all the lands of the empire were considered theoretically as belonging to the emperor, but by the beginning of the T'ang dynasty there was a strong and ever-increasing movement towards the recognition of the right of private possession of landed property. However, when the T'ang finally unified the empire they refused to recognise this development and adopted a rigid system of state-controlled land tenure which was directly opposed to the spirit of the times.

This was the *chün-t'ien* system which, like so much else in the institutions of the T'ang, had been developed under the barbarian dynasties of northern China during the preceding period of division.[2] It had been enforced for the first time in 486 by the emperor Hsiao-wen Ti of the Northern Wei, and was based on a scheme submitted by his minister Li An-shih.[3] The system bore certain resemblances to the land policy imposed under the Chin,[4] sharing the main objective of the older system of allocating lands on a broad social basis to encourage its exploitation. With modifications of detail, the *chün-t'ien* system was retained by the Northern Ch'i, Northern Chou, and Sui dynasties in their turn,[5] and from the latter was inherited by the T'ang.

The principle of the system was that each married couple[6] was entitled to a grant of land from the state for the duration of their working life. This land remained the property of the state, and was returnable when the couple reached an age at which they were no longer regarded as fully productive.[7] While the recipients held this land, they fell under the obligation of paying taxes and labour services in return.[8] Since money was little used under the northern dynasties, these taxes were paid in natural products.[9] One tax known as *tsu* was paid in grain, which was used to supply the needs of the armies and the capital and to pay official salaries. Another known as *tiao* was paid in cloth, which was the standard medium of exchange in this economically backward region.[10]

In many cases the cloth which was collected for the tax in kind was silk, and this added complication to the system of land grants since sericulture requires the cultivation of mulberries or other suitable trees to provide food for the silkworms, and such trees had to be planted permanently. It was not possible to grant land for this purpose on exactly the same basis as ordinary arable land, and the administration were forced to incorporate two separate types of tenure within their system. Tenure of arable land granted use and occupation of the lands for a specified period, at the expiry of which it reverted to the state and was granted afresh to other entitled persons. Such land was called 'open field' (*lu-t'ien*) under the Northern Wei, and 'personal share land' (*k'ou-fen t'ien*) under the T'ang. The tenure of lands planted with mulberries, on the other hand, was made hereditary within the family of the occupier, subject to a limitation of the total size of their holdings. Such land was at first known as 'mulberry field' (*sang-t'ien*) and later as 'land held in perpetuity' (*yung-ye* or *shih-ye*).[11]

Silk, however, was not the textile product in all areas. In much of the north-west and all of southern China the common textile was hemp. In such areas the Northern Ch'i and later dynasties made grants of land for the cultivation of hemp, and such lands known as 'hemp field' (*ma-t'ien*) were granted on the same hereditary tenure as mulberry fields.[12] There seems to have been no reason for this other than a desire for uniformity, and possibly the demand for a more permanent tenure of some lands in these less favoured areas. The result of this concession was very serious, for since hemp was grown as an annual crop, the original distinction of the two types of tenure lost its connection with the different needs of annual and permanent culture, and its *raison d'être* founded on agricultural technique. The two types of tenure were both applied to arable land, and this became a fatal weakness in the system as a whole.

The size of the land grants was generally large, and the nominal grant envisaged under the Northern Chou was almost seven times as large as the average farm holding in twentieth-century China.[13] The principal object of the scheme appears to have been the encouragement of the cultivation of as large an area as possible during a period of serious population decline in northern China.[14] At the same time, as is clear from the memorial in which Li An-shih set out his original scheme, it was also intended to limit the accumulation of vast estates by the great aristocratic families, and thus to prevent the appearance of influential territorial magnates powerful enough to defy the central government.[15] In this respect it was foredoomed to failure since the officials whose duty it was to enforce the system were the very people who were most interested in consolidating their social and economic position by building up landed properties, and such policies of limitation had already been proved unenforceable under the Later Han.

The modifications which the system underwent during the century and a half before its adoption by the T'ang reflected to a limited extent the changes in social conditions which were gathering momentum. For example, grants of land in respect of slaves were abandoned when the latter ceased to be a major factor in agricultural production,[16] and in the same way grants in respect of cattle also ceased when the foreign dynasties of nomadic origin came to an end.[17] However, in its essentials the land system adopted by the T'ang and incorporated in the *Land Statutes* in 624 was the same as that of the Northern Wei, although the social and economic circumstances in which it was now to be enforced were vastly different from those for which the primitive system had been devised.

The land law of early T'ang times has been preserved in considerable detail. The general administrative rules on the subject were laid down in the *Land Statutes* (*T'ien-ling*). Various articles in the *Code* provided sanctions to be used in the case of certain specific breaches of these rules,[18] and a general provision covered other infringements of the *Statutes*.[19] All these rules are translated in full in part I of the appendix

3

to the present chapter. The basic provisions of the system were as follows:

(*a*) Every male between the ages of 18 and 60 was to be granted 100 *mou* of land (about 13·3 acres). Of this 80 *mou* was to be 'personal share land' and 20 *mou* 'land held in perpetuity'.[20]

(*b*) Old men of over 60 years of age and disabled persons were entitled to 40 *mou*. Such land was 'personal share land'—at least after 737.[21] Persons in this category were not liable to taxation, but were responsible for their own support.

(*c*) Widows were granted 30 *mou* on similar grounds. In cases where they acted as head of household, that is when there was no taxable male in the family, they were entitled to a further 20 *mou*. This allowance for the head of household seems later to have been extended to members of other non-taxable personal categories.[22]

(*d*) Under the *Statutes* of 624, personal share land reverted to the state when the occupier reached the age of 60, while land held in perpetuity was transferred to his legal heirs on his death.[23] The *Statutes* of 737, however, incorporated a provision that lands held in perpetuity had to become part of the personal share land of the inheritor. This was presumably a device to prevent lands becoming truly hereditary, but this ruling tacitly abandoned the distinction between the two forms of tenure based on the different types of cultivation.

(*e*) Districts where there was enough land for the full legal entitlement of land to be distributed were classified as broad localities (*k'uan-hsiang*). Those where land was inadequate were classed as restricted localities (*hsia-hsiang*), and in such areas grants of personal share lands were halved, and certain other restrictions applied.[24] Some similar distinction had existed under the Sui dynasty.[25] It is clear evidence that the system was now being enforced in regions suffering from comparative over-population.[26]

(*f*) Merchants and artisans, the non-productive classes of traditional Chinese economic theory, were to be given small grants of land. However, in restricted localities (where the great majority of them lived) they were not entitled to any land at all.[27]

(*g*) Officials received large grants of land in perpetuity in accordance with their rank. These lands had to be purchased if they were held in a restricted locality.[28] Wang Kuo-wei suggested that this was merely a nominal right,[29] while Maspero contended that they had to be purchased in any locality,[30] but neither adduces any convincing proof. Whatever the truth may be, the other lands appertaining to official posts were certainly no fiction. These were in two categories, lands pertaining to office (*chih-fen-t'ien*), and lands of the public administration (*kung-chieh-t'ien*).[31] These lands were not, however, held personally by the official, but were attached to established offices. The produce from the lands pertaining to office formed part of the official salary, while that from the lands of the public administration provided for the up-keep of public buildings and similar expenses.[32]

(*h*) Buddhist and Taoist monks and nuns were entitled to reduced grants of land.[33] Since monks and nuns were exempt from taxation, such grants were made purely for their personal maintenance, and presumably were held and administered by the monastic communities.

(*i*) Bondsmen in the category *kuan-hu*[34] were to be granted one half of the personal share land due to a free man.[35] Those in the category *tsa-hu*[36] were granted the same amount of land as a free man. Since the former were not allowed a household register of their own, the nominal title to these lands must have been vested in the office under whose control they came.

(*j*) All persons were allowed a small additional amount of land in per-petuity for their house and garden.[37]

(*k*) A redistribution of lands was to be made annually by the county magistrate (*hsien-ling*), acting on detailed local information provided by the village headmen (*li-cheng*).[38]

(*l*) Nobody might own more than the amount of land to which he was legally entitled, and a sanction was provided for this rule in the *Code*.[39]

(*m*) The disposal of land was restricted. All sale of lands had to be carried out under official control,[40] and was allowed only under certain special conditions.[41] Leasing and mortgage of lands was also generally prohibited, although it was permitted in the case of lands presented as a gift by the emperor, and in the case of the lands in perpetuity owned by officials.[42] While a person might not acquire more than his legal entitlement of lands, if he resided in a restricted locality he was allowed to purchase additional lands up to the amount of his full legal entitlement as in a broad locality.[43] These rules, too, were covered by sanctions in the *Code*.[44]

This was the over-rigid system of land tenure which the T'ang sought to impose upon their newly consolidated empire in 624. The difficulties of enforcing it in regions with diverse physical environments and at varying stages of economic development must have been in-superable. Knowing as we do how dead laws were transmitted from generation to generation, and considering how little reference is made to the system in the historical writings of early T'ang, it once seemed not unreasonable to dismiss the whole system as a paper scheme which was never widely put into practice. Such an attitude was justified until the discovery at the beginning of this century of the manuscripts from Tun-huang and Turfan, which included a large number of relevant official documents.[45] These bear out the letter of the law with surprising exactness, and provide us with a new picture of T'ang local administrative practice.

The Tun-huang and Turfan Household Registers and the 'Chün-t'ien' Land System

The most important of these documents are a number of household registers (*hu-chi*). These documents were compiled every third year and set forth all the details about each household which had any bearing upon its legal status, its liability for taxation, and its entitlement to lands.[46] Besides being a register of all members of the family, it was also a register of all the lands in the possession of the household.[47] The registers were the basis for the census, and provided the information about every locality (*hsiang*) which was required by the financial administration. They were compiled by the county (*hsien*) authorities, who provided copies to the prefecture and to the central government.[48]

A considerable number of fragments of these documents were recovered from Tun-huang and Turfan, some of them quite long, and some mere scraps of a few lines. They have received a great deal of attention from Chinese and Japanese scholars, who were quick to see their importance, but have attracted little attention in the West.[49] The examples which concern us in discussing the *chün-t'ien* system date from about 690 to 769.[50] There are other examples dating from 891, but these are cast in an entirely different form, and belong to a period when the *chün-t'ien* system had been formally abandoned.[51]

These materials have to be used with caution. Both Tun-huang and Turfan were military outposts in Central Asian oases. Though it is possible that the area was less arid during the middle ages than it is today,[52] the registers themselves show us that many of the fields were bounded by the desert.[53] They also show that the area was covered by a dense irrigation network, for most properties are located by the name of the canal on which they were situated.[54] Under such conditions land must have been very scarce, and the environment anything but typical for China as a whole.

It is most unlikely that administrative methods in such frontier areas were identical with those in China proper. Among other problems, the authorities had to deal with a large non-Chinese element in the population, for many of the surnames found in the documents normally

6

refer to persons from Sogdiana and Bactria.[55] A mixed population of this type must certainly have had customs regarding land tenure and agricultural techniques widely different from those of the Chinese.

The documents, moreover, date from a period (690–769) when, as we know from other evidence, the rigid *chün-t'ien* system in metropolitan China was rapidly decaying, and being replaced by the recognition of permanent ownership of landed property and by the growth of great estates in private hands.[56] The latest of the registers were also compiled at a time when the Chinese authorities in Tun-huang had been cut off from contact with the central government by the Tibetan invasion of Kansu.[57]

There are thus ample reasons why we might expect these documents to show divergences from the letter of the law. Most surprisingly, the divergences which they contain are very few. The documents are drawn up in exact compliance with the rules in the *Statutes* and edicts on the subject, even down to the position of the seals.[58] The amounts of land to which each household was legally entitled are recorded in precise accordance with the *Land Statutes*.[59] The various changes in the limits of personal age categories which occurred during the eighth century are faithfully reflected in them.[60] Altogether they give the impression of a competent bureaucratic machine in good working order.

A number of features, however, need further consideration. Most of the families whose registers survive possessed very nearly the full amount of lands in perpetuity to which they were entitled,[61] but few held more than a small fraction of their entitlement of personal share land.[62] The extreme local shortage of land was certainly a factor in this situation, but it was more probably the direct result of the contemporary movement towards recognition of hereditary legal rights in landed property. This tendency is recognised by all writers on the legal history of the period. Niida Noboru, who has dealt with the question at some length,[63] concluded that the distinction in law between the two types of tenure tended to become less clear-cut as time went on,[64] and suggested that in cases where less than the legal maximum was held it was obviously to the holder's advantage to register most of his holdings as land in perpetuity in which he had the power of permanent possession and use.[65] Suzuki Shun held the opinion that lands were registered as lands in perpetuity up to the legal limit and that only the surplus holdings were registered as personal share land over which the holder had only the power of possession for a limited period.[66]

However much the distinction between the forms of tenure may have been reduced in practice, it still existed in law, and the law remained live enough to make it worth while to have lands officially registered in the more profitable category. Besides, from frequent mentions in the registers of lands which had reverted to the state (*huan-kung*), returned (*t'ui-t'ien*), or reverted on decease (*ssu-t'ui*), we may deduce the fact that official redistribution of lands was still enforced to some extent.[67] That these lands remained without an owner (presumably they were in the keeping of the local authorities) is evidence that the local land shortage was not extreme. Unfortunately it is not possible, save in a few instances, to tell under what circumstances these lands had reverted to the state.[68] But by no means all came from extinct families, and we thus know that redistribution was still carried on, and that permanent private possession of land was still not yet the universal rule.[69]

Besides the great preponderance of lands in perpetuity, the registers show certain other peculiarities. First, they contain an unbelievably high proportion of women.[70] This is certainly the result of an attempt at evasion of tax and labour service, for all women were tax-exempt. Probably either men have been falsely entered as women, or taxable males have been simply omitted from the lists. If in fact there was not enough land in the district for the full legal entitlements to be granted, men would willingly forgo their rights to a hypothetical land grant in exchange for the tangible advantage of tax exemption. This may, however, have been a purely local situation.[71]

Similar reasons may underlie the very large numbers of persons holding honorific rank (*hsün*).[72] Such ranks were originally granted as a reward for meritorious military service, but by the period when the registers were compiled they had become cheapened.[73] It has been suggested that some at least of the titles in the registers are fraudulent.[74] Such ranks gave the right of tax-exemption. They also carried with them the right to extensive holdings of land,[75] but in none of the existing cases does anyone hold more than a nominal fraction of his entitlement. It is probable that these prescribed amounts, like the sizes of fiefs,[76] represented maximum entitlements, and that the customary grants, where they were made at all, were very much smaller.

The existence of such irregularities proves some laxity among the lower ranks of the administration,[77] but also proves that the land and tax system was still working, at least nominally. People would not have risked the heavy penalties laid down in the *Code* for the falsification of official documents[78] had there been no concrete advantage to be gained by so doing. If we assume that the system was still nominally in force, however, the advantages were considerable. By the registration of their holdings as lands in perpetuity, occupiers gained the right of permanent possession and use of their land, which was the safest form of property in such a disturbed region. False registration as honorific officials or as women gained them not only tax exemption, but exemption from *corvée* labour and from military service, which must have been unusually onerous in a frontier garrison area.

The household registers, then, show us that until 769 the *chün-t'ien* system remained legally in force in the north-western frontier area, and although land grants were not made in accordance with the *Statutes*, redistribution was still practised on a limited scale, and the law was still live enough to make fraud worth while.

The Breakdown of the 'Chün-t'ien' System

With the exception of a few passages in inscriptions[79] the Tun-huang and Turfan documents are the only evidence that the *chün-t'ien* system ever existed save on paper. By the beginning of T'ang times the original aims of the scheme had been forgotten, and the system was looked on simply as a means of limiting the size of land-holdings.[80]

From the very beginning there was difficulty in enforcing it. One major difficulty was the problem of over-population. In Sui times a system of restricted localities had been imposed, under which the entitlement of land was reduced to 20 *mou* per person in congested regions.[81] In 644 the emperor visited a village in the environs of Ch'ang-an where the standard grant was only 30 *mou*, that is one half the legal entitlement for a restricted locality.[82]

The problem of overcrowding was especially severe in the Kuan-chung area. Here, around the capital, there was a great concentration of officials of high rank who were entitled to large holdings of land.[83] These lands, and the large areas which were held by the authorities as lands pertaining to office and lands of the public administration in respect of the officials employed at the capital, put a severe strain on the local economy. To relieve this region, in 636 the government abolished lands pertaining to office, and granted the lands so released to persons who had been forced to migrate from their native villages and had later returned.[84] However, since the rents from these lands had formed a portion of officials' salaries, the system had to be revived in 644 to prevent hardship to officialdom.[85]

The Kuan-chung region was not only the residence of a large proportion of the bureaucracy. It was also the home of many of the great aristocratic families who had ruled China since the Later Han dynasty. In T'ai-tsung's reign (626-49) there were complaints that these families were taking possession of great areas of fertile farmland.[86] The imperial family themselves were among the offenders, and at the very beginning of the dynasty the *Chiu T'ang-shu* records that the heir apparent Chien-ch'êng was accumulating lands and houses.[87] The great Buddhist houses too held large estates from the beginning of the dynasty, and continually increased their holdings through the gifts of pious laymen.[88] The trouble was not confined to Kuan-chung, for in 654 Chia Tun-i took action against rich persons with excessive land-holdings in the Lo-yang area[89] where, again, monastic holdings were very extensive.

One of the chief reasons for this widespread illegal acquisition of landed properties was the inadequacy of the laws governing the *chün-t'ien* system. During the period 624–737 the *Code* appeared in seven editions, and the *Statutes* were revised no less than twelve times.[90] Of the latter we still have fragments of the series of 624,[91] a digest of the series of 719,[92] and a very full abstract of those of 737.[93] In addition we have the complete Japanese statutes in *Ryō-no-gige* and *Ryō-no-shūge* which were modelled on the Chinese series of 651.[94] If these versions are compared it is obvious that, in general, the law incorporated in the *Statutes* remained static throughout the period.[95] Although the century 624–737 witnessed widespread and basic changes in the economic structure of the empire, none of the twelve revisions of the *Statutes* on the *chün-t'ien* system took the slightest heed of them. The case of the laws in the *Code* is even more surprising, for the articles of the *T'ang-lü shu-i* of 737 covering the *chün-t'ien* system were reproduced verbatim in the *Sung hsing-t'ung* of 963,[96] that is some 180 years after the system had been formally abandoned.[97]

Not only did the codifiers take no account of developments in contemporary society, but the very nature of the laws themselves was defective. Although illegal disposal of land and the possession of excessive holdings were punishable offences, there were a number of exceptional circumstances under which they were permissible. In any case the penalties were light, and it must be remembered that many of those who were in a position to break the law and accumulate property were able to benefit under one of the eight classes of legal privilege (*pa-i*), and thus commute the punishment into a money fine.[98] Only when it was too late, in 735, did the government at last impose a heavier penalty for such offences, making them equivalent to disobeying an imperial edict.[99]

The machinery of local administration, too, was unsuitable for the strict enforcement of the laws. The county magistrate (*hsien-ling*), who was nominally responsible, often had to administer a region containing 20,000 persons.[100] His official staff was very small, and had to deal with much petty business, nearly half of it being concerned with criminal matters.[101] In actual practice a great deal of responsibility fell on the village headmen (*li-cheng*). They drew up the lists of land for re-allocation, and prepared the statements (*shou-shih*) on the basis of which the household registers were compiled.[102] Although the magistrate was supposed to supervise land allocation in person,[103] he would inevitably depend upon the headmen's recommendations.

The headman, who thus exercised considerable power, was not a member of the official hierarchy at all, and it is more than probable that the law which he administered to his villagers was in the main customary.[104] Not only was this local administration too weak to oppose the powerful families in their accumulation of land, but it was unsuitable for the enforcement of a uniform system of tenure over the whole empire. This was especially the case in irrigated areas when family skill in the use of water must have been a strong factor in stabilising tenure on a hereditary basis.[105]

Local officials, the very persons who should have enforced the laws, were among the chief offenders. For instance, in T'ai-tsung's reign, Ch'ang-sun Shun-te became prefect of Tse-chou and redistributed a great quantity of fertile land which his predecessors in office had accumulated for themselves.[106]

The *chün-t'ien* system collapsed because, not only was it opposed to the current developments in Chinese society, but it was provided with inadequate sanctions for use against offenders, and was enforced by an administration many of whose members were themselves among the law-breakers.

The Problem of Vagrancy and Migration

Two closely interconnected problems arose from the inadequacy and subsequent breakdown of the *chün-t'ien* system. The first of these was the problem of farmers who, for a variety of reasons, fled from their homes and settled either on vacant lands where they no longer figured on the household registers, or on the great estates, where they became tenant-farmers or labourers. In any case they became families of whom no account was given in the official records, and thus represented a loss of taxation, of available *corvée* labour, and of potential military man-power. The vagrancy problem was most acute in Kuan-chung, and it was precisely in that province, equally vital as an economic and as a strategic area, that the government were most anxious to prevent such losses.[107]

The second problem was the accumulation of land in the hands of the rich and influential. The new owners sometimes gained possession of their holdings by driving out the small land-holders. This could be done by the misuse of official powers, by coercion, by illegal purchase, or by involving the owner in debt. In such cases the establishment of large land-holdings helped to cause vagrancy, but more frequently new estates were built up from land left vacant by farmers who had fled from their homes for other reasons.

The motives which caused this widespread migration are very complex. There was a continuous drift of population to the south from Han times onwards which continued until after the end of the T'ang dynasty, and fluctuated according to the conditions in the north.[108] The south attracted settlers not only because of the vast areas of rich vacant land available for agriculture, but also because it was a centre of commerce and mining.[109] In the troubled times before the Sui conquest this migration included not only farmers, but many members of the great aristocratic clans,[110] and at that period the south was economically further advanced than the north.

Pulleyblank has calculated that between the census of 609 and that of 742 the population of the four northern provinces Kuan-chung, Ho-nan, Ho-pei, and Ho-tung, which had contained 73·5 per cent of the total Chinese population at the earlier date, declined to such a degree that in 742 they only accounted for 53 per cent of the total for the empire. This decline was not merely a relative one. It represents a 28 per cent fall in the numbers of families in the area. During the same period the population of the southern provinces Chiang-nan, Ling-nan, Chien-nan, and Ch'ien-chung, which had previously contained only 12 per cent of the total population, increased very rapidly, and in 742 accounted for 34·2 per cent of the total for the empire. This increase was most marked in the lower Yangtze basin (that is, Chiang-nan, where the increase was almost fivefold) and in Szechuan (that is, Chien-nan, where the population rose two and a half times).[111]

These figures clearly show the north–south migration, but they cannot be taken at their face value. They derive ultimately from the household registers, and thus take into account only those settlers in the south who had been registered and thus had their position legalised. The illegal squatters (*k'o-hu*, etc.) represent a still further increase. On the other hand the dispossessed farmers who remained in the north working as casual labourers or tenant-farmers on great estates were also no longer registered, and the fall in population in the northern region was thus less than it appears.

The government was stubbornly opposed to this movement. It was generally recognised that Kuan-chung was seriously over-populated, and as early as 627 the counsellors advised the emperor to allow the people to migrate elsewhere.[112] But this suggestion was overruled on the grounds that it would denude the vital strategic area of its manpower. The *Code* contains a number of articles covering the cases of persons liable to military and other service who absconded from their homes.[113] Such cases were considered as very grave, and in some instances the death penalty was prescribed.

Some effort was made to relieve the land shortage around the capital. Lands pertaining to office were abolished on at least two occasions,[114] imperial properties were broken up and distributed among the landless,[115] and new land was brought into cultivation.[116] In addition, during the famine years the court frequently transferred to Lo-yang to relieve the strain on the resources of Kuan-chung.[117] Under the Empress Wu the capital was permanently established at Lo-yang, and during this period, in 691, several hundred thousand households were transferred to that area from the region around Ch'ang-an.[118]

The 680's brought an economic crisis to China, and at this time, it seems that the problem of vagrancy assumed dangerous proportions. In 685 Ch'ên Tzu-ang made a complaint about the migration of population from Shantung and the lower Yellow river (Huang-ho) plain.[119] Probably the various campaigns conducted during Kao-tsung's reign were the immediate cause of the problem.[120] In 695 Li Chiao made a memorial on the subject which pointed out that both the desire for a better livelihood and the wish to avoid military service were among the reasons for migration.[121] The Kitan invasion of Ho-pei in 696–8 and the rebellion which broke out in its support undoubtedly caused widespread disorganisation and migration. The brutality with which the rebellion was suppressed caused further disorder and discontent in that area.[122] At the same period we hear of migration being caused by official oppression, not only in the overcrowded province of Kuan-chung,[123] but even in the sparsely peopled province of Shan-nan.[124] In 711 Han Yüan again memorialised the throne on the subject.[125]

Though these memorials are evidence that there was growing official disquiet, none of them suggested any constructive measures which might have alleviated the situation. The earliest[126] effective suggestion for a solution came from Yü-wen Jung[127] who presented his first scheme to the throne in 721.[128] Although its exact terms are not known, his recommendations were passed on to the ministers for discussion, and an edict was promulgated allowing unregistered squatters 100 days in which to give themselves up and either return to their original home or be registered in the place where they had settled.[129] Those who failed to do so were to be rounded up and transported to the frontiers. This severe measure seems not to have been seriously enforced.

In the fifth month of 723 Yü-wen Jung was given an extraordinary appointment as commissioner for encouraging agriculture (ch'üan-nung shih) and given a staff of nineteen executive officers (ch'üan-nung p'an-kuan) who were sent out to every part of the empire to superintend a new scheme,[130] under which unregistered squatters who gave themselves up were to be given exemption from taxes for six years and instead would have to pay only a special 'light tax'.[131] This was a far-sighted measure, for instead of threatening past offenders, it allowed the migrant families to regularise their position on favourable terms.[132] The scheme was a success, and was even popular among the unregistered families,[133] and in 724 Jung was given further staff to assist him and was promoted.[134] Eight hundred thousand households of vagrants and a corresponding quantity of unregistered land were brought back on to the registers.[135] There is some reason to believe that these figures are exaggerated,[136] but if they are correct, these newly registered households accounted for no less than 12 per cent of the total population of 7,069,565 households recorded for 726.[137]

The motives which underlay this policy are not altogether clear. The traditional historians see Yü-wen Jung as the first of a line of oppressive financial specialists who, on the one hand, extorted money from the people to finance the extravagances of Hsüan-tsung,[138] and on the other undermined the authority of the regular bureaucracy.[139] Suzuki Shun recently suggested that it was an attempt to revive the *chün-t'ien* and registration systems, and thus put the finances of the state on a more solid foundation.[140] This is certainly true, but as Pulleyblank has pointed out it is also clear that political motives played almost as important a role.[141]

The policy roused strong opposition within the bureaucracy itself. This opposition was partly the result of resentment among local officials at Yü-wen Jung's being allowed to deal with the problem through special powers, and to override the customary methods of administration. But it was also a manifestation of a deep tension in the ruling class between the old aristocracy (of whom Jung was a representative), and the new class of bureaucratic officials who had risen to power during the latter half of the seventh century through the examination system.[142]

Whereas the position of the great aristocratic clans was already economically secure at the beginning of the dynasty, for the new officials the acquisition of landed property was essential in order to stabilise their economic position. Whether the examination candidates came from the new land-owning class, or whether the new land-owning class was formed by successful examination candidate officials,[143] the newly formed estates were more vital to the career-bureaucrats than to the aristocracy. Jung had already denounced one prominent official for excessive land-holding,[144] and this new scheme threatened not only the officials' lands, but their source of labour, the vagrant farmers.[145] This was the underlying cause of the opposition. At first Yü-wen Jung prevailed in his policy,[146] becoming vice-president of the Board of Finance in 725,[147] but in 727 he and his supporters fell from power.[148] This seems to have brought his scheme to an end, for although he returned to power for a short while in 729 there is no record of his having revived this policy.[149]

In 730 P'ei Yao-ch'ing[150] put forward a more severe scheme for the resettlement of vagrant households on vacant lands, where they would form state-controlled farming communities similar in organisation to military colonies (t'un-t'ien).[151] This scheme seems never to have come to fruition.

The question of vagrancy was not solved by Yü-wen Jung's policies. Admittedly the registers were brought up to date, and the financial administration given a temporary respite. But the opposition which the scheme had provoked should have shown the ruling classes that the chün-t'ien system could never be re-enforced while it was in direct opposition to the interests of the official class itself. In spite of this, however, no move was made to amend the system and introduce taxation laws more suitable to contemporary needs. In 735 an edict was promulgated formally reimposing the chün-t'ien system and providing increased penalties for offences against it,[152] and in 737 the system was again solemnly reproduced in new Statutes.[153]

The Problem of Great Estates

The growth of great land-holdings had long been recognised as one of the principal causes of vagrancy. The edict of 735 which reimposed the chün-t'ien system described its aims as 'to prevent the poor from losing their source of livelihood while the rich and powerful accumulate their lands'.[154] Estate-building was again attacked in an edict of 752, which, although it met with little success, gives us a clear picture of some of the ways by which these lands were obtained.[155] It mentions the taking over of fertile vacant lands 'on loan' from the local authorities, the establishment of 'pasturages' where there were in fact no animals, and illegal purchase disguised either by the falsification of the registers, with official connivance, or by falsely representing the transaction as a mortgage.[156] Not all estates were illegally obtained, however. During Hsüan-tsung's reign there are many instances of landed properties being given in reward for services, and such estates were not only quite legitimate, but could be freely disposed of.[157]

There is no doubt that there were always considerable amounts of land held outside the chün-t'ien system. It is significant that the Statute covering the compilation of the registers of cultivated lands (ch'ing-miao-pu) specifies that they are to include not only lands allocated under the system (shou-t'ien), but also wasteland borrowed temporarily (chieh-huang).[158] There is ample contemporary evidence that the large-scale exploitation of wasteland and hill-land was very common, and was a legitimate way of accumulating land which fell beyond the scope of the *chün-t'ien* re-allocation. Monastic estates were very commonly built up in this way.[159] It has recently been suggested that the term *tzu-t'ien*, which is mentioned in certain Tun-huang MSS., represents such personal lands, but the evidence is not entirely convincing.[160]

Unfortunately, it is difficult to say which regions were most deeply affected by the growth of great land-holdings. Most of the instances of which we hear were in the areas around the two capitals. But this may be simply the result of the disproportionate amount of space which is devoted to the metropolitan regions in the official histories.[161] It may, however, also reflect the concentration in those areas of the wealthy and privileged with connections in the central administration. These estates were for the most part pleasure gardens rather than economic investments,[162] and may perhaps be regarded as the rural counterparts of the city mansions (*chai*), etc. of the nobility.[163] Estates employed for large-scale agriculture were largely concentrated in the south and the Yangtze valley, where *chün-t'ien* tenure certainly never took very deep root, and to a lesser degree in Ho-pei, where society had been seriously unsettled by the Kitan invasions and civil war at the end of the seventh century.[164]

The outbreak of An Lu-shan's rebellion began an entirely new phase of the land problem. It led to a total breakdown of the registration system on which the whole complex of land tenure and taxation had depended.[165] The number of recorded households dropped from nearly 9,000,000 in 755 to less than 2,000,000 in 760.[166] This astonishing decrease is, needless to say, not indicative of a fall in population, but of a decrease in the area controlled by the central administration and of a decline of administrative efficiency. But the rebellion did lead to the virtual depopulation of large areas,[167] and further accelerated the existing population movements from the north.[168]

Under such conditions, with the sudden removal of effective government checks and the vacation of large areas of farmland, estate-building naturally flourished. The government took some steps to check these developments. In 757 they forbade the collection by local officials of tax debts of refugee families from their neighbours who had remained behind.[168a] In 760 the sale of abandoned lands to new owners was forbidden, and the collection of tax debts from neighbouring households prohibited, and local authorities were ordered to rent out the lands, taking the rents in lieu of the outstanding taxes. The original owners could obtain restitution of their property if they returned to their native place.[169] In 763 an edict laid the blame for the great current increase in vagrancy on powerful persons who had taken advantage of the disorder accompanying the rebellion to steal land, and imposed double penalties on offenders.[170]

Such legislation was stillborn. The dynasty survived An Lu-shan's rising only thanks to foreign intervention and to the assistance of powerful military figures who represented the same interests as those for which An Lu-shan himself had stood.[171] In the period immediately following the peace of 763 the authority of the central government was greatly restricted, especially in the provinces. Here, instead of the central administration being able to deal directly with the prefectures, as before 755, it now had to deal with them through the intermediary of the provincial governors. The latter introduced a new combination of military and civilian authority into local administration, and their powers increased steadily, at the expense of central power, until the end of the eighth century. These governors and their subordinate officers sprang in many cases from lowly origins, and to them the acquisition of lands was a means to social and financial security. The extent to which their local power could be abused in this way may be seen from the case of Yen Li, provincial governor of eastern Chien-nan, who, when he was impeached in 809, was found to possess no less than 122 estates.[172]

However, the new military men were not the only social group involved in the building up of new estates during this period. Civil officials in the central administration,[173] local officials both military and civil,[174] eunuchs,[175] and many private persons[176] pursued the same ends. The Buddhist foundations, too, continued to build up great properties.[177] The ownership of estates was thus spread over a much wider section of society than before, and the great landed property became a permanent and widespread feature of Chinese economic and social life.

Such land-holdings were known by a variety of names,[178] the most usual of which was *chuang-yüan*. This term was originally used for a country estate used as a pleasure-ground, and even after it began to be applied to lands held for purely economic purposes, it was still often used in the same way.[179] Such pleasure-resorts were an established feature of the life of the ruling class, and we know of many famous examples in late T'ang times.[180]

The internal organisation of estates at this period has been extensively studied by Katō Shigeshi,[181] Tamai Zehaku[182] and more recently by Sudō Yoshiyuki[183] who has thrown new light on T'ang conditions by comparison with those obtaining under the Sung.

Most *chuang-yüan* were probably fragmented holdings, built up as additional lands became available.[184] This was the case with the monastic holdings of which we have details, but these, accumulated by successive acts of pious charity, were perhaps a special case.[185] Later in the ninth century, we hear of cases where estates were bounded by natural features, such as watersheds and streams.[186] Such holdings were comparatively widespread in Sung times, when they sometimes included several villages, but could never be formed during the T'ang until the anarchic conditions of the late ninth century allowed the use of coercion on a scale impossible under rigid administrative control.[187] Besides the farm land itself, estates often included orchards, vegetable gardens, and mills.[188] The latter were a very profitable means of investment.[189]

The estates were normally worked by tenant-farmers recruited from dispossessed persons and vagrants,[190] by hired hands,[191] and occasionally by slaves.[192] Slaves employed as a labour force were not uncommon, and in one case at least Sung-time tenant-farmers were directly descended from the slaves who had farmed the same lands under the Late T'ang.[193] But the use of slaves was generally uneconomic, and the numbers of slaves owned by individuals very small; other types of semi-dependent persons were more often employed. Usually estates were worked by tenants, known as *chuang-k'o*, the precise relationship of whom with the land-owner is by no means clear. There is no suggestion that under the T'ang there was any tie between the tenant and the land he farmed as in the case of the *tien-hu* of Sung times.[194] However, the link was a very strong one. The *chuang-k'o* became a personal adherent of the estate owner, and in some cases even bore arms on his behalf.[195] The land-owner loaned him his seed, and rations, for which he was normally charged a high interest.[196] The tenant also lived in a house provided by the estate, often in a special tenants' settlement.[197] On a large estate, employing as many as 200 tenant households, such villages might be of a considerable size,[198] and they formed the nucleus of many villages and small towns of later times.[199] Already by late T'ang times some of these settlements were large enough to support their own shopkeepers[200] and innkeepers.[201]

19

The tenants were controlled by the estate's bailiffs[202] who collected their rents (*t'ien-tsu*) on behalf of the landlord. These rents usually represented about half of the crop, and were much heavier than the taxes levied on individual farmers.[203] In addition to this rent in kind (grain), separate levies in other commodities were made,[204] and the tenant was expected to perform certain labour services on behalf of the land-owner such as building and repairs to property.[205]

The owners of such estates had no particular privilege in the matter of taxation. Estates counted as part of the family property for the purpose of assessment of the household levy (*hu-shui*),[206] and were also taxed on an acreage basis for the land levy (*ti-shui*) collected in grain and the green sprout tax (*ch'ing-miao-ch'ien*) collected in cash. Tamai has shown that this rule was applied even to the relatives of the emperor,[207] while it seems that even estates held by the emperor himself were liable to tax.[208]

Two types of estate are worthy of special consideration. The Buddhist monasteries were great land-owners. When Buddhism was suppressed in 846 they were said to have held some tens of millions of *ch'ing* of land.[209] Since this is more than all the registered farmland of the empire a century before[210] this figure is obviously an exaggeration, but the total must have been very large. Among pious laymen, the practice of presenting lands to monasteries as an act of charity was so common that in 713 it had to be prohibited by law.[211] But even afterwards such gifts were constantly made not only by private individuals, but by emperors and members of the imperial household. The support in high places on which the monasteries relied led to an attempt in 811 to have these estates and certain other monastic properties made exempt from taxation.[212] This failed, and they remained technically taxable. However, Niida, who has studied this question closely, is of the opinion that the great temples were powerful enough to resist taxation in practice.[213]

Monastic estates were rented out to tenant-farmers in the same way as ordinary estates. The income was used in part to provide capital for the other monastic financial enterprises such as the pawnshops (*wu-chin tsang*).[214] These institutions were of considerable importance to the monasteries as they, unlike pawnshops owned by laymen, were tax-exempt.[215] Monasteries also commonly established mills.[216]

The position of the monastic communities as land-owners was temporarily altered by the persecution of 846. Vast amounts of confiscated land must have come into the market at this time, and may well have formed the nucleus of the estates built up in the middle ninth century by many provincial officials.[217] The policy of suppression did not, however, remain in force for long, and by the end of the century many of the monasteries had to a considerable extent recovered their losses.[218] By the beginning of the Sung they were once more a major factor in land-ownership.

Considerable lands were also in the possession of the state. The state acquired land in many ways, through confiscation, through land becoming ownerless, through presentation to the throne, and even by purchase.[219] Katō has studied in some detail an organisation, probably part of the imperial household and under the control of the eunuchs, known as the household commissioner for estates (*nei chuang-chai shih*) which administered such properties.[220] These same officials also controlled shops, mills, house property, gardens and tea estates, and salt works.[221] Their lands, in the same way as these miscellaneous properties, were for the most part rented out,[222] though they also provided a convenient source for imperial presentations[223] and were occasionally sold off.[224] These estates were subject to tax, presumably levied on their tenants, since an amnesty of 805 remitted arrears of taxes outstanding on such properties in the metropolitan district.[225] It is certain, moreover, that there were further properties in the possession of the imperial family which did not come under the effective control of the household commissioners for estates.[226]

In general, however, most of the *chuang-yüan* estates were in the hands of private individuals. At the beginning of the eighth century the majority of these were either members of the aristocracy or career bureaucrats. But later, with the breakdown of effective local administration from the centre, the social strata from which the estate-holders were drawn grew wider, and we find military officers, local petty gentry,[227] members of the non-ranking lower bureaucracy, and even merchants, holding estates. By the middle of the ninth century it is clear that the great estate was an accepted feature of rural organisation.

Nevertheless, it would be quite wrong to consider the *chuang-yüan* as a new system of land tenure. Especially misleading is the resemblance to the European manorial system, and to the Japanese *shōen*.[228] Under the T'ang the administration took no legal action whatever to regulate or regularize either the position or the management of such estates. They seem simply to have accepted the growth of such great holdings and recognised the principle of private ownership of land and the right to its disposal as an accomplished fact. But in law the rules of the *chün-t'ien* system remained in force[229] and the doctrine of the emperor's ownership of all land remained unquestioned.

The only attempt made by the government to reimpose rigid control over land tenure was the stillborn scheme of great fields (*ta-t'ien*) proposed by Chao Tsan in 783 as an emergency measure in a time of crisis.[230] This embodied no original ideas and was clearly modelled on the well-fields (*ching-t'ien*) of the *Chou li*. Otherwise, the central government seem to have acquiesced in the growth of private properties, and were able to do so without serious damage to their finances thanks to the *liang-shui* tax reform which divorced the taxation and land-allotment systems.

The *liang-shui* reform, by removing the discrimination between native families and settled vagrants in matters of taxation, also made less urgent the government's concern with the problem of vagrancy. The problem itself remained, however, and was aggravated by the deflation of the currency after 785, which increased the tax load several-fold in the course of two or three decades.[231] It seems that the migration from the north-west to the south-east continued, but the statistics require very careful interpretation.[232] To some extent the hard-pressed peasant-farmer may have found a more acceptable solution to his problems in becoming a tenant or dependant under the protection of a powerful land-owner, rather than in flight to a new province. There is also some slight evidence that by the ninth century the more hospitable 'frontier areas' in central China were filling up, and it was no longer so easy for squatters to establish themselves. Moreover, the population of the Yangtze valley bore a particularly onerous tax load.[233]

Under the *liang-shui* system, the problem of vagrancy became a local one. The reform fixed an overall assessment of taxes for each administrative area, and thus migration from a county or prefecture meant that the same total taxes had to be levied on a diminished number of taxpayers. Arrangements for re-allocation of the tax load were by no means effective.

In some areas considerable areas of land seem to have been temporarily abandoned, and the government showed some concern to settle people on such lands to maintain production. In 821 an Act of Grace ordered that lands left vacant by migrants should be granted to regular soldiers with dependants, who were exempted from tax for three years.[234] In 841 another edict dealt with the disposal of such abandoned lands, which were at first to be rented out, so that there would be no question of their reverting to waste, and later granted to new owners.[235] In 845 much of the second-rate land belonging to the monasteries[236] was distributed to their former dependants and slaves.[237] In 848 an edict ruled that when lands became vacant the neighbours, or local people without land of their own, could work it as tenants and become full owners after five years.[238] This rule was reimposed in 870.[239]

It is clear that the primary purpose of all these measures was to settle persons who were not already taxpayers on vacant land and thus make them liable under the *liang-shui*. This purpose is mentioned specifically in the Act of Grace of 821 and in the edict dissolving the monastic estates in 845. But as a generalisation, we may suggest that the administration's interest in land tenure diminished when the proportion of the state income provided from non-agrarian sources enabled them to depend on taxes other than those on land. This situation was forced upon the government by the loss of effective control in the provinces after 756.

CHAPTER II

DIRECT TAXATION

In the state's relationship with the land, the T'ang dynasty witnessed a complete revolution. Beginning with a theoretical adherence to a system under which land remained the possession of the state, and was granted to productive taxpayers on more or less limited tenures, by the ninth century *de facto* rights both of possession and of disposal of landed property were accepted in practice, even though the fiction that 'all land in the empire is the emperor's' and that it was subject to distribution under the *chün-t'ien* was maintained even in the Sung *Code*. In this respect the T'ang is a transition from the controlled systems of land allotment characteristic of the period of division in the third to sixth centuries, to the free tenure of land leading to the accumulation of estates and growth of tenancy which has characterised the Chinese economy since the ninth century.

The taxation structure underwent a revolution perhaps even more complete. During the T'ang there was a transition from the fixed head-taxes, which had been imposed during the period of division, to a system of progressive taxation based on assessment of property on the one hand, and of land levies based on the areas under cultivation on the other, which remained the fundamental tax system of the empire until the *I-t'iao-pien fa*[1] reform in the sixteenth century.

At the beginning of the dynasty, almost the whole of the revenues of the state were derived from a system of direct taxation supplemented by labour services. This system, commonly referred to by the names of its three principal component taxes *tsu-yung-tiao*, was adopted from the institutions of the semi-barbarian northern dynasties of the fifth and sixth centuries together with the *chün-t'ien* system of land allotment with which it was intimately connected.[2] The basic rules of the system were first promulgated in an edict in 619,[3] and then incorporated in an expanded form in the *Taxation Statutes* (*fu-i-ling*) of 624.[4] They were retained, with little significant alteration, in the subsequent series of *Statutes* down to and including those of 737.[5] The system was backed by specific sanctions written into the *Code*,[6] and provided with detailed supplementary rules in the *Ordinances* of the Board of Finance (*hu-pu-shih*).[7] The most important relevant extracts from these bodies of codified administrative law are translated in appendices (pp. 140–53).

The system consisted of four basic liabilities, a tax in grain (*tsu*) and a tax in kind (*tiao*) paid in terms of cloth, together with two separate types of labour service, the regular annual *corvée* (*cheng-i*) and miscellaneous labour service (*tsa-yao*).[8] The amounts payable by each taxable individual were fixed, and took no account of his personal circumstances, since the system assumed that each taxpayer had received an equal grant of land from the state. The grain tax was very light, amounting to two *shih* (about 2·8 cwt.) of millet. This represented the product of only some two or three *mou* of land out of a total entitlement of 100 *mou*, although of course the normal size of actual holdings was much smaller than this. The tax in kind amounted to a length of 20 ft. of silk or 25 ft.[9] of hempen cloth in respect of each individual taxpayer, together with a small supplementary payment (*chien-tiao*) paid in silk floss, silk thread or hemp thread.[10] For the regular annual *corvée* each taxpayer was liable to twenty days' service. But this was normally avoided by the payment of a *corvée* exemption tax (*yung*), paid in cloth together with the tax in kind. Payment of this exemption tax was so common that it and the tax in kind, being paid in the same commodities, were frequently treated as a single category (*yung-tiao*). In theory the *corvée* exemption tax represented the cost of hiring a substitute for the period of labour service.[11] It was also permitted to provide an actual substitute from among the household's personal adherents.[12] The miscellaneous labour services stood somewhat apart from the three other basic obligations, being labour services not on behalf of the central government, but of the local authorities,[13] and were levied on a wider category of persons.[14] They are given separate treatment below.

For the normal taxes, the unit of taxation was the taxable individual (*k'o-k'ou*). The individual was not however the taxpayer, as all taxes were levied on the head of the household. Any household containing taxable individuals became a taxable household (*k'o-hu*).[15] In general, all males who did not come under one of the categories of physical disability[16] or in one of the categories for exemption were liable to tax and labour service while they were classed as adult (*ting*) in their household register. The limits of this age-category varied during the course of the dynasty, but were normally from twenty-one to fifty-nine years of age.[17] Since lands were also granted to adolescent males (*chung-nan*), that is, persons of eighteen to twenty years of age,[18] grants of land preceded liability to full taxes by some three years. During this interval, however, the adolescent male was already liable to miscellaneous labour services and various special services.[19] It is implied in one source at least that nobody who had not received a land allotment would be liable to taxation, as had been the case under the Sui statutes.[20]

Although the unit of taxation under the T'ang was always the individual adult male, it is clear from the form of the taxes (grain produced by the man, cloth woven by the wife) that the unit originally envisaged had been the married couple. This had been the case under previous dynasties,[21] when additional allowances of land were made on behalf of wives,[22] but under the T'ang all women were automatically tax-exempt, at least under the *tsu-yung-tiao* system itself.

It is thus utterly misleading to pay any heed to the analysis of the *tsu-yung-tiao* system made by the statesman Lu Chih at the end of the eighth century, that *tsu* was essentially a tax on land, *tiao* a household tax, and *yung* a tax on the individual.[23] All three taxes were taxes on the individual, but levied in different commodities—grain, cloth, and physical labour. The system was moreover adapted essentially to a backward economy where commodities were of more value than money in exchange, and to an agrarian society in which the majority of the taxpayers were primary producers.

Very many persons were exempt from taxation under this system. All persons related in the most distant way with the imperial clan, and members of families with noble titles,[24] all officials and many persons serving in subordinate government posts,[25] all holders of official rank[26] were exempt. In the same way all Buddhist and Taoist clergy were given exemption,[27] and the *Code* contains specific penalties for use against those who became ordained simply to evade tax and labour services.[28] Exemption was also granted to persons whose moral conduct had singled them out for official commendation, and such exemptions were extended to their whole household.[29]

In addition to these categories of persons who were permanently exempt, limited remissions of tax were granted rather freely. Apart from remissions made by Act of Grace from time to time, either on ceremonial occasions or as a consequence of natural disasters, the *Statutes* contained rules for automatic remissions in certain circumstances. For instance, specific periods of remission or exemption were prescribed where persons were retained on labour service beyond the normal period,[30] where they moved their residence from one region to another,[31] where there was a crop failure,[32] when slaves received manumission,[33] when persons returned from abroad[34] or when foreigners took service with the Chinese.[35] In addition all persons performing military service or the more arduous labour services involving regular turns of duty (*se-i*) received temporary exemption from their basic tax liabilities under the *tsu-yung-tiao* system.[36] The households of such persons were listed in the registers as 'taxable households not at present contributing' (*k'o-hu chien pu-shu*).[37] To judge by the household registers and *corvée* lists preserved from the Tun-huang area, such persons accounted for a considerable proportion of the registered male population. But since Tun-huang was a vital frontier garrison, military and labour services must have been unusually onerous in the area, and the situation can hardly have been typical for all of China.[38]

Taxation, moreover, fell only upon the registered population—the households described as 'resident households',[39] who were included in the annual tax registers (*chi-chang*). These households represented only a part of the total population, for there were many 'settler households' (*k'o-hu*)[40] who remained unregistered and consequently untaxed. The re-registration of population carried out by Yü-wen Jung in 724 brought into account settler households amounting to some 12 per cent of the total registered population,[41] and subsequently it was estimated that between 20 and 10 per cent of the farming population still remained unregistered.[42] The number of such unregistered families must have been very considerable, though perhaps not so large as some recent estimates have suggested.[43] Beside totally unregistered households, there is every reason to suppose that within the registered households there was a great deal of fraudulent misrepresentation, by which taxable adults were either omitted entirely from the record, or recorded in some non-taxable category.[44]

To keep losses through non-registered households and partial declaration of members of registered households down to a minimum, regular and accurate census-taking was essential. Even more necessary was an efficient and rigorously controlled local administrative machine reaching down to the village level, where the actual business of registration and tax collection was carried on. As I have suggested in the previous chapter, the lowest level at which the state bureaucracy functioned was the county (*hsien*), the official staff of which was totally inadequate to carry out themselves the routine work of registration, land allotments and tax collection.[45] This routine was performed by the sub-bureaucratic village administrations of headmen (*li-cheng*) who were closely identified with local interests and who themselves usually came from the more prominent local families.[46] Moreover, these headmen normally dealt with the subaltern officials (*hsü-li*) of the county government who were themselves for the most part from local families[47] and whose interests were by no means identifiable with those of the central power. The officials of the county *yamen* normally came into the picture only in case of disputes, although they bore responsibility for the administration down to the lowest level.[48]

In general, then, the *tsu-yung-tiao* system may be characterised as a complex of head taxes levied throughout the empire at a uniform rate. It was a far from satisfactory system. Being based on the fiction that every taxpayer had received an equal land allotment under the *chün-t'ien* system, it was completely divorced from economic reality, taking no notice of differences between diverse regions, or between individuals. The richest and most productive classes in the empire—the officials and other tax-exempt groups with the entitlement to build up large land-holdings within the law, the monasteries who were able to accumulate huge inalienable holdings of land and to take a prominent part in finance and industry with their capital, the merchants and the artisans who generally held no lands—all were left untouched by the system. In effect the whole tax load as levied under the *tsu-yung-tiao* system was borne by the small farmers, on whom the uniform tax rate, levied without regard to their wealth or productive capacity, weighed the more heavily the poorer they became.

However, as a result of a series of recent studies, it has become clear that there was in fact much more diversity in the field of taxation than is apparent from the *Statutes*. The most drastic suggestion has been that the whole apparatus of *chün-t'ien* land allotment and *tsu-yung-tiao* taxation was never employed as laid down in the laws, except in the north of China, while in the south the taxes were replaced by a heavy grain levy on the acreage of cultivated land and a *tsu* grain tax graded according to the categories of households.[49] But the evidence for such a sweeping generalisation is inconclusive, although it is clear that there were many regional differences within the system. The most striking case was that of the border areas with non-Chinese populations, where entirely separate forms of taxation suitable for the local pastoral economy was prescribed in the *Statutes*.[50] In the wild southern border province of Ling-nan there was a grain levy in rice which, while preserving the adult male as the object of taxation, varied the tax rate in accordance with the category of the household, that is with its relative wealth.[51] In the Yangtze valley (Chiang-nan) it was customary to convert the grain tax into cloth, presumably in order to reduce transportation costs. There is some doubt when this practice arose,[52] but tax cloths paid in lieu of grain tax in Chekiang and dated 684 have been discovered at Turfan, proving that the system was already in force in the seventh century,[53] and it is likely that the T'ang adopted this from the practice under previous dynasties.[54] Other regions also regularly paid their *tsu* and *tiao* taxes in special commodities, for instance in silk cloth in I-chou (Ch'engtu, Szechuan), silk thread in Annam, and salt in coastal districts,[55] or even in cash as in Yang-chou.[56] Moreover, the *Statutes* granted the Department of Public Revenue authority to order any prefecture to pay its taxes in terms of other commodities in case of need.[57]

Very little is known of the details of these types of substitute taxes, but in the case of the payment of hemp cloth in place of the grain tax an important refinement was added to the system. This was the collection of the tax at a progressive rate in accordance with the household category, not at a uniform rate for all taxable individuals.[58]

The household categories (*hu-teng*) were assigned from the earliest years of the dynasty, and were a rough assessment by the officials of a district of the wealth, property and size of individual households.[59] This assessment was revised every third year, in the year preceding the compilation of the household register, on which it was entered.[60] There were nine categories, the great bulk of the population falling in the eighth and ninth categories.[61] These categories were of great significance in a household's financial obligations outside the basic *tsu-yung-tiao* taxes, as I shall make clear below.[62] They also affected liability to the basic taxes, under certain conditions.

For example, during the seventh century members of households belonging to the two lowest categories who had served as militiamen (*fu-ping*) and who, although they had remained taxable persons were not required to contribute while serving, were allowed to retain this privilege after being retired, although theoretically they should have lost it when they were taken off the army registers.[63] They were only required to pay grain tax. Moreover, certain fragmentary tax lists (*chi-chang*) dating from the end of the seventh century would seem to suggest that households of the lowest categories, with little land and few members, sometimes received exemption from *yung* and *tiao* taxes, and contributed only the grain tax (*tsu*).[64] Later, during the eighth century a certain number of the poorest families in each locality (*hsiang*) were given exemption from grain tax and *yung*, being required only to contribute the tax in kind (*tiao*).[65] The number of such families entitled to exemption in each locality was later increased, until it amounted to roughly 5 per cent of the population.[66] Moreover, the authorities were forbidden to select for service men who were the only adult in households of low categories, since loss of their services would cause great hardship to their dependants.[67] It is likely that the increasing number of persons entitled to exemption during the latter part of Hsüan-tsung's reign reflects the rapid increase in registered population, resulting in larger revenues.[68] During the same period, the Acts of Grace granting temporary remissions of tax also began to make special concessions to low-category households with little land,[69] or with single adult male members.[70]

It was not here, however, that household categories had their deepest influence. Beyond the *tsu-yung-tiao* system itself there existed a number of supplementary fiscal obligations which were levied not at a universal rate, but in accordance with the household grades. These obligations were known collectively as selective impositions (*ch'ai-k'o*).[71] The most important of these impositions was the household levy (*hu-shui*) to which I shall revert shortly. But in the early years of the dynasty, it is probable that special labour services (*se-i* or *fan-i*) were a far heavier burden on the tax-paying population.[72]

The problem of such special duties is one of the most complex in the whole field of T'ang finance. Being mostly local in character they were not specified in the *Statutes*, a large proportion of which have survived, but in the *Ordinances*, of which hardly anything remains extant. Moreover, there is a great confusion between these special duties and the miscellaneous labour services performed on behalf of the local authorities (*tsa-yao*), about which we are almost equally ill-informed.[73]

Most of the special labour services involved regular recurrent turns of duty in a specific type of employment, usually lasting for two months in every year. Most of these services, but not by any means all of them, were performed locally.[74] There were great numbers of such duties, running into hundreds of thousands,[75] and in any given area the proportion of taxpayers with such responsibilities was rather high.[76] However, selection for such a special duty, which was normally made on the basis of the household's category, was by no means an unmitigated disadvantage. The large proportion of special duty men did not actually perform any duty in person, but merely paid an exemption tax (*tzu-k'o*), usually of 1500 or 2000 cash per annum. For this contribution—a small enough sum for a relatively well-to-do household—the taxpayer received exemption not only from miscellaneous local labour service (*tsa-yao*), but also from selection for military service.[77] Thus selection for special duties was in one respect advantageous.

In other cases, where the duties had to be performed, but it was inconvenient to have a constant change-over of the persons performing them, a different system was employed. Permanent employees were assigned actually to perform the duty, while commoners from households in the higher categories were assigned as *t'ieh-ting*, that is persons responsible for the payment of a maintenance grant (*tzu-chu*) for the support of the permanent employee.[78] Such an assignment too carried exemption from *corvée* and military service.

Various other minor charges, made in respect of special recurrent duties which came normally to be performed by professional employees, such as, for instance, the transport of taxes (*tsu-chüeh*) and granary storage (*ying-chiao*) were paid as supplementary taxes levied according to the grade of household.[79]

The income from these payments in lieu of special duties was not inconsiderable. According to Tu Yu[80] they accounted for more than 8 per cent of the national income in the *T'ien-pao* period (742–56), though this figure includes other forms of minor taxation and it would be more realistic to take these payments as accounting for something less than 5 per cent of the total.

Less important as a source of income, though of greater historical significance, was the household levy, which was known under a variety of names, *hu-shui, shui-ch'ien* or *shui-hu-ch'ien*. This was a money tax collected from all households at a rate varying in accordance with the household category. There were no privileged exceptions as in the case of the *tsu-yung-tiao* taxes; an edict of 701 clearly specifies that it shall be levied on 'all from the nobility downward'. It was a money tax, the proceeds being used to provide official salaries, army funds, etc.

The rate was not the same from year to year, but the system provided for a heavy levy (*ta-shui*) every third year, and a light levy (*hsiao-shui*) annually, in addition to which a separate levy (*pieh-shui*) was collected each year to help pay for local officials' salaries.[81]

The tax was a rather light imposition. During the *T'ien-pao* period the average rate for the whole empire was only 250 cash per household, the annual rate for households of the eighth category averaging 452 cash, and that for one of the ninth category only 222 cash.[82] At contemporary prices, these household rates were far less than either the *tsu* or *tiao* tax for a single adult.[83] The total revenue which it brought in was only some 2,000,000 strings of cash, and Tu Yu calculated that it amounted only to one-twentieth or one-thirtieth of the revenue from the *tsu-yung-tiao* taxes.[84]

However, the tax had an importance far exceeding the small part it played in the total revenue. It was virtually the only tax which was levied alike on all households, and was almost the only source of revenue from landless townsmen, in particular the merchant class. Moreover, it incorporated the very important principle of progressive taxation dependent on an assessment of the wealth of the taxpayer, and thus provided a model for the later *liang-shui* reform.

The category of a household, and thus the economic position of a family, had then a considerable effect upon its liability to various types of taxation. This naturally led to attempts at evasion. In 696, 742 and 744 edicts had to be issued prohibiting the illegal division of families during the lifetime of the head of the household, so as to reduce their category.[85] Another edict, promulgated in 730, prohibited merchants from consorting with officials in the hope of having their household category reduced,[86] and in 741 and 745 the procedure for the periodical assessment of household categories was tightened up.[87]

A further supplementary tax also abandoned the fixed rate for every taxable individual. This was the land levy (*ti-shui*) which originated not as a tax in the ordinary sense, but as a compulsory contribution of grain to provide stocks for the relief granaries (*i-ts'ang*) which had been established as a result of a memorial presented by Tai Chou in 628 to build up reserves of grain in every locality as an insurance against crop failure.[88] The levy was made at the rate of 2 *sheng* for each *mou* of cultivated land in the possession of a household, and this total was assessed according to a special land register called a *ch'ing-miao pu*. This, unlike the household registers which included only the lands granted under the *chün-t'ien* allocation, included all cultivated lands, however acquired.[89]

For a short while after 651 the tax was collected in accordance with the household's category, as had been the case with a similar levy under the Sui.[90] The collection on the basis of acreage under crops was soon restored, but a levy on the basis of the category of household was retained in the *Statutes* of 719 in the case of landless merchants.[91]

At the end of the seventh century, with the continual growth of state expenditure, the government began to misapply these stocks of grain and to use them for current expenditure, and the term land levy (*ti-shui*) for the contribution of grain first appears in 705.[92] This practice was forbidden by an edict of 716[93] and prohibited under the *Statutes* of 719,[94] but it continued nevertheless, and during the reign of Hsüan-tsung when the demand for grain was greater than ever before, the land levy became a most important source of income. Tu Yu's assessment of the state revenues during the *T'ien-pao* period gives the annual income from the land levy as 12,400,000 *shih* compared with 12,600,000 *shih* from the *tsu* tax.[95] Its growth in importance may be judged by the increasing frequency with which it occurs as an item remitted by Acts of Grace. First mentioned in 680, it then recurs in 709, 723, 725, 729, 730, 731, 732, 733, 734, 735, 736, 739, 740, 747 and 748.[96] The majority of these Acts of Grace were local in application and made as a result of natural disasters. The remission of the land levy under such circumstances suggests that it had come to be regarded as a tax rather than as a contribution towards relief funds.

The land levy was a particularly important source of revenue in the Yangtze valley, where, since the *tsu* tax was paid in hemp cloth and not in grain, it was the only source of revenue in grain. Thus the vast bulk of the grain transported from the Huai and Yangtze valleys during the reign of Hsüan-tsung came from the land levy.[97] This source provided the capital with up to 4,000,000 *shih* (more than a quarter of a million tons) of grain annually.[98] In spite of such misapplication of funds from the relief granaries for revenue purposes, they still contained enormous stocks of grain, amounting in 749 to almost two-thirds of the total grain reserves at the disposal of the government and representing more than five years' income from the land levy.[99]

Both the taxes levied according to an assessment of the wealth of households and the land levy, assessed on actually cultivated lands, could still be enforced locally even when the registers held by the central authorities had ceased to reflect the true state of affairs. The deterioration of the registration system began already in the *T'ien-pao* period,[100] perhaps as a result of the permanently applicable orders issued by Li Lin-fu in 736 which fixed standing tax quotas for each prefecture.[101] According to Tu Yu's assessment of the empire's revenue, the number of taxable individuals in the empire, 8,200,000 in all, was less than the total number of households and represented only 17 per cent of the total population of 52,919,000 persons.[102] Since all males were taxable from the age of twenty-one to sixty, unless they belonged to one of the privileged classes (who can hardly have amounted to more than 2 per cent of the population), this figure can be accounted for only by a phenomenally low expectation of life (well below thirty years), or by a great proportion of the population having avoided registration as taxable individuals.[103] If we consider that the proportion of the total which might reasonably be expected to have fallen within the limits of taxation is about 20–21 per cent, the number falsely registered must have run into millions, and to this figure must be added those who evaded registration entirely.[104]

The only taxes which were able to derive revenue from these persons were the household levy and the land levy, which were based on economic realities and not on individual personal status, as defined in the household registers. They may thus be considered as first steps by which the government began to base its financial system upon actual wealth and productivity instead of upon the theoretically equally endowed taxable adult envisaged by the primitive *tsu-yung-tiao* system. The An Lu-shan rising brought these developments to a sudden climax. In the widespread dislocation of the administrative and financial systems which ensued, the registration system and the land allotment ceased to be effective, while the extensive depopulation and migration which followed the initial campaigns destroyed the entire basis of the *tsu-yung-tiao* taxes as previously levied.[105]

In the attempt to meet the unprecedented need for revenue the government tried a series of temporary expedients. First of these was the sale of official certificates of ordination as Buddhist or Taoist priests, which status entitled the holder to tax exemption. This was first tried in 755 by Ts'ui Chung,[106] and revived in 757 by Cheng Shu-ch'ing and P'ei Mien, who extended this very short-sighted method of raising funds to the sale of official credentials of rank and of honorific or noble titles[107] which gave entitlement to tax exemption in the same way. Ordination certificates were again openly sold by the authorities after the recovery of the capital by the imperial forces.[108] At this same period forced loans were levied on the powerful merchants of the Yangtze valley cities and of Szechuan,[109] and various taxes were imposed on the production of commodities, for instance, on salt and on hemp.[110] **1568713**

More ambitious schemes to solve the financial crisis were also put into operation. The first of these, a debasement of the coinage which was put into effect in 759, had no result other than the aggravation of the serious inflationary situation already caused by the war.[111] The second, the imposition of a monopoly tax on salt, was eventually so successful that within twenty years it was producing over half the annual cash revenue of the state, but in its initial stages the income from this source remained insignificant.[112]

The government made some attempt to revive the old taxation and land-allotment systems. Persons who had fled from their homes were offered inducement to return by the promise of new land grants and remission of taxes.[113] This proved unsuccessful, and edicts were vainly issued in an attempt to prevent the usurpation of vacated lands by the rich and powerful,[114] and to prohibit local officials from driving into flight the remaining settled population by charging to them the arrears of taxes owing from their neighbours who had already fled.[115] Local officials were even permitted to rent out vacated lands, taking the rent in lieu of tax arrears.[116]

However, all these attempts to bolster up the old system failed dismally, and local officials were placed in an impossible position, since the quotas of tax expected from each prefecture and laid down in the permanently applicable orders since 736 still had to be produced, even where the registered population formally liable to taxation was reduced to a fraction of its former size.[117] The central authorities, too, when they wished to make any reform had to work on registration documents twenty or thirty years obsolete.

It is hardly surprising, then, that the decades from 760 to 780 saw direct taxation becoming less and less important in the face of the growing revenue from the salt monopoly. It is even less surprising that no constructive attempt seems to have been made to revive the *tsu-yung-tiao* system after 766, and that direct taxation became more and more a matter of the taxes levied on households' property and cultivated land. There were, of course, a great variety of minor and local impositions, many of them levied at the initiative of the provincial governors who now became the dominant figures in local administration.[118] But in general it may be said that the trend in tax policy towards taxes on property and cultivated land continued from the end of Hsüan-tsung's reign, the essential distinction being that the central authorities no longer had sufficient authority outside the capital region and some areas in south-east and southern China effectively to impose any system.

The land levy continued to be an important source of income. An edict promulgated in 763 required that it should be paid at the old rate of 2 *sheng* per *mou*.[119] In 765, under Ti-wu Ch'i, this was replaced by a 10 per cent tax on the total harvest in the metropolitan district, but this law was rescinded in the next year.[120] At about this same time the land levy was divided into two instalments known as the summer levy (*hsia-shui*) and autumn levy (*ch'iu-shui*). These terms have been mistakenly understood to have referred to the new 'green sprout tax', to which I shall revert below.[121] But this is manifestly wrong, as the latter was a money tax, while these levies were collected in grain, and their connection with the land levy seems proved beyond reasonable doubt.[122]

The summer and autumn levies are first mentioned in 769, when land was divided for purposes of taxation into three categories, superior, inferior, and cultivated wasteland.[123] On these categories the autumn tax was 1 *tou*, 6 *sheng* and 2 *sheng* per *mou* respectively,[124] while in 769 the summer tax for the following year's wheat crop was reduced to 1 *tou*, 5 *sheng* and 2 *sheng* for the three categories of land.[125] The edict announcing this reduction states clearly that it was the land levy which was in question, and it seems reasonable to infer that the summer tax was levied on the wheat crop, while the autumn tax was presumably levied on the millet harvest. If this was the case, the two levies were made in respect of different lands, and each *mou* was taxed only once per annum. This was the opinion of Katō Shigeshi,[126] but the source material is too scanty to arrive at any definite conclusion.

In 770 a further edict set the rate for the summer levy at 6 *sheng* and 4 *sheng* (no rate was fixed for cultivated waste), and that for the autumn tax at 5 *sheng*, 3 *sheng* and 2 *sheng* per *mou*.[127] Although the rates were thus reduced, they still remained very much above the standard 2 *sheng* per *mou* in force in 763. As all the material concerning these taxes refers to the metropolitan district of Ch'ang-an, I am inclined to believe that the summer and autumn levies were a form of the land levy enforced only in that area, but here again final proof is lacking.

While the land levy itself was undergoing these modifications, a second form of taxation on the acreage under crops, but this time levied in cash instead of grain, developed. On this question, also, there is a lack of adequate source material, and there is a further complication in that there were at first two such taxes, the green sprout money (*ch'ing-miao-ch'ien*) and the acreage money (*ti-t'ou-ch'ien*). The green sprout money was first levied in 758–60 to provide cash for the money salaries of the bureaucracy.[128] In 766 the rate was 10 cash per *mou*, and this was increased to 15 cash in 768 as the revenue had ceased to be adequate,[129] following a 20 per cent rise in official salaries at the beginning of that year.[130] The income from the tax was only 47,516 strings at this date, and thus it can have been collected only in a very restricted region, as this represents the tax on only some 3,100,000 *mou*.

The origins of the *ti-t'ou-ch'ien* are very obscure, and we know little about it until 770 when it was amalgamated with the green sprout money. At this time its rate was higher than that of the green sprout money, at 25 cash per *mou*.[131] The new combined tax was known either as *ch'ing-miao-ti-t'ou-ch'ien* or simply as green sprout money (*ch'ing-miao-ch'ien*) and was levied at the rate of 35 cash per *mou*,[132] representing a slight overall decrease.

In 773 the combined rate was 15 cash in the provinces, and 30 cash in the metropolitan district. The latter is said to have been 'formerly increased', and it was now reduced to the same level as the provincial tax.[133] Since the provincial rate in 773 was the same as the rate for the green sprout money alone before 700, it looks very much as if the *ti-t'ou ch'ien* was amalgamated with the green sprout money only in respect of the metropolitan district, the 'former increase' having been the result of the amalgamation of the green sprout money with another purely local money tax.

In any case the rates of these taxes were by no means onerous, since during the 760's and 770's grain prices, especially in Kuan-nei, were very high. A figure of 1000 cash per *tou* is commonly cited before 770, and although prices fell somewhat between 770 and 780 they remained very high.[134] It appears that these taxes, moreover, were not collected by the local authorities, but by censors specially deputed for the duty by the central administration.[135] Later the president of the censorate was given overall authority for these taxes, and given the concurrent title of commissioner for the money and goods from the levies on land (*shui-ti-ch'ien-wu shih*).[136] Such abnormal methods were necessitated by the almost complete lack of central authority in the provinces, and by the considerable powers exercised over local affairs by the provincial military governors.

The household levy remained a very important source of income. After the rebellion it proved a convenient means of raising prefectural tax quotas, and in many areas the rates—especially on households of the higher categories—were excessively onerous.[137] In 769 the whole system underwent a thorough revision, which attempted to increase the taxes paid by the merchants and artisans and by the officials. The former were taxed two grades above their nominal household category, whilst the latter were taxed in accordance with their honorary rank, which was usually higher than the rank in which they were actually employed. The estates possessed by officials in their place of employment, as well as those in their home district, were made subject to taxation. The measure also attempted to bring within the scope of taxation all unregistered migrant settlers, who were very numerous in central and southern China, where many people had sought refuge during the rebellion.[138] It also took strict account of the owners of the large estates (*chuang-yüan*) which were becoming increasingly widespread.[139] The only persons who received any measure of relief under the new law were the military, and this may represent a concession in favour of the class who had suddenly became the real source of power in the provinces.[140]

Under the new measure the tax rates were higher than had been the case before the rebellion. But the rates which had commonly been enforced in the provinces in the preceding years were drastically reduced,[141] and if the greatly reduced purchasing power of money is taken into account, the new rates probably represent a decrease in terms of the actual commodities in which most taxes continued to be levied.

To summarise the position at the end of Tai-tsung's reign in 779, while theoretically the *tsu-yung-tiao* taxes remained in force, the administrative machinery necessary for their enforcement had to a large extent broken down, and where they were still collected they were not levied equitably on all the population. In their place the central government had come to rely on the taxes levied in grain or money upon all cultivated lands, and in cash upon the property assessment of households, while the provincial governors raised revenue through a variety of irregular and unauthorised taxes imposed on their own authority. But the most important development of the period immediately after An Lu-shan's rebellion was not the new emphasis upon land and property taxation, but rather the phenomenal growth of indirect taxation levied through the salt monopoly, a source of revenue with the collection of which not even the most powerful of provincial magnates could interfere. By 779 the proportion of the central revenues produced by direct taxation was less than half.[142]

Upon the death of Tai-tsung, a new group of ministers was appointed by his successor.[143] Prominent among these was Yang Yen, a bitter personal enemy of Liu Yen who had been the head of the financial administration throughout the reign of Tai-tsung and who had been principally responsible for the growth in importance of the salt monopoly at the expense of normal methods of direct taxation.[144] Yang Yen set out deliberately to reverse the policies of his predecessor. This was not simply the result of personal motives. There is no doubt that the new reign awakened hopes of a revival of imperial authority, and as one aspect of the restoration of such authority was visualised the revival of the power of the properly constituted offices of the bureaucracy over the irregularly appointed financial specialists of the salt administration on the one hand and over the eunuchs who had come to control the treasuries on the other.[145] Yang Yen's reforms are to be understood in this context. His purely administrative reforms are dealt with elsewhere,[146] but by far the most important and lasting of the measures introduced during his brief tenure of office was a new reformed system of direct taxation, known as the two-tax system (*liang-shui fa*).[147]

The traditional view of the *liang-shui* reform represented it as an entirely novel approach to the problem of taxation. It is now generally accepted that it was more in the nature of a rationalisation and unification of existing methods of taxation than a revolutionary new scheme,[148] but nevertheless its effects were far-reaching. It greatly simplified the chaotic tax structure of the preceding twenty years, and enabled the whole system to be administered through the regularly constituted bureaucracy, without having constant resort to the appointment of extraordinary commissioners. It laid the foundation for a revival of central authority under Hsien-tsung (805–20) by providing the state with a practical means of deriving direct taxation from provinces over which it had little real authority. It also brought taxation into line with contemporary social developments, enabling the state to derive revenue from all the productive classes, not from the peasantry alone. As the basic system of taxation, it served successive dynasties for seven centuries.

The documents relevant to this measure are translated in full in appendix II, 5. Yang Yen suggested the reform in a long memorial almost immediately after his appointment as Great Minister in 779.[149] General assent to the implementation of such a plan was contained in an Act of Grace promulgated at the beginning of 780,[150] and in the second month of the same year an edict appointed commissioners (ch'u-chih shih) who were to enforce the new system in the provinces, followed a few days later by a directive giving the detailed orders which they were to implement.[151]

The tsu-yung-tiao taxes were at last formally abolished, though not without some misgivings,[152] and the hypothetically equally endowed peasant taxpayer was finally abandoned as the basic unit of taxation.[153] In place of the old system, a new household levy (hu-shui), based as before on an assessment of the size and property of every household, was universally imposed without question whether households were natives of the locality where they resided or settlers from elsewhere. At the same time a land levy (ti-shui) was imposed, collected on the basis of all lands actually under cultivation in 779. All the miscellaneous taxes which had been levied during the preceding reigns were abolished, and the new taxes were to be levied in two instalments, one in summer and one in autumn.[154]

There was thus no actual innovation in the system of taxation which was introduced. Both the household levy and the land levy had been enforced as supplementary taxes for many years, and had been growing in importance at the expense of the tsu-yung-tiao taxes since the beginning of the century. The collection of taxes in two separate annual instalments had been practised during Tai-tsung's reign in the contribution of the land levy and the green sprout tax. However, the measure of rationalisation and simplification effected by the liang-shui reform was very considerable. Instead of the many different taxes which had previously been levied at different times and even by different authorities, the taxpayer now had only two basic liabilities, the household and land levies, both of which were assessed on his property and productive capacity, and were collected together at the times when he was likely to be best able to meet the demands of the tax-collector.

The reform was not, however, primarily designed to benefit the tax-payer. The unification of taxes and their collection at specified times also represented a great saving to the authorities, and it is from the point of view of administrative rationalisation that the reform was of the greatest importance. The commissioners sent to the provinces in 780 fixed, in collaboration with the provincial governors and their sub-ordinate prefects, overall tax quotas for each province and for each prefecture within the province.[155] Once this quota (*o*) was assessed, the central government was concerned only that it received this total, and the provincial authorities were allowed considerable latitude in the manner in which the tax was collected. The actual tax rate, both for the household levy and for the land levy, varied from province to province, and from one prefecture to another within any given province.

Prefectural tax quotas had existed before 780, as we have already seen. However, there is no doubt that the quotas imposed under Li Lin-fu's permanently applicable directive (*ch'ang-hsing chih-fu*) of 736 were designed as a rough general guide, eliminating the necessity of assessing local revenue in detail each year, but were rigidly based on the registered population of each prefecture and were envisaged as liable to adjustment in the light of population increase or decrease, rather than as permanently fixed amounts. The new quotas were not so much a device to eliminate an annual assessment as a compromise between the central authorities and the provincial governors, fixing the annual revenue which the former might expect from the latter.

The adoption of this quota system meant in fact that actual financial administration, the assessment of tax rates, the equitable collection of taxes from the most productive elements of society and re-allocation of taxes to bring taxation into line with social changes, was decentralised and these powers, formerly exercised by or under the strict control of the central government, now devolved upon the provincial authorities. The latter were now admitted to be intermediaries in the collection of taxes, as they had been in effect for some two decades. A further compromise between the central and provincial powers may be seen in the manner of disposal of tax revenue. All the tax income of a province was divided into three categories, *shang-kung* which was sent to the capital and placed at the disposal of the central government, *sung-shih* or *liu-shih* which was retained by the provincial governor as his revenue, and *liu-chou* which was retained in the prefecture of origin to meet local expenditure.[156] This arrangement recognised the right of the provincial governors to dispose of a fixed proportion of the revenue from their provinces, while it also assured the central government of a fixed income from each province. The central government was thus assured of a regular income from direct taxation, even from provinces within which they had little real authority.

The adoption of the quota system meant that the rates of taxation varied from one locality to another. Although in actual practice there had been variable local tax rates before 780, these had been the result of the administration's failure to take account of the widespread changes in population which followed on An Lu-shan's rebellion, and there had always been, in theory at least, a universal rate for each tax applicable throughout the empire. This was no longer the case under the *liang-shui* system, and it became possible to grade tax rates in accordance with the productivity of different regions.[157]

The rates for the land levy were fixed in terms of grain, as had previously been the case. Those for the household levy were assessed in cash, though, since there was an acute shortage of currency, the tax was still normally collected in commodities (in particular in cloth) as had been the case before.[158] Some scholars in the past have laid undue stress on the importance of the *liang-shui* reform as the beginning of money taxation in China.[159] This is not strictly true, for the household levy had always been assessed in cash. But it did mean an important change in that a tax assessed in terms of cash now became a basic category of taxation.[160] Actual money taxation (taxes both assessed and levied in terms of cash) was still some centuries in the future. T'ang China's coinage was neither sufficient nor stable enough to provide the basic medium for taxation, and it is debatable whether assessments in terms of a highly unstable currency marked any real progress.

The Act of Grace of 780 expressly forbade the collection of a single cash beyond the quotas for the *liang-shui*, and abolished all other taxes old and new.[161] However, in the event this was not carried into effect. It seems that the system of miscellaneous *corvée* duties on behalf of the local authorities (*tsa-yao*) survived with little change.[162] Labour service, as before the reform, seems to have been allocated on the basis of household categories.[163] In addition, the green sprout tax and the *ti-t'ou-ch'ien* continued to be levied as a supplementary money tax on the same lands which were taxed in grain under the land levy.[164] Other surcharges and supplementary taxes were also added to the household levy, the most important being the liquor monopoly tax.[165]

These supplementary charges also seem to have been levied on a graded scale depending upon the household category,[166] and thus bore a direct relationship with the basic tax assessment. There was no longer the multitude of petty levies and irregular impositions which had made it impossible for the taxpayer during Tai-tsung's reign to be certain of his total obligations.

On a short-term basis, the new measure achieved what had been hoped. In the first year of its operation it produced revenue exceeding the total income from all sources in 779, including the profits derived from salt.[167] The central government was thus enabled temporarily to relegate the salt administration to a comparatively minor position, and to re-establish the authority of the regularly constituted central financial offices.[168]

Unfortunately, however, the new system was introduced at a most unhappy moment. The accession of Te-tsung was shortly followed by a series of rebellions among the provincial governors of Ho-pei, who may well have seen the new regime as a threat to their autonomy.[169] For a time the rebels threatened the dynasty, and although they were eventually suppressed they placed a severe financial strain on the government, which did not have the enormous reserves upon which their predecessors in 755–6 had been able to draw in the face of An Lu-shan's rising. The new tax system had thus had no time to settle down before it was called upon to face a major financial crisis.[170] This led to the introduction of various forms of emergency taxation and the re-establishment of the salt monopoly as a major source of revenue.[171]

All might still have been well had the regime restored after the failure of the Ho-pei rebellions been a strong one. However, Te-tsung's reign gradually declined into another period of very weak central authority, and the compromise which had been effected between the central government and the provinces under the *liang-shui* reform proved ineffective when it became clear that the central government was powerless to press its claims. The number of provinces which continued to contribute taxes declined until at the end of Te-tsung's reign the emperor exercised no financial control whatsoever in a third of the provinces, and could depend for a regular tax income only upon the provinces of the Yangtze valley[172] (see map 8, p. 117). The only income received from the defaulting provinces came in the form of irregular tribute offerings,[173] and there were many illegal impositions levied by the provincial authorities in excess of the *liang-shui* quotas.[174]

43

In this situation the government fell back on the well-tried alternative source of revenue, indirect taxation of salt and other commodities.[175] The salt administration recovered its former prestige and supplied most of the financial experts employed at court. Even the Department of Public Revenue, which was mainly concerned with direct taxation, became involved in various small-scale temporary expedients for raising funds.[176] Little was done to reform the *liang-shui* system, since the government was powerless to enforce any reform. The only person who consistently pressed for a reform of the abuses which had arisen was Lu Chih.[177] But although his criticisms were very much to the point he was very soon replaced in office by others who were willing to leave aside such broad questions and to concentrate on short-term schemes for raising funds.[178]

The abuses were in fact very considerable. There were certain anomalies in the drafting of the new laws. The most important of these was that while land was subject to the land levy, and to the supplementary green sprout tax, it was also included in the property of a family in assessing the household category, and so affected liability to household levy as well.[179] Thus, although the adoption of the household levy as a basic form of taxation meant some modification of the old reliance on revenue levied from the peasantry, those with lands still bore more than their fair share of the tax burden. Similarly, although the reform swept away the old distinction between resident native households and settlers, making all equally liable for taxation, the selection of persons for labour service still took no heed of any save resident households.[180] As a result it became advantageous to settle away from one's native place simply to avoid *corvée* liability.[181]

More serious than these faults in drafting the new system was the failure to provide any effective machinery to keep the assessments of both household and land levies in line with changing circumstances. In theory the re-classification of households was still carried out every third year, under the old *Statutes*. But there is little doubt that this was seldom done, although edicts insisting upon it were issued in 788,[182] 807,[183] 819,[184] and 821.[185] We read of numerous cases where local officials proceeding to their new posts found that classification had been neglected,[186] in one case for as much as twenty years.[187] Such neglect could lead to considerable hardship. A family who had been wealthy in 780, and given a high tax assessment, would still have had to pay the same assessment years later, even if they had fallen on hard times.

In many cases their only recourse was to flight, in which case their assessment was re-allocated (*chün-t'an*) among the other families in the locality, causing an all-round increase of taxes. Such a process could lead to wholesale migration.[188] After it became clear that the reintroduction of the triennial re-classification of households was impossible, the government attempted as a last resort in 825 to increase the period to five years.[189] But this was no more successful, and the problem remained unsolved in the absence of strong central control over the activities of local officials.

An equally difficult situation arose with regard to the land levy. The levy was collected in respect of cultivated lands registered in 779. As in the case of the re-classification of households, however, the local officials failed to keep track of changes of ownership, and in many instances land changed hands while the responsibility for paying the land levy remained with the original owner.[190] By the ninth century, as a result, in some areas the owners of great estates were paying the land levy on only 20 or 30 per cent of their lands.[191]

Another policy introduced still further complications. After the end of the rebellions in Ho-pei, the government, in order to encourage the cultivation of more land, began to assess local officials for promotion, taking into account the amount of land brought into cultivation during their tenure of office. Such newly cultivated lands were exempted from land taxes,[192] which made it advantageous for people to abandon their lands and take up new land elsewhere.[193] Every such move meant further confusion in the tax registers. There was a time limit on such tax exemption, but it is not clear precisely what the period was in the early years of this policy.[194] In 841 an edict ordered that exemption should last for five years, after which the land would be assessed to produce its share of the local quota of the land levy.[195]

These problems of the reassessment of taxes were essentially a matter for the local administration.[196] The quota system, however, encouraged local officials to raise their required quota by extortion rather than to attempt regular readjustment of the taxes of individual households. It is likely that only a minority of local officials followed the more difficult course.[197] By the early years of the ninth century in many regions the tax quota was being levied, without pretence of equity, on a small minority of those theoretically liable for taxation,[198] while the rest of the households were subjected to irregular taxation at the hands of the local sub-bureaucracy.[199] There was very little that the central government could do to remedy this state of affairs, for even after the temporary recovery of central power in Hsien-tsung's reign, although governmental authority over the provinces was strengthened, direct authority over the prefectures and counties remained weak.

In cases of obvious hardship, the best the government was able to do was to attempt to re-allocate the tax quotas. Sometimes taxes were re-distributed among the prefectures in a single province,[200] and such re-allocations were also made among the counties within a prefecture,[201] or even among the lands within a county.[202] In spite of these measures, many areas had enormous arrears of taxation, and such arrears affected the quotas due for despatch to the capital rather than the sums set aside for local expenditure.[203]

By far the most serious problem raised by the introduction of the *liang-shui* system was, however, nothing to do with the administrative machinery through which it was enforced, and was the direct responsibility of the central power. This problem arose out of the assessment of tax quotas in money terms. In 780, and the years immediately following, China was in the last stage of a period of serious inflation which had lasted since 763.[204] After 785, with the rebellions in Ho-pei suppressed, prices fell steeply and a long period of deflation began.[205] The tax rates fixed in terms of cash in 780 had never been intended to be paid entirely in money,[206] but were assessed with a view to payment in commodities (in particular in cloth) at the current inflated prices. These inflated rates were then further increased by 20 per cent in 782 to meet the cost of the campaigns against the rebels,[207] and later increased still further in the highly productive regions of Szechuan and the Yangtze delta.[208] When the market-price of the commodities in which the taxes were actually paid began to fall steadily, more and more goods had to be levied in order to fulfil the cash quotas laid down in the period of inflation. At the same time the cash quotas demanded from individual households actually rose as the provincial registration systems became defective.[209]

Even when this did not occur, and the money quotas remained constant, the actual tax load rose proportionately as commodity prices fell. Already by 794 Lu Chih estimated that the tax load when paid in silk cloth had doubled since 780.[210] But although many writers in the early years of the ninth century gave this situation as the cause of rural distress and vagrancy,[211] no move was made either to reassess the tax quotas in terms of commodities, or to reduce the cash assessments to offset the effects of deflation. By 820 it was estimated that the tax load when paid in silk had increased fivefold over the preceding forty years.[212]

The governments of the time, quite correctly, saw this problem as essentially part of the larger problem of acute shortage of currency.[213] Their attempts to deal with this are discussed below in chapter IV. In taxation policy, as in money policy in the broader sense, the authorities strove to keep as much money as possible in active circulation, and also encouraged a return to reckoning in terms either of commodities alone, or of commodities used together with money. In 809,[214] and again in 811,[215] edicts were promulgated ordering the use of money and cloth together in tax payments, as had been done in the case of large commercial transactions.[216] However, it became clear that this half-measure would not meet the case, and in 819 and 820 a number of memorials were presented advising the collection of taxes entirely in kind.[217] In 821, the Act of Grace issued on the accession of Mu-tsung ordered that this should be done.[218] Unfortunately, it is not clear whether the basic assessments were translated into commodity terms. It seems that it merely prohibited officials from demanding payment in cash (which had been a contributory factor in the general shortage of money), and thus left the basic problem unsolved.

However, after 820 the deflationary situation was eased, and there are no further complaints on the subject. The system of direct taxation remained virtually the same until the fall of the dynasty. As before, there were abuses—the collection of illegal impositions,[219] the neglect of reassessment of the household and land levies, and the need for the re-allocation of taxes to meet the local quotas.[220] But the actual situation in any given district came to depend more and more upon the local administration, and it is impossible to generalise about the empire as a whole.

The *liang-shui* system then introduced several new administrative difficulties, and brought into being a vast new problem in its relation with the currency. The governments of the late eighth and ninth centuries were not powerful enough to ensure equitable enforcement of the system in the provinces, and its statesmen did not grasp the full implications of assessing taxation in money terms. Nevertheless, the reform did provide the central government with a viable means of raising direct taxation, and although they were powerless to act against provinces which persistently defaulted in payment, the government derived sufficient revenue through the new system to enable them during the reign of Hsien-tsung to re-establish central authority over much of the empire, and to prolong the dynasty for another half century and more. Moreover, the reform represents a very important step in financial policy, by introducing money-assessed progressive taxation as a basic form of tax, and by establishing a system which remained in force until replaced by taxes assessed and paid in silver under the Ming.

CHAPTER III

STATE MONOPOLIES AND
TAXES ON TRADE

When, in the confused period immediately following the outbreak of An Lu-shan's rebellion, the administration was faced with the need for new sources of revenue to make good the enormous losses of stores suffered at the fall of Ch'ang-an and to replace the income normally derived from direct taxation, one of the schemes put forward was the imposition of a monopoly tax on the sale of salt. Such a tax was no innovation, for a monopoly on salt had been enforced as long ago as Former Han times. Under Ti-wu Ch'i, who founded the institution, and Liu Yen, who made it the basis of an extremely powerful new financial machine, the salt monopoly proved very successful, and later statesmen attempted to extend the monopoly principle to two other items which figured largely in the list of common consumer goods, tea and liquor. In the latter case there was also a Han-time precedent for monopoly trading, but the monopolies on tea and liquor proved to be failures, for reasons which I shall discuss below.

Such monopoly taxes were very attractive to governments which had only slender authority in the provinces, since to ensure a steady revenue it was necessary only to control strictly the regions of production. The merchants, who had to buy their stock from the government and pay the monopoly tax on it, passed on this tax to the consumer as part of a greatly increased retail price. The government could thus collect such taxes indirectly through the agency of the merchants from the people in areas over which they had but limited authority, and where they could not hope to operate an efficient system of direct taxation.

For such a system to function satisfactorily, the production of the goods concerned had to be limited to specific areas, and to be of such a nature that it could be easily controlled. Salt fulfilled these conditions, since production was a large-scale industry, necessitating large areas of salt pans and considerable capital equipment. It was, moreover, a necessity of life, so that the greatly increased prices resulting from the levying of the monopoly tax could not cause the consumers to boycott the goods, or greatly to reduce their consumption. Liquor fulfilled none of these conditions, while in the case of tea the attempt to bring all production under the control of the authorities proved a disastrous failure. Neither commodity ever became more than a minor source of revenue.

The Salt Monopoly

At the beginning of the dynasty, salt does not seem to have been subject to any general form of taxation. We know from the *Hsin T'ang-shu* that during the early years of the dynasty the prefectures on the sea coast paid their *tsu* tax either in salt or in light commodities of high value purchased with the price of salt, the whole system coming under the control of the Court of Agriculture.[1] The same source speaks of the directorate (*chien*) for the salt pools in Shensi,[2] but these are mentioned nowhere else. These salt pools, which were the most important centre of production inland in northern China, were of considerable importance. In 710[3] and 713[4] commissioners were appointed to be responsible for their exploitation. But the authority of these commissioners was purely local, the posts being filled concurrently by the local prefects, and after 727 by the military governors of the province.[5] At the most important of these salt pools, that of An-i in P'u-chou, military colonies (*yen-t'un*) exploited by the labour of troops working under military discipline were established in 721 by Chiang Shih-tu.[6] Similar colonies were set up elsewhere in the next two decades, and detailed rules for their exploitation, dating from 737, are preserved.[7]

The third major area of production apart from the coastal region and the Shensi salt pools, was Szechuan, where much salt was produced from salt wells.[8] This production was taxed, a cash quota being allocated to each producing prefecture. This quota was payable either in cash or in terms of grain.[9]

In 721 Liu T'ung memorialised the throne about the possibility of taxing salt and iron as had been done under the Han.[10] The court seems to have been generally in favour of the adoption of his scheme, and Chiang Shih-tu and Chiang Hsün were actually despatched to make the practical arrangements for its enforcement. But the scheme eventually came to nothing, and in the next year an edict ordered that control over salt and iron was to revert to the local authorities, who were to 'collect a tax in accordance with the *Statutes* and *Ordinances*'.[11] It is by no means certain what this implied, since the only ruling on the subject among the preserved fragments of the *Statutes* is a very vague rule covering all mining and similar production.[12]

Before the An Lu-shan rising, then, the policy of the government on salt administration was by no means clear-cut. The coastal regions had some system of taxation in salt carried out at the prefectural level, whose details are unknown. The salt pools had a system of controlled production, or exploitation under official control by the local authorities or the provincial military administrations, and in Szechuan there was a fixed quota money tax levied on each prefecture.

After the outbreak of the rebellion, Ti-wu Ch'i, a former subordinate of the transportation commissioner Wei Chien, became financial adviser to the emperor. Among the many emergency schemes which he devised for the temporary raising of revenue, he advocated a monopoly on salt. It is probable that he had already had some dealings with salt administration at the salt pools while he was employed in the Department of Public Revenue, but there is some doubt whether in fact the scheme was one of his own devising.[13] It is also by no means clear when the plan was first put into effect.[14] It seems likely that it was first enforced locally in 756–7 and extended in 758 to the empire as a whole—or to those parts of the empire under effective control.[15] In the latter year Ti-wu Ch'i was appointed commissioner for the monopoly on salt and iron (*chu-chou chüeh-yen-t'ieh shih*). The inclusion of 'iron' in the title is merely a reference to the Han-time precedent. Under the T'ang the monopoly was confined to salt, and there was never any question of a monopoly tax on iron production.

Under Ti-wu Ch'i's system all salt producers, and any migrant families who wished to adopt this means of livelihood, were placed under the control of the commissioners, becoming state employees (*ting-hu*) and being granted permanent exemption from *corvée* duty. In every area of production directorates (*chien*) were established, to which the producers were compelled to sell all their salt: sales to other persons and illicit production were made punishable offences. The officials of the directorates resold the salt to the merchants adding a tax to the normal price. This tax was very severe, being some ten times the market value of the salt.[16]

Although the descriptions of the new organisation would suggest that it was strictly enforced, the revenue from the salt monopoly remained a relatively small item in the empire's revenues until the end of the hostilities, amounting only to some 600,000 strings of cash.[17] In 763, however, Liu Yen, who had previously held control of the Salt Commission from 760 to 762, was reappointed to the post which he held almost without a break until 779.[18] Under his administration the Salt Commission grew into a powerful organisation with manifold interests, as I shall show in a later chapter,[19] while the revenue from salt increased to such an extent that by 780 it was providing more than half of the cash revenue at the disposal of the central authorities.[20]

His system of management followed roughly the same lines as that established under Ti-wu Ch'i. The account given by *Hsin T'ang-shu* tells us that the producers sold salt directly to the merchants.[21] But since the same text tells how the merchants had to pay a surcharge to the *officials* if they made their payments in silk instead of cash,[22] it is clear that the officials were intermediaries. All the other sources say that the officials of the directorates (*chien-kuan*) sold the salt to the merchants as before.[23] In addition to the monopoly tax, the merchants were often forced to pay transit taxes on their goods. These transit taxes were often levied by local officials on their own responsibility, and Liu Yen sought the suppression of this abuse, which tended to force prices even higher.[24]

The new administration seems to have been very sensitive to the demands of the market, and managed to keep prices at a fairly constant level.[25] In this they were greatly assisted by the very intimate links forged by Liu Yen between the salt administration and the Transport Commission, which formed a unified system. While the salt administration met the costs of grain transport, the transportation commission could convey the salt stocks of the Salt Commisssion without charge.[26] In the more remote areas of the south a system of price-controlled salt (*ch'ang-p'ing-yen*) was established, by which the officials of the administration built up locally stocks of salt which, when trade was interrupted and prices consequently rose, could be sold off at less than the current price, but still show a profit since they had been built up when prices were low.[27]

The administrative organisation of the Salt Commission became very complicated. The centre of the commission was at Yang-chou, the southern terminus and receiving point for the canal traffic between the Yangtze and Huang-ho. The commission had agents (*liu-hou*) at a number of provincial centres and in the capital. These controlled in turn the branch offices (*yüan* or *hsün-yüan*) which were established at important centres of trade to supervise the marketing of salt to local merchants and to control illicit traffic, and the directorates (*chien*) in charge of production. The branch offices and directorates each controlled subordinate units known as *ch'ang* which were the lowest-grade centres for distribution and the control of production respectively (see map 3). These offices employed numerous personnel,[28] many of whom were officials seconded from other offices or holding sinecure ranks in the regular bureaucratic machine, but many more were irregular appointments made by the commissioners on their own authority.

From 766 Liu Yen and Ti-wu Ch'i divided between them the financial control of the empire, the former controlling the Yangtze and Huai basins, the latter the north and Szechuan.[29] After Ti-wu Ch'i fell from power in 770 Liu Yen gained financial control of Szechuan as well.[30] This division of the empire into two separate spheres of financial influence lasted until the end of the dynasty, the Salt and Iron Commission remaining the dominant authority in the south, while the Department of Public Revenue and the Board of Finance retained their authority in the north, after 792 regaining control of Szechuan.[31]

The commissioners of salt and iron thus had no powers of administration over production from coastal Ho-pei or from the salt pools of southern Shensi, and did not always control the production from the salt wells in Szechuan. Salt production in Shensi, however, was also subject to a monopoly tax, although this was levied at a different rate from that imposed in the coastal region[32] and salt prices were considerably higher than in the south.[33] Production was supervised by commissioners for the salt monopoly (*chüeh-yen-shih*) subordinate to the Department of Public Revenue. But in 780 the income from this area's salt production was only one-eighth of that from the coastal salt production of the Salt and Iron Commission,[34] amounting only to 800,000 strings. This income was directly at the disposal of the central financial authorities, which was not the case with the revenue derived from the Salt and Iron Commission.

When Yang Yen came to power in 780 he attempted to reverse all the policies employed by Liu Yen in the preceding period. In an attempt to revive the power of the central government and the regular bureaucracy, he attempted to bring all the tax income of the empire once more under the control of the Board of Finance, and to restore direct taxation as the basic source of revenue through the *liang-shui* reform. The salt

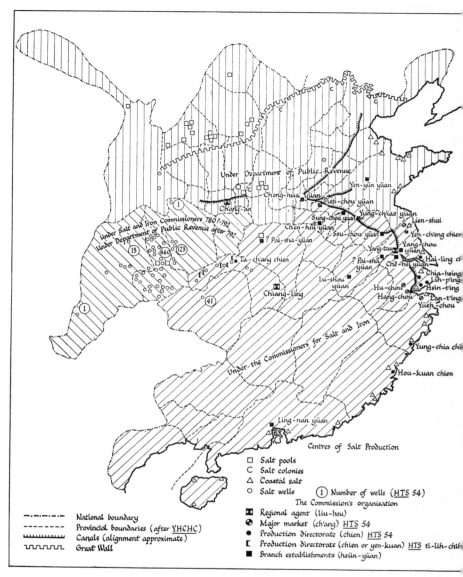

Map 3. Centres of salt production, and the administrative network of the Salt and Iron Commission.

54

administration was temporarily suspended, but later in the same year an edict was promulgated by which the 'profits from the mountains and marshes, which appertain to the emperor' were to revert to the control of the Salt and Iron Commission.[35] The only important one among these commodities was salt, and it is obvious that the government found itself unable to do without the income derived from the salt monopoly which previously had amounted to at least half of the income derived from the *liang-shui* taxes in 781–3.[36]

With the outbreak of the rebellions of the north-eastern provinces in the early 780's, the need for revenue from salt became even more urgent, and the monopoly tax was increased from 100 to 200 cash per *tou* in 782.[37] This clearly caused considerable hardship, for in 784 the executive departments of the central government and the Public Revenue Department, which had by that time become the dominant authority in the financial field, were ordered to give their advice on its reduction.[38] Nothing, however, was ever done about it, and the tax was further increased, first to 300 and then to 360 cash per *tou*.[39] In the north the rate under the direct control of the Public Revenue Department rose to 560 cash.[40] Since the period in question was one of acute progressive deflation the tax rate expressed in real values rose even more steeply than is at first apparent. In any case these figures represent only the increase in the wholesale price paid by the merchants to the officials, and probably the increase in price to the consumer was greater still. The problem of deflation led Pao Chi, who was commissioner from 782 to 785, to accept the practice of taking luxury goods from merchants on a barter basis in transactions over salt.[41]

During the two decades from 786 to 805 the salt administration fell into disorder, especially during the period in office of Li Ch'i, who became commissioner in 799.[42] Like his immediate predecessors, Li Ch'i was concurrently both commissioner for salt and iron and also provincial governor of the rich province of Che-hsi at the mouth of the Yangtze, and he seems to have used much of the income from the salt monopoly to make personal tribute offerings for the emperor's personal treasury, rather than to have placed it at the disposal of the financial authorities.[43] By his time the monopoly tax had grown so onerous, as the result of the increase in its rates and the continued deflation of the currency, that, as in the case of the *liang-shui* tax, it became the custom to levy the tax at fictitious accounting rates (*hsü-ku*). Where the nominal tax was 1000 cash, the actual amount paid in cash was frequently as little as 300 cash.[44] In spite of the increase in tax rates, the total income from the salt monopoly actually fell during the period 780–805.[45] In the hope of increasing the amount of salt passing through the official channels, Li Ch'i himself at one point reduced the monopoly tax by 10 cash per *tou*, but almost immediately after increased it again.[46] Smuggling and illicit production were rampant.[47]

On the accession of Hsien-tsung in 805, Tu Yu, an elder statesman with vast financial experience, was made commissioner for salt and iron,[48] and under his administration and that of his very able successor Li Sun,[49] the whole system was overhauled and reformed. The rate of the monopoly tax was reduced to 250 cash per *tou* in the Yangtze region and 300 cash in the north.[50] Punishments for illicit dealings were reduced,[51] and the system of price-controlled salt (*ch'ang-p'ing yen*) was extended to further regions.[52] The revenue from salt again reached and surpassed the high level of 780, and in 809 this income was for the first time placed at the disposal of the Public Revenue Department for the purpose of the annual budget.[53] What the previous arrangement had been is by no means clear, but the reform was obviously a part of the contemporary strengthening of the central finance administration as part of the general reaction against the autonomous power of the provinces which characterised the reign of Hsien-tsung. From 811 to 817 the salt administration remained in the hands of Wang Po.[54] The Salt and Iron Commission had by this time become so powerful in the southern region that their agents were responsible even for the collection of direct taxation in their areas.[55]

The Department of Public Revenue retained its authority over production of salt from the pools of southern Shensi, and jealously guarded their authority against the Salt and Iron Commission.[56] Illicit production seems to have been a particularly urgent problem in the northern region, and the laws against offenders were more drastic than in the south,[57] especially after Huang-fu Po memorialised the throne to revive the harsh laws of the early years of Te-tsung's reign.[58] Illicit extraction of salt from alkali soil was stringently prohibited, and in 828 laws were enacted to prohibit a new method of extracting salt from the ashes of a salt-bearing marsh plant.[59]

During the early years of the ninth century, several of the small salt pools in northern China came into the control of the provincial or military authorities.[60] Previously, provincial governors had also controlled the production in the coastal prefectures of Ho-pei and

Shantung, which had been a most important area of production in the early T'ang period, and again became very large producers during the tenth century. At the end of Hsien-tsung's reign the revival of central authority had proceeded to a point where it was feasible for the monopoly system to be extended to this region also. Following a memorial of Huang-fu Po,[61] in 819 the Salt and Iron Commission established three branches in Shantung.[62] But this caused great trouble, and in 821 the Department of Public Revenue and the local provincial authorities were ordered to look into the matter.[63] As a result of their deliberations, in 822 an edict ordered the salt administration of the region to revert to the control of the provincial governors.[64]

In 822 the newly appointed vice-president of the Board of Finance, Chang P'ing-shu,[65] suggested a wholesale reform of the salt monopoly by which the officials themselves would have sold salt direct to the consumers without allowing the merchants to be intermediaries, and the reimposition of very strict laws for use against offenders.[66] The proposals were bitterly opposed by Wei Ch'u-hou and by Han Yü, both of whom defended the existing system in long memorials[67] which are among the most informative documents on the monopoly system which we possess (see appendix III, 1), and the proposals were rejected.

After 830 there is little information about the workings of the salt monopoly. We are told that Yang Ssu-fu made certain reforms during his period in office as commissioner from 837 to 840.[68] We know no details of these reforms, but we do know that at this period, when the control of the Salt Commission was exercised concurrently by successive chief ministers, the day-to-day control of the more important southern production centres was deputed by them to the provincial governor of Che-hsi in the Yangtze delta area. Although this is said to have resulted in doubled production, it seems to have been a purely temporary and local arrangement.[69]

In 847 the Salt and Iron Commission presented a long memorial requesting a new series of laws to control illicit production and other abuses, and to impose a harsher scale of punishments.[70] This was accepted. There is some uncertainty as to whether this was the reform of the salt system elsewhere attributed to Ma Chih, commissioner from 847 to 848.[71] P'ei Hsiu, who became commissioner in 851, is also said to have drawn up new laws on the salt administration, but once again no details have survived.[72]

After 850, although the organisation of the Salt and Iron Commission and of the Public Revenue Department seems to have survived, salt production, especially in northern China, seems to have become for the most part a source of revenue for the various provincial military administrations. Even the important salt pools at P'u-chou came into the hands of the military governor of Ho-chung, and the only revenue derived from their salt by the central government at Ch'ang-an was tendered as provincial tribute. An attempt to restore central authority over them ended in complete failure.[73]

Total income from salt

(Figures in strings of 1000 cash)

Date	Ho-chung (Department of Public Revenue)	Chiang-Huai (Salt and Iron Commission)	Total
762	—	—	600,000[a]
779	800,000	6,000,000	6,800,000
779–80?	—	—	9,000,000[b]
785–805	—	—	3,600,000
786	—	2,630,000	—
805	—	3,010,000[c]	—
806	—	4,510,000	6,000,000+
807	—	5,220,000	—
808	1,500,000	7,270,000	8,770,000
809	—	7,220,000	—
810	—	6,980,000	—
811	—	6,850,000	—
812	—	6,780,000	—
829	1,000,000	—	—
847–60	1,210,000	3,600,000	4,810,000

[a] *HTS* gives 400,000.

[b] Figure given by *Yü-hai*, 181, p. 20a, citing Tu Yu's lost *Li-tao yao-chüeh*, and by *T'ung-tien*, 10, p. 59c, without date.

[c] These are figures in real values. The fictitious value (*hsü-ku*) accountancy figures for 805–12 range from 18,000,000 to 20,000,000 strings.

It is clear that even before the final breakdown of central authority in the second half of the ninth century, the state's revenue from salt was declining. As the table above shows, the income in Hsüan-tsung's reign (847–60), even after the reforms of P'ei Hsiu, was little more than half of that collected during the early years of Hsien-tsung's reign.

The Liquor Monopoly

The success of the monopoly on salt as a means of raising revenue, and the very large proportion of the national revenues which it was producing by the end of Tai-tsung's reign, led the administration, who were facing a serious financial crisis, to attempt to extend the system to liquor production in 782. It has been generally assumed that the liquor monopoly tax, which was imposed from this time until the end of the dynasty, was similar in its operation to the monopoly tax on salt, but it is quite clear that this was not the case.

As in the case of the monopoly on salt there was a good historical precedent for a monopoly tax on liquor, as this had been one of the measures imposed by the Former Han under Wu-ti.[74] However, before the An Lu-shan rising, the only action taken by the authorities with regard to liquor was the periodical banning of the use of grain for fermentation in times of famine.[75] This was merely a policy designed to relieve the temporary shortage of grain.

After the rebellion, when the administration experimented with a large variety of irregular forms of taxation in an attempt to swell their much diminished revenues, all households engaged in the production of liquor were registered in 763 and made liable for the payment of a monthly tax. All other persons were forbidden to engage in the trade.[76] In 770 wine shops, most of which produced their own liquor, were divided into three categories for the contribution of the tax.[77] This system of taxation was abolished together with many other forms of supplementary taxation after the liang-shui tax reform in 780.[78]

In 782 the rebellion of the provincial governors of the north-east caused a very serious financial crisis at the capital, since the government had not had any opportunity to build up adequate reserves in the preceding two decades. A series of emergency measures were enforced, among which was the imposition of a state monopoly on the manufacture and sale of liquor.[79] The whole trade was to come under official control and the common people were forbidden to deal in wine. It appears that the producer families, like those engaged in salt production, were to become state employees, for they were granted exemption from corvée in the same way. At first the system did not apply in the capital, but in 786 it was enforced there also.[80]

However, the liquor trade proved much more difficult to control than had that in salt. The technique of manufacturing wine was so simple and primitive that anyone could easily make it, providing that he could obtain grain and ferments—both of which were universally available.[81] The control of all centres of production by the authorities was thus quite impossible. As a result the administration of the monopoly was by no means uniform. Each province was assessed a quota of wine-monopoly money (*chüeh-chiu-ch'ien*) which it was expected to contribute. In some areas this money was raised by officially controlled dealings in liquor, as envisaged by the original measure. In others there was simply a monopoly on the production of ferments, and in many provinces it became the normal custom to impose the responsibility for contributing the wine monopoly money as a supplementary money tax upon households other than those actually engaged in the business.[82]

An Act of Grace promulgated in 807 put an end to the official participation in the liquor trade,[83] but in effect this seems only to have been a temporary suspension, for official wine shops are again mentioned in a memorial from the Board of Finance in 817,[84] and in 819 Li Ying presented a memorial requesting the prohibition of official trade in liquor.[85] Although in fact this had been the system which had been envisaged when the monopoly was first introduced, the commentary appended to his memorial in *T'ai-p'ing yü-lan* and *Ts'e-fu yüan-kuei*[86] gives the impression that such official participation in trade was merely an arbitrary means of producing revenue adopted by certain provincial authorities, and states that the normal means of raising the liquor monopoly had been to collect it from 'all households in accordance with the *liang-shui* tax'.

This was the normal practice during the Five Dynasties and the Sung, and it is quite clear that there was already a close connection between the wine monopoly money and the system of direct taxation by the beginning of the ninth century. This is borne out by a long memorial presented by the Board of Finance in 817, and by numerous Acts of Grace and edicts granting tax exemption, which mention the wine monopoly money as a supplementary item of direct taxation in cash, similar to the green sprout tax (*ch'ing-miao-ch'ien*).[87] From another memorial presented in 811 it would seem that there were two forms of the tax commonly levied, one called the 'regular levy' (*cheng-shui*) and presumably collected from the households engaged in the trade, and the other collected from the population in general as a supplementary money tax.[88]

Towards the end of Hsien-tsung's reign there appears to have been a crisis, which was undoubtedly connected with the general financial crisis brought about by the steady growth of deflation. In 817 the Board of Finance requested that the provincial governors should be prohibited from collecting the liquor monopoly money as an item of direct taxation, while at the same time engaging in official trading in wine.[89] In 819 Li Ying memorialised the throne requesting that the official liquor shops should be abolished, and the collection of the liquor monopoly money as a supplementary direct tax should become the universal system.[90] The consensus of opinion at court seems to have been in favour of Li Ying's proposal,[91] and this memorial was allowed in spite of a counter-memorial from the governor of his province, against whose policies the original memorial may well have been directed.

When in 820 Yüan Chen drew up a general survey of taxation on behalf of the Chancellery he drew attention to the great confusion which had reigned in the administration of the liquor monopoly, and again requested that a uniform system should be adopted, under which the total quotas assessed for each province should be everywhere collected as a money tax supplementary to the *liang-shui* contribution and levied on all families whose assessment reached a certain figure.[92]

In 821 the whole monopoly was suspended by an Act of Grace, and it is possible that it had been suspended previously.[93] The liquor monopoly money does not again figure among the items of tax remitted by Acts of Grace until 833, but the system must have been revived shortly after its suspension for in 823 a provincial governor requested that the 'offence of breaking the liquor monopoly laws' should be abolished.[94]

In spite of all these efforts at reform, official trading in liquor continued widely. In 830 Wei Tz'u, governor of Hu-nan, requested permission to engage in official trading in wine to replace the revenue formerly obtained by collection of the liquor monopoly money as a direct tax.[95] But in the very next year he asked leave to abandon this enterprise in his provincial capital of Hung-chou,[96] and in the same year the governor of the neighbouring province Chiang-hsi, P'ei I, requested permission to close down the official wine shops in his province.[97] In 834 an edict officially abolished monopoly dealings in the capital city where, it confesses, the whole scheme had proved impracticable.[98] The official participation in the wine trade may thus be generally described as a failure, especially in the large cities, where it must have been virtually impossible to control illicit production and sales.

The imposition of a monopoly tax on ferments and the opening of official liquor stores, as a temporary substitute for the direct tax, was again permitted in 846.[99] After this, it appears from an edict promulgated in 901, the military governments in the provinces generally administered a monopoly tax on ferments, and this became a widespread form of taxation. In 901 it was attempted to revive the old system of a graded tax imposed on all liquor-producing households, but since by this time the government in Ch'ang-an was entirely powerless this can have been enforced only on the most restricted scale.[100]

The liquor monopoly was never more than a minor source of revenue. The only total figure for income from this source is that given for 834, when it produced some 1,560,000 strings, of which sum one-third represented the cost of manufacture.[101] This figure represents only a sixth of the net profit from the salt monopoly, which paid for the expenses of the state transportation system into the bargain,[102] and if the figure quoted was in fact reckoned at the fictitious accounting values commonly employed during the period, the proportion would have been even less.

The Taxation of Tea

The phenomenal growth of the trade in tea during T'ang times has already received a certain amount of attention. We shall see later that the tea merchants played an important part in the development of an apparatus for credit transfers, and were closely associated with the provincial authorities. It is hardly surprising then that the government in the latter part of the eighth century should have attempted to raise revenue from this very flourishing trade.

As in the case of the liquor monopoly tax, the first move in this direction was made as an emergency measure during the financial crisis of the 780's. In 782 Chao Tsan suggested the imposition of a 10 per cent tax on the production of tea, lacquer, bamboo and timber.[103] The ostensible purpose of this tax was the provision of funds for the price-regulating granaries (*ch'ang-p'ing-ts'ang*) which he wished to extend and to establish in many provincial centres.[104] However, the critical financial situation forced the government to use the income for current expenditure, and the taxes were suspended in 783 when the rebels forced Te-tsung to flee from the capital to Feng-t'ien.[105]

In 793 Chang P'ang, the commissioner for salt and iron, presented a memorial suggesting the imposition of a tax on tea to replace the losses in direct taxation caused in the previous years by extensive floods and to build up financial reserves in case of a recurrence of such natural disasters.[106] In 794 Lu Chih asked that the income from this tax should be used to provide funds for the relief granaries (*i-ts'ang*), but it was diverted into the ordinary treasuries for current expenditure.[107]

This new tax was not a tax on production as its forerunner had been, but a tax on trade. Tea was divided into three qualities, on each of which a tax amounting to 10 per cent of the average price was levied.[108] This system was controlled by the salt and iron commissioners, who dominated the areas in Anhwei, Chekiang, and Fukien where much of the production was concentrated.[109] In Szechuan and Shan-nan, which were also flourishing centres of production, especially for fine quality teas,[110] and where the salt and iron commissioners no longer held financial control after 792, the Board of Finance administered the tax through their provincial branches (*yüan*).[111] The Salt and Iron Commission established special subordinate branches called *ch'a-ch'ang* with the specialised responsibility for the levying of the tea tax. The total annual income at this period was some 400,000 strings, or approximately 12 per cent of the current income from salt.[112]

There is little further information about the tea tax until in 818 the salt and iron commissioner, Ch'eng I, drew the attention of the central government to the abuse by which provincial governors had established transit warehouses, the use of which was made compulsory for tea and salt merchants, who had to pay heavy storage and transit dues.[113]

On the accession to the throne of Mu-tsung in 821, the rate of the tea tax was increased to 15 per cent.[114] This measure, which was suggested by the new salt and iron commissioner Wang Po, was strongly attacked by Li Chüeh,[115] but the emperor was temporarily in dire need of funds, and his opposition was disregarded.[116]

The merchants retaliated to the increase of the tax by increasing in their turn the size of the standard catty (*chin*) of tea, on which the tax was levied. After 821 they increased the size of the catty from the normal 16 ounces (*liang*) to 20. This process became a vicious circle. The tax was probably increased by Ling-hu Ch'u when he succeeded Wang Yai as salt and iron commissioner in 835,[117] and was again increased on the accession of Wu-tsung in 840.[118] By the time Yü Tsung became commissioner in 865, the merchants in their turn had increased the size of the standard catty to no less than 50 ounces, and he was forced to introduce a supplementary tax on surplus tea (*sheng-ch'a-ch'ien*) at 5 cash per catty, after which the use of the normal standard measures was restored.[119]

The state also participated directly in the production of tea. As has been pointed out in an earlier chapter, tea-gardens were among the properties administered by the household commissioners for estates (*nei chuang-chai shih*). These tea-gardens were presumably part of the private property of the imperial family, and must have produced some part at least of the tea which was continually presented to deserving courtiers, and part of the stock of 300,000 catties of tea which the emperor's private treasury disposed of in 817 to the Department of Public Revenue.[120] These tea-gardens belonging to the royal household were transferred to the control of the local authorities in 821,[121] the emperor continuing to receive large quantities of tea as an item of tribute.[122]

In 835 Wang Yai and Cheng Chu attempted to establish a state monopoly in tea production. A Tea-monopoly Commission (*chüeh-ch'a shih*) was set up with Wang Yai as commissioner, and all production was ordered to be confined in future to state-controlled plantations. The common people were ordered to transplant all their tea-shrubs to official plantations, and to destroy all their stocks of prepared tea.[123] This scheme caused extensive unrest, but, as Wang Yai and Cheng Chu fell from power almost immediately after, it is improbable that the scheme was ever put into effective operation.[124]

The events of the next few years are rather confused. Although Li Shih is said to have revived the old tax system in 836, other sources inform us that control was only restored to the Salt and Iron Commission in 840.[125] We know from a memorial of Ling-hu Ch'u presented in 835 that production had been disrupted, and this may have been the reason for the appointment in 838 of a eunuch as special commissioner for tea production in Hu-chou.[126]

In 839 there was a suggestion by Ts'ui Tan that the whole system should be scrapped, and that the tea tax should become a supplementary money tax linked to the *liang-shui* taxes in the same way as the liquor monopoly money, but this was rejected on the grounds that it would have led to increased direct taxation.[127]

In 740 a memorial from the Salt and Iron Commission complained about the rapid growth of illicit dealing in tea, that is, transactions made direct from the grower to the merchant without the employment of the brokers through whom the tax seems to have been charged.[128] After the tax rate was increased by Ts'ui Hung, this abuse became more and more common. In 848 an Act of Grace ordered some reform of the system to be made,[129] and in 852 P'ei Hsiu revised the administration of the tax. He first requested the prohibition of illegally imposed storage and transit charges by the provincial authorities,[130] and then drew up a series of rules in twelve articles to deal with the problem of illicit trading.[131] We are told that, as a result of his reforms, the tea tax brought in twice the revenue which it had in the time of Chang P'ang, but, as it appears that the total income was still only 603,370 strings, this seems to be an exaggeration,[132] and to the end of the dynasty the income from the tea tax remained a very minor item of revenue, while the provincial authorities continued to raise their own revenue from the trade by the illegal imposition of further local surcharges.

CHAPTER IV

CURRENCY AND CREDIT

It is clear from what has been said above about the change of emphasis in taxation, and the great growth of indirect taxes levied on or through trade, that during the T'ang commerce, in spite of the lowly position reserved for the merchant in traditional economic theory, became increasingly more important. This expansion of commerce called for a stable and sufficient currency, and the administration attempted in vain to supply this demand and at the same time maintain their monopoly of coinage.

The Manufacture of Coinage

This was a privilege reserved for the government. At the very beginning of the dynasty an exception to this rule was made, when two of the imperial princes and one of the important supporters of the emperor in his rise to power were granted hearths and the right to cast coin, as a reward for their services.[1] Another exception of the same nature was made in favour of An Lu-shan in the middle of the eighth century.[2] Apart from these cases, the principle that 'currency is the privilege of the ruler'[3] was always maintained, and although there was an attempt to allow free manufacture of coinage in 734, this was unsuccessful.[4]

The government's privilege was protected by heavy legal sanctions. The edict of 621, which first set up mints, imposed the death penalty on counterfeiters, and enslavement on their families.[5] Under the T'ang *Code*, dating in its present form from 737,[6] the casting of copper coin by private individuals was punishable with exile beyond 3000 *li*, while even making preparations for such casting was punishable with two years hard labour. The defacement of coin by paring down or grinding away the metal was punishable with one year of hard labour.[7] These penalties were increased by special edicts from time to time, the death penalty being frequently imposed.[8]

The actual manufacture was carried on by mints called coinage directorates (*ch'ien-chien*). The first of these were set up in 621 at

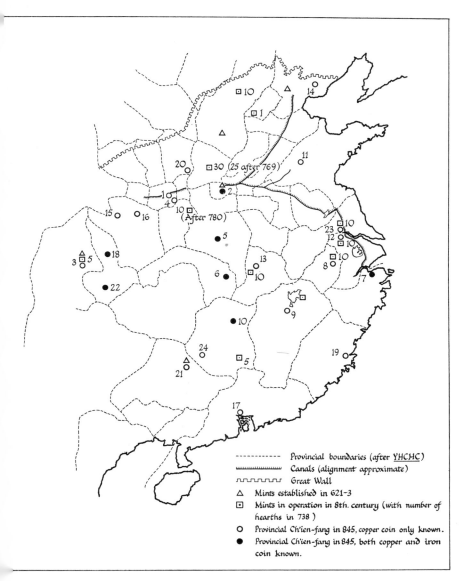

Map 4. Distribution of mints.

Numbers in roman refer to mint-marks listed in appendix IV, 2.

Lo-yang, T'ai-yuan, Yu-chou and Cheng-tu. Another was added to these in 623 at Kuei-lin.[9] It seems from the commentary to the *T'ang liu-tien* that besides these mints in the provinces, the Directorate of Imperial Workshops (*shao-fu-chien*), which was in nominal control over their activities, also had ten hearths, presumably at the capital, under their direct control.[10] When the latter were closed down for a while in 679, owing to a belief that there was too much money in circulation, the provincial mints were taken away from the directorate's control.[11]

The Directorate of Imperial Workshops was a body whose main concern was the manufacture of luxury goods for the imperial household, official insignia, ceremonial objects and so forth. The organisation for casting coin, as described in the *T'ang liu-tien* and the *Monograph on Officials* in the *Chiu T'ang-shu*,[12] was very loose. *T'ang liu-tien* makes a distinction between the provincial mints and those foundries directly controlled by the directorate, and I think one may safely assume that this organisation refers only to the former.

The provincial mints were staffed entirely by members of the official hierarchy of the local prefectures, who combined responsibility for the minting of money with their regular duties.[13] They seem to have employed the labour services of the local people, rather than employ professional artisans on a permanent basis. This was not altogether unreasonable, as the mints were all situated in copper-producing areas, where there were presumably a large number of people with the necessary metallurgical skill who were presumably employed as special duty *corvée* labourers (*fan-i*) of the category of artisans (*tsa-chiang*). But we know from the advice which Wei Lun offered to Yang Kuo-chung in the late 740's[14] that this system was wasteful and inefficient. Wei advocated the permanent employment of professional artisans, and it appears that his suggestion was put into practice.

In the early eighth century there were a considerable number of mints in operation, to judge by the account in the *T'ang liu-tien* dating from 739 which lists ten mints with a total of eighty-nine hearths. Both *T'ung-tien* and *Ts'e-fu yüan-kuei* give an almost identical list for the *T'ien-pao* period (742–55),[15] with eleven mints and ninety-nine hearths.

We may deduce the fact that loose control and careless methods of manufacture were causing trouble in the 730's from the appointment, in 737, of the first commissioner for the casting of coin (*chu-tao chu-ch'ien shih*), who had general responsibility for the whole business.[16] Such commissioners continued to be appointed until 770.

After the An Lu-shan rising the control of the Coinage Commission came into the hands of Liu Yen and Ti-wu Ch'i in turn. From 765 until its abolition in 770 they divided control on a geographical basis, Liu Yen controlling the south, and Ti-wu Ch'i the north.[17] During this period, too, regional coinage commissioners were appointed; in 760 one for the capital environs, and in 764 one for Chiang-hsi, which contained important sources of copper.[18]

In the latter eighth and early ninth centuries the manufacture of coinage seems to have come under the control of the Salt and Iron Commission, since we know from *Hsin T'ang-shu* that prior to the suppression of the Buddhist monasteries in 843–5 the salt and iron commissioners maintained a regular staff for minting cash.[19] As they were the most powerful financial organisation in the south, where the bulk of the copper was produced, this was not unnatural. The organisation was changed again in 845. The suppression of the monasteries suddenly released a great quantity of copper in the form of images, bells, gongs, etc. The metal obtained was ordered to be cast into coin, but the regular staff were unable to deal with the rush of work. As a result local mints called *ch'ien fang* were set up under the control of the civil governors of the provinces.[20] We can trace a number of these mints, for they put their names on the reverse of the coin which they cast.[21] Previously the mints had sometimes put signs on the reverse of coins, which have been taken for mint marks, but these have never been identified.[22]

The coinage which this organisation produced was of a comparatively high quality. The currency situation at the end of Sui times had been chaotic.[23] The *K'ai-yüan t'ung-pao* coins which were produced from 621 onwards to provide a stable medium of currency[24] remained the standard coin throughout the dynasty. The weight of officially cast coin of this type tended to increase, at least until the An Lu-shan rebellion. At first it was fixed at 6 catties 4 ounces per 1000.[25] But *T'ang liu-tien* says that[26] 'many of those recently (i.e. in 739) cast weigh 7 catties (per 1000)', while a calculation from the figures given in *T'ung-tien* gives a weight of 7 catties 2 ounces.[27]

The cost of these coins was extremely high, and the minting of cash was not a source of profit to the government. According to the

T'ung-tien it cost 750 cash in metal alone to manufacture 1000 cash, setting aside entirely the costs of fuel, labour, and transport to the capital where most of the coin was put into circulation.[28] According to a memorial presented by Han Hui in 780 the cost of coins had at that time reached double their face value, though this seems partly to have been due to the high cost of transport from the mints in the south of the Yangtze basin to the capital.[29]

As a result of the high value of the metal content of the coinage it became a profitable business for the people to break up and melt down money, not only to recast it into debased coin, but simply for the sake of the metal, which was in very short supply. This made a constant inroad on the amount of money in circulation. The pattern of the coins, which were cast in very simple moulds, made counterfeiting very easy. The fact that most of the mints were operated by unskilled labour presumably made it impossible to introduce a more complicated design.

The Use of Cloth and Precious Metals as Currency

The *K'ai-yüan t'ung-pao* coins were of one denomination, and that a low one. There were three attempts during the dynasty to mint coins of higher denominations,[30] but these coins had only a token value, and their introduction must be viewed rather as schemes to debase the currency for a temporary profit than as plans to provide the much-needed high-value coin. All failed very rapidly.

To supply the need for a medium of currency suitable for use in large transactions, where copper cash were too bulky[31] and cumbersome, it was the practice in T'ang times to employ either silk cloth or precious metals, in the latter case usually silver.[32] The use of these media of exchange has been discussed in most painstaking detail by Katō Shigeshi in his monumental work *On gold and silver in T'ang and Sung times*.[33] According to his findings silk and precious metals were used in every variety of transaction, both public and private, for the payment of large sums. The use of silk was more widespread at the beginning of the dynasty, and it seems that silver began to replace it as the usual medium for payment of large sums after An Lu-shan's rebellion and especially during the ninth century.

The government also made wide use of silk for very large payments. For instance, the armies used silk in making 'harmonious purchases' (*ho-ti*) of grain,[34] while the government paid enormous quantities of silk cloth to the Uighurs in return for horses after the suppression of An Lu-shan and Shih Ssu-ming and the loss of their own breeding grounds to the Tibetans.[35] For such payments there was a very ample source, in that the tax in kind (*tiao*) and *corvée* exemption tax (*yung*) were paid in cloth. The great care exercised over the standard size and quality of tax cloths[36] may be attributed in part at least to the fact that the standard length of silk or hemp was an item of currency, a defective length being equivalent to a debased coin.

The government never minted a silver coinage, in fact the *Code* specifically states that the laws against counterfeiting did not apply to casting silver.[37] The only official mention of silver coins is in *T'ang liu-tien*, where the collection of taxes in silver cash amongst the submitted barbarians is mentioned.[38] As Katō has pointed out, this probably refers to Persian or Indian coinage which was in common use in Central Asia.[39] The minting of silver coins on behalf of Yang Kuei-fei is also mentioned,[40] but these were only in the nature of curiosities. The normal form in which silver circulated was not a coin but an ingot *ting* of a standard 50 ounces.[41] Gold was used either in the form of ingots or of dust.[42]

As there was no official silver or gold currency, and the quality of ingots was variable, a type of business grew up specialising in dealings in the precious metals, and in making appraisals. These were known as *chin-p'u*, *yin-p'u*, or *yin-chiang-p'u*; and were organised in closely-knit guilds (*yin-hang*, *chin-yin-hang*).[43]

The government collected a considerable amount of silver as local tribute from the various southern prefectures which were the chief producers. A list of the places offering silver and gold has been compiled from the *Ti-li chih* of the *Hsin T'ang-shu* and from the *Yüan-ho chün-hsien t'u-chih* by Katō.[44] In addition there was a tax on mines, which seems to have been levied in silver. Under P'ei Hsiu in the middle of the ninth century this annual tax in silver came to 25,000 ounces.[45] But the details regarding this are far from clear, owing to lack of information.

The export of coin was illegal under the T'ang, but great quantities of copper cash were exported.[46] The trading of gold with foreigners was forbidden in 714,[47] and of silver in 780.[48] Nevertheless, there was some trade in precious metals, which seem to have been imported from Korea and Japan.[49]

The Development of Credit Organisations

There were three separate ways in which credit transferences were made in T'ang times. The first and best known of these was the so-called 'flying money' (*fei-ch'ien*) or 'convenient exchange' (*pien-huan*). Balázs makes rather too strong a claim to the importance of this as an early form of paper money. In fact the *fei-ch'ien* was a type of bill of exchange. Its development arose out of the great increase in trade in the latter half of the T'ang dynasty, and from the lack of a convenient currency for large sums. There was a great deal of trade between the south and the capital, the most important single branch of which was the tea trade. Miyazaki long ago pointed out the connection between the growth of the tea trade and the development of flying money.[50] The increasing dependence of the central government on taxes paid by the southern provinces in money rather than in actual commodities was also a contributory factor.

The system worked as follows. The provincial governors at this time maintained their own chancelleries, the 'memorial-offering courts' (*chin-tsou-yüan*) in the capital. The merchants from the south paid money which they had made from the sale of their goods at the capital to these agents, who used it to pay the tax quotas due from their provinces to the central government. In return they issued the merchant with a certificate, that is, the *fei-ch'ien*. When he returned to the south, he presented this certificate to the provincial authorities who paid him the equivalent sum of money. By this means the merchant avoided the risk and trouble of carrying his profits back in the bulky form of copper cash or silk, and the provincial authorities were saved the considerable trouble of transporting their tax money to the capital.[51] There was probably some connection, too, with the policy of the T'ang administration of restricting the flow of money from one region to another.[52]

By the beginning of the ninth century, this system was widespread. It was forbidden by an edict in 811.[53] The suspension caused great inconvenience, and in the next year the government allowed the same type of credit transfer to be made by merchants through the 'three offices', that is, the Board of Finance, the Department of Public Revenue and the Salt and Iron Commission, all of which maintained provincial branches, instead of through the provincial authorities.[54] This change is clearly an indication of the recovery of the powers of the central financial authorities from the provincial governors, which took place in this period. According to one account the government at first tried to make a profit on these transactions by charging a commission, but the merchants would not accept this, and the authorities were obliged to make the credit transfer at 'a string for a string'.[55] Later on, it appears that the local branches of the financial administration were not so prompt in paying the merchants as they should have been, for in 867 a memorial from the vice-president of the Board of Finance sought to prevent such abuses.[56]

The sources on the flying money system are so fragmentary that it is very difficult for us to visualise the documents themselves. However, Niida has drawn some very convincing conclusions by deduction from the descriptions of their Sung equivalents, the *pien-ch'ien*.[57] He considers that they were not promissory notes, as had been suggested, but bills of credit, for the person who issued the bill was not the one who was to pay it. He considers that they were payable at sight, and that the names of the three parties concerned were entered on them.[58] He also considers that at the same time as issuing the bill, the issuer sent a confirmatory document to the paying authority, which had to be matched with the bill itself before payment.[59] These bills can hardly have been readily negotiable and it is quite misleading to call them 'the first paper money'.

The other forms of instruments of credit arose from the activities of the institutions which Yang Lien-sheng[60] has called proto-banks. These were of two types. The first, which went under the names of *kuei-fang*, *chiu-kuei*, or *chi-fu-p'u*, were a sort of safe-deposit firm.[61] The second were the gold- and silversmiths' shops (*chin-yin-p'u*) mentioned above.[62] Both of these issued notes of credit and promissory notes which were negotiable, and from which the first true paper money later derived. The more important, at least in late T'ang and early Sung times, seem to have been the *kuei-fang*, which issued two types of credit instrument. The first was a certificate of deposit, which was known in Sung times as the *chiao-tzu*. These have been the subject of a series of studies by Katō Shigeshi and Hino Kaisaburō,[63] who have shown that they took the form of promissory notes. In Sung times they came to be circulated as money, especially in Szechuan. The second type was a sort of cheque called *t'ieh* or *t'ieh-tzu* which could be drawn on the firm by customers whose goods they had in safe keeping.[64]

It is difficult to know how widespread the use of such credit instruments was in the confused situation of the latter ninth century. It is tempting to connect their appearance with the shortage of money and the lack of a currency for high denominations. What is certain, however, is that they remained private issues of the proto-banks. The first government issue of paper money began with the issue of official *chiao-tzu* in Szechuan in 1024.[65]

Government Money Policy

The two great problems which faced the administration in the monetary field were counterfeiting and the shortage of money. The two were complementary, for although counterfeit coin tended to drive good money out of circulation, money was so scarce that illicit coin was necessary to supply the needs of commerce.

When the dynasty came to power, the coinage was in a chaotic state,[66] and after the introduction of the new currency in 621 it must have taken some time before there was a sufficient supply of coinage. At the time the empire was recovering from the effects of a long period of warfare and dislocated production. However, about 630 the situation seems to have improved, and grain prices fell to 3 or 4 cash per *tou*.[67] Prices remained low until about 665, when grain was still only 5 cash per *tou*.[68] With the very scanty material at our disposal, it is difficult to assess to what extent these low prices were the result of abundant production, and to what extent they were due to the scarcity of money. Both factors were certainly involved.

Counterfeiting had already begun to flourish at this early period. In 660 an edict was promulgated ordering the officials to buy in illicit coin at the rate of 1 good cash for each 5 counterfeit coins.[69] Even when the rate was subsequently reduced[70] the people refused to part with their money at a loss. This method of dealing with counterfeit coin was used frequently during the dynasty, grain or cloth rather than good cash being usually issued in exchange for counterfeit coin.[71] As Kanei has pointed out,[72] these exchanges were usually made at a rate calculated to yield a profit to the authorities.[73]

In spite of these measures, and the imposition of the death penalty not only for the counterfeiter himself, but for his family and neighbours,[74] counterfeiting continued, especially in the Yangtze valley, where the money economy was most firmly rooted[75] and where official control was relatively slack.

In 666 the government cast a new coinage called *Ch'ien-feng ch'üan-*

pao which had a face value ten times that of the *K'ai-yüan t'ung-pao* coins, though its metal content was little greater.[76] This may have been a plan to increase the amount of currency in circulation and provide the much needed coin of higher denomination, but it seems more than likely that it was simply an attempt to debase the coinage. It was probably the result of the shortage of funds caused by the growth of the official body, and by the campaigns against the western Turks,[77] and against Korea.[78] The effect on trade of this debasement was very serious, and although the new coinage was speedily abolished, it ushered in a period of high prices.

During the latter half of Kao-tsung's reign, as a result of the foreign campaigns and internal developments the economic situation remained strained. Not only was production very low owing to a series of bad harvests,[79] but the problem of vagrancy began to assume serious proportions.[80] At the same time, the current high prices of commodities were misinterpreted by contemporary statesmen, and taken as evidence that there was too much coin in circulation,[81] and minting was suspended. It is clear that the years 679–83 were a period of serious financial crisis, and the price of rice rose to between 200 and 400 cash per *tou*.[82]

In face of this the government introduced extremely severe laws against counterfeiting, and at the same time cut down its own production of coin,[83] both measures being designed to strengthen the position of the coinage. However, counterfeiting seems to have flourished under the empress Wu. In the period *Ch'ang-an* (701–4) the use of the better kinds of counterfeit coin was permitted by the government.[84] In 713, according to a memorial offered by Yang Hsü-shou, debased coin of a standard too low for use elsewhere was at that time permitted in the markets of the capital.[85] It seems that in the early days of the eighth century, the demand for money had so far exceeded the supply that the government had to relax the law in order not to bring trade to a standstill.

This policy did not survive for long. In 717 Sung Ching requested that the former strict ban on counterfeit money should be reimposed.[86] This was done in the next year and Sung Ching sent a censor to the Yangtze and Huai valleys, where the problem of counterfeiting was extremely serious, and where a large number of types of bad money were in circulation.[87] The result of this mission, however, was not what had been anticipated, for many people threw away or concealed the bad coin in their possession in order to avoid punishment, and a serious shortage of cash followed. As a result of this trade was brought to a standstill, and the prohibition had to be relaxed.[88]

The reign of Hsüan-tsung was generally a period of low prices.[89] This was due to a number of reasons, among them a series of good harvests and the great improvements in communications brought about in the 730's. Undoubtedly the shortage of money and its high value was also a factor. In 723 Chang Chiu-ling memorialised the throne that the people should be allowed freely to make coin.[90] Such a suggestion could hardly have been made, save in a period of severe shortage of currency. His suggestion, however, was strongly opposed and not adopted.[91]

At the beginning of the T'ien-pao period (742) the coinage was of relatively good quality. But a great spate of counterfeiting again broke out, this time involving the export of good coin from the capital to the south, where it was melted down and recast into counterfeit.[92] This resulted in another attempt to take very bad coin out of circulation, and to issue good coin to replace it, in 752.[93] But inconvenience to commerce ensued and an edict shortly followed allowing the free use of all save a few of the worst types of counterfeit money.[94] Part of the trouble was due to the refusal of the government to allow the interchange of bad and good coin at different prices.[95]

One of the emergency measures introduced by Ti-wu Ch'i after the outbreak of the An Lu-shan rising was the minting in 758 of new coins of high denominations and comparatively low metal content called Ch'ien-yüan chung-pao. The new coins were in two denominations, of 10 cash and 50 cash, weighing 10 and 20 catties per 1000 respectively, compared with 6 catties and 4 ounces per 1000 for the ordinary K'ai-yüan t'ung-pao coins.[96] Apart from the dislocation of commerce which naturally followed this debasement, there was a new outbreak of counterfeiting, the old single cash being melted down to make copies of the new high value coins.[97] Prices, already very high as a result of the scarcity of goods caused by the war, rose even higher, the price of a tou of rice reaching 7000 cash.[98] Prices in general seem to have remained very high until about 785.[99] It became obvious that the plan had failed completely, and at the end of 759 its author, Ti-wu Ch'i, was disgraced.[100] In the next year the old K'ai-yüan t'ung-pao were raised to a token value of 10 cash, while the new coins were reduced to 30 and 10 cash in value respectively.[101] In 762 the heavier new coins were made equivalent to 3 cash, and the lighter ones to 2 cash.[102] This was approximately the worth of their metal content. Later in the same year they were all made to circulate at par with the ordinary cash,[103] and reckonings at the previous token prices were forbidden.[104] This resulted in their being taken out of circulation and melted down for the value of the metal.[105]

While the rebel Shih Ssu-ming was in control of Lo-yang he too carried out a debasement of the coinage, casting coins with a nominal value of 100 cash.[106]

Under Liu Yen's financial administration, a policy was developed of using the tax produce of places so remote that the costs of transporting their tax goods to the capital were prohibitive to buy locally the raw materials needed for minting cash. By this means over 100,000 strings were produced annually. This money was sent to the great commercial centres in the Yangtze valley where the demand for cash was very great, as well as to the capital.[107]

A new problem arose at this time. This was a severe shortage of copper,[108] which became so expensive that it was profitable to melt down money and make implements from the metal.[109] In 772 the first of a series of edicts prohibiting the manufacture of copper utensils of various sorts was promulgated.[110]

A new era in the history of currency was begun with the reform of the tax system in 780. Taxation in money was no new thing, for the household tax and the exemption tax for special labour services had been collected in money since early in the dynasty, while since the suppression of An Lu-shan the green sprout tax had been collected in money, and the indirect monopoly tax on salt—now the biggest single item of income—was also reckoned in cash. After the reform, however, a fixed local rate for the unified *liang-shui* tax was assessed for every province.[111] This rate was fixed, in so far as the household tax was concerned, in terms of cash. Now in 780 the empire was in the last stages of the long period of inflation and high prices which had followed the rebellion. According to Li Ao, in 780 a *tou* of grain still cost 200 cash.[112] After the rising of the Ho-pei governors in the early 780's the price reached famine levels of 500 and 1000 cash.[113] Cloth was also very dear, fetching 3000–4000 cash per length.[114]

In 787 there was a sudden fall in grain prices, reflecting the end of hostilities, the reopening of transport from the south, and a series of good harvests from 785 onwards. The price of rice fell to 150 cash per *tou*,[115] and that of millet to 80 cash.[116] By the beginning of the ninth century these prices fell still further to an average of 50 and 20 cash per *tou* respectively.[117] This period of deflation lasted until the middle of the ninth century, and the hardships which it caused to the people, whose taxes had been assessed on a money basis during the inflationary period, made it a critical administrative problem.

Besides, in this period money seems to have gained a great deal of ground as the predominant form of currency. Kanei[118] links this up with the destruction of the government's stocks of tax cloth during An Lu-shan's rising, but I am more inclined to believe that it was the result of the natural economic development of society. The disadvantages of cloth as a medium of exchange were already clearly set out in an edict of 734,[119] and with the growth of trade these must have grown more acute. The shortage of money in circulation thus not only caused distress to the people who paid taxes fixed at inflated rates with goods at deflationary prices, but also had an adverse effect on commerce.

The primary cause of the shortage was the failure of the government to manufacture enough coinage. Whereas in the *T'ien-pao* period, when the demand was lower, the annual output of the empire's mints had been 327,000 strings,[120] in 804 the annual production was 135,000 strings,[121] in 821 it was 150,000 strings,[122] and in 834 less than 100,000 strings.[123] Many of the mints were abandoned in the period after An Lu-shan's rebellion. In 780, following a memorial of Han Hui, the production of coin in the mints in the Yangtze valley, which had fallen away from 100,000 strings annually[124] to some 45,000, was abandoned as uneconomical, as the cost of producing a string of cash had reached double its nominal value. This centre of production was replaced by that of Shang-chou, not far south of Ch'ang-an, where production was cheaper, and the annual total was increased to 72,000 strings.[125] But the shutting down of the southern mints resulted in a shortage of money in the Yangtze and Huai valleys,[126] and in 808 they were revived and again went into production on a small scale.[127] In 811 some additional hearths were put into production in the northern mint at Yü-chou.[128] But, as the previously cited figures show, the total production remained quite inadequate.

One of the reasons for the low production of coin was the severe shortage of metal. Copper production totalled 266,000 catties in 806,[129] while under Hsüan-tsung (847–60) it reached only 655,000,[130] compared with 14,605,969 catties under the Sung in 1078.[131] It seems that at the beginning of the ninth century many miners started working silver mines rather than mining copper. In 808 the Salt and Iron Commission, who were in general control of mining operations,[132] attempted to prohibit silver mining and to employ the miners in copper mining and minting.[133] But this policy was a failure and had to be abandoned in the next year.[134]

The minting of money was only one of the many uses to which copper was put. As previously remarked, the high price of copper made it profitable for artisans to melt down money and make utensils from the metal. During the period of acute money shortage there was a whole series of edicts proscribing the use of copper for utensils, and the breaking up of cash for this purpose. In 793, following a memorial of Chang P'ang, the casting of all articles save mirrors was forbidden.[135] In 794 the price of copper was limited to 160 cash per catty (compared with the current price of 600 cash quoted by Chang P'ang), which was roughly the value of the equivalent amount of coin by weight. At the same time those who broke up coin were made guilty of the crime of counterfeiting.[136]

In 820, when the shortage of money again reached a crisis, a scheme was put forward by which the local authorities and the armies were to collect in copper utensils and cast them into money.[137] In 825 it was specifically forbidden to break up money to make Buddhist images, and offenders were to be considered as counterfeiters.[138] In 829 an edict prohibited the use of copper save for mirrors, chimes, nails, rings and handbells, and imposed the death penalty on offenders.[139] However, these laws could not be enforced, and the drain on the currency continued.[140]

A further drain on the currency took the form of a large-scale export of cash. This was strictly forbidden, but Kuwabara has drawn attention to Abu Zeyd's *Diary*, which records that in the late ninth century Chinese coins were in use around the Persian Gulf.[141] The *Tzu-chih t'ung-chien* records that in 820 there was a considerable amount being taken abroad[142] and that copper cash were replacing other forms of currency in the marginal backward territories within the empire.[143] This was especially the case in the south.[144]

To deal with this shortage of cash in circulation the government employed a number of policies. The first was that already used earlier in the dynasty, of issuing money from the state treasuries and buying in cloth or grain with it. In 813 500,000 strings of cash were issued from the palace treasury [145] and used to buy in cloth at 10 per cent above the current price. [146] The government presumably hoped that they would thus not only increase the total of money in circulation but also force up the market price of cloth. In 817 a further issue of 500,000 strings was made, this time to be exchanged for goods at current market prices. [147] It seems, from a passage in *Hsin T'ang-shu*, that under Wen-tsung (827–41) a further edict permitted provincial governors to make similar exchanges of money for grain. [148]

The purpose of these issues was to keep as much money as possible in circulation. Another policy designed for the same purpose was the limitation of the hoarding of currency. The first edict of this sort was issued in 808. [149] This ordered the merchants who had money hoarded up to bring it out and exchange it for goods. In 812 the memorial requesting the resumption of the credit transference system also asks that the prohibition of hoarding shall be rigorously enforced. [150] In 817 another edict was issued prohibiting, under pain of very heavy punishments, the accumulation of more than 5000 strings of ready cash. [151] This time the prohibition did not apply only to merchants but also to officials of all ranks, royal princesses, and to the temples. They were given a time limit of a month, which could be extended to two months in the case of very large sums, in which to dispose of their money. After this they were to be liable to confiscation and punishment. However, the local administrations proved incapable of enforcing the law, and although it seems to have caused some initial panic [152] amongst the provincial magnates, some of whom possessed enormous sums, in the end it was not enforced. [153] A new edict issued in 830 reaffirmed this law, and imposed a rather more generous time limit of one to two years. [154] But this also was not, in the end, enforced.

Beside trying to keep as much money as possible in circulation, the government at this time attempted to restore the former position of silk cloth as an item of currency, and thus to reduce the importance of money. This reactionary idea lies behind a great many of the contemporary writings on economic problems, and eventually found expression in the reassessment in 821 of the tax rates and quotas in terms of commodities. [155] It was, of course, a rational reaction to the hardship caused by the monetary situation after 780, with money taxation being imposed in a society which had still not yet developed a universal money economy, and where the consequent instability of the currency could cause great hardship to the primary producers. Another way in which the importance of silk cloth as currency was bolstered up was by the insistence on its use together with cash in transactions involving large sums. This scheme had previously been tried in 737.[156] It was now revived, although in private economy silk cloth as currency seems by this time to have been largely replaced by the precious metals, in particular by silver. In 804 the use of cloth and various commodities together with money was made compulsory in market transactions.[157] In 811 the use of such mixed currency was made obligatory in transactions totalling 10 strings or more, and the financial authorities were ordered to fix the proportions in which commodities and cash were to be employed.[158] In 830 it was ordered that in transactions involving 100 strings or more, half the sum should be paid either in cloth or in grain.[159]

Such were the schemes devised by the government to deal with the currency shortage. The people themselves evolved two further methods of counteracting it, both of which were viewed with official disfavour. The first of these was plainly illegal. This was the appearance of a great amount of 'lead and tin coin' which presumably circulated at a lower price than good copper coin. In 781 a memorial complained of the great amount of such coin in the Yangtze and Huai region.[160] In 811 the military governor of Ho-tung requested permission to cast copper cash in order to do away with lead and tin coin in his province.[161] Edicts prohibiting its manufacture and use were issued in 807,[162] 809[163] and 819.[164] Anyone possessing such coins were ordered to hand them over to the authorities, and large rewards were promised to informers. In 829 a new series of severe penalties was imposed for transactions involving such coin, under which the death penalty was imposed for a transaction where the sum exceeded 10 strings.[165] We know that these laws were still in force in 846.[166]

The second method which was devised, was the use of 'short strings' of less than a thousand cash to represent a token value of a full string. This was known in T'ang times by a variety of names such as *tuan-ch'ien*, *tien-mai*, *ch'u-mai-ch'ien*, and *sheng-mai*.[167] It was not an innovation, but seems to have arisen during the southern dynasty of Liang (502–66). If my reading of an edict of 750 is correct,[168] at that date the system was officially tolerated, and the standard number of cash used for a string fixed at 980. This was still the standard rate in 809, although the use of less than the nominal number of cash for a string had been prohibited by an edict of 793.[169] This prohibition was re-enforced in 809 and the heads of guilds and brokers were made responsible for its imposition.[170] Another edict in 819 dealt with offences against the prohibition by the subordinates of various powerful authorities.[171] In 821, however, an edict recognised that it was impossible to enforce the prohibition, and imposed a standard rate of 920 cash for a string.[172] This standard fell towards the end of the dynasty, and in 904 was 850 cash only, while in Lo-yang 80 cash passed current for 100.[173]

However, in spite of all these schemes, the basic problem remained, the fact that there was too little coin being made, and too little copper from which to make it. In 845 the suppression of the Buddhist monasteries released a great quantity of copper in the form of images, bells, chimes and various fittings. Whether or not the primary motives underlying the suppression were economic ones, one of its chief results was the partial solution of the shortage of money.[174] The copper confiscated was ordered to be cast into money and, as there were no adequate facilities for doing this, special coin factories (ch'ien-fang) were set up in the provinces. The new coinage was sufficiently plentiful for the authorities to revive payment of salaries entirely in cash instead of in half commodities, half cash as before.[175] There seems to have been some reluctance on the part of the public to accept the new currency, as in 846 an edict ordered that the new coin should be used exclusively in trade. The old cash were suspended from use for three years, and were to be handed in to the officials.[176] But this measure was never enforced. When Hsüan-tsung came to the throne in 847, the policy of the previous reign was reversed. The new coins, which could be easily distinguished because they bore the name of the provincial mint on their reverse, were ordered to be taken out of circulation and cast into images again.[177] This too cannot have been strictly enforced, to judge by the innumerable surviving examples of these coins, and should probably be seen as part of the reaction against the anti-Buddhist measures as a whole.

After 847 the sources give us no information about the coinage. In the troubled times at the end of the dynasty, the minting system probably fell into disorder. As we have already seen, the number of coins used for a string had fallen to 850 and even 800, by 905. At the same time the manufacture of debased coinage continued on a large scale. At the beginning of Sung there was an iron coinage in use in Szechuan, and we possess iron coins made by a number of the provincial ch'ien-

fang, presumably at the end of T'ang times. These mostly come from the mints of the central Yangtze basin and Szechuan.[178]

During the five dynasties, all the problems besetting the coinage continued. The melting down of coin, and the copper shortage which brought it about, lasted into Sung times. So did the use of short strings and of tin and lead coin.[179] But, in spite of the failure of the government to provide an adequate coinage, it is clear that during the T'ang not only did a general money economy continue rapidly to develop, but that the government took great strides in bringing their financial policy into line with these developments.

CHAPTER V

THE TRANSPORTATION SYSTEM

From the Han period onwards the economic centre of gravity of the empire gradually shifted from the north-west to the Yangtze basin. This phenomenon had caused no administrative difficulties during the Six Dynasties, when the two regions were politically independent of one another. However, when the empire was again unified under the Sui and T'ang, the political and strategic centre of the state remained in the north-west, while the most important area of production was in Ho-nan and in the Huai and Yangtze valleys.

Since the Kuan-chung area was over-populated and was liable to droughts and crop failures as a result of its rather variable climate, it was essential to be able to import large quantities of grain and other commodities from the south. These imports were necessary not only for the provisioning of the armies on the northern frontiers, but also to make up the deficiency in local production which was caused by the great concentration of government officials and other non-productive classes in the region around the capital. It was this situation which made the transport system so important to the T'ang administration.

The Sui under Yang-ti had rebuilt and integrated a system of canals which linked the Huang-ho with the Yangtze and with Hang-chou bay. In the north a further canal joined Lo-yang with the region of modern Peking, which was a vital strategic centre. The T'ang thus inherited a ready-made transport network linking the south and the north of the great Chinese plain. However, the last necessary link in the system, the connection between this north–south route through Ho-pei, Ho-nan and the Yangtze valley and the capital at Ch'ang-an, was defective.

The Huang-ho, which provided the most natural link, was unsuitable for navigation, and was blocked at San-men by practically impassable rapids. As a result it was customary at the beginning of the dynasty to employ overland haulage on the eighty-mile stretch between Lo-yang and Shan-chou.[1] Haulage costs for this stage of the journey were very high, reaching 500 cash per *shih* of grain.[2] From Shan-chou, water transport could follow the Huang-ho to its junction with the

Wei-ho, and then either ascend the Wei-ho itself or the Ts'ao-ho canal following its southern bank to Ch'ang-an.

In the first years of the dynasty, the administrative system was comparatively simple, and a large proportion of the troops were organised under the militia system.[3] This meant that they were virtually self-supporting, and thus, although many of them were concentrated in the Kuan-chung area,[4] they did not put an undue strain on the state finances, or on the local economy. At the beginning of the dynasty

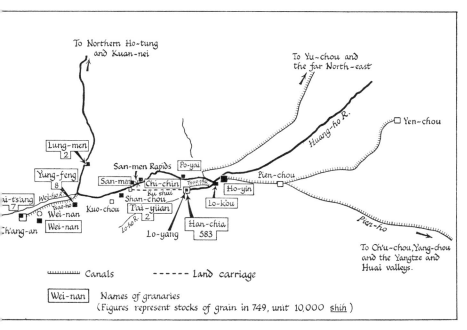

Map 6. The transport system in the region of Ch'ang-an and Lo-yang.

then, the amount of grain which needed to be transported to the capital was comparatively small, amounting to some 200,000 *shih* per annum most of which came from Ho-nan.

However, from the reign of Kao-tsung onwards, the militia system fell into decay, and the militias were gradually replaced by professional soldiers (*chien-erh*) and levied troops (*chao-mu*). These were not part-time soldiers, part-time farmers, as the militias had been, but formed a regular standing army which had to be provisioned and clothed by the state. The additional burden on the economy of Kuan-chung could only be borne with the aid of imports from the south.[5] The strain on the economy was increased by the growth of the official body during the reigns of the empress Wu, Chung-tsung and Jui-tsung,[6] for official salaries were the largest item of state expenditure after the upkeep of the armies.[7]

In the period prior to the accession of Hsüan-tsung, the need for efficient transport of goods, especially of grain, to Kuan-chung was an ever-growing problem. In years of crop failure this need was imperative.

The crux of the problem, as we have seen, was the difficult stage of the journey between Lo-yang and Shan-chou. The most straight-forward solution of this difficulty was to make passable the rapids at San-men, thus opening up direct water transport from the Yangtze to Ch'ang-an. In 656 an attempt was made under Ch'u Lang to open a land route through the San-men mountains,[8] but this was a failure. Later Yang Wu-lien cut a tow-path along the cliffs, so that boats could be dragged up the rapids, but this was arduous and very dangerous.[9] Thus, although improvements were made to the canal up the Wei-ho valley in 672,[10] the haulage of goods from Lo-yang to Ch'ang-an remained difficult and costly.

The problem of improving this route to a point where it could deal adequately with the grain supplies needed to provision Ch'ang-an and the armies in Kuan-chung in time of famine seemed insoluble. The government therefore adopted the plan of transferring the entire administration to Lo-yang in times of crop failure. Lo-yang, the eastern capital, was the terminus of the water route to the south, and provisions could thus easily be transported there. It would have seemed logical for the government to have settled there permanently, but strategic motives, political inertia, and the fact that most of the important families supporting the administration were from Kuan-chung, prevented this.

The economic motives underlying the visits of the emperors to Lo-yang have been clearly demonstrated by Ch'üan Han-sheng in his work on the canal system.[11] We may therefore gain some idea of the precarious economic conditions in Kuan-chung from the fact that, after the establishment of Lo-yang as the eastern capital in 657, Kao-tsung spent eleven years out of the next twenty-six there. These transferences of the court were often made under very bad conditions,[12] and must have been ruinously expensive, for the whole government travelled with the emperor. The places through which they passed were so ravaged that they usually had to be given remissions of taxes to assist their recovery.[13]

The empress Wu resided permanently in Lo-yang except for the years 701–3, but it is almost certain that this was due to political rather than economic reasons. It seems that Chung-tsung transferred the capital back to Ch'ang-an in 706 mainly because of the influence of the Wei empress. His ministers put forward powerful economic arguments against such a course,[14] and again in the next year the empress dissuaded Chung-tsung from returning to Lo-yang only by employing a monk to frighten him.[15]

At the beginning of Hsüan-tsung's reign the transport problem again became acute. In the very first year of his reign he intended to go to Lo-yang, and published an edict to that effect,[16] but probably political expediency intervened, for he seems never to have gone. At the same time Li Chieh, the prefect of Shan-chou, was appointed commissioner for land and water transport (*shui-lu chuan-yün shih*)[17] and was made responsible for the route from Lo-yang to Shan-chou, which he reorganised so that it could deal with 1,000,000 *shih* of grain per year.[18] His authority is usually considered to have been confined to the stage between Lo-yang and Ch'ang-an, which was placed under direct government control. He may also have had some powers over the main canal, for in 714 he rebuilt an important haul-over on the Pien canal, which lay outside his jurisdiction as governor of Lo-yang.[19] However, the haulage on the canal, as distinct from such constructional work, remained the responsibility of the local authorities in the tax-producing areas.

In spite of Li Chieh's work, Hsüan-tsung was forced to transfer the government to Lo-yang in 717 because of a crop failure in Kuan-chung and the inability of the transport organisation to provide relief. He spent nine of the next twenty years in Lo-yang, during which period the government was uprooted ten times.[20] These moves became more and more expensive with the growth of the administrative machine.

Just before the last of them, in 734, the emperor summoned P'ei Yao-ch'ing, who had some years previously memorialised the throne on the reorganisation of transport, to give his advice on the improvement of the system.[21] Yao-ch'ing's plan was accepted, and he was appointed a 'great minister', with the title of commissioner for transport from the Chiang-huai Region and Ho-nan (*Chiang-huai Ho-nan chuan-yün tu-shih*). During Hsüan-tsung's last stay in Lo-yang he carried through a reorganisation of the system which enabled the emperor to dispense with these difficult and expensive journeys in the future.[22] Until the time of P'ei Yao-ch'ing, the prefectural authorities had borne responsibility for transporting their taxes to Lo-yang. The only exception to this had been in the case of Chiang-nan, where, because of the great distances involved, the local prefectural authorities were only responsible for their taxes as far as Yang-chou, the remainder of the journey being made under the direct control of the central government, and paid for out of the taxes themselves.[23]

It was therefore necessary for the prefects to hire transport, and this necessitated the levying of an additional tax called *chüeh-chih* to meet the expense.[24] Under the *Code*, it was forbidden for the authorities to hire transport within the area under their jurisdiction,[25] and technically at least transport was controlled by special duty officers called *kang-tien*. In actual practice it seems that professional seamen were employed, and where the *kang-tien* were in charge there were frequent cases of mis-application of the goods in transit, as we know from an edict of 721.[26]

Although there were official regulations on the distances to be covered in a day's journey by various forms of transport, boat traffic was very prone to hold-ups owing to shallow water or contrary winds. Such delays were especially common on the last lap of the journey, from the junction of the canal and the Huang-ho to Lo-yang where the difficult waters of the Yellow river had to be traversed.[27]

When the crews reached Lo-yang, they were sometimes ordered to take on their cargoes of grain to supply the armies in the north-east centred on Yu-chou.[28] As they only carried sufficient provisions for the return trip to Lo-yang, this additional journey of over a thousand miles caused great hardship. In the eighth century this canal route to the north of Ho-pei was supplemented by the coastal sea route.

P'ei Yao-ch'ing's first reform was to make the ships coming from the south stop at the junction of the canal and the Huang-ho. They un-loaded their grain cargoes into a newly established granary at Ho-yin (see map 6 on p. 85) and then returned to their prefecture. This meant that their crews avoided the hazardous waters of the Huang-ho, for which local crews or pilots had previously had to be employed, and that they were no longer liable to make the further journey to the north of Ho-pei.

Responsibility for transport from Ho-yin to Ch'ang-an and Lo-yang was taken over by a new commission for transportation. The two routes were separated. Traffic for Ch'ang-an was sent along the 'northern route'. This was entirely a water route apart from a short land haulage of about 5 miles around the rapids at San-men. The journey was divided into stages, at the end of each of which the grain was paid into one of a series of transit granaries where it could be stored until conditions were favourable for the next stage of the journey.[29]

By this means, although land haulage was not altogether avoided, the distance was reduced from the 80 miles from Lo-yang to Shan-chou up the Ku-shui valley to the 5 miles separating the Chi-chin and San-men granaries at the eastern and western ends respectively of the San-men rapids.[30]

As before, grain supplies for Lo-yang were sent up the Ts'ao-ch'ü canal to the Han-chia granary (see map 6 on p. 85), where very large stocks continued to be built up.

It appears that the new system was extremely successful. In three years of operation over 7,000,000 *shih* of grain were transported, more than twice the maximum load of the previous land route. At the same time transport costs were reduced by 300,000 or 400,000 strings of cash.[31]

This improvement in grain supplies from the south coincided with abundant harvests in Kuan-chung itself. To protect the farmers from the effects of the glut of grain, the government imposed 'harmonious purchases' (*ho-ti*) of grain at prices above the market value,[32] and as a further measure of relief allowed the population of Kuan-chung to pay all taxes in grain.[33] Because of this, the transport system of P'ei Yao-ch'ing was suspended in the sixth month of 737.[34]

We are told that under P'ei Yao-ch'ing's former subordinate Ts'ui Hsi-i 1,800,000 *shih* of grain were transported in a year, and that this figure was subsequently reduced by several hundred thousand *shih*.[35] It is not clear whether this was transported by water or overland. It has been assumed that the old system was revived, and that Lo-yang again became the terminal point for the tax boats.[36] However, the northern water route must also have remained in use, as in 741 Li Ch'i-wu cleared a channel for shipping through the San-men. His attempt at making possible through-traffic seems to have been more effective and safer than the one previously made by Yang Wu-lien, but the new channel soon silted up and was abandoned.[37]

There is a tantalisingly vague account of the reorganisation of transport between Lo-yang and Shan-chou in 750 under P'ei Hsiang. This appears to have been a reorganisation of the route laid out by Li Chieh, following the valley of the Ku-shui, tributary of the Lo, but divided into shorter stages to reduce the strain on the oxen.[38] During the years after 737 Ch'i Huan attempted to improve the southern part of the Pien canal itself, and to change the crossing of the Yangtze south of Yang-chou so as to make passage easier.[39]

From 741 onwards Wei Chien was employed as prefect of Shan-chou, a post which carried with it the concurrent title of Commissioner for Land and Water Transport.[39a] In 742–3 he constructed a new canal running parallel to the southern bank of the Wei river linking Ch'ang-an with the Yung-feng granary at the junction of the Wei river and the Huang-ho. This canal, which followed the lines of an abandoned Sui-time predecessor the Ts'ao-ho, facilitated the last stage of the journey to the capital where a new dock for the transport boats was constructed.[40] The total quantities transported to the capital again grew very large, and in 744 the amount of grain transported from 'east of the passes', that is from Ho-nan and the south-east, reached 4,000,000 shih.[41] There seems to have been such an abundance of grain that the ti-shui from the south was no longer sent to the capital as grain, but was converted into 'light commodities', that is, goods with a high value relative to their bulk.[42] In 743, in celebration of his success, Wei Chien organised a great exhibition of these tax goods in his newly completed dock at Ch'ang-an, the Kuang-yün t'an.[43]

Wei Chien also made a reform of the organisation for payment of transport costs, making rich households (designated ch'uan-t'ou or ch'uan-hu) responsible for the boats and their cargoes. This policy, aimed at the wealthy classes, may have contributed to his downfall.

As a result of these reforms, the supply of grain in the Kuan-chung area was exceptionally good in the last years of Hsüan-tsung's reign, which was generally a period of low prices. Thus it was no longer found necessary for the government to be transferred to Lo-yang, though it seems from an edict of 744 that such transfers were still contemplated.[44] Since Lo-yang was no longer a part-time residence of the court, it declined in importance. However, as always Lo-yang and the province of Ho-nan as a whole remained the most important area in which stocks of government grain were accumulated. In 749 Ho-nan contained over a quarter of the total stocks of grain held by the government, while the great Han-chia granary in Lo-yang held a total of

5,833,400 *shih* in contrast to a mere 71,270 *shih* in the great granary in Ch'ang-an. The Kuan-chung area held rather slender reserves, totalling only 8,000,000 *shih* or 8 per cent of the total stocks in the empire[45] (see appendix v, 3).

With the An Lu-shan rising the T'ang dynasty was faced with an entirely new economic and financial situation. The whole of the north and north-east was lost to the rebels, which meant not only a loss of territory, but a very considerable loss of revenue. At the same time there was much trouble with the border nomads, and large armies had to be maintained in the north-west. These troops consumed all the taxes from the north-west, and more besides. Thus the central government was faced at the same time with a great increase in expenditure, and a loss of much of the revenue from the northern regions.

Under these conditions supplies from the south, and the transport link by which they could be sent to the capital, became more and more essential. This dependence upon transported supplies did not end with the suppression of the rebels in 763, for even after this date many of the governors of provinces, especially in the north-east, remained semi-autonomous, and rendered no taxes to the government in Ch'ang-an.[46] The central government thus depended upon the south not only for bulk grain supplies, but also for the cloth with which to pay the exorbitant demands for their Uighur allies[47] and to a lesser extent for weapons, as most of the empire's metal production was concentrated in the south.

It was thus a serious blow to the government when An Lu-shan overran Ho-nan and cut the canal route from the Huai river.[48] Even when Lo-yang was recovered from the rebels with the aid of the Uighurs at the end of 762, Shih Ch'ao-i's troops were still operating near Sung-chou and again cut the canal.[49]

As a result of this the government was forced to use the alternative link between north and south, the Han valley route.[50] This route, which entailed the crossing of high passes, was not suitable for bulk grain traffic, and was much more expensive than the Pien canal route. Ti-wu Ch'i had suggested in 756 the establishment of tax commissioners in the south, who were to convert the taxes into light commodities and send them to the capital by this route.[51] But although the region through which it passed was not involved in the main rebellion, the Han valley route, too, was cut off in 756–7 by the rising of K'ang Ch'u-yüan and Chang Chia-yen at Hsiang-chou, and again in 760 by the rebellion of Chang Chin at the same place.[52] As this route was so vital, Mu Ning was made deputy commissioner of transport and salt and iron to control transport along it. He was also made governor of O-chou (modern Wu-chang) so that he could control the collection of taxes from the south, O-chou being the southern collecting centre for this route, much as Yang-chou was for the main canal.[53]

The relief given to Kuan-chung by this means was not great. The situation was very grave, for the ravages of the rebels in the first stages of the rising had been followed by a disastrous drought and a plague of locusts in 758.[54] Owing to migration of the population, much land went out of cultivation, and the irrigation system was seriously neglected, while the armies, which in peace-time had been partly self-supporting, now made great demands on the local economy. The position was not improved by the expedients employed by the government to raise revenue, especially by the attempt to debase the coinage.[55] During 760–3 the price of grain is said to have reached 1000 cash per *tou*. There was another year of poor harvests in 763,[56] and the revival of the canal became an urgent matter.

Liu Yen was sent to examine the situation. From the long letter which he wrote to the chief minister Yüan Tsai we know what difficulties he had to overcome.[57] The canal had been neglected since 755 and had not been dredged or repaired. The region through which it passed had been depopulated since the early stages of the fighting[58] and was suffering from an acute labour shortage. In addition the canal was totally undefended against marauders.

His first step was to clear out the channel, a task accomplished only with the aid of the local military authorities.[59] His next reform was a complete change in the provision of payment for transport. Previously, as we have seen, the costs had been borne in turn first by the taxpayers in general as a surcharge on their taxes, and then by selected rich families and merchants. Liu Yen created a new and powerful Transport Commission (*chuan-yün shih*) which was intimately linked with the Salt and Iron Commission. The cost of transport was borne directly by the commission, and paid for from the profits of the new salt monopoly.[60] At the same time the policy of making the local authorities provide special servicemen as labour for transport was abandoned.[61] The special servicemen from the prefectures were replaced by permanent professional crews. This was necessitated by the depopulation of the area traversed by the canal. To protect the cargoes in transit, guard-posts were established at regular intervals[62] and the boats sailed in convoys of ten under the command of army officers.[63]

Liu Yen carried the system of transport in relays begun under P'ei Yao-ch'ing one stage further. The journey from the south was divided into four stages: (1) the Yangtze, (2) the canal, (3) the Huang-ho, (4) the Wei-ho. As the conditions on each of these sections were different, he constructed special types of boats for use on each, and trained special crews for each stage of the journey.[64] To provide the huge fleets necessary ten shipyards were set up at Yang-tzu county in Yang-chou, the central depot of the transport and salt administrations.[65] The construction programme was planned on a long-term basis.[66] We can gain some idea of its scale from the account in *Hsin T'ang-shu*, which informs us that on the Pien canal alone there were 2000 craft, each with a capacity of 1000 *hu*.[67] For the Huang-ho special boats were built able to ascend the rapids at San-men.[68]

As a result of these reforms not only was transport restored, but its cost greatly reduced. There was a 75 per cent saving on the cost of transport of grain from Yang-chou to Ho-yin, and a similar proportion was saved on a stretch south of the Yangtze where boat transport had been substituted for land haulage. Even on 'light commodities' there was a saving of more than 40 per cent.[69] The total annual saving was reckoned at 100,000 strings of cash. Moreover, the whole enterprise now came under the control of a powerful independent authority, who undertook the whole journey from the south, not merely the difficult stretch from Ho-yin onwards as had been the case in Hsüan-tsung's reign.

However, the total amounts transported annually were by no means as large as in the days of P'ei Yao-ch'ing and Wei Chien. *Hsin T'ang-shu* and *Tzu-chih t'ung-chien* quote annual totals of 1,100,000 and 1,000,000 *shih* respectively, but these seem to refer to particularly good years. The average of 500,000 *shih* given in *Chiu T'ang-shu*[70] is substantiated by other independent sources[71] and is probably nearer the truth. This is only 20 per cent of the total under P'ei Yao-ch'ing, and only 12½ per cent of that under Wei Chien. Although *Hsin T'ang-shu* claims that 'after this, even though there were floods and droughts in Kuan-chung, prices did not rise very high', it appears that the whole of Tai-tsung's reign was a period of high prices, especially of grain.[72] It is thus tempting to suppose that the organisation of transport was still not wholly adequate, or at least that the demand for grain imports in Kuan-chung was considerably less than before.

The most serious problem from which transport suffered at this period was one over which Liu Yen had no control. This was the continuous friction between the central government and the various semi-independent provincial governors. The chief trouble centre, as it was throughout the dynasty, was Ho-pei and Shantung, and the disturbance had only to spread a little way for it to dislocate traffic on the canal. During Liu Yen's own tenure of office transport was interrupted in 767 by Chou Chih-kuang,[73] who forcibly detained a great quantity of tribute goods, and again in 777 as a result of the rebellion of Li Ling-yao.[74]

These difficulties were only short-lived, but after the fall of Liu Yen, the much more serious revolt of the provincial governors of Ho-pei, which broke out in 781, again cut the canal.[75] Though communications were reopened by the end of the year, they were again broken in 782 by the forces of Li Na and Li Hsi-lieh.[76] In 783 the emperor was driven from the capital and fled to Feng-hsiang and then to Liang-chou. The armies under Li Sheng, which recaptured the capital in 784, had to be supplied with provisions by armed convoys sent from the Yangtze delta by Han Huang, himself an important provincial governor.[77] Even after the capital was recaptured conditions seem to have been very bad for some time.[78]

In 792 Lu Chih, who had recently become chief minister, suggested a drastic cut in the amount of tax grain to be transported from the Yangtze valley to the north. He planned to exchange much of the tax grain used to supply the armies in Kuan-chung for silk, which was to be transported in its stead and used for making local procurements of grain (ho-ti) in Kuan-chung itself. It is interesting to see that he estimated that the saving on the cost of transportation would exceed the value of the grain which would no longer be sent to the north.[79] It seems that his plan was at least partially put into effect.[80] The reform must have been rescinded after Lu Chih's fall in 794, but at the end of the century the total amount of grain despatched from the south was only 400,000 shih, of which only a part would have reached Ch'ang-an.[81]

In order to protect strategic points along the route, the government had established powerful garrisons at Pien-chou and Hsü-chou, but under the very weak central government of Te-tsung these garrisons themselves became sources of trouble. In the period 792–8 that at

Pien-chou mutinied five times,[82] and such risings must have interrupted communications seriously. It was only by the appointment of a powerful and ruthless commander at Pien-chou, and the establishment of a separate transport commissioner for this stretch of the journey, to supplement the control of the Transport Commission itself, which was centred at Yang-chou and was at this period headed by the provincial governors of the Yangtze delta region, that such troubles were prevented from recurring.[83]

The accession to the throne of Hsien-tsung in 805 once again changed the internal situation of the empire. A reaction began against the excessive local autonomy which had characterised the reign of Te-tsung, and the provincial governors were subdued in turn.[84] The canal was essential for transporting taxes from the south to provision the campaigns necessary to suppress these local governors, and the system was overhauled under Tu Yu and Li Sun between 805 and 809. Under the administration of the latter the annual total of grain transported again reached the level of Liu Yen's time, but even so the total for 810 was only 400,000 *shih*, as little as in the last years of Te-tsung's reign,[85] and this fell to 200,000 in the next few years in spite of construction works carried out on the canal by Tu Ya, the governor of Huai-nan.[86]

Not only was the total amount small, but the proportion which was lost or stolen *en route* was very high. When Wang Po was put in charge of the business in 811 he suggested imposing the death penalty on anyone who lost more than 10 per cent of his cargo.[87] Later, Huang-fu Po suggested an even more drastic scale of punishments,[88] and in 819–21 his nominee Liu Kung-ch'o again advocated heavier penalties.[89] But these laws failed to have any effect, and between 70 per cent and 80 per cent of the total is said never to have reached its destination.

The revival of the transport organisation under Li Sun did not last very long. In 822 there was a fresh outbreak of trouble at Pien-chou,[90] during which the depot of the Salt and Iron Commission was looted, and a great amount of tax goods stolen elsewhere.[91] During the whole period up to 850 'the powerful officials who controlled the Transport Commission annually sent off not more than 400,000 *shih* of grain from the Chiang-huai region. But not 30 or 40 per cent of this actually reached the granaries on the Wei river.' This was mostly due to inefficiency and dishonesty amongst the transport personnel, for every year at least seventy ships were lost.[92] At this time, too, piracy and wholesale plunder of shipping and merchants were rife, both on the Yangtze and the canal.[93]

During the period 836–41 a system of permanent convoy officers was established. It was their duty to escort the money for the *liang-shui* tax to the capital, and they were encouraged by being granted accelerated promotion in proportion with their success.[94] But this reform had no effect on the grain transport system. In 851 P'ei Hsiu made some reforms which seem temporarily to have revived the system, and in three years 1,200,000 *shih* were transported. But this revival again was very short-lived,[95] and efficiency once more declined.

Later the system fell into still worse disorder. In 868 an army from the region of Hsü-chou on the canal, which had been sent to fight the forces of Nan-chao, mutinied and fought their way home across southern China. When they reached Ho-nan, they completely dislocated all traffic before they were finally suppressed.[96]

At this period, too, the methods of ship construction adopted by Liu Yen were abandoned, and smaller and cheaper boats were built, which proved inadequate for their task.[97] The shipping shortage was aggravated by a campaign which was in progress in An-nan, to provision which the Salt and Iron Commission had to charter a great many ships from the Yangtze region.[98]

In 875 the revolt of Wang Hsien-chih, followed by that of Huang Ch'ao, again broke down communications between the capital and the Yangtze. Although this rising was eventually put down, for the remainder of the dynasty the emperor's authority was confined to Szechuan and parts of the Han and Yangtze valleys.[99]

In 880 a last attempt to reorganise transport was made. The agent at the branch of the Transport Commission at Yang-tzu was appointed commissioner for the despatch of transport (*chuan-yün shih*).[100] Such officers are mentioned in the *Annals* in 900 and 904, the holders being in each case provincial governors from the southern region who were loyal to the throne.[101] Their duties were simply to collect and deliver what tax income they could to the capital. But with them transport was not a regularly organised business, but an attempt to do the best they could in extremely difficult circumstances. As it says in *T'ang hui-yao*, 87, 'From this time (885) the transport routes from the south were cut off'. It seems certain that state transport on any considerable scale was never resumed after Huang Ch'ao's rebellion.

CHAPTER VI

THE FINANCIAL ADMINISTRATION

The history of the financial administration during the T'ang divides clearly into three main periods. The first of these extends from the beginning of the dynasty until about 720. The second covers the period from 720 until the rebellion of An Lu-shan in 755, and the third, which may be further subdivided, from this date until the end of the dynasty. The first period was characterised by the continuance of the rather primitive institutions adopted from the preceding Northern Dynasties. In the second these institutions were rationalised to some extent, and supplemented by a general growth of specialised offices. In the third period specialisation of financial control developed further, and tension arose between these specialised authorities and the regular organs of the central government. At the same time the central government was engaged in a continual struggle with the provincial magnates for the control of revenue.

The Period 618–720

During the first century of their rule the T'ang preserved the financial organisation which they had inherited from the Sui and their semi-barbarian northern predecessors. This system was almost entirely unspecialised, and many duties requiring specialist skills, such as transportation, the manufacture of coinage, manipulation of grain prices, etc., were left in the hands of the local authorities who were already overburdened with a multitude of other responsibilities.

The structure of this administrative machine was intimately connected with the systems of land allotment, registration, and taxation which the T'ang had taken over from the same source. With its lack of administrative specialisation it was no more suited to the needs of a highly complex society than were these rather primitive measures, and like them, it was supplemented by newer institutions more in line with the realities of the time from the eighth century onwards. However, while the obsolete land allotment and taxation systems disappeared during the decades following the An Lu-shan rebellion, the original financial organisation remained in being until the end of the dynasty, although its power was curbed by the emergence of new administrative organs.

Regarding this first period we are generally well-informed about the details of the administrative machine. The functions and personnel of the different departments are described at length in the *T'ang liu-tien* and in the *Monographs on Officials* of the two standard histories of the period, which are for the most part based on this work. However, these accounts are frequently vague and confusing and in any case only deal with the theoretical responsibilities of each post. Material on the actual operation of the system, which would enable us to make a more precise appraisal of the relative importance of the various offices, is very sparse before the *K'ai-yüan* period (713–41).[1]

The Central Organisation

The Board of Finance. The chief financial organ of the central government was the Board of Finance (*hu-pu*), one of the six boards subordinate to the Department of State (*shang-shu-sheng*) which formed the essential executive machinery of the empire. The internal organisation of the Board is best shown in the following diagram.

DEPARTMENT OF STATE

BOARD OF FINANCE
President
2 vice-presidents

BOARD OF FINANCE	DEPARTMENT OF PUBLIC REVENUE	DEPARTMENT OF TREASURY	DEPARTMENT OF GRANARIES
2 chief secretaries	1 chief secretary	1 chief secretary	1 chief secretary
2 under-secretaries	1 under-secretary	1 under-secretary	1 under-secretary

The president (*shang-shu*) and vice-presidents (*shih-lang*) of the Board had nominal control only over matters of general policy. The president normally held the post concurrently with other high offices, and with certain notable exceptions was usually little more than a figurehead. To a lesser extent this was also true of the vice-presidents, but the latter were more commonly selected from experienced finance officials, and at least from the beginning of the eighth century seem to have been the effective executive heads of the Board. Day-to-day business as opposed to general policy was in the hands of the chief secretaries (*lang-chung*) and under-secretaries (*yüan-wai lang*) of the four subordinate departments, each of which had its own large establishment of clerks, book-keepers, accountants, ushers and other subordinates, details of whom—in all probability highly idealised—may be found in *T'ang liu-tien*.[2]

The Board of Finance was not only the name for the whole organisation, but also designated the most important of its four constituent departments. This department had a larger establishment of personnel than the others, and during the early years of the dynasty was certainly the most influential of the four. As its name during the early years 'Department of Population' (*min-pu*) suggests, its primary responsibility was the registration system and the records of population and taxation.

The registers were compiled in the following way. Each year the village elders (*li-cheng*) collected statements (*shou-shih*) from households giving particulars of all changes relating to the status of individuals and households in respect of the law and of fiscal responsibility. From these annual statements the prefectural and county authorities compiled two different series of registers destined for the central government, besides various lists of persons liable for labour service and taxation for their own local use.[3] The first series of documents compiled for the central authorities were the nominal tax rolls (*chi-chang*), which were compiled annually and gave a complete schedule of all taxes due for the current year. The second, the household registers (*hu-chi*) were compiled once every three years, and contained all information relevant to the legal status of every inhabitant of each locality. Copies of these registers were kept on file in the Board of Finance for twenty-seven years,[4] and provided the central government with its most accurate picture of the population and tax load of each local district. So important were these documents that when the emperor moved from Ch'ang-an to his secondary capital at Lo-yang all these bulky files had to be transported to and fro.[5]

After the An Lu-shan rising and the subsequent growth of fresh forms of taxation and the decay of the land allotment system, the system of detailed registration fell into complete chaos and lost its importance, since the local authorities preferred to collect taxes in the light of actual conditions rather than according to long-obsolete registers.[6] At the same time the rise of the provincial governors who became for the first time intermediaries in the collection of revenue further reduced the value of detailed local registers to the government in the capital, who could do little more than allocate quotas of taxes to be collected in each province. Furthermore, the primacy of the department made sense only in the light of the very rigid economic theory to which the early T'ang governments attempted to adhere. The classical policy of 'regulating expenditure by measuring income' was applicable only where the income was adequate for all likely contingencies, and where no extraordinary and unavoidable expenditure was called for. The rigidity with which this principle was followed grew less during the early years of the eighth century, and after the rising of An Lu-shan there was no question of attempting such a course. It was now a matter of survival or disintegration to obtain sufficient funds from whatever source was available to meet current expenditure. Under such conditions the Board of Finance itself lost much of its importance while the Department of Public Revenue, whose function was the production of an annual budget, gained in influence. In 782 Tu Yu drew attention to the change in the relative importance of the two departments and suggested that the complement of officials employed in the Board of Finance itself should be reduced to that of the other subordinate departments.[7]

The Department of Public Revenue (Tu-chih). This was always a very important body, having the responsibility for drawing up a sort of budget every year: 'Annually they are to calculate what is to be expended and to pay out what is necessary.'[8] At the beginning of the dynasty internal responsibility within the department was divided, the chief secretary being in charge of income and the under-secretary of expenditure.[9] The president and vice-presidents of the Board had no say in the detailed workings of the department, but were only called upon to seal documents. In the early years the methods used in drawing up the annual budget seem to have been extremely unwieldly, for detailed directives were drawn up annually for each prefecture laying down the amounts of tax to be collected, payments to be made out of local funds, tax-exemptions, transportation expenses and miscellaneous expenditure which might be incurred. In 736 Li Lin-fu, considering that this procedure was unduly laborious and clumsy, rationalised the system by abolishing these detailed annual assessments, and replaced them by a set of permanently applicable directives (*ch'ang-hsing chih-fu*) which laid down permanent quotas and rules for tax collection, transportation, etc., and left the department only to draw up annually the detailed budgets of local expenditure.[10]

Having overall control of the disposal of revenues, the department grew rapidly more important as the financial situation of the empire became more complicated and precarious. Eventually its position as a subordinate office of the Board of Finance became insufficient, and to bolster up its authority statesmen holding other offices were appointed to 'control the business of the Public Revenue Department' (*p'an tu-chih shih*).[11]

The two other subordinate departments divided between them the duties of collecting and storing the tax revenue of the empire.

The Department of Treasury (*Chin-pu*). This department controlled the tax income in money and in cloth which was widely used as currency in large-scale transactions. The department maintained permanent staff both in Ch'ang-an and in Lo-yang, and had further personnel who attended the emperor as part of his personal retinue. Most of the payments which the department made were in respect of official salaries in money, and these were subject to the approval of the Secretariat (*chung-shu-sheng*). All incomings and outgoings were accompanied by vouchers (*wen-t'ieh*) which were accounted for at the end of each quarter. There was also a complicated system of wooden tallies (*mu-chieh*) for use in dealings between the various divisions within the department itself, the Court of Treasury, and the Chiu-cheng palace.[12] These were designed to facilitate interdepartmental accounting.

The Department of Granaries (*Ts'ang-pu*). This was a similar body controlling the income in grain from the *tsu* tax and from the converted funds of the charitable granaries. It was also nominally responsible for the charitable granaries (*i-ts'ang*) and the price-regulating granaries (*chang-p'ing-ts'ang*) of the empire. The former were established at the beginning of the dynasty, but after the beginning of the eighth century were converted into a source of supplementary taxation in grain.[13] The latter were established on a permanent basis in 655[14] and were later placed under the control of special commissioners. The Granary Department maintained staff in both capitals and personnel attached to the emperor's retinue, as the Department of Treasury did. They were linked by a tally system for interdepartmental accounting with the Court of Agriculture, and its subordinate directorates controlling the great Yung-feng and T'ai-yüan granaries.[15]

Each of these two departments was duplicated in function by other offices. While the T'ang administration was based on the system of six boards as developed under the Northern Dynasties, there existed side by side with this the older system of nine courts surviving from Han times. In many cases the authority of these bodies overlapped that of the boards, and it is almost impossible to delineate the separate areas of responsibility of the different offices.[16] What is certain, however, is that these courts were by no means functionless survivals with no real power, but were real and independent authorities—sometimes more powerful than their parallel body among the six boards.

The Court of Treasury (T'ai-fu ssu). This was a department parallel with the Department of Treasury in the Board of Finance, but entirely independent of it. As can be seen from the system of interdepartmental tallies it worked in close collaboration with the latter department and with the imperial treasury in the Chiu-ch'eng palace which was under the control of the Court of Agriculture. In actual fact it seems to have been considerably more important than the Department of Treasury, for it controlled the treasuries of the Left and the Right (*tso-yu-tsang-shu*) which received the tax income in money and cloth from the empire, and the goods sent in as tribute (*kung*) respectively.[17] In the historical sources, these treasuries are mentioned very much more commonly than is the Department of Treasury. The court also had some degree of accounting supervision over tax income, a duty which its president shared with members of the censorate. There was a very close link in fact between the court and the censorate. Both were strongholds during Hsüan-tsung's reign of the aristocratic party which advocated realist financial measures, and for many years it was controlled first by Yang Ch'ung-li and then by his sons, who were famed for their exacting control of finance.[18] By 738 this office had become so important that special commissioners (*ch'u-na shih*) were appointed to supervise it. These commissioners, again, were provided from the censorate.[19]

A further field for which the court was responsible was the supervision of the markets of the capital, and the price-control offices (*ch'ang-p'ing-shu*), which attempted to regulate the prices of grain in the capitals.[20]

The Court of Agriculture (Ssu-nung ssu). This was a most important office which had a large number of subordinate offices (*shu*) and directorates (*chien*) and widespread administrative ramifications. For the present purpose, however, it is enough to say that its main function was the collection and storage of grain income. Like the Court of Treasury it seems to have been more powerful than the parallel department under the Board of Finance. A subordinate office (*t'ai-ts'ang-shu*) controlled the great granary in Ch'ang-an,[21] and various separate directorates (*chien*) responsible to the court controlled the other major granaries, T'ai-yüan, Yung-feng, Lung-men, etc.[22] The officials of these granaries were held responsible under very detailed rules for damage and deficiencies, and had to render regular accounts for their stocks.[23] All issues of grain, most of which was used for army rations and salaries of officials, were made under the control of the Department of State.

The court also controlled some of the colonies (*t'un-t'ien*) in metropolitan China,[24] and thus controlled some actual grain production as well as storage and distribution.

These were the offices which were directly concerned with the gathering of revenue, and the distribution of the state's income. Such a complicated business involving vast sums of money and enormous quantities of grain and other commodities needed a rigorous system of supervision and accountancy. Each of the offices kept its own accounts, but two further authorities were responsible for supervision and auditing.

The Department of Judicial Control (Pi-pu). This was one of the subordinate departments of the Board of Justice (*Hsing-pu*). According to the *Monograph on Officials* in the *Chiu T'ang-shu*, 'the duties of the chief secretary and under-secretary are to control accounting for the salaries of the officers of the various departments, for public buildings, for cases of corruption and for the payment of money fines. They are to investigate the use of convict labour, the extent of impositions, amounts of commodities owing to the state, and they are to have a complete knowledge of the current expenditure in the capital and in the provinces, and to exercise general control over it.'[25] The prefectures rendered their accounts to the department annually for audit. These accounts were sent in at various dates according to the distance of the prefecture from the capital. In the environs of the two capitals a slightly different system was in force, and the department audited the accounts of the counties as well as those of the metropolitan administrations.[26] This organisation survived the An Lu-shan rising, but after 780 accounts were audited first by the financial service of the prefecture, then by the executive officers of the provincial civil governor (*kuan-ch'a p'an-kuan*) of the province, and lastly by the department.[27]

The Censorate. This body had the power of supervision over the whole bureaucratic machine, and was one of the most powerful offices in the empire. In the field of finance, it had a supervisory duty of the first importance—that of controlling the activities of the chief storage departments, the Great Granary and the Treasury of the Left. This duty was at first performed by examining censors (*chien-ch'a yü-shih*) and later by censors of palace affairs (*tien-chung yü-shih*). Censors with this special duty were appointed for the first time in 731.[28] The date of transfer of the duty to the censors of palace affairs was after 731[29] and probably before 736 when commissioners for income and expenditure (*ch'u-na-shih*) were first appointed. Since the latter were always appointed from the censorate, it would seem that they were merely performing their old duties under a new title.[30] It seems from a memorial of 827 that the normal practice was to depute a senior censor to act as Inspector of the Great Granary (*chien t'ai-ts'ang shih*) and a junior censor to act as Inspector of the Treasury of the Left (*chien tso-tsang-k'u shih*).[31]

It was also a part of the duties of the examining censors when they made their tours of inspection in the provinces to look into the accounts and documents of the local finance authorities.[32] They thus exercised a general power of inspection over the local finance officials, but this was not a regular annual inspection of accounts like the audit conducted by the Department of Judicial Control.

The Local Organisation

During the first half of the dynasty, the local authorities with whom the central government had direct dealings in matters of finance were the prefectures (*chou*) or their equivalents the administrations (*fu*) in centres of major importance, and the protectorates (*tu-hu-fu*) and governments-general (*tu-tu-fu*) in areas of military importance on the frontiers. The provinces (*tao*) during this period were simply convenient divisions of the empire which were used as units for periodical inspection. They had no permanent governor, nor administration, and played no part as intermediaries in the dealings of the central offices with the prefectures.

Beneath the prefectures were their constituent counties (*hsien*). The precise relationships between prefectures and the subordinate counties is by no means easy to establish, but, in general, business from the counties was submitted to the capital through the prefecture. The ranking personnel of the counties, however, were all appointed directly by the central government, and the central authorities were able to interfere directly in the affairs of a county without consulting the prefecture.

Both the prefect (*tz'u-shih*) and the county magistrate (*ling*) were nominally responsible for all the financial business, tax collection, allocation of lands, and registration of population and lands within the area under their jurisdiction.[33] In both cases, however, such financial matters were only a part of the responsibilities laid upon them. Both prefect and magistrate were also responsible for a wide range of other matters, and spent a great deal of their time in dealing with legal cases. Generally speaking, they intervened personally only in cases of disputes, the day-to-day administration falling upon their subordinate Services of Finance (*hu-ts'ao* in the prefectures, *ssu-hu* in the counties), and Services of Granaries (*ts'ang-ts'ao*; *ssu-ts'ang*). The former were in charge of registration, certificates of tax exemption, and all the business carried out at the central level by the principal sub-department of the Board of Finance. The latter were responsible for the active tax administration, the storage and collection of taxes, and for various other duties such as the supervision of markets, upkeep of official buildings, etc.[34] For brief periods there were also established Services of Land-control (*t'ien-ts'ao*; *ssu-t'ien*) to control the allocation of lands.[35]

At the beginning of the dynasty the prefects were also responsible for a variety of specialised tasks such as transportation of taxes and the minting of money, besides their routine responsibilities as tax-collecting agents.

As in every period, T'ang local officials were very heavily overburdened with multifarious responsibilities, and had subordinate staff whose numbers were insufficient to deal effectively with every detail of financial administration. Beneath the county there was no administrative system staffed by members of the bureaucracy, and the magistrate had to depend, in his direct contact with the people under his administration, upon his own subordinate staff (*li*), most of whom were local people, on the one hand, and on the sub-bureaucratic rural administration of the villages on the other. The heads of these local rural subdivisions were not members of the official class at all,[36] and their position, together with the precise status of their administrative subdivisions, seems never to have been precisely laid down. It is very probable that they varied widely from one region to another, and were largely fixed by custom.[37]

Most important among them, to judge from surviving administrative documents, were the village elders (*li-cheng*) who were responsible for providing the data for the registers, for the allocation of land, the supervision of agricultural methods, and payment of taxes.

Such persons were identified with the interests of the local population from amongst whom they were chosen, rather than with those of the central administration. Since the county magistrates were forced to deal with the population at large through this organisation, at this level the representatives of the central power were forced to adapt their policies to the realities of local conditions, and undoubtedly there was widespread compromise and modification of administrative practice. The details of such local administrative practices seem to have been codified by the prefectural governments.[38]

The Period 720–55

A new period in the history of the T'ang financial administration began shortly before 720, and lasted until the An Lu-shan rising. During this period, partly as a result of the growing complexity of the state economy, and partly as a result of purely political factors, a series of financial experts were given very extensive powers which they wielded not through any of the established posts in the official hierarchy, but by virtue of extraordinary appointments as commissioners (*shih*). Such titles gave them power to co-ordinate a whole field of activity, for which no regular appointment gave the required authority.

While these men changed the pattern of administration to some degree, the old organisation continued to exist and to function. They do not seem to have created any large permanent organisation to encroach upon the authority of the Board of Finance, for although they had staffs of assistants, their duties were essentially the efficient co-ordination of existing offices. The only exceptions to this were the commissioners for transportation.

Before the appearance of the commissioners, the regular way of dealing with such problems of co-ordination had been the despatch of censors, and throughout this period there is a close connection between the commissioners and the censorate.[39] For example, in 718 Hsiao Yin-chih, a censor, was sent to the south to deal with the problem of counterfeiting.[40] In the same way when in 719–20 it was proposed to impose taxes on salt and iron to provide a fresh source of revenue, no new organisation was set up to implement the policy, but two prominent financial officials, Chiang Hsün and Chiang Shih-tu, were specially appointed vice-presidents of the censorate, in order to look into the business.[41]

The earliest posts as commissioner were given as concurrent appointments to provincial officers in respect of local duties. Thus some of the provincial governors on the northern frontiers were given posts as finance commissioners (chih-tu shih) and a small subordinate staff to deal with financial matters,[42] while the prefects of Shan-chou were appointed commissioners for land and water transport to supervise transportation between Lo-yang and Shan-chou after 713.[43]

The first appearance of a powerful commissioner with empire-wide authority was that of Yü-wen Jung. He was given extraordinary powers to deal with the land question and the connected problem of unregistered squatters who evaded taxes. He was made vice-president of the censorate, while the envoys whom he despatched to the provinces were made supplementary censors. However, he was also given the title of commissioner for the encouragement of agriculture (chüan-nung shih), and later those of commissioner in charge of taxation and the land levy (kou-tang tsu-yung ti-shui shih), and commissioner for various types of population settlement (chu-se an-chi hu-k'ou shih). Under his control he had a number of executive officers for encouraging agriculture (chüan-nung p'an-kuan).[44] It is not clear whether the latter were identical with the supplementary censors, but we do know for certain that in the case of Yü-wen Jung himself the old and new systems were combined, his title as vice-president of the censorate giving him standing within the regular hierarchy, and his titles as commissioner denoting his special fields of responsibility. The connection of the censorate with the new commissioners is deeper than this, however. As Pulleyblank has suggested, the granting of extraordinary powers to Yü-wen Jung and his successors was more than merely an attempt to increase efficiency in the financial field. They were, in fact, an attempt by the old Kuan-chung aristocracy to curb the growing power of the new official class who had risen through the examination system by striking at the very roots of their economic power.[45] It is not, I think, without significance that one stronghold of the aristocratic party in Yü-wen Jung's time was the censorate.[46]

Censors continued to play an important part in financial affairs. Their control over the treasuries had been established by the beginning of the period. Yang Ch'ung-li (another member of the aristocracy) was permanent president of the Court of Treasury from about 713 to 733.[47] When his sons were put in charge of the Court of Treasury and the Court of Agriculture on his retirement,[48] they too were appointed examining censors (*chien-ch'a yü-shih*) to perform their tasks. About 736 their authority was bolstered up by giving them the additional title Commissioner for Income and Expenditure (*ch'u-na shih*). This title was held by censors until it became a dead letter with An Lu-shan's rising.[49]

When P'ei Yao-ch'ing reorganised the transportation system in 734–7, he was appointed transport commissioner for the Chiang-huai region and Ho-nan (*Chiang-huai Ho-nan chüan-yün shih*).[50] Under him the responsibility for the last stages of transport to the capital was transferred from the local authorities to the central government. The complicated organisation of transit granaries, fleets of barges, and carts for land haulage seem to have been under the direct control of the commissioner, and not under any existing office. Thus arose the first permanent commission with a permanent staff. P'ei Yao-ch'ing had two deputy commissioners, and his organisation must have employed a very large personnel.[51] He was succeeded in 737 by Hsiao Chiung, one of his deputies, and then by Wei Chien.[52] The latter, like P'ei Yao-ch'ing, was a member of the aristocratic party, being related by marriage with two of the imperial princes, and with Li Lin-fu.[53] Under him the connection with the censorate was continued, for he was himself vice-president, and both of his executive officers were concurrently censors.[54] After his fall the commission came into the hands of Yang Kuo-chung.

A second permanent commission, though by no means such an

important one, was that for the manufacture of coinage. The old system, under which this was performed by *corvée* labour under the supervision of the prefects, had proved both cumbersome and impracticable.[55] In 737 Lo Wen-hsin was appointed the first commissioner for the coinage of the empire (*chu-tao chu-ch'ien shih*). We possess no details on the organisation under his control. Both he and his successor Yang Shen-chin were members of the censorate.[56]

The ministers who exercised wide financial powers during the *T'ien-pao* period all held multiple titles of commissioner. For instance, Wei Chien was commissioner for land and water transport (*shui-lu yün shih*) and also commissioner for transportation of taxes from Chiang-huai and along the canal (*kou-tang yüan-ho chi Chiang-huai tsu-yung chuan-yün shih*); Yang Shen-chin besides being commissioner for income and expenditure (*ch'u-na shih*) and commissioner for coinage (*chu-ch'ien shih*), was also commissioner for taxation from all commanderies (*chu-chün tsu-yung shih*); Wang Hung was commissioner for population and special services (*hu-k'ou se-i shih*); while Yang Kuo-chung is said to have accumulated more than forty titles as commissioner. But these titles referred to special fields of responsibility rather than to the control of any specific organisation.

The chief alterations in actual financial practice have already been noted. But under Wang Hung an important innovation was made in that for the first time a considerable proportion of the revenues of the empire were paid directly to the emperor's personal treasury, the *nei-k'u*, without going through the regular channels (that is, the Court of Treasury). This practice was continued during and after the rebellion, and since the personal treasuries *Nei-k'u* and *Ta-ying ts'ang* were controlled by the eunuchs this led to the growth of interference by eunuch officials during the ensuing decades.[57]

The Third Period, from 756 Onwards

The outbreak of the An Lu-shan rising meant the beginning of a totally new administrative period. In the financial field this is especially the case. The loss of power over the provinces by the central government, and the disintegration of the old land, registration, and tax systems which had depended on close supervision by the central authorities, changed the entire situation. During the first few years of warfare, the chief concern of the government was with a series of short-term measures to provide for current expenditure.

The widespread breakdown of control in the provinces led to the appointment of commissioners with wide special power to control tax collection. In 756 Ti-wu Ch'i, a former subordinate of Wei Chien, came into financial prominence, and was created commissioner for taxation in the Chiang-huai region (*Chiang-huai tsu-yung shih*) and also appointed a censor.[58] Such commissioners for taxation continued to exist until 765, when, following a memorial from Ti-wu Ch'i, they were replaced by executive officers (*p'an-kuan*) or inspectors (*hsün-kuan*), who were to be deputed for the task from their subordinate staff by the provincial governors.[59] From Liu Yen's biography it seems that he established provincial taxation commissioners who concurrently held other offices); and that these were later replaced by professional tax-collectors.[60] This probably refers to the same reorganisation.

Owing to the urgent needs of the government various extraordinary methods of raising revenue were tried. In most cases censors were employed in these missions. For example, Ts'ui Chung, a censor, was sent in 755 to sell testimonials of ordination as priests, which gave tax exemption, as an emergency means of raising revenue.[61] Two other censors were sent to the Yangtze valley in 737 to raise forced loans, and to sell official ranks.[62] In 758–60 censors were employed to put the new green sprout tax into force.[63] Their employment in such cases was still a common practice in 779, when an edict was issued clarifying the position of censors employed in this way with regard to their regular duties.[64]

Commissioners for coinage and for transportation continued to be appointed. But the centralised organisation of transport was destroyed when the canal system was overrun by the rebel forces.[65] An alternative route was organised up the Han valley, but this was less satisfactory. Owing to some troubles in that area, too, a special deputy commissioner Mu Ning was appointed to control the traffic, but this was only a temporary appointment to deal with a crisis.[66]

By far the most important of the emergency finance measures was the imposition of the monopoly on salt. The new period of financial administration may well be said to begin with the appointment of Ti-wu Ch'i as salt and iron commissioner (*yen-t'ieh shih*) in 758.[67]

The salt monopoly was the only source of revenue which did not need close and effective control in the provinces for its efficient operation. The system devised by Ti-wu Ch'i was that the commissioners should strictly control the producers of salt, compulsorily purchase all their output, and sell it off to retail merchants with the addition of a heavy tax to the price. The merchants would thus pass on the tax to the consumers.[68] Since the areas of production were fortunately limited, and also situated in regions where central authority was still fairly strong, this scheme was quite practicable. Besides salt was a necessity, and the people could not resist the increased prices caused by the imposition of the tax. The monopoly was so successful that within twenty years it was producing over half of the annual revenues, and from 760 to 780 the history of finance is to all intents and purposes the history of the salt administration.

The backbone of the organisation built up by Ti-wu Ch'i was the system of directorates (*chien*) which were established in all producing districts. These controlled the producer-households (*ting-hu*) and conducted the sale of salt to the merchants.[69]

Until the end of hostilities the salt monopoly remained a relatively minor source of income.[70] After the fall of Ti-wu Ch'i in 759, control of the commission passed to Lü Yin[71] and then to Liu Yen.[72] After the temporary disgrace of the latter in 761, it came under the nominal control of the Great Minister Yüan Tsai, but most of his financial duties were delegated to Liu Yen.[73] In 763 Liu Yen was created a Great Minister and commissioner for public revenues, salt and iron, transport and taxation.[74] Apart from a temporary disgrace when he was involved in the fall of the eunuch Cheng Yüan-chen,[75] he remained the most prominent financial minister throughout the reign of Tai-tsung.

His work of financial reorganisation began in 763 when hostilities ended. Yüan Tsai sent him on a tour of inspection to the south, to restore the canal system. We still possess his report, in the form of a long letter to Yüan Tsai.[76] His solution of the problem was the close co-operation of the transport organisation with the salt and iron monopoly. The profits on salt were utilised to pay for the maintenance of the canal and the barge fleets, the transport system being taken completely out of the hands of the local authorities.[77] This proved convenient, for the chief areas of salt production were around the Yangtze delta, and the centre of the transport network was Yang-tzu county in Yang-chou, where the canal joined the Yangtze. This became the central depot for both the salt administration and the transport commission.

Ti-wu Ch'i's system of directorates controlling production was maintained, though improved in detail. The chief innovation was the establishment of a chain of branch offices (*yüan*) on the route to the north, which seem to have been shared by both the salt and the transport authorities. These branch offices served mainly as distribution centres, where salt was sold to merchants, but were also control points for illicit traffic in salt.[78] The branch offices controlled minor distribution centres called *ch'ang*, and also controlled a chain of local salt stores in the Yangtze region. There were also four further *ch'ang* which are mentioned by name in *Hsin T'ang-shu*, 54. Since these were all in large cities, they are unlikely to have been subordinate centres of production, and were possibly big local salt markets.[79]

The personnel of this organisation must have been very numerous. Though we know the names of many offices, the details of their duties are unknown. Many of them were probably outside the official class altogether, and the higher grades were probably filled by persons holding sinecure ranks in other departments.[80]

In 765 the financial control of the empire was divided between Liu Yen and Ti-wu Ch'i on a purely geographical basis.[81] Liu Yen controlled the southern provinces, while Ti-wu Ch'i controlled the north and Szechuan. Ti-wu Ch'i was also given the title of salt and iron commissioner, but since the salt production of the salt pools of Shensi and the salt wells of Szechuan remained under the Department of Public Revenues,[82] this meant little, and when he fell from power in 770, his successor in control of the north, Han Huang, no longer held the title.

As a result of this, during the latter part of Tai-tsung's reign the pattern began to emerge of two separate financial regions. The north was controlled first by Ti-wu Ch'i and later by Han Huang, chiefly through their positions in control of Public Revenues,[83] while the south was ruled continuously by Liu Yen through his position in control of the Salt and Iron Commission. In 779 Han Huang was finally dismissed after a series of troubles,[84] and Liu Yen gained complete control of the empire's finances. But shortly afterwards Tai-tsung died. Among the new Great Ministers was Yang Yen, who was bitterly opposed to Liu Yen on personal and political grounds.[85]

During the preceding twenty years there had been considerable changes in the central financial administration. I have spoken above of the shift of power within the Board of Finance from the Board itself to he Department of Public Revenues. The treasury departments had also been seriously affected. Not only was the tax income precarious, but under Ti-wu Ch'i the depredations of the powerful generals reached such a pitch that, for safety's sake, taxes were no longer paid into the regular treasuries but, as had been done to a lesser degree under Wang Hung, paid into the personal treasury of the emperor (*nei ying-k'u-sang*). This department was under the control of eunuchs.[86] The regular treasury departments fell into disuse, and the posts in them became sinecures.[87]

Yang Yen attempted, during his brief period in power, to undo all the work of Liu Yen. The first of his plans was to restore the responsibility for financial matters to the original offices. It is plain from his memorial on the subject that this measure was not only dictated by enmity towards Liu Yen, but was designed to curb the power of the eunuchs over finance.[88] An edict was issued, following this memorial, restoring the power over tax income to the Treasury of the Left (*tso-tsang-k'u*), and limiting the amount paid into the palace treasury.[89] A further edict on similar lines was issued in 780, when Liu Yen's titles as commissioner were finally suspended.[90] At the same time the offices of commissioner for public revenue and for transport were abolished.

The Board of Finance had been in a state of advanced decay for so long that there was no adequate organisation left for dealing with business. The Chancellery and Secretariat were ordered to find suitable candidates to fill the lapsed posts,[91] while, to fill the vacuum in the administration, two temporary officials were placed in charge.[92] By the third month, the deficiencies of the revived financial administration had become so obvious that Yang Yen was forced to revive Liu Yen's system. Han Hui, the younger brother of Han Huang, was appointed vice-president of the Board of Finance in control of Public Revenues.[93] Tu Yu, who had been put in charge of the revived Department of Treasury, was now put in control of transportation from the south.[94]

More successful was Yang Yen's attempt to regularise taxes, and restore direct taxation as the main source of revenue. The *liang-shui* system was by no means an isolated reform. It represents an attempt to bolster up the central power of the bureaucratic machine against the attacks of the provincial governors on the one hand, and the eunuchs on the other. As such it must be considered as part of the first reaction of the central power against sectionalism, an attempt which was

8

thwarted temporarily by the rebellion of the Ho-pei governors, which for a while threatened the central government as seriously as had that of An Lu-shan.

In spite of this the new division of taxes into allocations for central and local expenditure assured the central government of a regular income beyond that from the salt monopoly which had already reached its optimum level, and enabled the central government to relieve the pressure of taxation in the areas close to the capital.

The details of the *liang-shui* reform are dealt with elsewhere, but the scheme had considerable effects in the administrative field. First, it recognised the provincial governors as intermediaries in taxation. The governors were each responsible for collecting a quota. Local quotas and rates were assessed by envoys despatched by the central government (*ch'u-chih shih*), in consultation with the provincial governors and the prefect.[95] Likewise the governors became intermediary authorities in the audit of accounts.[96] The governors paid their provinces' taxes into the treasuries through their chancelleries (*chin-tsou yüan*) in the capital. Thus the *liang-shui* reform meant the end of the direct financial relationship between the central administration and the prefectures.

The whole administration of the new tax was placed under the Department of Public Revenues.[97] This confirmed the growing authority of the office, which in the period 780–805 developed into a powerful and independent authority with a multiplicity of interests, on the lines of the Salt and Iron Commission. The latter authority suffered something of an eclipse from 780 to 786, for, when its posts were revived in 782, they were specifically subordinated to the Public Revenue Department.[98] The various ministers who controlled financial matters during the war with the provincial magnates Tu Yu,[99] Chao Tsan,[100] P'ei Tien,[101] and Yüan Hsiu[102] were all in the Public Revenue Department.

The salt and iron administration began to revive after the appointment of Han Huang as commissioner for public revenue, salt and iron and transport in 786, shortly before his death.[103] He delegated the duties on the salt monopoly to his deputy commissioner, Pan Hung. In 789 it was proposed to make the latter a Great Minister, but he was passed over in favour of the more forceful Tou Shen, who had formerly been his subordinate.[104] The latter was nominally in charge of financial matters, but delegated most of the authority to Pan Hung, promising that he would eventually be appointed to the post. However, when the time came to hand over, he wished to give the office to Chang P'ang instead. Pan Hung said that the latter was not suitable—an opinion which came to the ears of Chang P'ang, who was bitterly resentful.[105]

Shortly before Tou Shen and his party were disgraced in 792,[106] they made a compromise arrangement, by which Chang P'ang was created salt and iron commissioner, but was made subordinate to Pan Hung, who was appointed commissioner for public revenues.[107] The animosity between the two made this arrangement unworkable. Hung refused to hand over the files of the Salt and Iron Commission,[108] and, since the two could never agree over the appointment of subordinate officials, many posts fell vacant.

The situation was eventually solved by dividing the control of finances between them on a geographical basis, Pan Hung being given control over Ho-tung and the provinces of Szechuan, and Chang P'ang control over the south.[109] They even divided control over the collection of the *liang-shui* tax on a regional basis. Thus the financial administration was once more split into two regions, this time permanently. Pan Hung died shortly after, and was replaced by the oppressive and rapacious P'ei Yen-ling,[110] under whose administration the two regions grew more and more separate.[111] In 794 Yen-ling had Chang P'ang dismissed, and he was replaced by Wang Wei, a prominent governor in the Yangtze delta area.[112]

The appointment of the commissioners for salt and iron from amongst the southern governors cut their administration off completely from the central government. Both Wang Wei's successor, Li Jo-ch'u,[113] and Li Ch'i, who followed him,[114] were powerful figures in the south-east, and under them the regional nature of the Salt and Iron Commission was consolidated. The centre of the salt administration was fixed either at Yang-chou or Jun-chou, and its interests in the capital were attended to by an agent (*liu-hou*), who had much the same responsibilities as the chancellery of a provincial governor.[115]

On the death of Te-tsung in 805 the empire came into the hands of Wang Pi and Wang Shu-wen. They dismissed Li Ch'i, and made the veteran Tu Yu commissioner both for public revenue and for salt and iron. However, Wang Shu-wen acted as his agent in the capital, and thus kept control in his own hands.[116] When Hsien-tsung succeeded to the throne, and the Wangs fell from power, Tu Yu remained for a while in charge of finance, and was then replaced at his

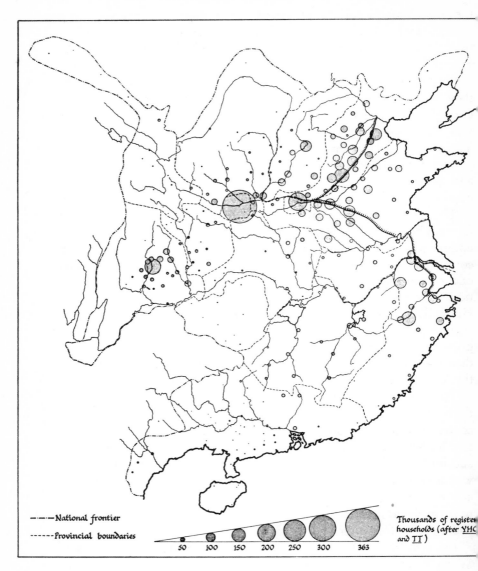

Map 7. Registered population in the *T'ien-pao* period (742–56).

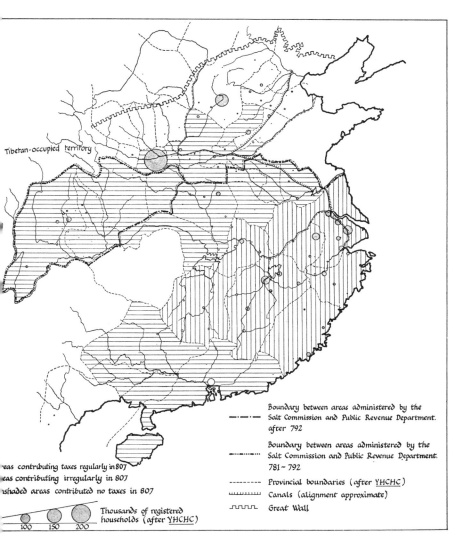

Map 8. Registered population in the *Yüan-ho* period (probably 812) and areas under effective administrative control.

For the boundaries of the areas administered by the Public Revenue Department and the Salt and Iron Commission between about 781 and 792, see note 82 to p. 112.

Figures for the number of households registered in Huai-nan, Ching-nan, Chin-hang, most of Shan-nan hsi-tao and Ling-nan are missing.

117

own request by Li Sun.[117] The latter overhauled thoroughly the salt and transport systems.

The importance of the Salt and Iron Commission at this period was very great, for, as we know from the account of the national budget for the *Yüan-ho* period compiled by Li Chi-fu, the only provinces which could be depended upon to pay their taxes annually were those in the Yangtze valley and the south-east, the area where the commissioners were in control of direct taxation.[118] A glance at maps 7 and 8 will show the far greater proportion of taxpayers in southern China after 755, and that the great preponderance of tax-producing registered population was in the area controlled by the Salt Commission. Under Li Sun, too, the profits on salt again reached the high level of Liu Yen's time. In 807 this money was for the first time brought under the control of the Public Revenue Department for accountancy purposes.[119] At the end of the eighth century the Salt and Iron Commission had gone into all variety of other business. It controlled the minting of money,[120] mining production,[121] the taxation on tea and other goods, and the imposition of transit taxes.[122]

At the same time, the Public Revenue Department had carried out a similar expansion of its interests in the north. As always, they controlled the taxation of salt in the north, and from 792 that of Szechuan as well.[123] The administration of the salt pools was carried on by commissioners (*chüeh-yen shih*) with their own regular staff,[124] who performed the same duties as the directorates in the south. The public revenue commissioners also maintained branch establishments (*hsün-yüan*) just as the salt and iron commissioners did in their area. The great expansion of the department had been carried out under P'ei Yen-ling. By 806 they had 'by degrees taken over the duties of various offices, and established staff on a large scale. Their business was multifarious, and difficult to control.'[125] Tu Yu requested in 805 that building works, the manufacture of textiles, and the provision of fuel should once again become the responsibility of the regular offices, and later in the same year he requested the abolition of the special granaries set up by the Public Revenue Commission under P'ei Yen-ling.[126] In 808 the staff of the department was reduced,[127] but later restored.[128]

In 810 an edict recognised the division of the empire between these authorities, when it made the agents (*liu-hou*) of the Salt and Iron Commission at Yang-tzu and at Chiang-ling commissioners responsible for the *liang-shui* tax in the Yangtze valley, and the head of the Public

Revenue branch in Shan-nan (west) commissioner for the *liang-shui* tax in Szechuan.[129]

At this time the practice began of referring to the *San Ssu*, the 'three offices', meaning the Board of Finance, the Salt and Iron Commission, and the Public Revenue Department.[130] The heads of these three offices frequently made joint memorials on financial matters, and although the influence of the respective offices fluctuated from time to time, they remained in joint control of central financial affairs until the end of the dynasty. The provincial military authorities, however, gained more and more financial power, as the central government grew weaker after the middle of the century.

In this third period the trend towards professionalism in finance, which we have seen beginning in Hsüan-tsung's reign, was maintained and strengthened. I have dealt with this matter in detail elsewhere, but to sum up, the position was this. Practically all the statesmen who controlled the two most important offices, the Salt and Iron Commission and the Public Revenue Department, had previous financial experience. The exceptions were all either mere figureheads (for example, Tou Shen, Li Yung, Liu Kung-ch'o), or temporary stop-gap appointments (Chi Chung-fou, P'ei Chün, Li Yüan-su, etc.). The only truly exceptional case was Li Ch'i, and he was appointed through bribery.

Not only had most of the candidates, and all the important figures amongst them, previous experience in finance, but a great many of them had prior service in the Salt and Iron Commission, a large proportion of the more prominent persons being protégés of former commissioners. This self-perpetuating tendency was much more marked in the semi-independent Salt Commission, and only extended to the Public Revenue Department in the short period of irregular administration, 796–805, which followed the tenure of office by P'ei Yen-ling. But in the Salt Commission it was the rule rather than the exception and in the period 780–830, former employees of the commission were in control for twenty-eight years out of fifty. It is interesting that the period when such persons were not in charge (786–806, with the exception of a short period 798–9) was a period of decline both in the influence and in the revenue of the commission.

Thus we may say that during T'ang times the central administration of finance, at first carried out by the Board of Finance and its satellite offices, was completely changed after the beginning of the eighth century by the emergence of specialised organs of administration. This change was accelerated after An Lu-shan's rising, when the decay of the old taxation system led to the old organisation's being replaced as the real authority by two new financial organisations, the Salt and Iron Commission, which was dominant in the area of production in the south, and the Public Revenue Department, much more closely tied to the traditional administrative pattern, which controlled the northern region where the political and strategic interests of the government were concentrated.

Besides these the old organisation continued a shadowy existence, generally maintaining the balance between its two powerful new rivals and emerging into prominence at intervals under the influence of some powerful statesman, or by the influence of a president who concurrently controlled public revenue.

Local Administration

Important as were the changes in central finance administration during the eighth and ninth centuries, the greatest alterations in the administrative system were those which took place in the local administration.

The most far-reaching of these changes was the establishment throughout central China of provincial governments whose heads, unlike the prefects of the early part of the dynasty, were in control of regions large enough to provide for a considerable degree of autonomy. The majority of the provincial governors bore a number of concurrent titles, usually combining that of 'military governor' (*chieh-tu-shih*), with that of 'civil governor' (*kuan-ch'a-shih*). In both capacities such a governor was provided with a large establishment of subordinates. While as military governors the rulers of the provinces challenged the military power of the central government, in civil matters they exerted a much more powerful influence on the old-established local government of the prefectures and counties, many of whose responsibilities and powers they arrogated for themselves.[131] The details of this change are too complicated for discussion here, and in any case varied greatly in different regions.

Generally speaking, the provincial government became an intermediate link in the chain of command from the capital to the county. Edicts and other orders were relayed to the local executive authorities through the province and not direct, as had been the case previously. At the same time the provincial governments began to take responsibility for the annual merit-ratings of the local officials in the prefectures and counties under their jurisdiction, and thus to exercise control over them. Generally speaking, the central government jealously guarded the right to appoint county and prefectural officials, but there is little doubt that powerful governors were able to veto appointments which they considered unsuitable, and some of the more powerful among them did actually appoint local officials without the consent of the central government. In the late ninth century some local posts in the more autonomous provinces even became hereditary.[132]

Such direct control over and interference with the established local authorities, however, was not the most dangerous infringement of their authority. Much more significant was the establishment by the provinces of new offices and authorities, directly responsible to themselves, which rivalled the prefectures and more particularly the counties in certain administrative fields.

Much of the county magistrate's time was taken up with legal business of various types. Here the province encroached severely on the magistrate's traditional authority. One of the offices under the military governor was the *ma-pu-yüan* or *ma-pu-ssu*, which was originally responsible for military discipline and summary justice, a sort of provost marshal's office. As time went on such offices and the officials employed in them came to deal with many legal offences committed by civilians, which had formerly been dealt with under the summary jurisdiction of the magistrates. These new officials were often simply personal adherents of the governor, seconded to their duties from his personal force, the *ya-ch'ien-chün*. It is thus extremely unlikely that such persons had either legal training or experience. However, the members of the staff of the *ma-pu-yüan*, in particular the *tu-yü-hou*, controlled not only criminal law, but even civil matters—for instance, registering the titles to land.[133]

In the county magistrates' second most important field of activity, finance, the province again took a hand. The governor's staff included *k'ung-mu-kuan*, a sort of registrars who were responsible for detailed administrative routine, and in particular for financial business.[134] Like the personnel of the *ma-pu-yüan*, most of these officials were personal adherents of the governor, though in this case they were mostly civilians. Some of them were deputed to look after financial affairs in important towns within a province. Others were in charge of tax collection, sometimes with the title of commissioners for levying rations (*liang-liao shih*).

While these offices of the provincial administration were encroaching on the powers of the counties from one direction, a further curtailment of their authority was caused by the establishment of centres of local power under the direct control of the province and staffed with provincial personnel, which remained completely outside the jurisdiction of the prefecture–county network. Most important of these centres were the garrisons (*chen*). At first these were outposts in important strategic centres with detachments of troops from the provincial armies. But later these garrisons began to become centres of civil administration rivalling the local counties in power. They were frequently sited at places where transit taxes were collected from merchants, and where there were important rural markets. They were most commonly staffed from among the personal adherents of the governors, and were in many cases under military command.[135]

These local representatives of the provincial administration were not the only authorities which arose in the provinces to rival the old-established county administrations. The central government's financial agencies were reluctant to leave too much authority in the hands of prefectures and counties, since such authority could so easily be annexed by the provinces who posed a potential military threat to the government at Ch'ang-an. Thus the Public Revenue Department, the Commission for Salt and Iron, and the Board of Finance established local agencies in the provinces to look after their interests. It is impossible to describe these systematically, as the sources are so fragmentary, but it is clear that, beside the branch establishments (*hsün-yüan*) maintained in important centres, there were many branch offices designated as *yüan* or *wu* established to control special business such as mining, military colonies, markets, customs controls, coinage, or tax collection in important localities.[136]

The position of these offices was complicated, for although they seem to have been directly responsible to the central authority, they often seem to have been staffed by the members of county or prefectural administrations acting concurrently. But there can be no doubt that their existence weakened the financial authority of the prefectural and county administrations.

The repercussions of these changes on the lowest scale sub-bureaucratic rural administration in the villages and those of the widespread social changes which followed the growth of provincial autonomy and the wider diffusion of political power must have been considerable. But the material available to clarify this question is not adequate for us to formulate any conclusions at present.

The local administrations must have varied very considerably, the forces of change being much stronger in the north, where military authority and the employment of personal adherents in important posts were much more the norm than was the case in southern and central China, where things went on much as in the early part of the eighth century until the last three or four decades of the dynasty. But we may make the generalisation that during the period from 756 to the end of the dynasty there was a general decentralisation of authority from the centre to the provinces, and a further decentralisation of local authority with the establishment in the ninth century of garrison administrations independent of the counties and under direct provincial control. In the course of these changes the position of the county magistrates, who in the early years of the dynasty had been most important figures in local administration, was generally weakened, and was not restored until the re-establishment of firm central administration under the Sung.

APPENDIX I

1. THE FRAGMENTS OF THE 'LAND STATUTES'

The following is a translation of the fragments of the *Land Statutes* (*T'ien-ling*) of the early T'ang reconstructed from various quotations by Niida Noboru and printed in his *Tōryō shūi* (1933), pp. 607–58. The fragments have been arranged where possible in accordance with the order of the rules in the Japanese statutes *Ryō-no-gige* and *Ryō-no-shūge*. Niida's reconstruction follows in the main that of Nakada Kaoru, in 'Tōryō to Nihon-ryō to no hikaku kenkyū' (*Hōseishi ronshū*, I, pp. 677 ff.). The abbreviations used here are listed in the Bibliography (pp. 343–5).

Art. 1. Land which is one double pace wide, and 240 double paces long constitutes one *mou*. One hundred *mou* are one *ch'ing*.

SOURCES: *CTS*, 48, p. 3*a*; *TLT*, 3, p. 31*b*; *TT*, 2, p. 15*c*; *TFYK*, 495, p. 21*a*; *STCSKS*, 65. *CTS* reflects the *Statutes* of 624, *TLT* those of 719. The latter three sources, all of which are based on the digest of the *Land Statutes* in *TT*, 2, specify that they refer to the 737 *Statutes*.

NOTES: The versions in *CTS* and *TLT* begin by defining the double pace (*p'u*) as equivalent to 5 feet (*ch'ih*). The commentary to *Ryō-no-shūge*, 12, p. 345, cites this definition as belonging with the other measurements of length in the *Miscellaneous Statutes* (*Tsa-ling*).

Art. 2. The tax in grain (*tsu*) shall be assigned in sequence according to whether the harvest in the prefecture concerned is early or late, and taking into account whether transport thence is difficult or easy, and the road distant or short. When the harvest in the prefecture is completed the grain should be despatched. Collection should begin in the eleventh month, and contribution finished by the 30th day of the first month. [In those prefectures of Chiang-nan from which the taxes are transported by water and where in the winter months the water is shallow and it is difficult to take boats up the haul-overs they may be transported in the fourth month or later, the contribution to be completed by the 30th day of the fifth month.] Where the tax is collected in by the prefecture itself, contribution must be completed by the 30th day of the twelfth month. If the locality (*hsiang*) is without millet, they may pay in rice or wheat, making payment in accordance with when the crops ripen, not within these time limits. Should a [taxpayer] die before his grain is placed in the granary in cases where he contributes to the local prefecture, or before it is sent off on the road in cases where the grain is allotted elsewhere, it shall be returned.

In places where hulled grain is stored one *hu* of unhulled grain may be converted and 6 *tou* of hulled grain collected in its stead. Conversion in terms of miscellaneous products should always accord with the local products, and should follow current prices in the locality (*hsiang*) concerned.

NOTE: This passage is divided into two by *TT*, and other matter inserted. The subject-matter would suggest that the article belonged rather to the taxation statutes. However, the Japanese statutes (*RSG*, 12, pp. 347–8; *RGG*, 9, p. 107) include an article parallel to the first part in the land statutes.

Art. 3 (A). All adult (*ting*) and adolescent (*chung*) males shall be granted one *ch'ing* of land. Crippled and disabled persons shall be granted 40 *mou*; Widowed wives or concubines 30 *mou*, and where they are the head of their household 20 *mou* in addition. A fifth of the lands granted shall be land in perpetuity (*shih-ye*), the other four-fifths personal share land (*k'ou-fen t'ien*). On the decease of the holder the lands in perpetuity will be granted to his heir, but his personal share land shall be returned to the authorities and granted again to other persons.

SOURCES: *CTS*, 48, p. 3*a*; *THY*, 83, pp. 1530–1; *TCTC*, 190, p. 5982. All refer to the 624 *Statutes*. Niida, *op. cit.* pp. 609–10, further accepts *WHTK*, 2, p. 41*b*, as a source and adds from it a passage dealing with restricted localities and fallow lands which does not appear in the other sources. In fact *WHTK* here is verbatim quotation from a passage in *HTS*, 51, p. 1*b*, which does not specify that the rules come from the 624 *Statutes*, and which is in any case reworded. Such rules were, however, very probably included in the 624 *Statutes*, since the rules on restricted localities had been in force under the Sui, and are incorporated in *RGG*, which is presumed to derive from the 651 *Statutes*, of which all trace is now lost.

Art. 3 (B). In the system of granting lands there are various distinctions. Adult and adolescent males shall be granted one *ch'ing* [adolescent males of eighteen years and above shall receive grants as adults]. Old men (*lao-nan*), cripples and disabled persons shall be granted 40 *mou*; widowed wives or concubines 30 *mou*, and where they are head of their household half of the grant due to an adult male. Lands are divided into two categories, one called 'lands in perpetuity', the other called 'personal share land'. Of an adult's grant two parts shall be lands in perpetuity, eight parts personal share land.

SOURCE: *TLT*, 3, p. 31*b*. This is probably a résumé of the relevant article in the 719 *Statutes*. The comment (in square brackets) may refer either to a modification of the system added after 719, or to a supplementary *Ordinance* defining the extent to which adolescents should benefit from grants.

125

Art. 3 (c). Adult males shall be granted 20 *mou* of lands in perpetuity, and 80 *mou* of personal share land. Adolescent males of 18 years and above shall be granted lands in the same way as adults. Old men, cripples and disabled persons shall be granted 40 *mou* of personal share land; widowed wives and concubines 30 *mou* of personal share land. Where their forebears have possessed lands in perpetuity these shall be taken into account among the personal share lands. When male or female infants, children, old persons, cripples or disabled persons, or widows are heads of their household, they shall in every case be granted 20 *mou* of lands in perpetuity and 20 *mou* of personal share land. Where grants are to be made in an unrestricted locality, they should in all cases follow the prescribed amounts. But when grants are to be newly made in a restricted locality, the person will receive only one-half of the personal share land to which he would be entitled in an unrestricted locality. If the personal share land which he is granted is poor land requiring fallow periods then he shall be granted double. [But in an unrestricted locality land which needs three or more years of fallow should be granted according to the local practice.]

SOURCES: *TT*, 2, p. 65 c; *TFYK*, 495, p. 21 a–b; *STCSKS*, 65. The second two are probably secondary, deriving from *TT*. It is likely that the version in *HTS*, 51, p. 1 b; *WHTK*, 2, p. 41 b–c, also derives from this summary of the *Land Statutes*, although it is rephrased.

NOTE: The three versions of this statute form the basis of the *chün-t'ien* system, and show a development of more precise rules especially concerning the categories of land.

Art. 4. Grants of lands in perpetuity (*shih-ye*): princes of the blood, 100 *ch'ing*; serving officials of the 1st rank upper division, 60 *ch'ing*; prince of commanderies (*chün-wang*) and serving officials of the 1st rank lower division, 50 *ch'ing*; dukes of states (*kuo-kung*) and serving officials of the 2nd rank upper division, 40 *ch'ing*; dukes of commanderies (*chün-kung*) and serving officials of the 2nd rank lower division, 35 *ch'ing*; dukes of counties (*hsien-kung*) and serving officials of the 3rd rank upper division, 25 *ch'ing*; serving officials of the 3rd rank lower division, 20 *ch'ing*; marquises and serving officials of the 4th rank upper division, 14 *ch'ing*; earls and serving officials of the 4th rank lower division, 11 *ch'ing*; viscounts and serving officials of the 5th rank upper division, 8 *ch'ing*; barons and serving officials of the 5th rank lower division, 5 *ch'ing*; 'great pillars of the state' (*shang chu-kuo*), 30 *ch'ing*; 'pillars of the state' (*chu-kuo*), 25 *ch'ing*; superior *hu-chün*, 20 *ch'ing*; *hu-chün*, 15 *ch'ing*; superior *ch'ing-chü-tu-wei*, 10 *ch'ing*; *ch'ing-chü-tu-wei*, 7 *ch'ing*; superior *chi-tu-wei*, 6 *ch'ing*; *chi-tu-wei*, 4 *ch'ing*; *hsiao-chi-wei* and *fei-chi-wei*, 80 *mou*; *Yün-chi-wei* and *Wu-chi-wei*, 60 *mou*. Persons holding nominal office (*san-kuan*) of the 5th rank and above will be given the same grant as a serving official of equivalent rank. If a person holds an official rank, a noble title, and an honorific rank simultaneously, and is entitled to a grant in respect of each of them, he shall not be granted all these amounts, but only the largest of them. If a family possesses lands inherited from their forebears in excess of the personal shares to which the members of the household are entitled, if it is not a restricted locality they may receive it in their turn. If there is a surplus this should be returned to the authorities, while if there is insufficient they should be given a further grant.

SOURCES: *TLT*, 3, pp. 32*b*–33*a*, quoting the *Statute* of 719. *TT*, 2, pp. 15*c*–16*a*; *TFYK*, 495, pp. 21*b*–22*a*; *STCSKS*, 65 from *Statute* of 737. The beginning is cited as a *Land Statute* (*t'ien-ling*) in an edict of 788 preserved in *THY*, 92, p. 1671, and *TFYK*, 506, p. 20*a*.

Art. 5. All lands in perpetuity are to be handed down to the holder's descendants, and do not come within the scope of reverting to the state. Even if the descendant commits a crime entailing the loss of his name the lands he has inherited are not to be recovered from him.

SOURCES: *TLT*, 3, pp. 33*a*, quoting *Statute* of 719. This version lacks the second part. I correct 不在此授之限 in the Kuang-ya shu-chü edition to 不在收授之限. *TT*, 2, p. 16*a*; *TFYK*, 495, p. 22*a*; *STCSKS*, 65, all quote 737 *Statute*.

Art. 6. All lands in perpetuity held within the household should be planted with fifty or more mulberries to each *mou*, and ten or more of both elms and jujubes. The planting of these should be completed within three years. If the soil of the locality is unsuitable it is permissible to plant appropriate trees in their place.

SOURCES: *TT*, 2, p. 16*a*; *TFYK*, 495, p. 22*a*–*b*; *STCSKS*, 65, *Code*, 13, art. 8. All derive from 737 series. Parallel in *WHTK*, 2, p. 41*b*–*c* (Niida, art. 6A).

Art. 7. Lands in perpetuity granted to officials of the 5th rank and above may never be received in a restricted locality. They are allowed to take possession of ownerless wastelands which are in a broad locality to fill out the amount. (However, if they buy inherited or donated lands to fill out the full amount, this is permissible even in a restricted locality.) It is permitted for lands in perpetuity of officials of the 6th rank and below to be provided by granting them lands which have reverted to the state in their own locality. But if they too desire to receive lands in a broad locality, this is allowed.

SOURCES: *TLT*, 3, p. 33*a*, gives a fragmentary version of the 719 *Statute*. *TT*, 2, p. 16*a*; *TFYK*, 495, p. 22*b*; *STCSKS*, 65, preserve the version of 737.

Art. 8. Lands which are to be given as an imperial donation, if their situation is not specified, shall not be granted in a restricted locality.

SOURCES: *TT*, 2, p. 16*a*; *TFYK*, 495, p. 22*b*; *STCSKS*, 65, all from 737 *Statute*.

Art. 9. All persons who should receive grants of land in perpetuity who retire or are dismissed while holding official's rank or honorific rank, shall return the lands appertaining to the office they have left. (If they are not dismissed completely, they shall return land corresponding to their reduction in rank.) Those who are struck off the roll of officials will be granted lands in accordance with the rule for personal shares. Anything apart from this, and any donated land they might possess shall be returned. If there is anybody in his own family who possesses rank or noble title and having little personal share land is entitled to receive it, he shall be granted the land in his stead. If there is any surplus beyond such entitlement, this shall revert to the state.

SOURCES: *TT*, 2, p. 16a; *TFYK*, 495, p. 22b; *STCSKS*, 65. All cite 737 *Statute*.

Art. 10. In all cases where persons are entitled to receive lands in perpetuity by reason of official rank or nobility, and die without requesting that it be granted, or without its having been granted to the full, their heirs may not request it to be granted retrospectively.

SOURCES: *TLT*, 3, p. 33a (719 *Statutes*); *TT*, 6, p. 16a; *TFYK*, 495, p. 22b; *STCSKS*, 65 (737 *Statute*).

Art. 11. All those who inherit noble titles shall only receive the lands in perpetuity possessed by their father and grandfather, and are not entitled to make a request for a separate grant. If the father or grandfather has died without requesting a grant, or without receiving the full amount, then they may be granted a half less than the lands given to those first receiving a fief.

SOURCES: *TLT*, 3, p. 33a–b (this omits the first sentence), from 719 *Statutes*; *TT*, 2, p. 16a; *TFYK*, 495, pp. 22b–23a; *STCSKS*, 65, from 737 *Statutes*.

Art. 12. Where there is sufficient land for everyone within the borders of a prefecture or county to receive his share, this is a broad locality (*k'uan-hsiang*). Where there is not sufficient it is a restricted locality (*hsia-hsiang*).

SOURCES: *TLT*, 3, p. 32b, from 719 *Statute*; *Code*, 13, art. 1; *TT*, 2, p. 16a; *TFYK*, 495, p. 23a; *STCSKS*, 65; *PSLT*, 23, p. 78a, from 737 *Statute*.

Art. 13. Where the lands in a restricted locality are insufficient, it is permitted that persons may transfer to a broad locality and receive a grant of land there.

SOURCES: *TT*, 2, p. 16a; *TFYK*, 495, p. 23a; *STCSKS*, 65; *PSLT*, 23, p. 78a, from 737 *Statute*. There is an identical rule in *RGG*, 9, art. 14, p. 109, and this article was thus almost certainly included in the 651 *Statutes*.

Art. 14. Those who are entitled to be granted lands for gardens and dwellings will be granted 1 *mou* for three free persons or less, and 1 *mou* for each three additional persons. They will be granted 1 *mou* for five bondsmen or less, and 1 *mou* for each five additional persons in this category. None of this land shall come within the limits of the personal shares or lands in perpetuity. Gardens and dwellings in the suburbs of the capitals and of prefectural and county towns do not come under this rule.

Sources: *TLT*, 3, p. 32*a*, from 719 *Statute*; *TT*, 2, p. 16*a*; *TFYK*, 495, p. 23*a*; *STCSKS*, 65, from 737 *Statute*.

Art. 15. When a common person dies, and his family are too poor to pay for his funeral, they are permitted to sell lands in perpetuity. It is also the same in the case of persons moving their residence. Those who are transferring to a broad locality of their own free will are also allowed to sell their personal share lands. The sale of land for use as homesteads, stores or mills is allowed even when the persons concerned are not moving away.

Sources: *TT*, 2, p. 16*b*; *TFYK*, 495, p. 23*a–b*; *STCSKS*, 65, from 737 *Statute*. Compare the similar rule given in a commentary to *Code*, 12, art. 14.

Art. 16. No person may buy land beyond his entitlement. However, if he lives in a restricted locality, it is permissible for him to obtain lands up to the standard for a broad locality. Persons who sell their lands may not request a further grant.

Sources: *TT*, 2, p. 16*b*; *TFYK*, 495, p. 23*b*; *STCSKS*, 65, from 737 *Statute*.

Art. 17. In all cases of the sale and purchase of lands, a report should be sent to the official under whose jurisdiction the case comes. At the end of the year the lands will be placed under the new holder in the registers. If a sale or purchase is made improperly without a report being rendered, the price will be confiscated and not recoverable, and the lands will revert to the original owner.

Sources: *TT*, 2, p. 16*b*; *TFYK*, 495, p. 23*b*; *STCSKS*, 65 from 737 *Statutes*. For a slightly different version, see *Code*, 13, art. 1, commentary.

Art. 18. All those whose professions are those of merchant or artisan will receive a half share of both lands in perpetuity and personal share lands. But those who dwell in restricted localities will be granted none whatever.

Sources: *TT*, 2, p. 16*b*; *TFYK*, 495, p. 23*b*; *STCSKS*, 65, from 737 *Statutes*.

Art. 19. In all cases where a person, in the course of performing his duties to the state, is missing among the foreign tribes and does not return, if he has any kinsmen living with him, his own allocation of land will be recoverable by the state only after six years have elapsed. On the day he returns he shall again receive a grant as in the first instance. If he himself dies in the course of his duties, his lands will not be recoverable by the authorities, even if his sons and grandsons have not reached adult status. If he is wounded in battle, and becomes crippled or disabled, his lands will not be recoverable or reduced, but he will be permitted to retain them in full until death.

Sources: *TT*, 2, p. 16*b*; *TFYK*, 495, p. 23*b*; *STCSKS*, 65; *PSLT*, 10, p. 37*a*, from 737 *Statutes*.

Art. 20. Persons may not rent out or mortgage lands. In case of infringement, the price will be confiscated and not recoverable, and the land returned to the original owner. If a person is employed on distant duty away from his home, and has no one to keep his lands in cultivation, he is allowed to rent out or mortgage them. Lands in perpetuity of the officials, and lands donated by the emperor are not within the scope of this prohibition, should the owner wish to sell or rent them.

SOURCES: *TT*, 2, p. 16*b*; *TFYK*, 495, pp. 23*b*–24*a*; *STCSKS*, 65, from 727 *Statute*. Compare the commentary of *Code*, 12, art. 14.

Art. 21. In granting personal share land the authorities should strive to grant it in a convenient and nearby place. Lands should not be granted at a great distance. If, owing to the change (of boundaries) of the prefecture and counties, the lands which they had controlled come within the borders of another administrative division, or if they join together with an irregular (dog-toothed) border, it is permitted to continue to follow the former rule. Town dwellers who have no lands in their own county are permitted to receive a grant in another.

SOURCES: *TLT*, 3, p. 32*a*, from 719 *Statute*; *TT*, 2, p. 16*b*; *TFYK*, 495, p. 24*a*; *STCSKS*, 65, from 737 *Statute*. The last sentence is also quoted in the commentary to *RSG*, 12, art. 18 (p. 362) as a *Kai-yüan Statute*.

Art. 22. Beginning on the first day of the tenth month the village headman should compile a list, from his previous investigations, of all lands which should revert to the state, or be granted. During the following eleventh month the county magistrate should assemble all the persons who should either return or receive lands, and make the grants before them all. This should be completed during the twelfth month.

SOURCES: *TLT*, 3, p. 32*a*; *TLT*, 30, p. 35*a*, from 719 *Statute*; *Code*, 13, art. 8, commentary refers to 737 *Statute*; *WHTK*, 3, p. 45*a*, quotes the opinion of the Sung scholar Ch'eng Hui that this was the text of the T'ang *Statute*.

Art. 23. In granting of land those liable to taxation and *corvée* shall be put before those who are not liable, those without before those with a little, and the poor before the rich. But if in a household which is returning land there is anybody who is entitled to come forward and receive a grant, then he shall be permitted to receive it himself in the first instance, even if he is not liable for tax and *corvée*. If there is any land left over after this, it shall revert and be reallotted.

SOURCES: *TLT*, p. 32*a–b*, from 719 *Statute*; *Code*, 13, art. 8, commentary from 737 *Statute*. The fullest quotation of the latter section is in the commentary to *RSG*, 12, art. 22 (p. 236), where it is cited as a T'ang *Statute*.

Art. 24. All Taoist clergy who have 'received Lao Tzu's Classic' or any higher degree shall be granted 30 *mou* in the case of monks and 20 *mou* in the case of nuns. Buddhist priests and nuns who have taken their complete vows shall also accord with this rule.

SOURCES: *TLT*, 3, pp. 31*b*–32*a*, from 719 *Statute*; *PSLT*, 26, p. 20*a*, from 737 *Statute*.

Art. 25 (A). Bondsmen of the status *tsa-hu* will, according to the *Statutes*, be exempted from tax on reaching old age, and be granted lands on becoming adults in the same way as the common people.

SOURCE: *Code*, 3, art. 2, from 737 *Statute*.

Art. 25 (B). The lands received by bondsmen of the category *kuan-hu* will be a half of the personal share land of a commoner.

SOURCE: *TLT*, 3, p. 32*a*, from 719 *Statute*.

Art. 26. In all cases where lands are encroached upon by rivers which do not return to their original courses, the lands which are newly left dry shall be first granted to the families who have suffered from the encroachment. If the new land is in the borders of another county, they should act according to the law on reversion and granting lands. If the two banks of the river are under separate jurisdictions, a decision shall be made following the regular course of the river. If there are any who are entitled to receive their lands at a distance, do not employ this rule.

SOURCE: *Sung hsing-t'ung*, 13, p. 4*a*, cites this as according to the *Land Statute* (*T'ien-ling*). As *RGG*, 3, art. 28 (p. 112), and *RSG*, 12, art. 26 (p. 369), have versions almost identical with the first sentence, we may accept that much at least as a T'ang *Statute*.

Art. 27. If any person borrows land and does not plough it for a period of two years, a person with the necessary ability may be permitted to borrow it instead. If he does not perform the work himself, but divides it with another person, then the land will be loaned in turn to the actual cultivator. If the cultivator is unable to plough and plant it after three years, although these lands may have been cultivated previously, the land shall revert, in accordance with the ordinances, and be regranted.

SOURCE: *RSG*, 12, art. 27, commentary (p. 370), cited as *K'ai-yüan Statute*.

Art. 28. In all cases of disputed lands, where a settlement has been reached, the person who has already ploughed and planted the land shall have the benefit of the crop, even if the decision is later reversed. Where it had been ploughed but not planted, the new owner shall repay the cost of the labour. Where a decision has not been reached, and the land is ploughed and planted by force, the right to the crop will follow the decision over the land.

SOURCE: *Sung hsing-t'ung*, 13, p. 3 *b*. There is an identical rule in *RGG*, 9, art. 30, p. 113, so this *Land Statute* must go back to early T'ang times.

Art. 29. All the services in the capital have Public Administration Lands (*kung-chieh t'ien*). The Court of Agriculture (*ssu-nung ssu*) shall be granted 26 *ch'ing*; the Department of Palace Services (*tien-chung sheng*), 25 *ch'ing*; the Directorate of Imperial Workshops (*shao-fu chien*), 22 *ch'ing*; the Court of Imperial Sacrifices (*t'ai-ch'ang ssu*), 20 *ch'ing*; the administrations of the metropolitan districts of Ch'ang-an and Lo-yang, each 17 *ch'ing*; the Court of Treasury (*t'ai-fu ssu*), 16 *ch'ing*; the Boards of Officials (*li-pu*) and of Finance (*hu-pu*), each 15 *ch'ing*; the Board of War (*ping-pu*) and the Intendance of the Inner Palace (*nei-shih sheng*), each 14 *ch'ing*; the Secretariat (*chung-shu sheng*) and the Directorate of Works (*chiang-tso chien*), each 13 *ch'ing*; the Board of Justice (*hsing-pu*) and the Supreme Court of Justice (*ta-li ssu*), each 12 *ch'ing*; the Central Department of State (*shang-shu tu-sheng*), the Chancellery (*men-hsia sheng*), and the Grand Secretariat of the Left of the Heir Apparent (*t'ai-tzu tso-ch'un-fang*), each 11 *ch'ing*; the Board of Works (*kung-pu*), 10 *ch'ing*; Court of Imperial Conveyances (*t'ai-p'u ssu*) and the Emperor's Library (*pi-shu-sheng*), each 9 *ch'ing*; the Board of Rites (*li-pu*), the Court for the Reception of Foreigners (*hung-lu ssu*), the Directorate of Waterways (*tu-shui-chien*) and the Intendance of the Household of the Heir Apparent (*t'ai-tzu chan-shih fu*), each 8 *ch'ing*; the Censorate (*yü-shih t'ai*), the State University (*kuo-tzu-chien*) and the counties under the metropolitan administrations, each 7 *ch'ing*; the Guards of the Left and the Right (*tso-yu wei*), and the services for the Heir Apparent's Palace (*t'ai-tzu chia-ling-ssu*), each 6 *ch'ing*; the Court of Imperial Insignia (*wei-wei-ssu*), the Guards *hsiao-wei*, *wu-wei*, *wei-wei*, *ling-chün-wei*, *chin-wu-wei*, and *chien-men-wei* of the Left and Right, and the Secretariats of the Left and Right of the Heir Apparent (*t'ai-tzu tso-yu-ch'un-fang*), each 5 *ch'ing*; the Guards of the Heir Apparent (*t'ai-tzu tso-yu-wei-shuai-fu*) and the Imperial Observatory (*t'ai-shih chü*), each 4 *ch'ing*; the Court for the Imperial Clan (*tsung-cheng ssu*), the *chien-niu* Guards of the Right and Left, the Heir Apparent's Court of Conveyances (*t'ai-tzu p'u-ssu*), and his Guards *ssu-yü*, *ch'ing-tao*, and *chien-men* of the left and right, each 3 *ch'ing*; the service of the harem of the Heir Apparent (*nei-fang*) and his Palace Guard *nei-shuai-fu* and *shuai-keng-fu*, of the Left and Right, each 2 *ch'ing*.

SOURCES: *TT*, 35, p .202*b*; *WHTK*, 65, p. 592*a*. Both presumably derive from the 737 *Statutes*.

Art. 30. Lands of the Public Administration for provincial offices. Superior governor general (*tu-tu fu*), 40 *ch'ing*; secondary governor general, 35 *ch'ing*; inferior governor general, protectorate (*tu-hu fu*), or superior prefecture, 30 *ch'ing*; medium prefecture, 20 *ch'ing*; directorate for a palace (*kung-chien*) or inferior prefecture, 15 *ch'ing*; superior county, 10 *ch'ing*; medium county, 8 *ch'ing*; lesser medium county (*chung-hsia hsien*), 6 *ch'ing*; superior pasturage (*mu-chien*) or superior garrison (*chen*), 5 *ch'ing*; inferior county, medium or inferior pasturage, bamboo plantation (*ssu-chu chien*), medium garrison, and the militias of the armies (*chu-chün che-chung-fu*), 4 *ch'ing*; foundries (*ye-chien*), granaries (*ts'ang-chien*), inferior garrisons and superior control posts (*kuan*), 3 *ch'ing*; market directors (*hu-shih-chien*), military colonies (*t'un-chien*), superior outposts (*shu*), medium control posts and fords, 2 *ch'ing* (but fords under the control of the Directorate of Waterways shall not receive a separate grant); inferior control posts 1 *ch'ing* 50 *mou*; medium and inferior outposts, sacred mountains and the holy rivers, 1 *ch'ing*.

Sources: *TLT*, 3, pp. 33*b*–34*a*, from 719 *Statute*; *TT*, 35, p. 202*b*; *WHTK*, 65, p. 592*a*, from 737 *Statute*.

Art. 31. The lands pertaining to office (*chih-fen t'ien*) of serving civil and military officials of the capital. 1st rank (*p'in*), 12 *ch'ing*; 2nd, 10 *ch'ing*; 3rd, 9 *ch'ing*; 4th, 7 *ch'ing*; 5th, 6 *ch'ing*; 6th, 4 *ch'ing*; 7th, 3 *ch'ing* 50 *mou*; 8th, 2 *ch'ing* 50 *mou*; 9th, 2 *ch'ing*. These lands should all be granted within 100 *li* of the capital. The lands appertaining to office of all officials of the metropolitan district of Ch'ang-an and Lo-yang, and of the counties of the capital should also accord with this rule. (But if there are few lands within 100 *li* of the capital, and they wish to have them granted beyond this distance, it is also permitted.)

Sources: *TT*, 2, p. 16*a*; *STCSKS*, 65; *TT*, 35, p. 202*b–c*; *WHTK*, 65, p. 592*a*, from 737 *Statute*. But as an edict of 618 (see *THY*, 92, p. 1659; *TFYK*, 505, p. 18*a*) mentions the same amounts, this rule was probably incorporated in identical form in the 624 *Statutes*.

Art. 32. Lands pertaining to office for officials serving in the prefectures, protectorates, and administrations of princes (*ch'in-wang-fu*): 2nd rank, 12 *ch'ing*; 3rd, 10 *ch'ing*; 4th, 8 *ch'ing*; 5th, 7 *ch'ing*; 6th, 5 *ch'ing* (the counties of the environs of the capital also accord with this); 7th, 4 *ch'ing*; 8th, 3 *ch'ing*; 9th, 2 *ch'ing* 50 *mou*. For officers of garrisons, fords and control posts, holy mountains and rivers and of directorates in the provinces: 5th rank, 5 *ch'ing*; 6th, 3 *ch'ing* 50 *mou*; 7th, 3 *ch'ing*; 8th, 3 *chi'ng*; 9th, 2 *ch'ing* 50 *mou*. For colonels of the three guards (*chung-lang chiang*), and commanders of superior militias (*tu-wei*), 6 *ch'ing*; commanders of medium militias, 5 *ch'ing* 50 *mou*; commanders of inferior militias and lieutenant-colonels (*kuo-i*), 5 *ch'ing*; deputy commanders of militias, superior, 4 *ch'ing*; medium, 3 *ch'ing* 50 *mou*; inferior 3 *ch'ing*; the chief administrators (*chang-shih*) and adjutants (*pieh-chiang*) of militias, superior, 3 *ch'ing*; medium or inferior, 2 *ch'ing* 50 *mou*; colonels of the guards of princes (*ch'ia-wang-fu tien-chün*), 5 *ch'ing*

50 *mou*; deputy colonels (*fu tien-chün*), 4 *ch'ing*; personal guards (*ch'ien-niu pei-shen*) of the emperor and of the heir apparent, 3 *ch'ing*. (Military and civil officers in the administrations of princes shall be given grants in their normal place of residence, where they are serving in an administration beyond the borders.) The service of weapons (*ping-ts'ao*) in [superior] militias, 2 *ch'ing*; medium and inferior, 1 *ch'ing* 50 *mou*; in the provincial armies, majors (*hsiao-wei*), 1 *ch'ing* 20 *mou*; captains (*lü-shuai*), 1 *ch'ing*; lieutenants (*tui-cheng*) and sub-lieutenants (*fu*), 80 *mou*. All these grants should be given within the boundaries of the prefecture or county in which they hold their command. Officers from major downwards who are serving in their native county or within 100 *li* of their homes shall not be given a grant. The lands are to be leased to the people to work and plant. When autumn and winter come, the authorities shall receive a share of the crop, and nothing more.

SOURCES: *TLT*, 3, p. 34*a–b*, from 719 *Statute*; *TT*, 2, p. 16*a–b*; *TT*, 35, p. 202*c*; *WHTK*, 65, p. 592*a–b*; *STCSKS*, 65, from 737 *Statute*. Confirmed by a MS. table of officials discovered at Tun-huang (P. 2504), though with some slight differences in the amounts. See Niida's note, *loc. cit.* p. 650.

Art. 33. Lands for relay and postal stations should be granted as close to them as possible. For each horse 40 *mou* shall be granted. If it is a place where there are pastures besides the relay station this amount shall be reduced by 5 *mou* per beast. For relay horses (*ch'uan ti-ma*) they shall grant 20 *mou* each.

SOURCES: *TT*, 2, p. 16*b*; *TFYK*, 495, p. 23*a*; *STCSKS*, 65, from 737 *Statute*.

Art. 34. For all lands pertaining to office, where an official assumes his post before the 30th of the 3rd month in the case of dry fields, or the 30th of the 4th month for paddy fields, the crop shall go to the incoming official. If the appointment is made after this date they shall belong to the outgoing official. With wheat fields, the limit is the 30th day of the 9th month. If the outgoing officer has himself had the land ploughed but not planted, the incoming officer shall repay him for this labour. If he has already planted it the law on the apportionment of the grain tax shall be followed. If the value is 6 *tou* or less they shall accord with the previous arrangement. If it is more they must not exceed 6 *tou*, and in all cases they shall only take what is willingly given, and may not forcibly apportion it.

SOURCES: *TLT*, 3, pp. 34*b*–35*a*; *TT*, 2, p. 16*b–c*; *TT*, 35, p. 202*c*; *TFYK*, 506, p. 3*a–b*; *THY*, 92, p. 1692. The sense of this article, especially of the last half, is by no means clear. However, the difficulty may be solved by the analogous *RSG*, 12, art. 32 (pp. 375–6), which at least makes it clear that it refers to change-over of officials.

Art. 35. Those princes of the imperial house who are sent out to the frontiers are to be granted 1 *ch'ing* to make a garden. If there is no land which can be opened up within the city, then a convenient grant may be made in a nearby city. If there is no public land, they may take land from the commoners to fill this amount, giving them good land elsewhere in return.

SOURCES: *TT*, 2, p. 16*c*; *TFYK*, 495, p. 34*a*; *STCSKS*, 65, from 737 *Statute*.

Art. 36. Regarding all military colonies (*t'un*); those attached to the Court of Agriculture shall each consist of from 20 to 30 *ch'ing*. Those attached to the prefectures, garrisons and armies shall each consist of 50 *ch'ing*. All cases of the establishments of colonies shall be decided by the Department of State (*shang-shu-sheng*). In the case of the re-establishment of old colonies their boundaries shall be fixed according to their former boundaries. Those which are newly established shall in all cases be formed by taking wasteland or large holdings of unregistered lands. Even if the colony is reckoned as 50 *ch'ing*, in places where periodic fallow (*i-t'ien*) is practised, in each case the circumstances may be taken into consideration and the size increased in accordance with the resources of the locality. For the officers of the colonies they shall take honorific officials of the 5th rank or above, unemployed military officers, or civil or military officers of the 8th rank or above who have previously assisted in prefectures, counties, garrisons or outposts on the frontiers, and select suitable ones to fill the posts. Their annual merit assessments will depend upon the amounts of grain which they collect.

SOURCES: *TT*, 2, p. 19*b–c*; *TPYL*, 333, p. 5*a*, from 737 *Statute*. *TPYL* cites it as from *T'ang-shu*, and it was thus accepted in error by Ts'en Chien-kung as a lost fragment of *CTS*, 48. The same applies to arts. 37 and 38.

Art. 37. Regarding military colonies in areas where oxen are employed. Since the land is sometimes hilly, sometimes plateau, valley or marsh, sometimes hard and sometimes soft, the power needed to cultivate it is not uniform. Where the soil is light, one ox shall be allotted for every 1 *ch'ing* 50 *mou*. Where the soil is heavy, one ox for every 1 *ch'ing* 20 *mou*. If within the colony there are some places with heavy soil and some with light, this rule should still be adhered to. For paddy fields, one ox should be allotted for every 80 *mou*.

SOURCES: *TT*, 2, p. 19*c*, from 737 *Statute*; *TYPL*, 333, p. 5*a*, cites it as from *T'ang-shu*.

Art. 38. Regarding agricultural colonies (*ying-t'ien*), if they have surplus lands beyond 50 *ch'ing* for which men and oxen have been allotted, the grain which they collect from them shall be reduced according to the area. In the case of barley, buckwheat, dried root vegetables, etc., they should work out the equivalent in terms of millet, in order to fix the grades of [contribution].

SOURCES: *TT*, 2, p. 19*c*, from 737 *Statute*; *TPYL*, 333, p. 5*a*.

Art. 39. Niida gives as art. 39, the reflection in the commentary of *Code*, 27, art. 8 of a *Statute* covering the burning off of stubble fields. As this is not direct quotation, I do not include it.

2. ARTICLES FROM THE 'CODE' ('T'ANG-LÜ SHU-I') RELATING TO LAND TENURE

Code, 12, *art.* 14. Any person selling personal share land will be punished with a beating of 10 strokes for 1 *mou*. For every additional 20 *mou* the punishment will be increased by one degree. The maximum penalty is a flogging of 100 strokes. The land will revert to the original owner. The price paid for it will be confiscated and not recoverable. Where the person is entitled to sell, this law is not to be employed.

[*Commentary:* Personal share land: that means, all lands received by a person which are not lands in perpetuity or lands for houses and gardens. Those who improperly sell them: the Rites say: 'Lands are not to be sold'; one receives them from the state, and thus one may not privately sell them oneself.[1] Offenders will receive a beating of ten strokes for the first *mou*, the punishment to be increased by one degree for each additional 20 *mou*, the maximum penalty being a flogging of 100 strokes. Thus the sale of 1 *ch'ing* 81 *mou* entails the maximum penalty. The land reverts to the original holder, and the price paid for it is confiscated and not recoverable. In cases where one is entitled to sell: that is, in the case of lands in perpetuity, where the family is poor and it is sold to defray funeral expenses, or in the case of personal share land, where it is sold to provide the cost of a homestead, or a mill, or store, or something of like sort, or where one was moving from a restricted to a broad locality, one is allowed to sell it according to the Statutes. Those who wish to sell donated land also do not come within the scope of the prohibition. The lands in perpetuity of officials of the fifth rank and above, and of honorific officials, are also allowed to be sold. Therefore it says, 'do not employ this law'.]

Code, 13, *art.* 1. Any person possessing more than the permitted amount of land will be punished with a beating of 10 strokes for the first *mou*, the punishment to be increased by one degree for each additional 10 *mou* up to a flogging of 60 strokes, and after that by one degree for each additional 20 *mou*. The maximum penalty is one year of hard labour. If it is committed in a broad and unrestricted place, then there is no offence to answer for.

[*Commentary:* The law laid down by the ruler is that the farmers' land shall be 100 *mou*, the officials shall have lands in perpetuity in accordance with their rank, while the old, the young and widows shall each have their degree for receiving lands. If the locality is not broad and unrestricted, they are not permitted to possess lands beyond these limits. Those who possess more than the permitted amount will be punished with a beating of 10 strokes for the first *mou*, the punishment to be increased by one degree for each 10 additional *mou* up to a flogging of 60 strokes and thereafter by one degree for each additional 20 *mou*. At 1 *ch'ing* 51 *mou* the maximum penalty of one year's hard labour is reached. Also according to the *Statutes* 'A place where there is sufficient land for the people to receive what is due to them is a "Broad locality", and one where there is not is a "restricted locality"'. If they possess such lands in a broad and unrestricted place, there is no offence. That is, if there are still surplus lands after the people have all received their full share, the important thing is to open up land, and extract the maximum produce from it. Thus, even if their possessions are very large, the *Code* assigns no punishment for the owners. They should still report such matters and establish a record. If they take possession of such lands without filing a request, then they should be punished for not reporting what ought to be reported.]

Code, 13, *art.* 2. Any person who illegally cultivates public or private lands (which do not belong to him) shall be punished with a beating of 30 strokes for the first *mou*. The punishment shall be increased by one degree for each additional 5 *mou* up to a flogging of 100 strokes, and after that by one degree for each additional 10 *mou*. The maximum penalty is 18 months' hard labour. If the land is waste the punishment shall be diminished by one degree. If the offence is committed forcibly, the punishment shall be increased by one degree. The crops shall belong to the officials or to the rightful owners. [*Comm*. The crops involved in cases under the following articles shall be disposed of by this rule.]

[*Commentary:* Since lands cannot be moved they are not the same as cases of true stealing, and therefore it says 'Any person who illegally ploughs and plants public or private lands shall be punished with a beating of 30 strokes for one *mou* or less. The punishment is to be increased by one degree for every 5 *mou*. For over 35 *mou* they shall receive a flogging of 100 strokes. Beyond this the punishment shall be increased by one degree for each 10 *mou*. For over 55 *mou* they shall receive the maximum penalty, of 18 months' hard labour. For wasteland the punishment shall be reduced one degree: that is for waste and uncultivated lands, which are on the registers, the punishment will be reduced by one degree from that applying to land under cultivation. If they cultivate it forcibly the punishment is increased one degree in either case, that is, the maximum is 2 years' hard labour for cultivated land, and 18 months' for wasteland. The crops in each case are to belong to the officials or to the owner: that is, all the crops, hay, etc., shall be collected and returned either to the officials or to the owner. In the following articles the crops shall accord with this rule: that is, in cases of laying false claims or illicit exchange, robbery of private lands, illicit cultivation of grace land and of such sorts, the crops in the case shall revert to the officials or to the owner. In a case where someone has illicitly cultivated another's land, and some of it is waste and some cultivated, or some was taken by stealth and some by force, if it was from one family and the rules for punishment do not cover it exactly, it shall be judged according to the rule that the heavier offence absorbs the lighter. Where they have illicitly cultivated the lands of two or more families, they should only try them for one. The crimes are assimilated, not accumulated, and they are given only the heaviest single penalty. If kinsmen have robbed one another, they should be judged by the law on kinsmen stealing one another's property, according to their affinity.]

Code, 13, *art.* 3. All persons who wrongfully lay claim to public or private lands, or exchange or sell it, shall be punished with a beating of 50 strokes for the first *mou* or less. The punishment shall be increased by one degree for every additional 5 *mou* up to a flogging of 100 strokes, and thereafter by one degree for every additional 10 *mou*. The maximum penalty is 2 years' hard labour.

[*Commentary:* Any person who illicitly lays claim to public or private land and calls it his own land, or who privily exchanges it or illicitly sells it to somebody else, for the first *mou* shall be punished with a beating of 50 strokes, to be increased by one degree for each additional 5 *mou*. Any who [steals] over 25 *mou* shall be given a flogging of 100 strokes. Beyond this, the punishment shall be increased by one degree for each 10 *mou*. Anyone who [steals] 55 *mou* or more shall receive the maximum penalty of 2 years' hard labour. The section of the *Code* on robbery says that in the case of pens or folds one has to move them from their normal place. In the case of ordinary objects you must move them from their place. Now [for land], although we refer to it as stealing, in establishing the law we need some specific rule. Since land is not moved from its place, the principle involved differs from that concerning movables. Thus there is no reckoning up the value to assess punishment, and no system of dispensing with half of the sum involved. 'Wrongfully lay claim' means either that possession has been taken (if it has not yet been taken, then they shall assess punishment according to the law concerning cases of wrongful claims to slaves or movable property) or in the case of exchange, the transaction must have been completed. In the case of illicit sale, the purchase must have been completed. According to the *Statutes*, where land is improperly bought or sold without the rendering of official documents, the price is to be confiscated and not recoverable, while the standing crops shall belong to the [original] landlord.]

Code, 13, *art.* 4. Any person holding official rank who encroaches upon private lands shall receive a flogging of 60 strokes for the first *mou* or less. The punishment shall be increased by one degree for each additional 3 *mou* up to a flogging of 100 strokes, and thereafter by one degree for each additional 5 *mou*. The maximum penalty shall be 2 years' and 6 months' hard labour. In the case of gardens or vegetable gardens the punishment will be increased by one degree.

[*Commentary:* When the *Code* says 'holding official rank' it means someone who is in office and wielding authority. When they encroach upon the private lands of the common people they shall receive a flogging of 60 strokes for the first *mou* or part of a *mou*. The punishment shall be increased by one degree for each additional 3 *mou*. For more than 12 *mou* they shall receive 100 strokes. Beyond that it shall increase by one degree for each 5 *mou*. For over 32 *mou* they shall receive the maximum of 2½ years' hard labour. Gardens and vegetable gardens means places where they plant nut or fruit trees or plant vegetables or roots and which are enclosed by a fence or a wall. Their fertility is different, and thus the punishment is increased one degree. If they steal some ordinary land, and some garden, the punishment scale is not the same. They should then accord with the law of the heavy offence absorbing the lighter one. If they take official lands, or the lands appertaining to their post, and exchange it with the land of private individuals, then the law for deciding the case shall accord with the principle laid down in the article preceding. If they obtain [lands] as a repayment of money lost by the people in business, then they shall be tried in accordance with the law of frauds committed by persons acting in a supervisory capacity. If officials rob one another, they shall use the same rule as for ordinary persons. If when a person has been in office he encroaches upon, or exchanges land, and then leaves office before the case comes up, the punishment shall be assigned according to [the position he held] at the time of committing the offence.]

APPENDIX II

1. FRAGMENTS OF THE 'TAXATION STATUTES'

Translation of Niida's reconstruction of the *Taxation Statutes* (*Fu-i-ling*).

Art. 1. All taxable households shall pay annually a grain tax (*tsu*) of two *shih* of millet for each adult male family member. The tax in kind (*tiao*) shall be paid in damask, thin silk, coarse silk, or hempen cloth, according to what is produced in each locality. In the case of damask, thin silk and coarse silk, [each adult male shall pay] a length of 20 feet. In the case of hempen cloth the length shall be 25 feet. Those who contribute in silk fabrics shall pay a supplementary tax in kind (*chien-tiao*) of 3 *liang* of silk floss, and those who contribute in hempen cloth 3 *chin* of hemp. Both hempen cloth and silk should be 1 foot 8 inches in width. A length of 40 feet [of silk] constitutes a 'piece' (*p'i*); 50 feet of hempen cloth constitutes a 'length' (*tuan*); 6 *liang* of silk floss constitutes a 'bundle' (*t'un*); 5 *liang* of silk thread constitutes a 'hank' (*hsüan*); 3 *chin* of hempen [thread] constitutes a 'bundle' (*li*). If a particular household's contribution does not amount to a complete 'piece', 'length', or 'bundle', it should be made up together with the contributions of their neighbours. If in the hemp paid annually as [supplementary] tax in kind there is a surplus, 1 *tou* of millet may be contributed in place of 1 *chin* of hemp, and collected together with the grain tax. The grain tax of the prefectures of Chiang-nan shall be converted and paid in terms of hempen cloth.

SOURCES: *THY*, 83, pp. 1530–1; *CTS*, 48, p. 3*a*; *TT*, 6, p. 33*a*; *TFYK*, 487, pp. 16*b*–17*a*; *TFYK*, 504, p. 33*b*. All reproduce parts of the *Statutes* of 624. *TLT*, 3, p. 35*b*, reproduces the *Statutes* of 719 and possibly part of the relevant *Ordinance* (*Pieh-shih*). *Code*, 13, art. 10, p. 117; *TPYL*, 626, p. 3*a*, and *Hsia-hou Yang suan-ching*, 1, p. 7*a*, reproduce passages from the *Statutes* of 737.

NOTE: There are a great number of variants, but it seems difficult to establish the differences between the various series of *Statutes*. Niida suggests (*Tōryō shūi*, p. 662) that the versions deriving from the *Statutes* of 624 and 719 under which the length of hemp to be contributed per adult male was 24 feet, were altered in the *Statutes* of 737 to a length of 25 feet. The 737 *Statutes* incorporate the rule that the grain tax from Chiang-nan should be converted and paid in hemp cloth (*TT*, 6, p. 1*b*) which does not appear in the surviving fragments of the earlier series. Pulleyblank, *The background of the rebellion of An Lu-shan*, p. 35 and note 67 (pp. 130–1), suggests this was a reversion to an earlier practice, as attested by the seventh-century tax cloths recovered from Turfan. However, I see no reason to consider the insertion of this rule as a change in the text of the *Statutes*. Our knowledge of the earlier versions is confined to abbreviated quotations, and since the rule in question was irrelevant in Japan it is impossible to check the surviving texts against the versions in *Ryō-no-shūge* and *Ryō-no-gige*. Thus it is perfectly possible either that the rule, being only of regional application, was omitted from the summaries of the earlier series, or even that the rule comes not from the *Statutes* themselves, but from the supplementary *Ordinances* relevant to this *Statute*.

Art. 2. The commodities for the tax in kind (*tiao*) should all be inscribed and stamped.

SOURCE: This rule is added to the passage summarising art. 1 in *TLT*, 3, p. 35*b*, *Statutes* of 719. Niida makes it a distinct article, on the analogy of the *Taxation Statutes* in the Japanese *Ryō*.

Art. 3. The contribution of all the goods for the *corvée* exemption tax and tax in kind shall begin in the first 10 days of the eighth month of each year, and their payment completed by the 30th day [of the same month], and in the first 10 days of the 9th month they should be despatched to the prefecture. If anyone dies during the period while the tax boats and carts have still not set out, his goods shall be returned [to his household]. The expenses of transportation shall be borne by the families contributing *corvée* exemption tax and tax in kind. It is permitted to hire at a fair price (*ho-ku*) persons to deliver the goods. Regarding the levying of the necessary expenses for packing, the goods required are to be provided out of a payment in lieu of the *corvée* exemption tax and tax in kind. The prefectural offices are to send them off under escort. They may not hire transportation at their convenience to pay the goods in.

SOURCE: *TT*, 6, p. 33*c*, *Statutes* of 737.
The text of *TT* has been supplemented by Niida with some clauses from the parallel article in *RSG*, 13, pp. 387–9.

Art. 4. Every adult male[1] shall perform 20 days' labour service (*i*) annually, with 2 days extra in years including an intercalary month. From those who perform no actual labour,[2] the *corvée* exemption tax *yung* shall be collected. This shall consist of 3 feet of either heavy or light silk, or 3 feet $7\frac{1}{2}$ inches of hempen cloth in respect of each day's service. Where it is necessary that persons should be retained for [additional] *corvée* (*liu-i*),[3] after the completion of 15 days their tax in kind (*tiao*) should be remitted; after 30 days both their tax in kind and grain tax (*tsu*) should be remitted. (If the number of days of labour is small, they shall be granted remission proportionate to the number of days worked.)[4] Together with the regular annual *corvée* [this additional labour service] must not exceed 50 days in all. Those who wish to send their retainers (*pu-ch'ü*) to do labour service in place of themselves are permitted to do so.[5]

SOURCES: *CTS*, 48, p. 3*a*; *TFYK*, 487, p. 16*b*; *THY*, 83, p. 1531; *Statutes* of 624; *TT*, 6, p. 33*c*, *Statutes* of 737; *TLT*, 3, pp. 35*b*–36*a*, *Statutes* of 719.

Art. 5. Apart from rations for the journey [to the place where labour service is to be performed], each labourer shall provide his own rations in accordance with the number of days he shall labour.

NOTE: This rule is lost in all the Chinese sources. The *Shaku* to *RSG*, 13, p. 389, however, preserves it. The passage reads as follows: 'The *Shaku* says "Why does the commentary to the *Statute* say 'for the first ten days' *corvée* no official rations shall be provided"'.' The T'ang *Statute* reads 'Apart from the rations for the journey each labourer shall provide his own rations in accordance with the number of days he shall labour...', thus we know that the present article of the statute (i.e. that corresponding to art. 4 here) has combined two articles of T'ang into one. The text given by Niida follows the earlier printed editions of *RSG* which read 各唯役賣和糧. The emendation proposed by Kuroita in his edition in the *Kokushi Taikei* of 准 for 唯 gives better sense, as does the insertion of 日 after 役 in accordance with the Kanazawa Bunko MS.

Art. 6. All foreigners who have submitted and been registered should be divided into nine grades. Those of the fourth grade and above will become superior households (*shang-hu*), those of the seventh grade and above secondary households (*tz'u-hu*) and those of the eighth grade and below inferior households (*hsia-hu*). In the superior households there shall be a tax on each adult (*ting-shui*) of 10 silver coins,[6] in secondary households one of 5 silver coins. Inferior households shall be exempt. In the case of those who have already been registered for two or more years, in superior households each adult shall contribute two sheep, in secondary households one sheep. In inferior households three households together should jointly contribute one sheep.

[*Commentary:* In places where there are no sheep, the price may be converted into terms of goods of high price and small size, in accordance with the value of white sheep. If there is a military campaign and the [barbarian households] are ordered themselves to provide saddle-horses, if these are employed for thirty days or more, the current year's contribution of sheep will be remitted.][7]

SOURCES: *CTS*, 48, p. 3*a*; *TFYK*, 487, p. 16*b*; *WHTK*, 2, p. 41*c*, *Statutes* of 624; *TLT*, 3, pp. 36*b*–37*a*, *Statutes* of 719.

Art. 7. In the various prefectures of Ling Nan, there shall be a levy of rice amounting to 1 *shih* 2 *tou* on superior households, 8 *tou* on secondary households, and 6 *tou* on inferior households. If they are households of the *I* or *Liao* barbarians, each shall contribute a light tax at half of this rate.[8]

Those Koreans from Koguryo and Pakche in the various prefectures who are liable for assignment to military service shall all be exempted from tax and labour service.[9]

SOURCES: *THY*, 83, p. 1531; *TFYK*, 487, p. 16*b*; *CTS*, 48, p. 3*a*; *WHTK*, 2, p. 41*c*, *Statutes* of 624; *TLT*, 3, p. 37*a*, *Statutes* of 719.

Art. 8. Regarding all taxation and labour service. Each year when the tax registers (*chi-chang*) arrive at the Department of State, the Department of Public Revenue shall assign the works necessary during the coming year, and must complete the reporting of them to the throne by the 30th day of the 10th month. If there is any case where it is necessary to convert contributions into terms of other commodities this matter should be decided at the same time as in previous payments of commodities. If there is anything required by the armies, which is not at the time available in the storehouses, an account of it should be drawn up and reported to the throne. The authorities may not levy such things on the subjects immediately.

SOURCE: *TT*, 6, p. 33 *b–c*, *Statutes* of 737.

Art. 9. Every household from those of princes and dukes downwards should annually draw up a separate 'green sprout register' (*ch'ing-miao pu*) in accordance with the total average under crops of lands allocated them [under the *chün-t'ien* system] and 'borrowed wasteland', etc. These shall be reported to the Department of State by the prefecture before the 7th month. When it comes to the time of levying taxes, the taxpayers shall make a supplementary payment of 2 *sheng* of millet on each *mou* to provide funds for the charitable granary (*i-ts'ang*).

In broad localities (*k'uan-hsiang*) it will be collected according to actually cultivated land: in restricted localities (*hsia-hsiang*) according to (what is already levied?). If the region experiences loss of 40 per cent or more of its crop half shall be remitted. If 70 per cent or more it shall be totally remitted. The households of merchants who have no land or who have not sufficient land, in the case of first grade households (*shang-shang-hu*) shall be taxed 5 *shih* of grain, and second grade households and below reduced by 1 *shih* to each grade, fifth grade households 1 *shih* 5 *tou*, sixth grade households 1 *shih*, seventh grade households 7 *tou*, eighth grade households 5 *tou*. Ninth grade households and households which have all absconded, together with I and Liao barbarians who pay the reduced tax, shall not come within the limits of taxation. Those who contribute at half rate shall pay half of the load of an inferior household. Where a locality has no millet, it is allowed to pay miscellaneous grain stuffs to make up the amount.

SOURCE: *TLT*, 3, pp. 53 *a*–54 *a*, *Statutes* of 719.
NOTE: The corresponding Japanese statute (*RSG*, 13, p. 395) gives equivalents for 1 *tou* of millet as follows: 2 *tou* of rice, 1 *tou* 5 *sheng* of barley, 2 *tou* of wheat, 2 *tou* of large beans and 1 *tou* of small beans. It also says that this was to be collected at the same time as the grain tax (*tsu*). It seems likely that the T'ang *Statutes* contained similar rules. The second half of this passage, given as Commentary in *TLT*, may again come from an *Ordinance*, not the *Statutes*.

Art. 10. Whenever meritorious subjects have been rewarded with the grant of fiefs of maintenance,[10] these shall be made up of taxable households (*k'o-hu*). In accordance with the number of households granted, the prefectural and county authorities, together with the officials of the 'state' or 'fief',[11] shall hold the registers and together collect the grain tax and tax in kind. Each shall accordingly assign the authorities of the prefectures and counties collecting these taxes also to collect the costs of transport (*chüeh-chih*) according to their distance. Afterwards these costs shall be charged to the fief authorities. The labour service[12] involved shall also be accounted for in accordance with this rule. Those who actually form part of the fief of maintenance shall pay *corvée* exemption tax (*yung*).[13]

SOURCES: *TLT*, 3, p. 40*b*, *Statutes* of 719.

Art. 11. Regarding all lands,[14] whenever there is a place which suffers disaster through flood, drought, insect pests or hail, the prefectural and county authorities shall inspect the circumstances in accordance with the land actually in cultivation, make a list of the damage and report it to the Department of State.[15] If more than four parts out of ten [of the crop] has been ruined, the grain tax (*tsu*) shall be remitted: if the damage exceeds six parts out of ten both grain tax and tax in kind (*tiao*) shall be remitted. If the damage exceeds seven parts out of ten all taxes and labour services shall be remitted. If the mulberries or hemp have been completely ruined tax in kind shall be remitted in each case.[16] If there are any who have already contributed their taxes or performed their labour services, it is permitted for them to transfer the remission to the coming year.[17] After two years have elapsed they shall no longer be eligible for transfer of remission. For the remission to which they are entitled, the wheat and other sums should be totalled together, but given in separate quantities.[18]

SOURCES: *THY*, 83, p. 1531; *TFYK*, 487, p. 16*b*; *CTS*, 48, p. 3*a*; *TT*, 6, p. 33*a*; *WHTK*, 2, p. 41*c*, *Statutes* of 624; *TLT*, 3, p. 37*b*, *Statutes* of 719; *Code*, 13, art. 7; *PSLT*, 23, p. 84*a*, *Statutes* of 737.

Art. 12. In all frontier and distant prefectures where there are places inhabited by various foreign tribes such as the I and Liao who should contribute taxes and labour services, these should be carefully estimated according to the circumstances, and need not be made identical with those of the Chinese themselves.

SOURCE: *TT*, 6, p. 33*c*, *Statutes* of 737.

Art. 13. All employed officials who are entitled to remission of taxes should in each case await the arrival of their certificate of exemption (*chüan-fu*) and only then enter themselves on the registers as exempt. However, even when their certificate has not yet arrived, their official credentials (*kao-sheng*) may be verified, and where the case is obviously true, remission may still be granted. In the case of minor employees (*tsa-jen*) who have been retired and are liable to be entered [on the tax registers again], they shall be taxed in each case in accordance with the date of their retirement from the office to which they belonged.

SOURCES: *TT*, 6, p. 33*c*; *Code*, 4, art. 5, *Statutes of 737*. *RSG*, 13, p. 407, cited as *K'ai-yüan Statute* in a quotation from the *K'ai-yüan Ordinances*.

Art. 14. All persons who are entered [on the registers][19] during the spring quarter shall pay all their taxes and labour services [for the same year]. Those entered in the summer quarter shall be exempt from taxes but shall perform labour services. Those entered in the autumn quarter shall be exempt from both tax and labour service. If there is any fraud or attempt at evasion in order to escape tax or labour service, they shall pay all the taxes and labour services due during the current year without question of the date upon which they were entered on the register.[20] Runaway households who are entered on the registers should be treated in the same way.[21]

SOURCES: *TLT*, 3, p. 37*b*, *Statutes of 719*; *TT*, 6, p. 33*c*, *Statutes of 737*. *RSG*, 13, pp. 406–7, cited as 'according to the *Statutes*' in a quotation from the *K'ai-yüan Ordinances*.

Art. 15. All persons who dwell in restricted localities and move to their advantage to broad localities, if they move more than 1000 *li* from their original residence shall be given exemption for 3 years. If they move beyond 500 *li* they shall be given exemption for 2 years; if beyond 300 *li* for 1 year. After they have changed their residence once, no remission will be granted in respect of a further move.

SOURCES: *Code*, 13, art. 9; *TT*, 6, p. 33*c*, *Statutes of 737*.

Art. 16. All those who have been held captive among the barbarians and succeed in returning shall be granted 3 years' exemption from tax if they have been held captive for more than 1 year, 4 years' remission if more than 2 years, and 5 years' remission if more than 3 years. Barbarians who seek to adopt civilisation will be granted 10 years' remission.

SOURCE: *TT*, 6, p. 33*c*, *Statutes of 737*.

NOTE: *WHTK*, 13, p. 142*b*, gives a somewhat confused version of this article conflated with the next two articles, reading 'Those households of the four barbarians who submit will be registered in broad localities and given tax exemption for ten years. Slaves who are manumitted to become free men shall be granted three years' tax exemption. Those who have fallen among[22] the barbarians, if they return after one year, will be given exemption for three years,...etc.'

Art. 17. I and Liao barbarians who are newly pacified and entered on the household registers shall be given tax exemption for 3 years.

SOURCE: *RSG*, 13, p. 409 (cited as *K'ai-yüan Statute*).

10

Art. 18. All retainers (*pu-ch'ü*) and slaves[23] who are manumitted and entered on the household registers shall be granted tax exemption for 3 years.

SOURCES: *TT*, 6, p. 33*c*; *WHTK*, 13, p. 142*b*, *Statutes* of 737.

Art. 19. All filial sons and obedient grandsons, righteous husbands and chaste wives, whose minds and conduct are well known in their locality, shall be reported by the prefecture and county to the Department of State, who shall report it to the throne. Their dwellings shall be given a distinguishing sign, and all those on the same household register shall be granted exemption from taxes and labour service.[24] If there are any possessing absolute sincerity and who has been given some favourable response from Heaven, he shall be granted liberal rewards in addition.[25]

SOURCES: *RSG*, 13, p. 406, quoted as *Statute* in a quotation from the *K'ai-yüan Ordinances* (see app. III, art. 5*a*); *TLT*, 3, p. 38*a*, *Statutes* of 719; *TT*, 6, p. 33*c*; *WHTK*, 13, p. 142*b*, *Statutes* of 737.

Art. 20. All members of the imperial class who are registered with the Department of Imperial Genealogy, and all kindred of the fifth degree or closer of the empress, empress dowager or grand empress dowagers, kindred of consorts of the first rank and above, kindred of all civil and military serving officials of the third rank and above, the kindred of those of great merit living in common, and the kin living in common of dukes of states (*kuo-kung*), shall be exempt from tax and labour service.[26]

SOURCES: *TLT*, 3, p. 38*a*, *Statutes* of 719; *WHTK*, 13, pp. 142*a–b*; *Code*, 12, art. 12, *Statutes* of 737.

Art. 21. All officials of the sixth rank and below, both in the capital and in the provinces, and all those holding official posts of various sorts in the offices at the capital are entitled to exemption from taxation and *corvée*.

SOURCES: *TLT*, 3, p. 38*a*, *Statutes* of 719; *THY*, 58, pp. 1012–13; *TFYK*, 474, p. 13*b*, *Statutes* of 737 as cited in a memorial of Ts'ui Yüan-lüeh dated 826.

Art. 22. All adults serving their parents (*shih-ting*) according to the *Statutes* are exempt from labour service and contribute only grain tax and tax in kind.

SOURCE: *Code*, 3, art. 8, *Statutes* of 737.

Art. 23. All persons who have been struck off the register of officials but have not yet had this confirmed[27] shall be exempt from labour service and from contributing grain tax, and shall not come within the scope of miscellaneous labour services or conscription (*tien-fang*).

SOURCE: *Code*, 3, art. 3, *Statutes* of 737.

Art. 24. The relevant office should estimate (this) and record it and send it to the Department of Public Revenue. At the time when the draft registers (*shou-shih*) are collected, households should be fixed in nine grades to determine the tax lists (*pu*).

SOURCES: *RSG*, 14, p. 422; *RSG*, 14, p. 423.[28]

Art. 25. In apportioning impositions (*ch'ai-k'o*), these should be laid on the rich and strong before the poor and weak, and on those households containing many adults before those containing few.

SOURCE: *Code*, 13, art. 10, *Statutes* of 737.

Art. 26. If there is any construction which is separate from the normal annual provision (*chih-liao*) or if the necessary labour force is large, the matter must be reported to the Department of Public Revenue for decision.

SOURCE: *RSG*, 30, p. 761.

Art. 27. All the tribute offerings from the prefectures should consist entirely of locally produced goods. Reckoning their value in terms of thin silk, at the most they should not exceed 50 lengths (*p'i*). All should be purchased out of official goods. [As the goods sent as tribute are extremely slight they may be easily supplied.]

SOURCE: *TT*, 6, p. 34c, *Statutes* of 737. The last sentence is probably not part of the *Statute* as Niida assumes, but a comment by Tu Yu.

2. 'FRAGMENTS OF THE ORDINANCES' ('SHIH') OF THE BOARD OF FINANCE

I have attempted below to assemble and translate all the known quotations from the *Ordinances* (*shih*) of the Board of Finance. As is well known, not only each of the Six Boards, but each of their sub-departments, had its own collections of *Ordinances*.[29] The fragments which I have located all come from the *Ordinances of the Board of Finance* (*hu-pu shih*) and from the *Ordinances of the Public Revenue Department* (*tu-chih shih*). There appears to be no surviving trace of the *Ordinances of the Department of Treasury* (*chin-pu shih*) or those of the *Department of Granaries* (*ts'ang-pu shih*).

It is probable that chapter 3 of *T'ang liu-tien*, devoted to the Board of Finance, contains many silent quotations from the *Ordinances*, in addition to the extensive quotations from the *Statutes* which have been identified by Niida. In particular, some passages from the commentary seem likely to have derived from the *Ordinances*, but as I have not yet been able to justify these identifications to my own satisfaction, this problem must await another occasion. However, it is perhaps worth pointing out that the section[30] giving the types of cloth and tribute goods contributed by various prefectures certainly derives from the *Ordinances*, since parallel passages are cited in *Wamyō ruiju-shō* beginning 'The *K'ai-yüan Ordinances* say' (*Kaigen-shiki iwaku*) or 'The *T'ang Ordinances* say' (*Tō-shiki iwaku*),[31] and as Niida has pointed out, these *Ordinances* were almost certainly part of those of the Board of Finance, and probably of the type known as *pieh-shih*, which supplemented articles in the *Statutes*, often giving rules for local application.[32] As may be seen from the examples below taken from *RSG*, such *Ordinances* frequently began by citing the *Statute* to which they were an amplification, and this adds a further layer of difficulty to any attempt to reconstruct the original *Ordinances*.

A. 'ORDINANCES OF THE BOARD OF FINANCE' ('HU-PU SHIH')

I. All regular adults (*cheng-ting*) who perform miscellaneous *corvée* (*ts'ung-fu*)[33] for 40 days shall be exempt from [labour service].[34] After 70 days they shall also be exempt from grain tax (*tsu*) and after 100 days shall be exempted from all taxation and labour service. When adolescent males (*chung-nan*) perform miscellaneous *corvée* after they have completed 40 days' labour, exemption shall be given for the [land levy][35] of the household. If there is no liability for land levy (*ti-shui*), the exemption may be transferred to one of the adult male members of the household.

SOURCE: *PSLT*, 22, p. 67*b*, ll. iv–v.

NOTE: Niida, *Hōseishi kenkyū*, 4 (1953), *loc. cit.* points out that this stood in an intimate connection with *Taxation Statutes*, art. 4 (see above). The passage is discussed in detail by Miyazaki Ichisada, 'Tōdai fueki-seido shinkō', *Tōyōshi kenkyū*, 14, IV (1956) pp. 1–24, and especially pp. 5–10.

II. All[36] men and women shall be 'babies' (*huang*) until three years of age, children (*hsiao*) until fifteen years of age, adolescent males (*chung-nan*) until twenty years of age, and shall become adults (*ting*) at twenty-one.[37]

SOURCE: *PSLT*, 22, p. 67 *b*, ll. v.

NOTE: Niida, *loc. cit.* points out that this is almost identical with an article in the *Household Statutes* (*Hu-ling*), *Tōryō shūi*, pp. 225 ff.

III. In all wasteland where there are mulberry or fig trees, no one may burn over the land.

SOURCE: *Sung hsing-t'ung*, 27, p. 8 *b*.

NOTE: Niida, *loc. cit.* points out the very close connection between this passage, *Code*, 27, art. 8, and the *Statute* quoted in the *Commentary* thereto.

IV. Where persons bring wasteland into cultivation, they may reap the harvest on their own account for two years, but thereafter must abide by the general rule.

SOURCE: *RSG*, 12, p. 372, cited as '*K'ai-yüan Ordinances*', ch. 2.

NOTE: See Takigawa Masajirō, *Shina hōseishi kenkyū*, pp. 110–11. *Li* here may refer to the specific body of law known by this title, or simply to 'normal practice'. The 'general rule' may well have been similar to that in the clause of *RSG* in the commentary to which it is quoted. This laid down strict time limits for the utilisation of 'borrowed wasteland' after which it would revert either to its original owner or to the state.

V A. According to the *Statutes*[38] 'all those on the same household register as persons who have had their family specially designated for filial piety and righteousness shall be exempt from taxation and *corvée*'.

Should the filial and righteous person himself die, or should his descendants not continue to live together with him on a common household register, or should the righteous family be divided, they shall in no case come within the scope of exemption.[39]

V B. According to the *Statutes*[40] 'those who are appointed to office and are not entitled to exemption from taxation and labour service should in all cases await the receipt of their certificate of exemption and only then enter themselves as exempt [on the registers]. In the case of subaltern employees who are discharged from their post and should be re-entered in the registers, they should in every case be taxed as from the date on which they left their office.'

The various persons who are employed on a personal basis (*pu*) are entitled to exemption as from the date of employment.

V C. According to the *Statutes*[41] 'those who are registered in the spring quarter shall pay both taxes and labour services. Those registered during the summer quarter shall be exempt from taxes but shall render labour services. Those registered in the autumn shall be totally exempt.'

Those who are taken off the registers in spring, then, shall be totally exempt, those taken off in summer shall pay taxes, those taken off in autumn shall be liable to both taxes and labour service.

In the case of all *fang-ko*, *chi-p'u*, *i-shih*, *po-chih*, etc.,[42] and persons in miscellaneous employment of all sorts who are entitled to exemption from taxation and labour service; if among them any are relieved or replaced or released from service, the two persons (i.e. the original holder of the post and his successor) shall be entitled to a year's exemption to be apportioned between them.

In the case of all types of person entitled to a selection examination (*hsüan-jen*) who are relieved or released or who are selected and given office, they shall be granted tax exemption in accordance with the rule for erasing persons from the registers. In each case the calculation of their entitlement shall be made in co-operation with the office to which they are attached.

S O U R C E : *RSG*, 13, pp. 406–7.

N O T E : These three clauses show perfectly how the *Ordinances* were dovetailed on to clauses from the *Statutes* which they expanded and made more specific. See Niida, *loc. cit.* pp. 203–4.

VI. The fifty-nine prefectures of Ling, Sheng, etc., are border prefectures, and in these continuous residence on the frontiers is essential.

S O U R C E : *Code*, 28, art. 15 (comm.).

VII. After the death of all persons holding a fief of maintenance (*shih-feng*) the goods which they have received from their enfiefment shall be divided according to the number of their sons, the legitimate heir receiving a double share. After reaching the generation of great-grandsons the division shall not be continued, and the fief shall descend only in the sub-family of the legitimate heir.

S O U R C E : Memorial from the Board of Finance dated 747, 6th month, quoted in *THY*, 90, p. 1645. Cited as abbreviated text of the *Ordinances of the Board of Finance*.

VIII. The periods of labour [for artisans employed by the Directorate of Imperial Workshops (*shao-fu chien*) and the Directorate of Works (*chiang-tso chien*)] shall be fixed according to the *Ordinances of the Board of Finance*.

S O U R C E : *TLT*, 7, p. 20a.

N O T E : Although this does not apparently quote the *Ordinance* itself, it is likely that the preceding passage (pp. 19b–20a) is a quotation from the *Ordinances of the Directorate of Works* (*shao-fu shih*).

B. 'ORDINANCES OF THE DEPARTMENT OF PUBLIC REVENUE' ('TU-CHIH SHIH')

I. For provisioning the armies in their campaigns,[43] if the prefectural storehouses are without the goods, they may each year pay out cloth for the tax in kind and *corvée* exemption tax . . .[44] and transportation cost and pay it into the prefecture. If there is not sufficient in the prefecture concerned by itself, they may allocate tax cloth from other prefectures which should be sent to the capital, so that the troops may have thick furs and wadded garments to wear.

SOURCE: *PSLT*, 16, p. 61*b*, ll. 12.

3. FRAGMENTS OF THE 'REGULATIONS' ('KO') OF THE BOARD OF FINANCE

Like the *Ordinances* the *Regulations* (*ko*) were issued in separate series[45] by each of the subordinate departments of the Six Boards, and by certain other offices. The fragments which I translate below all come from *Regulations* promulgated by one of the departments of the Board of Finance: one is quoted as from the *Regulations of the Board of Finance* (*hu-pu-ko*) itself, one from the *Regulations of the Department of Treasury* (*chin-pu-ko*), and one from the *Regulations of the Department of Granaries* (*ts'ang-pu-ko*). I have not located any surviving quotation from the *Regulations of the Department of Public Revenue* (*tu-chih-ko*). The last quotation is cited without its being specified from which section of the *Regulations* it derives, but from its subject-matter, which is closely connected with one of the surviving clauses of the *Ordinances of the Board of Finance*, we may safely assume that it too derives from the *Regulations of the Board of Finance*.

In addition to these short quotations, there is a long manuscript among the Tun-huang MSS. in the Stein Collection in the British Museum,[46] which has been tentatively identified by Niida Noboru as a fragment of the *Regulations of the Board of Finance*. However, this document raises a number of very difficult problems, as its form is by no means identical with the well-known fragment of the *Regulations of the Board of Justice*, and I shall leave this document for a separate study of the MS. fragments of the *Regulations* recovered from Tun-huang and Turfan.

A. 'REGULATIONS OF THE BOARD OF FINANCE' ('HU-PO-KO')

If any commoners who are not from frontier prefectures or who are attached to army administrations within 1000 *li* as 'attached households' (*tse-hu*)[47] wish to be registered in frontier prefectures and to reside there, in every case it shall be permitted for arrangements to be made with the authorities in the place in which they reside, who should report to the office in charge (in the place to which they wish to move) to grant them land in accordance with the number of adult family members, and to grant them remission of taxes for ten years. If there should be any military trouble in the prefecture in which they reside they must defend it, but they may not be selected for campaign or garrison duty outside it. This shall become a *Regulation* forthwith.

SOURCE: *PSLT*, 22, p. 66*b*.

B. 'REGULATIONS OF THE DEPARTMENT OF TREASURY' ('CHIN-PU-KO')

An edict[48] ordered the wild Chiang tribesmen of the prefectures of Sung, Tang, Wei, Hsi, etc.,[49] to come each year after the tenth month to P'eng-chou at the time laid down for setting up a market to trade with them. One senior assistant of the prefecture (*shang-tso*) should be deputed to establish a market-place and to supervise trade with them beyond the Ts'an-yai customs barrier, in accordance with the market system. The common people must not be allowed to have free intercourse with them.

SOURCE: *PSLT*, 24, p. 92*b*.

C. 'REGULATIONS OF THE DEPARTMENT OF GRANARIES' ('TS'ANG-PU-KO')

No place may on its own initiative pay out rewards for troops or authorise consumption of army supplies. If essential expenditure is permitted, a memorial must be submitted reporting the matter.

SOURCE: *PSLT*, 16, p. 61*b*.

D. 'REGULATIONS OF K'AI-YÜAN PERIOD'

'Righteousness' (*i*) is an absolute necessity. Those who for successive generations live in common, with the whole family imbued with harmony and reverence, where senior and junior preserve their proper precedence, where there is no selfish interest in the holding of property or in consumption, should be treated with respect by all, near and far, and the prefecture should pay its respects to them. The local authorities should make a personal investigation to acquaint themselves with the true circumstances, and specially appoint a commissioner to make an inquiry, and then report the matter to the throne in accordance with the *Statutes*. In the case of those who obtain a special banner of designation, the tax exemption accorded to them as a 'filial household' shall cease with the death of the filial son on whose behalf the honour was granted.

SOURCES: *RSG*, 13, p. 412. A fuller version of this same clause is to be found in the Stein MS. S. 1344, lines 6–9. The MS. dates the original edict from which this was compiled as 708. ix. 20. *RSG*, 13, p. 413, quotes a further passage from the *Edicts subsequent to the Regulations* (*ko-hou chih*), 13, making the matter even more specific.

NOTE: Although *RSG* does not specify from which section of the *Regulations* of K'ai-yüan times this passage comes, it is clear from its contents that it must be from those of the Board of Finance (cf. app. II, 2, art. VA of the fragments of the *Ordinances*, to which it is immediately relevant).

4. TU YU'S ACCOUNT OF THE STATE FINANCES IN THE 'T'IEN-PAO' PERIOD

Average number of registered households (*chi-chang hu*) in the empire, 8,200,000 +.

Average household levy from these approximately 2,000,000 + strings of cash.

[*Commentary:* In general there were few households of the higher categories, and many of the lower categories. As an average we calculate this figure at something below the rate for an eighth grade household. The tax levied on an eighth grade household was 452 cash: that levied on a ninth grade household 222 cash. We have taken 250 cash per household as an overall average rate.

During the six or seven years between 748 and 755 there were some differences in quantities of tax, increases and decreases. This is why we say 'average' (*yüeh*). All of the following categories should be understood in the same way.]

Average income from the land levy (*ti-shui*), 12,400,000 + *shih*.

[*Commentary:* Under the Western Han the amount of land cultivated by each household did not exceed 70 *mou*. We calculate this average total on the basis of this figure.]

Number of taxable individuals (*k'o-ting*), 8,200,000 +.

The *yung*, *tiao*, *tsu*, etc., contributed by them:

1. Average income from prefectures and counties producing silk and silk floss. Number of taxable individuals, 3,700,000 +.

Yung and tiao: average contribution of silk, 7,400,000 lengths (*p'i*); reckoned at 2 lengths per individual.

Of silk floss, 1,850,000 + hanks (*t'un*).

[*Commentary:* Each individual contributed 3 *liang*, and 6 *liang* made a hank (*t'un*). Thus the contribution of every two individuals made up into one hank.]

Tsu: in grain (*su*), 7,400,000 + *shih*.

[*Commentary:* Each individual contributed 2 *shih*.]

2. Average income from prefectures and counties contributing hemp cloth. Number of taxable individuals, 4,500,000 +.

Yung and *tiao:* average contribution of hemp cloth, 10,350,000 lengths (*tuan*).

[*Commentary:* Each individual contributed 2 lengths and 15 feet. Hence 10 individuals contributed 23 lengths between them.]

Tsu: an average of 1,900,000 individuals in the prefectures and counties south of the Yangtze paid hemp cloth in place of grain (*che-na pu*), contributing an average of 5,700,000 lengths (*tuan*).

[*Commentary:* In general this is calculated on a basis somewhat below the figure for an eighth grade household. Eighth grade households converted their *tsu* tax at the rate of 3 lengths 10 feet of hemp cloth per individual (*ting*), while ninth grade households converted at the rate of 2 lengths 20 feet per individual. We have taken 3 lengths as the overall average rate.]

An average of 2,600,000 individuals in the prefectures and counties north of the Yangtze contributed an average of 5,200,000 + *shih* of unhulled grain (*su*).

If we make a grand total of the *tsu, shui, yung,* and *tiao* taxes, each year on an average the income in money, grain, silk and hemp cloth was 52,200,000 + lengths of cloth, hanks of silk floss, strings of cash, and *shih* of grain. The various types of payment in lieu of special duties (*tz'u-k'o*) and income from various impositions are not included.

[*Commentary:* According to the figures for the *T'ien-pao* period, the annual income of the Department of Public Revenue of the Department of State in lengths of cloth, strings of cash, and *shih* of grain amounted to 57,000,000 +. Of this 53,400,000 were accounted for by the household levy, land levy, *yung, tiao,* and converted *tsu* tax. The payments in lieu of special duties (*tz'u-k'o*) and various impositions amounted together only to 4,700,000 +.]

The annual total of grain at the disposal of the Department of Public Revenue was 25,000,000 + *shih*.

[*Commentary:*

3,000,000 was converted into silk or hemp cloth to supplement the income of the treasuries of the two capitals.

3,000,000 was converted into hulled grain or beans to provide supplies (*liao*) for the imperial commissariat and for the kitchens of the various official departments, and all was paid into the granaries in the capital.

4,000,000 was converted into hulled grain in Chiang-nan and transported to the capital to provide official salaries and rations (*liang-liao*) for the various offices.

5,000,000 was retained in the prefectures of origin for official salaries or handed over as rations (*ti-liang*).

10,000,000 was either employed as rations for the armies of the military governors of the provinces, or stored in the granaries in the prefecture of origin.]

The annual total of hemp cloth, silk, and silk floss at their disposal was 27,000,000 + lengths and hanks.

[*Commentary:*

13,000,000 was paid into the western capital.

1,000,000 was paid into the eastern capital.

13,000,000 was used for the expenses of rewards for troops and the harmonious purchase of grain in the various provinces, together with the expenses for conveniently paying official salaries and expenses of the postal relay service in distant small prefectures.]

The annual total of cash at the disposal of the Department of Public Revenues was 2,000,000 + strings.

[*Commentary:*

1,400,000 went to provide salaries (*k'o-liao*) for officials serving in the provinces, and for the purchase of post-horses.

600,000 went to supplement the provision of army rations for the provinces through 'harmonious purchase' (*ho-ti*).]

From the *K'ai-yüan* into the *T'ien-pao* period, in opening up the frontier regions a great many honorific offices were established. Every year the expense of provisioning the armies increased day by day.

The expense of purchasing grain totalled 3,600,000 lengths of cloth.

[*Commentary:* Shuo-fang, 800,000; Lung-yu, 1,000,000; I-hsi, Pei-t'ing, 80,000; An-hsi, 120,000; Ho-tung, 400,000; pasturages, 400,000.]

Provision of clothing totalled 5,300,000 lengths of cloth.

[*Commentary:* Shuo-fang, 1,200,000; Lung-yu, 1,500,000; Ho-hsi, 1,000,000; I-hsi, Pei-t'ing, 400,000; An-hsi, 300,000; Ho-tung, 400,000; pasturages, 500,000.]

Special payments (*pieh-chih*) totalled 2,100,000.

[*Commentary:* Ho-tung, 500,000; Yu-chou, 800,000; Chien-nan, 800,000.]

Provision of rations (*kuei-chün shih*), 1,900,000 *shih*.

[*Commentary:* Ho-tung, 500,000; Yu-chou, 700,000; Chien-nan, 700,000.]

Grand total, 12,600,000.

[*Commentary:* Before K'ai-yüan times the expenditure on the frontier barbarians did not exceed 2,000,000 strings. But from that time onward the expense increased daily, eventually reaching this figure.]

The expenses of rewards and special payments are still not included in this total. At this time the financial offices (*ch'ien-ku chih ssu*) only concentrated on the extortion of taxes and invented multifarious categories such as 'surplus in conversion' and 'remaining profit'. Although the storehouses were abundantly full, the villages suffered distress.

[*Commentary:* The Department of Public Revenues of the Department of State was in general control of the current expenditure of the empire; during the period after An Lu-shan's rebellion in the reign-periods *Chih-te* and *Ch'ien-yüan*, commissioners for public revenue (*tu-chih shih*) were appointed. After the *Yung-t'ai* period, public revenue no longer had a commissioner. A transportation commissioner was appointed to control the provinces and the Public Revenue Department controlled the capital. At the beginning of the *Chien-chung* period the transport commissioners too were abolished, and control reverted to the Department of Public Revenue. Commissioners of Advancement and Disgrace were ordered separately to each province to collect population statistics and to fix the categories and amounts of taxes.

Each year in the empire as a whole there were levied some 30,000,000 strings of cash. Of this sum 20,500,000 strings went to pay expenses in the provinces, and 9,500,000 strings to provide for the capital.

The rice and wheat levied amounted to 16,000,000 *shih*, of which 2,000,000 *shih* were to supply the capital and more than 14,000,000 *shih* were granted to supply the expenses of the provinces.]

Source: *TT*, 6, p. 34*a–b*.

Note: Ikeda On, in a personal communication, suggests that this account is in fact manufactured from two separate sources. In the section dealing with revenue, the term *tsai* is used for years, while *chün* is used to refer to the commanderies, as would be natural in the *t'ien-pao* period. In the account of expenditures, however, the term *chou* is used for prefectures. This passage then probably refers to the last years of the *k'ai-yüan* period (713–41) rather than to 749.

5. DOCUMENTS RELEVANT TO THE 'LIANG-SHUI' TAX REFORMS

1. YANG YEN'S MEMORIAL TO THE THRONE

In the 8th month of that year (780),[50] the Great Minister Yang Yen presented a memorial to the throne saying: 'When our state first established the *Statutes* and *Ordinances*, they had the system of the *tsu-yung-tiao* taxes. But when it came to the *K'ai-yüan* period (713–41) Hsüan-tsung cultivated virtue according to the way, and made liberality and humanity the basis of his regime. Therefore the documents of registration were not compiled. The households of the people increased by degrees, the precautionary measures were not enforced. As individuals came to die there were no longer the former names. As lands changed hands there were no longer the former quantities. As families became richer or poorer the former property categories were no longer preserved. But the Board of Finance vainly used these meaningless documents and managed their business with old papers, and thus were unable to find out the true current state of affairs. Under the old system adults from the common people who served in the garrisons on the frontiers were granted exemption from their *tsu* and *yung* taxes, and were demobilised and returned home after six years. When under Hsüan-tsung there was trouble with the I and Ti barbarians, many of the garrison troops died and never returned home. The frontier generals, presuming upon the favour of the emperor, concealed their defeats[51] and did not report their dead. Therefore their names were not erased from the nominal rolls (*kuan-chi*). Coming down to the *T'ien-pao* period (742–55), Wang Hung became population commissioner (*hu-k'ou-shih*) and made the collection of taxes his special duty. He held that if such an individual was still included in his register then how could the person himself have gone away? He considered they were just concealing tax liability and failing to pay, and nothing more. Thereupon he would reckon up the accumulated *tsu* and *yung* taxes which their families would have paid in thirty years according to the old registers, giving exemption only for the six years [of military service]. The people of the empire suffered but had no one to whom they could appeal for help. Thus the system of the *tsu-yung* taxes had been in decay for a long while. Subsequently after the *Chih-te* period (756–8) war broke out in the empire. First there were military levies, which were followed by famine and pestilence. Taxes were levied and transported, and many minor labour services had to be performed together. The population was exhausted and diminished, while the household registers and maps became out-of-date and meaningless. Funds for the armies and the state depended upon provisions made by the commissioners for public revenue and transportation. The local military commanders in the provinces were provided themselves by the military governors and commissioners for local militia forces. The offices collecting taxation increased in numbers and nobody exercised overall control. On this the principles of government fell into decay. The court was unable to exercise supervision over the commissioners[52] and the commissioners were unable to exercise supervision over the prefectures. The tribute offerings (*kung-hsien*) from the provinces all went into the palace treasury (*nei-k'u*). Powerful ministers and cunning underlings took advantage of the situation to commit evil deeds. Some of them being entrusted with official goods to deliver as tribute took it as personal plunder for themselves, sometimes amounting to tens of thousands. In places where there were very many troops, such as Ho-nan, Shan-tung, Ching-hsiang, and Chien-nan, their commanders all liberally provided for themselves. The income from the regular taxes (*cheng-fu*) was not very large. The names of the ranks of petty officials were established temporarily in respect of the individual, and the size of their salaries depended upon how much they increased or decreased [official revenues]. Thus the types of imposition and taxes enforced came to number several hundreds. Those which had been [officially] abolished were not done away with. Those which reduplicated one another were not eliminated. New and old taxes were piled one upon the other, till one could not discover any limit. The common people received their commands and supplied what was demanded; their fat and blood were sweated away, and they had to sell their nearest and dearest.[53] Every ten days they had to pay in tax, and every month it had to be transported. They were never given any respite. The official underlings by their rapacity fed upon the people like silkworms [gnawing the leaves]. The rich and members of families with many adult members all became titular officials or monks or became tax-exempt by rendering special labour services. The poor had no such refuge open to them and so their adults remained [on the tax registers]. Thus liabilities were exempted for the superior classes, and taxes increased for their inferiors. By such means was the empire distressed and injured, and the people were dispersed and reduced to becoming vagrants, so that not four or five out of a hundred remained living in their own native place. Matters have gone on like this for thirty years.[54]

I therefore request the institution of a two tax system (*liang-shui-fa*) to unify these various types of levy [and saying]; 'When employing special *corvée* labour and whenever collecting in money, we should first calculate the amount necessary and then collect it from the people as tax, assessing expenditure to calculate income'.[55] Households should be registered according to their actual residence, with no distinction whether they are local families or immigrants. Persons should be distinguished according to whether they are rich or poor, not differentiated as 'adults' or 'adolescents'. In the case of travelling merchants who do not reside in one place, they should pay a one-thirtieth tax in whichever prefecture or county they are. The amount which is taken from them should be estimated so as to be equitable compared with the tax on local residents, to ensure that they do not have any unfair advantage. The tax on residents is to be collected in autumn and summer. Where there is anything unsuitable to local custom, it is to be corrected. The *tsu* and *yung* taxes and miscellaneous labour services (*tsa-i*) are all to be abolished,[56] but the total assessment of adult individuals liable for service (*ting-e*)[57] is not to be done away with. Expenditure and income should be reported as under the old *Ordinances* (*shih*). The tax on land should be equitably collected reckoned on the basis of the amount of land under cultivation in the fourteenth year of *Ta-li* (779). Collection of the summer tax (*hsia-shui*) must be made not later than the 6th month, and that of the autumn tax (*ch'iu-shui*) not later than the 11th month. After a year has passed, if there is any case where the population has increased and the tax been reduced, or where people have fled and the equitable state of affairs has been lost, the chief official should be promoted or demoted accordingly. Commissioners of advancement and disgrace (*ch'u-chih shih*) should in each case fix taxes equitably estimating what is suitable for local conditions and the size of the population.[58] The Department of Public Revenue (*tu-chih*) of the State Department (*shang-shu*) should be in overall control of it.

[Te-tsung thought this plan good, and enforced it.]

This document is translated from the text preserved in *T'ang hui-yao*, 83. Three short passages are inserted from parallel versions in *Ts'e-fu yüan-kuei*, 488, and in Yang Yen's biography in *Chiu T'ang-shu*, 118. There is, however, a major difference in form between the *T'ang hui-yao* version and the others. In the *Chiu T'ang-shu*, 118, biography of Yang Yen, the first part of this document (down to 'Matters have gone on like this for thirty years') is descriptive of the situation in the preceding decades. The actual memorial begins only with 'I therefore request...', and is introduced by the phrase '[Yang] Yen thereupon directed a petition to the throne earnestly discussing these evils. He then requested the institution...'. *Ts'e-fu yüan-kuei*, 488, also considers that only the second half is actually part of the text. The first half is relegated to a commentary. But it is not clear which document the editors of *Ts'e-fu yüan-kuei* took this to be. It is introduced simply as follows: 'In the second month [780] commissioners of advancement and disgrace were despatched to go to the various parts of the empire. They instituted the system of the double tax....'

There is no mention of 'request' and it seems that the compilers have taken it as the text of the directive for the commissioners. A similar error is found in the quotation of the document in *Chiu T'ang-shu*, 48 (*Financial Monograph*), where it is introduced as 'In the 2nd month of the 1st year *Chien-chung* (780) commissioners of advancement and disgrace were despatched to go to the various parts of the empire. *The edict said, in brief,....*' However, the edict regarding the commissioners was issued in the 1st month 780, and was quite different in form. It is translated below (document 3).

2. ACT OF GRACE OF 5TH DAY OF 1ST MONTH 780

General Act of Grace of the *hsin-wei* (5th) day of the 1st month 1st year *Chien-chung* (780)....[59]We ought to despatch commisioners for advancement and disgrace separately to the various provinces, to examine customs and to inquire about grievances. Since the 'troubles'[60] the types of taxes have become exceedingly multifarious. We depute these commissioners for advancement and disgrace together with the civil governors (*kuan-ch'a-shih*) of the provinces and the prefects (*tz'u-shih*), and the subordinates of the transportation commission (*chüan-yün suo-yu*) to estimate the households of the common people and immigrants, assess the numbers of adult male members and their property, and to fix their grades.[61] They should assess an equitable rate and institute a double tax which should be paid in annually. If there is anything in the local conditions of the place concerned which is unsuitable, then a special time-limit for contribution should be established. The different types of taxes old and new which have been in force in recent times should all be abolished. If anyone improperly collects a single cash as a separate levy beyond this double tax, he will be judged answerable under the law on official oppression as though he had raised taxes on his own authority.[62] The amounts of payments, etc., for the army administrations should be managed in accordance with the edict of the 7th day of the 8th month of the year *Ta-li*, 14 (779).[63]

This document is nowhere preserved in full, and my translation is made from a reconstructed text. The fullest version is that in *Ts'e-fu yüan-kuei*, 89, where the passage is shown in its true context as part of a lengthy Act of Grace marking the beginning of a new reign-period. Fragmentary versions, confined to the section under discussion, are preserved in *Ts'e-fu yüan-kuei*, 488, in *Chiu T'ang-shu*, 12, *T'ang hui-yao*, 78, and in two separate places in *T'ang hui-yao*, 83. The document is incorrectly described as an edict (*chih*) in *T'ang hui-yao*, 78, and *Ts'e-fu yüan-kuei*, 488, while *T'ang hui-yao*, 83, splits it in two, the first half being correctly described as an Act of Grace (*she-wen*) of the 5th day 1st month, while the second appears as a General Act of Grace (*ta-she*) dated in the 2nd month after the *Ch'i-ch'ing-tiao* issued on the 11th day. A second Act of Grace is not to be found mentioned elsewhere, and as it is most unlikely that two identical or partly identical documents of this type were issued in consecutive months, I presume that this is a mistake on the part of the compiler of the *Hui-yao*.

3. EDICT OF 2ND MONTH 780

In the 2nd month of the 1st year *Chien-chung* (780), commissioners of advancement and disgrace were sent out to different parts of the empire. Sou Ho, chief secretary of the Office of the Right[64] and concurrently serving censor, was sent to tour the capital district; Liu Wan, chief secretary of the Department of Regional Military Organisation, was sent to Kuan-nei; P'ei Po-yen, under-secretary of the Board of Justice, went to the provinces of Ho-tung, Tse-Lu and Tz'u-Hsing; Wei Chen,[65] chief secretary of the Department of Honorific Titles, was sent to the provinces of Shan-nan West, Chien-nan East and Chien-nan West; Chao Tsan, chief secretary of the Board of Rites, was sent to Shan-[nan] East,[66] Ching-nan, Ch'ien-chung and Hu-nan; Wu Ching-lun,[67] an Imperial Counsellor, was sent to the provinces of Wei-Po, Ch'eng-Te and Yu-chou; Lu Han, chief secretary of the Chancellery, was sent to Ho-nan, Tzu-Ch'ing and the metropolitan district of the eastern capital; Li Ch'eng,[68] chief secretary of the Board of Officials, was sent to Huai-hsi and Huai-nan provinces; the Imperial Counsellor Liu Tsai was sent to the provinces of Che-chiang East and West; Cheng Shu-tse, chief secretary of the Board of Justice, was sent to the provinces of Chiang-nan, Chiang-hsi, and Fu-Chien; and Wei Yen, under-secretary of the Board of Rites, was sent to Ling-nan and Wu-kuan.

The edict said,[69]

We have heard that under the saintly government of T'ang and Yü there was a scrutiny of the conduct of officials every three years, to degrade the inefficient and advance the intelligent ones. Those rulers who were propagators of the true teachings under the two Han dynasties commanded the eight envoys to purify the administration of the empire. Now we, having inherited the imperial sway, cherish the intention of delivering our instructions. Although within the nobles and ministers are diligent day and night, and without the barbarians and the protector generals remain entirely loyal, arms and armour are not yet at peace, the Jung and the Ti are not yet entirely subdued, our control is not yet fully exercised, and our laws are not yet made known. In the fiefs and the imperial domain, the commanderies and counties, taxation is not uniform. In the ranks of the armies, arduous labour and idleness are not equitably apportioned. This is the reason for which we spend the whole night in accumulated griefs, and for which our heart is full of trouble night and day. We therefore command the many officials to go and explain this for us; they should go to the four regions to make them obey our governance, and deal with their hundred problems to make them return to the correct way. The officials may not fail diligently to assist us in this matter of our profound regard.

The edict itself appears in two versions, one in *Ts'e-fu yüan-kuei*, 162 (section *Ming-shih*, 2) and the other in *T'ang ta-chao-ling chi*, 104, where it is undated and listed under the title *Ch'ien chu tao ch'u-chih-shih ch'ih*. There are a few trifling variants but none of any consequence. The preliminary list of the commissioners for advancement and disgrace is preserved only in the *Ts'e-fu yüan-kuei*. The *Tzu-chih t'ung-chien k'ao-i*, 17, tells us that the two *Veritable Records* which covered the first years of Te-tsung's reign were both defective at this point, the *Chien-chung Shih-lu* not having listed any of the names, while the *Te-tsung Shih-lu* omitted the commissioner sent to Ho-pei, whose name Ssu-ma Kuang reads as Hung Ching-lun, not Wu Ching-lun as in the text here.[70] There are a few other problems on the identities of the commissioners, which are discussed in the notes.

4. THE 'CH'I-CH'ING-T'IAO' OF THE 11TH DAY 2ND MONTH 780

It is requested that the commissioners for advancement and disgrace together with the civil governors of the provinces and the senior officials of the prefectures and counties be ordered to assess a tax to be collected twice annually in summer and autumn, on the basis of the amounts previously collected and in accordance with the categories fixed for each household, both natives and settlers, and with the amount of money in their possession. Widowers, widows, orphans and childless persons who are not supported or assisted shall be exempted in accordance with the edict.[71] The grain tax, tax in kind, and *corvée* exemption taxes (*tsu-yung-tiao*) on the adult male taxpayers are to be incorporated into the *liang-shui* taxes. The prefectures and counties should report the quota of taxable males which has been preserved, in accordance with the *Ordinances*.[72] Regarding the amounts of grain which should be collected, we request that they be equitably levied (*chün-shui*) on the total quotas of land on the 'cultivated land registers' actually under cultivation in 779. The summer tax is to be paid in by the 6th month; the autumn tax by the 11th month.

When the commissioners have completed the assessment of the taxes for each province, they should draw up a list of all the amounts which should be levied in its various constituent prefectures and administrations, with the time limits for collection; and the division between those amounts which should be retained locally and those which are to be sent in to the capital, and into those amounts to be paid in cash, cloth and grain, and these should be reported to the throne. These details should also be reported to the Department of Public Revenue, the Department of Treasury, the Department of Granaries, and the Department of Judicial Control.[73]

This document is the most important of all, for it is the detailed order which was to be implemented by the commissioners in the various provinces. It is preserved only in *THY*, 83, p. 1535.

6. TAX QUOTAS FOR SU-CHOU UNDER THE 'LIANG-SHUI'

The following information is extracted from the only surviving record of the detailed tax assessment of a prefecture under the *liang-shu* system. It is preserved in the early local monograph dealing with Su-chou, the *Wu-ti chi* written about 876 by Lu Kuang-wei, and the figures thus almost certainly date from the reign of I-tsung (859–73) or Hsi-tsung (873–88). The figures are of additional interest since they come from the area which was almost the sole regular source of revenue or the later T'ang emperors.

Su-chou controls 7 counties, 194 localities (*hsiang*) and 143,261 households.

Tax income from *liang-shui*, tea, salt and wine monopolies, 692,885,076 cash.

Disposal of revenue

(*a*) Deducted by provincial authorities and applied to 'purchase of pickled vegetables'.

107,720,246 (15·5 per cent)

County	Hsiang	Households	Tax quota	Average per household
Wu-hsien	30	38,361 (30 fang)	99,963,373	2,606
Ch'ang-chou	30	23,700 (30 fang)	98,576,576	4,159
Chia-hsing	50	27,054	178,076,120	6,582
K'un-shan	24	13,981	109,503,738	7,832
Ch'ang-shu	24	13,820	90,750,774	6,566
Hua-t'ing	22	12,780	72,182,431	5,648
Hai-yen	15	13,200	46,581,058	3,529
Total	—	142,896	695,634,070	4,856

NOTE: There is a discrepancy between the sums of population and tax given for individual counties and the global figures given for the prefecture.

(*b*) Retained in Su-chou for military expenses, 'pickled vegetables', clothing and rations.

178,349,098 (25·6 per cent)

(*c*) Retained for the military funds of the militia commissioner and despatched to the capital.

306,830,000 (42·1 per cent)

These figures leave 102,734,726 cash unaccounted for, or 15·4 per cent of the total revenue.

These figures show two very important facts. First, the heavy tax assessment of rural districts compared with urban (Wu-hsien, Ch'ang-chou) and industrial (Hai-yen) counties. Secondly, the comparatively low proportion of revenue taken by the province in comparison with that sent to the capital and that retained in the prefecture itself.

APPENDIX III

1. HAN YÜ'S MEMORIAL ON SUGGESTIONS TO REFORM THE SALT MONOPOLY

The following memorial, which comes from *Han Ch'ang-li chi*, ch. 40, pp. (vii) 55–60, is by Han Yü, and is entitled *Statement discussing whether it would be right to reform the salt system.*

[*Commentary:* In 822 Chang P'ing-shu¹ became vice-president of the Board of Finance and submitted a memorial requesting that the officials themselves might sell salt, by which means the country might be enriched and its military power strengthened, and set out the advantages of his proposal in eighteen articles. Of these sixteen can be seen in the present [document]. Po Lo-t'ien made a verse about 'P'ing-shu deciding the affairs of public revenue' which said 'In his calculations he could split an autumn hair: His underlings feared him like the summer sun'. Su Tung-po said, 'He was certainly a petty man'. According to the *Liu-shih chia-hsün* P'ing-shu was later ruined on account of financial malpractice, having a deficit of 400,000 strings of official moneys. It is appropriate that his policies should have come to such an end.]

Regarding the detailed suggestions on the salt system submitted by Chang P'ing-shu; I have received the imperial edict saying that there is a proposal to reform the salt system, which is of great value and worked out in detail, and ordering myself and others to set out the advantages and disadvantages of the scheme, and whether it is suitable for enforcement or not, and report them to the throne.

The detailed proposals for reform submitted by P'ing-shu have been given my careful consideration from beginning to end. I fear, however, they ought not to be put into practice. My assessment of their advantages and disadvantages is as follows, in each case following the specific proposal:

1. P'ing-shu requests that the prefectures and administrations be ordered to assign men personally to sell official salt, collecting the full market value in cloth. If the offices of the central government pay out their expenses according to the old rules, they will inevitably make a profit twice [that of old] or more.

I have now made a general estimate of the situation. Of the common people of any given place, many are poor and few rich. Apart from the prefectural town itself, those who buy salt with ready cash will be less than 2 or 3 out of ten; most of them will employ miscellaneous goods or grain and barter them [to obtain salt]. Salt merchants' profits go to the merchants themselves and there is nothing they will not take. In other cases they will sell on credit against amounts of grain, and agree to be repaid at harvest time. Using such methods [the people] receive assistance, and both parties gain some profit or advantage. If we were now to make the subordinate officers of prefectures and counties open up shop and sell [salt] themselves, the profits which they make will have no effect on themselves, yet if there is any crime involved, they will have to bear the punishment. If they cannot get ready cash or the highest quality cloth, they will be afraid that they will lose the official profit, and will certainly refuse to sell. After the reform of the system, the poor among the common people will have no means by which to obtain salt to eat. When [the officials] have sought for a profit and failed to obtain it, and when there is much resentment against them, they will naturally become guilty of failing to make the regular amount of profit on salt. I fail to see how [there will be] this so-called 'reaping a double profit'.

2. P'ing-shu also proposes that, for villages and hamlets in places far distant from prefectural and county towns, the authorities responsible [for the area] should take salt to the villages and sell it, saying that the common people [of these remote places] must not be made to lack salt.

I consider that these villages and hamlets far from their prefectural or county seats are often just three or five families living in a mountain valley. It would be impossible to make the official subordinates carry salt from house to house! If they carry too much they could not sell it all off; if they carry little they will not obtain much money. If one reckons it up, [the profit] will not be enough to pay just for their own rations while they are coming and going. Recently the merchants have often carried the [salt] on their own backs, and gone to barter it with the common people. The profit which they get over and above the fair price which they hoped for is only two or three cash. It is quite different from what would happen if the petty officials were sent out by the local officials. After they arrived in a village they would certainly demand some contributions from the common people, and though their profits would be slender, the harm they would do would be great. This too is something which should not be put into practice.

3. P'ing-shu also says that as the duties for which they are responsible are of great importance, the emperor's chief ministers should be ordered to act as commissioners (shih).

I consider that if the system were practicable, there would be no need to suppose the necessity for chief ministers acting as special commissioners, while, if the system were not practicable, even if chief ministers acted as commissioners for it they would not make matters any better. Besides, the chief ministers are those who should inspect the hundred offices and assess their merits and demerits. If they themselves became commissioners, and through their laxness there were deficiencies and corruption, who could be sent to deal with the matter? This too is something which should not be put into practice.

4. P'ing-shu also says that after his reform was put into effect the provisions of rations [*liang-k'o*] for the personnel of the salt offices [*yen-ssu*] could be stopped or reduced, so that annually 100,000 strings of cash could be collected in.

I consider that, after his reform was put into effect, there would be such abuses arising out of it, that I fear even the customary amount could not be raised. How could he still hope for a surplus profit?

5. P'ing-shu wishes to make the administrations and counties sell salt. Every month an additional 100,000 cash of *liao-ch'ien* will be assigned to the governor of the metropolitan district of Ch'ang-an, and additional 50,000 a month to the chief aides (*ssu-lu*) and to the magistrates of the two counties. Besides this, additional amounts will have to be assigned to all civil provincial governors, prefects, *hsien* magistrates, and their chief administrators, the largest sums amounting to 50,000 cash a month, the least amounting to 3000 or 5000. I calculate that the expense involved in this is already very great, but in addition there would be the provisions for rations (*liang-k'o*) for the clerks (*kuan-tien*), inspectors, labourers, and petty officials which do not come within these figures. If we make a grand total of what will have to be paid out each year it will be not less than 100,000 strings. I have as yet not seen any profit, but the expense will be very considerable. P'ing-shu also says that by stopping the ration allotments (*liang-k'o*) of the different types of minor employees in the salt offices, he could estimate to reduce expenses by 100,000 strings per annum. Yet I have just worked out that his new system would also cost 100,000. So not only will it effect a saving of 100,000 but it will also cost 100,000, so that the loss and the gain would be the same and there will be nothing left over.

P'ing-shu also suggests that the merit and demerit assessments of prefects and magistrates should be made according to whether they had sold much or little salt. Taking no heed of the normal practice, they would be promoted if they had sold a great deal, while if there was a deficit in the profit with which they were assessed, they would be punished in accordance with a detailed rule. Now the duties of a prefect and of a magistrate are essentially to reduce the sufferings [of those under him]. But if now their promotion is to depend only upon the amount of profit they make selling salt, and no further assessment is to be given on their good administration, this will miss the whole meaning of T'ang and Yü promoting the intelligent and demoting the obscure after their merit assessments for three years had accumulated.

6. P'ing-shu also requests that the price of salt be fixed at 30 cash per

catty (*chin*), with an additional charge of 2 cash per catty to pay the cost of porterage for each 200 *li*. The distance and difficulty of the journey to each place should be estimated and up to 6 cash added as the price of transport. If this is insufficient the officials shall pay out [some of the costs]. Thus nominally the price would be 30 cash per catty, but in fact it would be 36 cash. Now at present the price of salt in the capital is 40 cash per catty, and in the prefectures of the provinces it does not reach this. After the reform suggested the price might be a few cash lower, but there would be no great profit to the people. Where transport cost 5 cash the officials would have to pay a contribution of 2 cash as their share, and where it cost 10 cash this would amount to 4 cash. Thus in selling one catty of salt, the money obtained by the officials would be nominally 30 cash, but actually would be 28 cash at the most or 26 at the least. To strike an average, the money received for each catty would be no more than 26 or 27 cash. On the people's side, if we strike the average, each catty will cost 34 cash. Thus somewhere between the [profit to] the state and the [cost to the] individual there will be a loss of 7 or 8 cash on each catty. This profit will neither reach the people, nor will it return to the officials. The sum will mount up to an exceedingly great amount, such as cannot be calculated. Speaking from this point of view, it is not to be considered advantageous.

P'ing-shu also suggests that the local officials, at the season when agriculture is slack, should commandeer carts and oxen to transport salt and put it into the city granary (*tu-ts'ang*), and must ensure that no deficiency or interruption of labour is caused. Now if the prefectures and counties hire the carts and oxen at an equitable rate, the common people will certainly not be willing. Such business has to be assigned. Thus if the transport money is paid and the common people take their carts to transport salt, the authorities will at first always lack any sort of arrangement, and after they have all assembled and they can first transport the salt, when they get to the salt directorate (*yüan, chien*) and request to receive salt, they will have to wait for each cart to [go] in turn, and unless they employ bribes (*men-hu*) all will be held up, and by the time they are to pay the salt in [at the prefectural stores] yet another gift (*jen-shih*) will be required. Whenever hired labour is employed it is always like this. The common people would sooner cart goods for their private family and receive 5 cash than cart goods for the state and receive ten. If hire is not used, then it will be impossible to transport the salt. If it is used then it causes harm to the people. This again is something which should not be put into force.

7. P'ing-shu claims that by suspending or reducing the numbers of petty officers (*suo-yu*) in the salt administration, and collecting in their ration allotments (*liang-k'o*) he reckons on obtaining 100,000 strings of cash. He further says that there are already branch offices (*hsün-yüan*) and requests

that the largest and busiest of these should be chosen, and officials and subordinate officers left there to exercise management over the stores (*ts'ang*) and distribution centres (*ch'ang*). The vital centres should be firmly held, but the number of persons appointed should be small.

Fiscal privileges and ration allotments should be made [to them, but in case of abuse] they should rigorously apply the power of arrest. Any cases of loss or of trading by private individuals should be dealt with according to the detailed rules. Now the numbers of minor employees of the salt establishments controlled by P'ing-shu are very considerable. It is quite beyond reason [to suggest that] the ration allotments for those besides the persons considered suitable to be retained would still amount to as much as an annual sum of 100,000 strings. Recently the 'vital centres have been firmly held' and the numbers of people involved have been very large, yet there have still been the abuses of losses and private [illegal] trading. It seems quite impracticable in the light of common sense that the numbers of persons can be reduced and that it can then be said that the prevention of private trading will be possible.

8. P'ing-shu says that after the reform, there would certainly be an annual surplus in the national budget (*sui-chi*), and that although the daily expenses might still be insufficiently supplied, he would say that this is because for a year past, the profit from this tax had not yet been made an official responsibility, and that later the amount will be twice as much or greater.

This also is impracticable. At present the country's expenses are always said to be insufficiently supplied. If the tax profit from a single year was reduced or lost the harm would be very deep. Even if he says that the next year (the income) would be more, how can this be guaranteed? This too is something which is impracticable at a time when the accumulation of wealth in both public and private hands is still small.

9. P'ing-shu also says that the vagrants and evildoers grow richer while those who stay in their native place and devote themselves to their proper profession daily grow poorer. If the officials themselves were to sell salt, he says, everybody, no matter whether he was noble or base, rich or poor, a scholar, a farmer, an artisan, or a merchant, a Buddhist monk or Taoist priest or even a vagrant, would pay the officials money for what he ate (i.e. salt)· At the same time the family members and kin of the governors of the provinces and armies have exerted influence for one another and have not paid taxes, and were the officials themselves to sell salt, not a single one of this type of person would be omitted.

In my opinion, these various types of person have always bought salt to eat, even in the time when the officials have not sold it themselves. They did not have to wait for the officials to sell salt themselves before being able to eat salt. If we are to believe what P'ing-shu has said, [we must believe that] when the officials did not themselves sell salt, these types of persons did not buy salt to eat, and that only if the officials sold salt would they buy it to eat. Whether the officials sell salt or not, all of them will always buy salt to eat. So then if the officials were now to sell salt themselves there could be no profit to them. This is a case of what is called 'knowing the first part and not knowing the second' or 'perceiving what is near and not seeing what is more distant'. Now the state has a monopoly tax on salt, and sells it to the merchants, who pay the monopoly tax, and then sell it to the common people. This then is a case of all the common people of the empire, poor and rich, noble and base, already paying money to the officials. There is no necessity for them to pay over the money to the state directly from one hand to the other, before it may be considered as paying money to the officials.

10. P'ing-shu says that when the *liang-shui* tax system was first imposed, silk (*chüan*) cost 3000 cash a length, where now a length costs only 800 cash, so that the common people have been impoverished. Some borrow the value of their millet or wheat crops in advance, and when harvest comes, all their profit goes to repay their debts, and not a grain remains to provide their official taxes. If the officials themselves were to sell salt, the price of the salt eaten daily by a household of five persons would not exceed 10 cash, and this could be paid day by day, so that they would not be troubled and pressed [for outstanding taxes]. Thus there would no longer be the disaster of persons fleeing from their homes to escape their debts.

I consider that the sufferings and abuses of the common people do not all come about because the price of salt is high. If the officials were now to sell salt themselves, there would be little difference in price compared with that if they sold it to merchants according to the former statute. If we make a general estimate of the salt eaten by a family of five individuals, P'ing-shu's estimate is a rate of 10 cash per day. This means they would regularly spend 300 cash per month, and would thus consume a catty of salt every three days, or the equivalent of 10 catties per month. If the actual market price under the new system were not more than 3 or 4 cash per catty lower than under the former system, if we make a general estimate for a family of five persons, calculating by the rule set out by P'ing-shu, the cost will be only 1 cash per day or 30 cash per month less than under the old system. In a family of less than five persons the reduction will be even less. Thus, if the new reformed system is imposed, the common people will still not escape suffering and being driven to migrate. At the time when the taxes were first fixed (i.e. 780) one length of silk cost 3000 cash. Now, it costs only 800. Even were we to reform the salt system, the price of silk would not have been raised. As a result of such a reform, the family of five persons would obtain a profit of one cash daily. Would this enable them to avoid getting into debt, so that when the harvest came round they would not be subject to pressure and demands and after paying their official taxes they would still have a surplus left? As I see it the sufferings and abuses of the common people have lasted for a long while, but if they are not troubled by [government] actions, they will by degrees naturally improve. It does not depend on a reform of the salt system. Today silk is only 800 cash per length yet there are many of the common people who are still cold and without anything to wear. If we cause the price of silk to rise to 3000 cash per length, those without clothing will certainly be still more numerous. Moreover, the price of silk does not depend in the least on the salt system. If we speak of the matter on these grounds the salt system does not yet need to be changed.

11. P'ing-shu says, the amount of salt to be sold in each prefecture is not a little. Yet there may be some chief officials (*chang-li*) who neglect to give their personal attention to public business, so that their subordinates will tell them untruthfully that 'in the area under your jurisdiction there is nobody who will buy salt'. He requests, therefore, that inspecting officials of honesty and integrity be appointed to inspect the [officials] on the spot and verify the population. They should group them in mutual-responsibility groups, and issue them a year's supply of salt. They should be made to pay in the price of the salt quarterly. If the people (of the district) are numerous and the amount of salt sold is little, or if the price is paid in late or in a way offending the rules, he requests that the civil governor of the province be suspended, and his current appointment changed to a titular office, the prefects and below dismissed, together with their principal subordinates, and the other officials banished to distant places.

Now P'ing-shu originally suggested that the officials sold salt themselves in order to be lenient towards the people, and allow them some respite and enable them to avoid being driven to migrate. Yet now he would cause there to be a verification of the population, grouping the people in mutual responsibility groups and granting these salt, the price of which would have to be repaid quarterly. This is possible, but it does not agree with his former intention. The poor families among the common people consume very little salt, and there are some who eat food without flavouring for weeks and months at a time. If they are issued salt in accordance with the number of their individual members, and the price is collected from them at fixed seasons, all will have to pay in cash, whether or not it is practicable for them. If (as he suggests) in all cases of payment in arrears or any offence against the letter of the rules the civil governor and his subordinates will each be punished or banished, the officials and their subordinates, standing in dread of punishment, will be certain to employ severe punishments (themselves). Thus, I fear that as a result those living in the region will not be at peace, and the common people will in turn be driven to run away and migrate. This also is a major reason why the scheme is impracticable.

12. P'ing-shu requests that after the merchants' salt is paid in to the

officials, they should be prohibited from improperly seeking employment with the various armies or the provincial governors, managing their money and keeping shop, or administering their estates and mills, in order to seek their protection. He requests that the officials in the provinces be made to impose a rigorous examination, and should there be any offenders, the wealth in their possession should be paid to the officials, and a report again made about it. It should be sent to the local authorities to provide the needs of their subordinates. I consider that (now) the salt merchants pay the monopoly tax, and sell salt on behalf of the officials. Their profession is handed down from father to son, and they receive rich profits without effort. Comparing them with the ordinary common people, then their lot is truly more excellent. If now, when their livelihood has been taken from them, they are to be prohibited from seeking employment, or from handling money, keeping shops, or managing estates or mills on behalf of others, without knowing what crime they have committed, they will one morning find themselves reduced to desperate straits. If this measure were certainly to be enforced, the rich merchants and great traders would feel a grudge (against the state), and some would buy up valuable and expensive goods and flee with them to some rebellious region and support the robbers and brigands. This too is something which must be deeply considered.

13. P'ing-shu says that after his scheme was put into force the agents of the armies in the two markets (*liang-ching chün-jen*), the rich merchants and great traders would in some cases resort to bribery, interfere (in business) and start disputes. He requests that the authorities be ordered to seize and arrest (the offenders). If the principal is caught he should be summarily put to death by the officials on the spot. Where a group of persons are implicated in the same charge, they shall be given a summary flogging on the back of twenty blows. The offices and households under the armies should be investigated, and if there has been any secret leakage of salt, the offenders should all be punished in accordance with the rules relating to the prefectural or county authorities. In every case the officer or person informing about the offence should be rewarded. This clause, were it to be really enforced, would not only lead to a major loss of the people's goodwill, but it would also alarm those far and near. To practise such a rapacious policy which will harm the people, when we do not know how much profit will be received from selling salt, would truly be a great evil.

I report on the foregoing clauses. I have received the edict of the 9th day of the present month ordering myself and others to set forth the advantages and the disadvantages (of the scheme). I have carefully set them down and reported them. I humbly listen for the Imperial order.

2. MATERIAL ON THE PRODUCTION OF SALT

1. 'Hsin T'ang-shu', 37–43

The following list includes all counties given as producers of salt in the geographical monograph (*ti-li chih*) of *Hsin T'ang-shu*, 37–43.

Chapter 37 (Kuan-nei province)

T'ung-chou	Ch'ao-i hsien	There is a small pool (*hsiao-chih*) where there is salt.
	Feng-hsien hsien	
Ling-chou		Produces stamped salt (*yin-yen*).
	Hui-lo hsien	There is the Wen-ch'üan pool.
	Huai-yüan hsien	There are the three pools Hung-t'ao, Wu-p'ing, Ho-ch'ih.
Wei-chou	Wen-ch'ih hsien	There is one pool. Part of Ling-chou until 850.
Hui-chou	Hui-ning hsien	There is the Ho-ch'ih pool which produces salt after rain.
Yen-chou	Wu-yüan hsien	There is salt at the Wu-ch'ih, Pai-ch'ih, Hsi-hsiang ch'ih, and Ssu-wa yao ch'ih pools.
Hsia-chou	Shuo-fang hsien	There are two salt pools.
Yu-chou	Ch'ang-tse hsien	There is the Hu-lo salt pool.
Feng-chou		Produces stamped salt.

Chapter 38 (Ho-nan province)

Lai-chou	I-hsien	There are two salt wells.
	Chiao-shui hsien	
	Chi-mo hsien	
Ti-chou	Po-hai hsien	
Mi-chou	Chu-ch'eng hsien	
	Kung-hsien	

173

Chapter 39 (Ho-tung province)

P'u-chou	Chieh-hsien	There is the Yen-ch'ih pool and also the Nü-yen ch'ih pool.
	An-i hsien	There is a salt pool. With those in Chieh-hsien these constitute the Twin Pools (Liang-ch'ih).

(Ho-pei province)

Hsing-chou	Chü-lu hsien	There is a brine spring, whose water is boiled to produce salt.
Ts'ang-chou	Ch'ing-ch'ih hsien Yen-shan hsien	

Chapter 40 (Shan-nan province)

Kuei-chou	Tzu-kuei hsien Pa-tung hsien	
K'uei-chou	Yün-an hsien	There is a salt office (*yen-kuan*).
	Ta-ch'ang hsien	There is a salt office.
	Feng-chieh hsien	There is the Yung-an ching salt office.
Chung-chou	Lin-chang hsien	
Wan-chou	Nan-p'u hsien	There are two salt directorates of T'u-t'u chien and Yü-yang chien.
Chün-chou	Wu-tang hsien	There is a salt pool 100 *li* south-east of county town.
Ch'eng-chou	Shang-lu hsien	
Lang-chou	Lang-chung hsien Nan-pu hsien Hsin-ching hsien Hsin-cheng hsien	
Kuo-chou	Nan-chung hsien Hsiang-ju hsien Hsi-chung hsien	

(Lung-yu province)

Ch'in-chou	Ch'ang-tao hsien	
Wei-chou	Chang-hsien	There is a salt well 2 *li* south of the county town.
Liang-chou	Ku-tsang hsien	There is the Wu-hsing salt pool.
Sha-chou	Tun-huang hsien	There is a salt pool 47 *li* east of the county town.
Su-chou	Fu-lu hsien	There is a salt pool 80 *li* north-east of the county town.
	Yü-men hsien	Salt is produced at the Tu-teng shan mountain.
I-chou	I-wu hsien	There is a salt pool (Yen-ch'ih hai) 2 *li* south of the county town

Chapter 41 (Huai-nan province)

Yang-chou	Hai-ling hsien	There is a salt office.
Ch'u-chou	Yen-ch'eng hsien	There are 123 salt producing establishments (*yen-ting*).

(Chiang-nan province)

Su-chou	Chia-hsing hsien	There is a salt office.
Hang-chou		There are two salt directorates, the Hsin-t'ing chien and the Lin-p'ing chien.
Yüeh-chou		There is the Lan-t'ing chien salt directorate.
Wen-chou		There is the Yung-chia chien salt directorate.
Ch'üan-chou	Chin-chiang-hsien	
	Nan-an hsien	
Fu-chou	Lien-chiang hsien	
	Ch'ang-ch'i hsien	
T'ai-chou	Ning-hai hsien	
	Huang-yen hsien	
Ch'ien-chou	P'eng-shui hsien	

Chapter 42 (Chien-nan province)

Mei-chou	P'eng-shan hsien
Ch'iung-chou	Huo-ching hsien
	P'u-chiang hsien

Chien-chou	Yang-an hsien	
Tzu-chou	Pan-shih hsien	There is the Pao-chih ch'ih pool 70 *li* north of the county town.
	Nei-chiang hsien	
	Tzu-yang hsien	
	Lung-shui hsien	
Sui-chou	K'un-ming hsien	
Ya-chou	Lu-shan hsien	
Wei-chou	Hsien-ch'eng hsien	
Tzu-chou	Ch'i hsien	
	T'ung-ch'üan hsien	
	Hsüan-wu hsien	
	Yen-t'ing hsien	
	Fei-wu hsien	
	Yung-t'ai hsien	
	Fu-ch'eng hsien	
Sui-chou	Fang-i hsien	
	Ch'ang-chiang hsien	
	P'eng-ch'i hsien	There is the Hua-yen ch'ih pool.
Mien-chou	Pa-hsi hsien	
	Ch'ang-ming hsien	
	Wei-ch'eng hsien	
	Lo-chiang hsien	
	Shen-ch'üan hsien	
	Yen-ch'üan hsien	
P'u-chou	An-yüeh hsien	
	An-chü hsien	
	Lo-chih hsien	
	P'u-k'ang hsien	
Yü-chou	Pa-hsien	
	Pi-shan hsien	
Ling-chou	Jen-shou hsien	
	Kuei-p'ing hsien	
	Shih-chien hsien	
	Chi hsien	
Jung-chou	Ying-ling hsien	
	Kung-ching hsien	
	Tzu-kuan hsien	
Lü-chou	Chiang-an hsien	

Chapter 43 (Ling-nan province)

Kuang-chou	Tung-huan hsien
	Hsin-hui hsien
Ch'ao-chou	Hai-yang hsien
Ch'iung-chou	Ch'iung-shan hsien
Chen-chou	Ning-yüan hsien
Tan-chou	I-lun hsien

In general, the counties in Ho-nan, Ts'ang-chou in Ho-pei, Huai-nan, Chiang-nan and Ling-nan, shown above, produced salt by the evaporation of sea water, and were controlled by the commissioners of salt and iron. The production in Ho-tung, Kuan-nei, Lung-yu and Chün-chou in Shan-nan derived from salt pools and the extraction of salt from alkali soil. That in Shan-nan, Chien-nan and Ch'ien-chou in Chiang-nan derived from salt wells.

2. *From ' Hsin T'ang shu', 54*

The following comes from *Hsin T'ang-shu*, 54 (*Shih-huo chih*, 4), p. 1*a*.

Under the T'ang there were 18 salt pools (*ch'ih*) and 640 salt wells (*yen-ching*), all of which were under the control of the Department of Public Revenue. In the two counties An-i and Chieh-hsien in P'u-chou were five pools known collectively as the two pools (*liang-ch'ih*) from which 10,000 *hu* of salt were obtained annually. From this the capital was supplied. In Wu-yüan county of Yen-chou there were the Wu-ch'ih, Pai-ch'ih, Wa-ch'ih, and Hsi-hsiang ch'ih pools. In Ling-chou were the Wen-ch'üan ch'ih, Liang-ching ch'ih, Ch'ang-wei ch'ih, Wu-ch'üan ch'ih, Hung-t'ao chih, Hui-lo ch'ih, and Hung-ching ch'ih pools. In Hui-chou there was the Ho-ch'ih pool. These three prefectures contributed hulled grain in place of salt. In the protectorate-general of An-pei there was the Hu-lo pool from which 14,000 *hu* of salt were obtained annually. From this were supplied the Chen-wu and T'ien-te armies.

In Ch'ien-chou there were 41 salt wells; in Ch'eng-chou and in Sui-chou single salt wells, and in Kuo-chou, Lang-chou, K'ai-chou, and T'ung-chou 123 salt wells. These were all controlled by the branch office of the Public Revenue Department in Shan-nan Hsi-tao. In Ch'iung-chou, Mei-chou and Chia-chou there were 13 salt wells which were controlled by the branch office of the Public Revenue Department in Chien-nan Hsi-ch'uan. In

Tzu-chou, Sui-chou, Mien-chou, Ho-chou, Ch'ang-chou, Yü-chou, Lü-chou, Tzu-chou, Jung-chou, and Ling-chou there were altogether 460 salt wells which were controlled by the branch office of the Public Revenue Department in Chien-nan Tung-ch'uan.

The armies of Yu-chou, Ta-t'ung, and Heng-ye had salt-producing military colonies (*yen-t'un*). Each colony had both workers and soldiers and produced annually 2800 *hu* of salt. The smaller colonies produced 1500 *hu*.

The prefectures which lay on the sea-coast were annually exempted from contributing the tax in grain (*tsu*), and produced instead 20,000 *hu* of salt which they paid in to the Court of Agriculture (*ssu-nung ssu*). The prefectures of Ch'ing-chou, Ch'u-chou, Hai-chou, Ts'ang-chou, Ti-chou, Hang-chou and Su-chou purchased commodities of high value and little bulk with their salt, and sent these to the Court of Agriculture.

3. *T'ung-tien, 10*

The following is extracted from *T'ung-tien*, 10, p. 59 *b–c*.

In the Ch'ang-tao county of Ch'eng-chou is one salt well. The petty officials (*chieh-chi*) have a system of rewards and fines. In the ten prefectures of the province of Shu (Szechuan), Ling, Mien-chou, etc., there are in all 90 salt wells, the annual allocated production from which is equivalent to 8058 strings of cash.

Prefecture	Wells	Annual allocation (strings of 1000 cash)
Ling-chou	1	2061
Mien-chou	4	292
Tzu-chou	28	1083
Lü-chou	5	1850
Jung-chou	13	400
Tzu-chou	—	717
Sui-chou	—	415
Lang-chou	—	1700
P'u-chou	—	207
Kuo-chou	—	26

In a year when there is an intercalary month, an additional month should be added to the allocation to be provided from the prefectures. Payment is to be made by the month. It is permitted for payment to be made partly in cash and partly in grain. If payment is made in silver the value of one ounce (*liang*) is fixed at the special standard of 200 (cash). The allocation should be paid to the officials in accordance with the total sum. Any deficiencies shall be levied equally on all the producer households (*tsao-hu*).

The above passage from *Hsin T'ang-shu*, 54, probably refers to a date in the ninth century, as do the materials from the *Ti-li chih* of the same work. The material from *T'ung-tien* refers to the latter part of Hsüan-tsung's reign (737–55). Comparison of the two lists shows a spectacular increase in the number of salt wells in Szechuan during the late eighth and early ninth centuries.

APPENDIX IV

1. TABLE OF MINTS PREVIOUS TO 845

Prefecture	Name of mint	Number of hearths	Date
Lo-yang	—	—	621[1]
Ping-chou	—	—	621
Yu-chou	—	—	621
I-chou	—	5[2]	621
Kuei-chou	—	—	623[3]
Chiang-chou	(a) Fen-yang	30	—[4]
	(b) T'ung-yüan	(35 after 769)	
Yang-chou	(a) Tan-yang	10	—[5]
	(b) Kuang-ling		
Hsüan-chou	(a) Yüan-ling	10	738[6]
	(b) Mei-ken		
Jun-chou	—	10	738[7]
O-chou	Feng-shan	10	—[8]
Wü-chou	(a) San-ho	10	—[9]
	(b) Fei-hu	(15 after 811)	
Teng-chou	—	5	—[10]
Ch'en-chou	Kuei-yang	5	—[11]
		(2 after 808)	
Yang-chou	—	3	—[12]
Ting-chou	—	1	—[13]
Jao-chou	Yung-p'ing	—	—[14]
Shang-chou	Lo-yüan	10	780[15]

2. TABLE OF MINTS ESTABLISHED IN 845

The identity of the mints established in 845 by the provincial governments is known only through the mint-marks of a single character by which their coins were distinguished. The table lists all those known from coins reproduced in numismatic works. Nos. 1–22 are found in the *Ch'üan shih*, 5, of Hsiao Ling-yü. The same marks with the addition of no. 23 are listed by the *Ch'ien lu* of Liang Shih-cheng, and with both nos. 23 and 24 in the *Ku-ch'ien Ta-tzu-tien* of Ting Fu-pao (1938).

Mark	Place	Mark	Place
1. Ching	Ch'ang-an	13. O	O-chou
2. Lo*	Lo-yang	14. P'ing	P'ing-chou
3. I*	I-chou (Ch'eng-tu)	15. Hsing	Hsing-yuan
4. Lan	Lan-t'ien	16. Liang	Liang-chou
5. Hsiang*	Hsiang-chou	17. Kuang	Kuang-chou
6. Ching*	Ching-chou	18. Tzu*	Tzu-chou
7. Yüeh*	Yüeh-chou	19. Fu*	Fu-chou
8. Hsüan*	Hsüan-chou	20. Tan	Tan-chou
9. Hung	Hung-chou	21. Kuei	Kuei-chou
10. T'an*	T'an-chou	22. Ch'ang*	Ch'ang-chou[1]
11. Yen*	Yen-chou	23. Yang*	Yang-chou
12. Jun	Jun-chou	24. Yung	Yung-chou

The marks designated with an asterisk are found also on iron coins.

APPENDIX V

1. THE COURSES OF THE CANALS

1. *The Pien Canal*

The Pien canal (Pien-ho, or Pien-ch'ü) was the general name for the great waterway which connected the Huang-ho with the Huai river. As we have seen above, this was the major route by which supplies from the south were transported to the capital and to the northern garrisons.

In general the river pattern of the region through which it flowed was roughly the same in T'ang times as it is today. The Huang-ho flowed into the Chih-li gulf north of the Shantung peninsula, although between Meng-chou and P'u-chou its channel lay to the north of the present one. The Huai river, too, flowed in its modern channel at least as far as Hsü-i, and in the same general direction thereafter, but the Hung-tse lake was far smaller than in recent centuries, and the mouth of the Huai further to the north, near that of the modern Kuan river.

The provision of waterways linking these two great rivers was a comparatively simple engineering problem. The region is for the most part flat with a gentle slope from north-west to south-east. The watershed between the two systems is very close to the southern bank of the Huang-ho and the whole of Ho-nan is drained by a dense network of tributary streams flowing south-eastwards into the Huai. Owing to this low and ill-defined watershed, the Huang-ho has often been diverted in times of flood into a course discharging into the sea to the south of the Shantung peninsula. During the whole of the period from 1194 until 1853, when it established its modern course, the Huang-ho followed such southern courses, and at times became a tributary of the Huai. In the great floods of 1937 it discharged into the Huai, while in the disaster of 1887 the Huang-ho flowed into the Huai and thence into the Yangtze near Yang-chou. All these courses formerly taken by the Huang-ho in flood were possible routes for waterways, with virtually no physical obstacles to be overcome. Much of the waterway, therefore, was simply a canalised and straightened river bed, and once the initial canalisation had been completed the only major problems were those of maintaining a sufficient head of water, especially during the dry winter months, and of dredging the channels, which rapidly silted up owing to the very gentle gradients and the heavy silt load washed off the loess-covered uplands of western Honan.

Only in the two end sections of the canal, at its junction with the Huang-ho, and on the stretch linking the Huai with the Yangtze, were any considerable engineering works needed.

At the junction with the Huang-ho (Ho-k'ou) was a great dyke which prevented the Huang-ho from flooding out the Pien canal. This was known, after Liang Jui, the great Sui engineer who built it, as the Liang-kung Yen, or simply as the Pien-k'ou yen. It was constructed in 587, although in T'ang times it was generally believed to have been the work of Yü-wen K'ai, who was in charge of building the Pien canal itself under the Sui emperor Yang-ti.

There is considerable confusion over the precise location of the entry of the Pien canal into the Huang-ho. During the latter half of the dynasty, the junction was in the county of Ho-yin, which was specially established in 735 as a local administrative unit to control the great granary and trans-shipment depot of the same name which had been set up as a part of P'ei Yao-ch'ing's reforms. This new county was formed from parts of the former Ssu-shui, Jung-tse and Wu-chih counties, and its county seat is usually said to have been slightly to the east of modern Kuang-wu. The junction of the canal was said to have been 20 *li* west of the county seat, and 50 *li* north-east of Ssu-shui county.

The sources dealing with the abortive attempt to construct a new junction in 726 tell us that Liu Tsung-ch'i blocked up the old mouth of the Pien canal at Ssu-shui and constructed a new entry through the Liang-kung yen dam further downstream in Jung-tse county. Unfortunately, it is not clear whether Ssu-shui refers to the name of the county or to the river from which it takes its name, a small southern tributary of the Huang-ho. Katō Shigeshi took it that it was the river which was in question, and that the canal joined the Huang-ho *via* the lower course of the Ssu-shui. If this is correct the channel would have followed roughly the line of the modern Lunghai railway.

However, it seems to me more likely that the entrance was further downstream. To the north of the Ssu-shui mouth, the south-eastern bank of the Huang-ho is backed by a ridge of hills rising to some 200

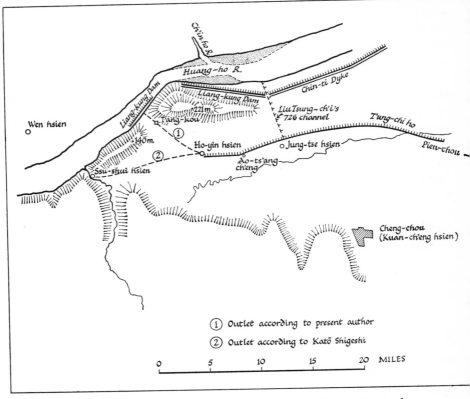

Map 9. The junction of the Pien canal with the Huang-ho.

metres, which would have been impassable by a canal. Prior to 735 the northern end of this ridge was certainly within the boundary of Jung-tse county, not Ssu-shui, and thus a junction here, which would have been physically possible, would not have fitted the information given in the texts. There is, however, one gap in this ridge, which would probably have fallen in Ssu-shui county, and provided a possible route. Moreover, to the present day this place has the very suggestive name of T'ang-kou—that is, T'ang canal. If this were not the entrance, and the junction was in fact north of the hills, it is difficult to see how the canal could have flowed immediately south of Ho-yin county town and then joined the Huang-ho 20 *li* to the east—even allowing for the very inaccurate use of directions which characterises medieval geographical texts, unless the traditional site of Ho-yin is wrong, and the town was in fact somewhere near the modern railway bridge over the Huang-ho at Yao-t'ou. In my opinion, however, the tradition is correct, and the information given corresponds neatly with an entrance near modern T'ang-kou (see map 9).

The new entrance made in 726 through the Liang-kuan dam by Liu Tsung-ch'i would then have followed roughly the line of the modern Huang-ho, joining the T'ang-period river somewhere opposite modern Wu-chih. We are told that this new entrance rapidly silted up, and if my identification is correct this would be accounted for by the extra silt load discharged just above this point by the Ch'in-ho. This stream drains a loess-covered area in southern Shansi, and even today its discharge forms great sandbanks in the Huang-ho. It is further significant that the old entrance at T'ang-kou in Ssu-shui county is upstream from the confluence of the Ch'in-ho, and would thus have been comparatively silt-free.

The name Liang-kung dam is used in reference to both the old and new junctions of the canal, and the dam must then have been of considerable length. It probably formed a strengthened western-most extension of the great Chin-ti dyke, which the Later Han had constructed from Jung-yang (that is, the area under discussion) to the sea coast along the southern bank of the Huang-ho. This dyke was 1000 *li* long, and provided with sluice gates every 10 *li* so that flood-water could flow back into the Huang-ho further downstream. By T'ang times the Huang-ho had shifted its course to the north and at Hua-chou the river bed was some 35 *li* north of the dyke.

The name Liang-kung-yen was used not only for the dam itself but also for the haul-overs constructed in it, on which vessels could be dragged up from the canal to the level of the river. Locks (*shui-cha*) were unknown in T'ang times, and first appeared in the mid-tenth century. There were also flood-gates which regulated the supply of water in the canal. The whole fell into disrepair early in the eighth century, and was rebuilt in 714 by Li Chieh. After this it was sometimes referred to as the New Dam (Hsin-yen) or Li Chieh's New Dam (Li Chieh hsin-yen). When the new opening in Jung-tse county was abandoned in 727, the old junction was again cleared out and repaired by Fan An-chi. After this there never seems to have been any attempt to move the entrance.

From Ho-yin county town the Pien canal flowed eastwards, for the most part in an artificial channel, passing north of Ao-ts'ang ch'eng in the west of Jung-tse county, through the south-western corner of Yüan-wu county and Yang-wu county, to the north of Chung-mu county and thus to Pien-chou, the modern K'ai-feng. This stretch of canal had been already established under the Later Han, although it had been often repaired and altered. It was known variously as the Pien-ho, Pien-ch'ü, T'ung-chi-ho, T'ung-chi-ch'ü, or as the Lang-tang-ch'ü (written in various orthographies). Pien-chou was a great route centre, where the north–south route from Ho-nan into Ho-pei crossed the east–west route to Shantung, and the north-west–south-east route of the Pien canal. Although the details are far from clear, canals joined Pien-chou with Ts'ai-chou and thus eventually with the Huai river to the south, and the Chan-ch'ü was built in 689 to link it with Ts'ao-chou and Yen-chou in western Shantung.

From Pien-chou to the Huai river there were a number of alternative waterways, and this fact has caused much confusion in the past. The principal routes were as follows:

1. *The Old Pien canal (Ku Pien-ho)*

This was a Han waterway, and possibly even older. It was employed spasmodically until Sui times when, because it was inconvenient for navigation, the new Pien canal or T'ung-chi-ch'ü was built under Yang-ti. In T'ang times it was abandoned and dried up, but it must have remained in reasonably good repair since in 781 Tu Yu advocated reopening it as an alternative to the new canal. This waterway is the one shown in error for the T'ung-chi-ch'ü in the T'ang volume of the *Li-tai yü-ti t'u*.

The canal left Pien-chou towards the south-west to Ch'en-liu county and Yung-ch'iu county, then turned north-eastward and passed 45 *li* north of Hsiang-i county, and then eastwards to K'ao-ch'eng county, Ning-ling county, Sung-ch'eng county and Yü-ch'eng county of Sung-chou. It then turned south-eastward again through Tang-shan and Hsiao-hsien counties to Hsü-chou where the canal joined the Ssu-shui. From this point onward the route followed the Ssu-shui to its junction with the Huai just above Huai-yin county town.

At Hsü-chou the canal passed through a gap in a southerly spur of the Shantung hills which reaches down into the centre of Ho-nan. Hsü-chou was a great and busy centre of trade, even in the days when the old Pien canal was in disuse.

2. *The Pien-ho (T'ung-chi ch'ü)*

This was the great canal constructed by Sui Yang-ti in 605 to replace the old Pien canal. The course followed by the new canal has been reconstructed by Aoyama Sadao, Ch'üan Han-sheng and more recently by Tsen Chung-mien, and the following agrees in the main with their conclusions.

From Ch'en-liu, a very important anchorage for shipping south-east of Pien-chou, the new canal branched off from the Old Pien canal, and followed the course of the Hui-chi-ho to Ch'i-hsien. It then cut across country to the east, passing to the north of the county towns of Sui-hsien, Ning-ling and Kuei-te. This is an extremely flat area with a very confused and much-braided drainage pattern, and the Sung scholar Shen Kua tells us that the silting of the canal gradually led to its being built up above the surrounding countryside. From Kuei-te the canal followed the course of the Sui-ho or one of the numerous parallel streams, to Yung-ch'eng county and then to the north of Su-chou through the southern gap in the central hill-belt of Ho-nan. It then followed the course of the suggestively named modern T'ang-ho, flowing to the north of a low ridge of upland to Hung-hsien. From this point the canal entered the Huai river. There are several possible routes by which it may have done so, either due south following the modern Ch'ung-ho to the west of the range of hills between Hung-hsien and the modern Hung-tse lake, or through the gap in these hills east of Hung-hsien, joining the Huai somewhere just above Yü-i. The problem is a very complicated one, since it is unknown just what the extent of the Hung-tse lake was in T'ang times, but I am inclined to support the second possibility on the evidence of place-names.

From Yü-i transport followed the Huai down to Lin-huai. This section of the route between Hung-hsien and Lin-huai was difficult and dangerous, and in the 740's Ch'i Huan constructed a new diversionary canal, the Kuang-chi-ch'ü, which went east from Hung-hsien and then skirted the north of the Hung-tse lake to join the Huai at Huai-yin. This new canal, however, was soon obstructed and was abandoned.

3. *The Kuo-ho*

This was a natural waterway which flowed into the Huai in north central Anhwei at Hao-chou. It joined the upper part of the Pien canal at Ch'en-liu, and was commonly used for navigation. The Japanese pilgrim Ennin appears to have travelled on this route in 845.

2. *The Shan-yang tu*

This canal formed the next link in the transport system, from the Huai to the Yangtze. It was already a very old waterway in T'ang times, and since it is still in existence, there is little question about its course. It ran almost due north and south between Ch'u-chou and Yang-chou, both great ports in T'ang times, and was connected with a network of waterways on the seaward side linking it with the innumerable salt works of Yen-ch'eng and Hai-ling. The junctions of the canal with the Huai and the Yangtze were protected by dams with haul-overs and sluices, and there were a number of haul-overs on the canal above Yang-chou.

3. *The Chiang-nan ho*

This too was an old-established waterway which linked Jun-chou on the Yangtze with Ch'ang-chou, Su-chou and Hang-chou. It followed much the same course as the modern canal, and was the chief artery of communication for this, the richest rice-producing area of T'ang China. Apart from some modification of the entry of the canal into the Yangtze in 737–8, no major changes seem to have been undertaken on this waterway in T'ang times.

4. *The Yung-chi ch'ü*

After Sui Yang-yi had constructed the new Pien canal in 605, in 608 he constructed yet another major waterway linking the Huang-ho with the vital strategic area around modern Peking. The establishment of its precise course is no easy matter, and the following account follows in the main that of Ts'en Chung-mien.

The canal joined the Huang-ho according to some accounts opposite Cheng-chou, according to others further downstream, in Wei county, the entrance being called Chi-men. The canal at first followed the Ch'i-shui (also called the Ch'ing-shui) which ran roughly parallel to the Huang-ho, and it is possible that there was more than one entrance. It passed through Chi-hsien and Li-yang counties and then turned north-east through Nei-huang, Kuan-t'ao, Yung-chi and Lin-ch'ing counties. At Wei-chou (probably at Ta-ming county) was a huge storage and transit depot. From Lin-ch'ing the canal went north to Pei-chou, where there was yet another storage depot known as the *Pei-k'u*, then through Ch'ing-yang, Wu-ch'eng, Chang-nan and Tung-kuang counties to Ts'ang-chou, and then north to Wen-an and Yung-ch'ing counties. The terminus of the canal is not known, but it must have been somewhere between modern Tientsin and Peking.

It is not clear how regularly this canal was used during the T'ang. It cannot have been altogether satisfactory, since it was supplemented by sea-transport during the early eighth century. There is no mention of any works on the canal, except at the supply depot of Wei-chou in 732. There is hardly any mention of the canal after the outbreak of the An Lu-shan rebellion.

NOTE: For a collection of source material on the courses of the canals see Aoyama Sadao, 'Tō-Sō Benga kō', *Tōhō gakuhō* (Tokyo), 2 (1931), pp. 1–49; Ch'üan Han-sheng, *T'ang-Sung ti-kuo yü yün-ho*, and Ts'en Chung-mien, *Huang-ho pien-ch'ien shih*, pp. 295–311. I am publishing shortly a detailed discussion of this question.

2. FRAGMENTS OF THE 'GRANARY STATUTES'

Translation of Niida's reconstruction of the *Statutes on Granaries and Storehouses* (*Ts'ang-k'u ling*).

Art. 1. The receipt of the tax in grain (*tsu*) is always to take place in the 'payment yard' (*shu-ch'ang*) in the presence of the officer of the granary and the officer responsible for transporting the tax. There shall be a minor official with an abacus to calculate the contents.

SOURCE: *TLT*, 19, p. 13 *b* (citing 719 *Statutes*). For a parallel compare the lost text of the Japanese Yōrō statutes cited by Niida, *Tōryō shūi*, p. 692, and the articles of Takigawa and Ueki quoted there.

Art. 2. The measures shall be made by the officials of the locality. The large ones are to measure 5 bushels (*hu*), the medium ones 3 bushels, and the small ones, 1 bushel. Their edges are to be bound with iron. They shall be officially tested for accuracy and certified and sealed. Only then may they be given out and used.

SOURCES: *TLT*, 19, p. 13 *b* (citing 719 *Statutes*), *Hsia-hou Yang suan-ching*, 1, p. 4 *a*.

Art. 3. In the case of converting (taxes) into equivalents in hulled rice, for 3 bushels of rice they shall pay as the equivalent in hulled rice 1 bushel and 4 pecks.

SOURCE: *Hsia-hou Yang suan-ching*, 1, p. 11 a.

Art. 4. The payments of grain for rations and salaries shall be provided from the regular granaries (*cheng-ts'ang*) in the district. In places where there are none, it should be reported to the Department of State, and they will be paid from nearby places. If there are no regular granaries nearby it will be permitted to provide the sums from the tax in cloth (*shui-wu*) or from goods collected by harmonious procurement (*ho-ti*) from the produce of military colonies, etc.

SOURCES: *THY*, 82, p. 1510; *TFYK*, 636, p. 11 b (both citing 737 *Statutes*).

Art. 5. All incomings and outgoings at the storehouses must be accompanied by vouchers, and these will be accounted for at the end of each quarter. In the cases where an order is received to make a payment, the matter should be referred to the Secretariat and then carried out. In the cases of the monthly salaries due to the officials, when authorisation reaches the responsible authorities (*so-yu*) they should forward it for review and then carry it into practice.

[*Commentary:* The former system was that the officials of the capital had guard-allowance (*fang-ke*), servant-allowance (*shu-p'u*), salaries (*feng-shih*), and miscellaneous expenses. In 732 there was an edict saying that, although the categories were very numerous, the amounts of materials were fixed beforehand, and this had led to the records becoming confused, because of which there had been abuses growing up. From that time onward they were to be unified, and all known as 'monthly salary' (*yüeh-feng*). If the amount of grain in store was the same as that which should make up the amount of salaries it should be reported, and thereafter become a permanent ordinance.]

They should also set up wooden tallies (*mu-chieh*) which should match with those of the office who should issue the goods in order to put in order their actions. They should subsequently match (the tallies) with the document of authorisation to make clear their reluctance to make issues or receive (goods).

[*Commentary:* The Department of Treasury established 110 wooden tallies. Twenty matched with those of the Court of Treasury, ten matched with the eastern capital, ten with the Chui-ch'êng palace, ten with the section of the Court of Treasury in attendance, ten with the section of the Department of Treasury in attendance and with the Department of Treasury at the capital, ten with the section of the Department of Treasury in attendance and with the eastern capital, twenty with the Court of Treasury's branch in the eastern capital, and twenty between the branch of the Department of Treasury in Lo-yang and that in the capital.]

SOURCE: *TLT*, 3, pp. 47*b*–48*b* (under-secretary of Department of Treasury). Cf. *TLT*, 19, pp. 17*b*–18*a* (Office for the Great Granary). 'The salaries of officials of the capital shall be paid out of the granaries in the capital.'.…'Whenever one issues public rations, one must receive an authority from the Department of State.' Both passages cite the 719 *Statutes*.

Art. 6. All millet may be kept in store for 9 years. Rice and miscellaneous grains may be stored for three years. [*Commentary:* When rice has been in store for 3 years a diminution of 1 *sheng* in each bushel (*hu*) is permissible. When it has been in store for 5 years or more 2 *sheng* (is permitted).]

SOURCE: *TLT*, 19 (office for the Great Granary) citing 719 *Statute*. Cf. *HTS*, 51, dealing with the Ever Normal Granaries (*ch'ang-p'ing ts'ang*), which reads 'Millet is stored for 9 years, rice for 5 years. In low-lying and damp localities, millet is stored for 5 years and rice for 3 years. All this was set out in the *Statutes*.…' Also cf. *STCSKS*, *Hou-chi*, 56, which has an almost identical passage.

Art. 7. All official slaves are to be granted government rations. Members of the category 'Official households' (*kuan-hu*) who come to do labour services in their turn of duty will also be treated in this way. These rations will be granted once per quarter. The rations will be 2 *sheng* per day for adults, 1 *sheng* 5 *ko* for adolescents and 6 *ko* for children. For those families who are retained on duty on a long-term basis, adults will be granted 3 *sheng* 5 *ko* daily, and adolescent males 2 *sheng*.

SOURCES: *TLT*, 3, p. 52*b* (under-secretary of Department of Granaries); *TLT*, 6, pp. 42*b*–43*a* (under-secretary of Department for Convicts). A passage in the *RGG* cites the *Granary Statutes* saying that the children in these categories were granted rations from the age of 4. Both *TLT* passages cite the 719 *Statutes*.

3. GRAIN RESERVES IN 749

The following three tables present the material contained in *T'ung-tien*, 12, pp. 70*c*–71*b*. Table A shows the stocks held in the great granaries in the metropolitan regions, table B the stocks brought in by 'harmonious purchase' (*ho-ti*), that is, state purchases of grain stocks made at a fair market price, and table C presents the reserves which were available in the various types of granary in the provinces.

TABLE A. *Metropolitan regions*

	shih
Pei-ts'ang[1]	6,616,840
T'ai-ts'ang	71,270
Han-chia-ts'ang	5,833,400
T'ai-yüan-ts'ang	28,140
Yung-feng-ts'ang	83,720
Lung-men-ts'ang	23,250
Total	12,656,620

NOTE: For the positions of these granaries see map 6, p. 85.

TABLE B. *Grain acquired by harmonious purchase*

	shih
Kuan-nei	509,347
Ho-tung	110,229
Ho-hsi	371,750
Lung-yu	148,104
Total	1,139,430

These stocks were at the immediate disposal of the central government, or of military forces dependent on the central power.

TABLE C. Provincial grain reserves in 749

Province	Total reserves	Cheng-ts'ang	I-ts'ang	Ch'ang-p'ing	Reserve per head of population (*shih*)
1. Kuan-nei	8,141,298	1,821,516 (23%)	5,946,212 (73%)	373,570 (4%)	1·75
2. Ho-pei	21,029,924	1,821,546* (9%)	17,544,100 (83%)	1,663,778 (8%)	2·05
3. Ho-tung	11,434,176	3,589,180 (32%)	7,309,610 (64%)	535,386 (4%)	3·07
4. Ho-hsi	1,090,468	702,065 (65%)	388,403 (35%)	—	—
5. Lung-yu	715,664	372,780 (52%)	300,934 (42%)	42,850 (6%)	2·27
6. Chien-nan	2,091,908	223,940 (11%)	1,797,228 (86%)	79,740 (3%)	0·5
7. Shan-nan	3,015,550	143,882 (5%)	2,871,668 (95%)	—	1·2+†
8. Ho-nan	22,527,641	5,825,414 (26%)	15,429,763 (69%)	1,212,464 (5%)	1·98
9. Huai-nan	5,605,276	683,252 (12%)	4,840,872 (86%)	81,152 (2%)	2·46
10. Chiang-nan	7,767,285	978,825 (13%)	6,739,270 (86%)	49,190 (1%)	0·75
Whole empire	96,062,220‡	16,167,400§	63,177,660	4,602,220	

NOTES

* This figure is suspiciously similar to that for Kuan-nei.
† The figure for the Ch'ang-p'ing ts'ang in Shan-nan is missing, and the average reserve was presumably higher.
‡ This is the figure given by Tu Yu, *TT*, 12, p. 70c. It includes reserves in certain centrally controlled granaries (see table 2). There is thus some discrepancy between this total and that of the three types of provincial granaries.
§ Tu Yu, *TT*, 12, p. 71c, gives the total as 42,126,184 *shih*. This is obviously corrupt.

POSTCRIPT TO THE SECOND EDITION

In the ten years which have elapsed since the completion of this book in 1959 both the T'ang period as a whole and its economic aspects in particular have continued to attract much scholarly attention. So much so that it would require a disproportionately lengthy bibliographical note to discuss fully all this new work and the many issues which have been raised. In this postscript I wish only to draw the reader's attention to the most important items in this new literature, and to those fields where it seems to me that considerable advances have been made. For convenience, I follow roughly the topical order of my chapter headings.

1. *The Land Problem*

The problem of land tenure and ownership, largely because of its broader implications for the nature of society as a whole, has always attracted a large share of attention from Chinese and Japanese scholars, and has continued to do so.

Almost all of the Chinese work in this field has been concerned with the long-standing and still unresolved controversies over the nature of the *chün-t'ien* and other land systems, their relationship to 'feudal society', and their inter-relationship with the *tsu-yung-tiao* tax system and the *fu-ping* militia organisation. Two symposium volumes have reprinted a very large number of articles from these almost exclusively theoretical controversies:

Li-shih yen-chiu pien-chi pu (eds.). *Chung-kuo li-tai t'u-ti chih-tu wen-t'i t'ao-lun chi* (Peking, 1957).

Nank'ai Ta-hsüeh Li-shih-hsi Chung-kuo ku-tai-shih chiao-yen-tsu (eds.). *Chung-kuo feng-chien she-hui t'u-ti suo-yu-chih hsing-shih wen-t'i t'ao-lun chi* (2 vols, Peking, 1962).

The second of these includes (pp. 725 f.) a full bibliography of articles connected with this topic published in China between 1949 and 1962. Very few of them are of any historical interest, largely because only a handful of Chinese historians are aware of the recent discoveries among the Tunhuang and Turfan manuscripts, or of recent Japanese scholarly work. By far the most important single Chinese contribution to this field is the excellent and provocative book,

Ho Ch'ang-chün. *Han-T'ang-chien feng-chien t'u-ti suo-yu-chih hsing-shih yen-chiu* (Shanghai, 1964)

which incorporates and supersedes the author's earlier book listed in the bibliography. It is important for the way in which it places the *chün-t'ien* system in its historical context as the last of a series of land policies designed

194

to maintain firm state control over the use of land, and also in its stress upon the close inter-relationship between these land policies and the state's military institutions, in particular with the *fu-ping* system. It also has an interesting discussion of the 'fiefs of maintenance' (*shih-shih-feng*) of the nobility and their place in the T'ang land and tax system. The author uses some of the older Tunhuang studies.

From Taiwan has come a useful general survey of the land, taxation and peasant problems:

Wu Chang-chüan. *T'ang-tai nung-min wen-t'i yen-chiu* (Taipei, 1963) which is generally traditional and orthodox in its approach, and which, like the work from mainland China, is very out of date in its secondary literature.

Most of the significant new work in this field has continued to come from Japan. A very interesting overall view of the problems which pre-occupy Japanese specialists on the land problem may be gained from the published transcript of a conference held at the Tōyō bunka kenkyūjo, Tokyo, in late 1963:

Zadankai. 'Kindensei wo dō miru ka?'. *Tōyō bunka*, 37 (1964), pp. 1–70. This also includes (pp. 55 f.) a very full and convenient bibliography of the literature on the subject in all languages.

There have been two excellent general surveys of the earlier pre-T'ang stages of development of the *chün-t'ien* system:

Hori Toshikazu. 'Hoku-chō no kinden-hōki wo meguru shomondai'. *Tōyō bunka kenkyūjo kiyō*, 28 (1963), pp. 45–131 which gives a very precise description of the successive forms of the system, and

Ikeda On. 'Kindensei—Roku-seiki chūyō ni okeru kindensei wo megutte'. *Kodaishi kōza*, 8, *Kodai no tochi seido* (1963), pp. 137–74, which is notable not only for an extremely lucid and imaginative account of the system as a whole, but for some original ideas on the environmental factors which helped to shape it. The same author has also contributed an equally good general account of the T'ang *chün-t'ien* system:

Ikeda On. 'Tōdai kindensei wo megutte'. *Hōseishi kenkyū*, 14 (1964), pp. 49–71.

An extremely detailed and wide-ranging study of the *chün-t'ien* and related problems has very recently been published by

Nishimura Genyū. *Chūgoku keizaishi kenkyū—Kinden-seido hen* (Kyoto, 1968) which is based on a close and extremely minute study of the documents from Tunhuang and Turfan dealing with land allocation, taxation and *corvée*. This replaces the author's earlier study of the *chün-t'ien* documents listed in the bibliography.

Nishijima Sadao's equally meticulous and detailed earlier article in *Tonkō Torohan shakai-keizai shiryō*, I (1959) was criticised in two excellent review articles:

Miyazaki Ichisada. 'Torufan hakken dendo monjo no seishitsu ni tsuite'.

Shirin, 43, III (1960), pp. 144–53.

Yang Lien-sheng. 'Ryūkoku daigaku shozō no Saiiki monjo to Tōdai no kindensei'. *Shirin*, 45, I (1962), pp. 28–34

and also in a very detailed review by Ikeda On in *Shigaku Zasshi* 69, VIII (1960), pp. 58–86. It has been recently incorporated in an extended, revised and corrected form in

Nishijima Sadao. *Chūgoku keizaishi kenkyū* (Tokyo, 1966).

(The article in question is in *ibid.* pp. 431–726.)

In general the discussion of the *chün-t'ien* system has continued to revolve around the evidence from Tunhuang and Turfan, and many points of difference exist over the detailed interpretation of the evidence, and particularly over how far these documents represent a situation typical for China as a whole. There has also been some controversy over whether the Turfan documents can be taken as showing that a form of the *chün-t'ien* system was already in force in the Kao-ch'ang kingdom centred on Turfan even before the T'ang conquest.

But by far the most interesting new development has been in the study of tenancy. This new discussion has arisen from the discovery by an archaeological team from the Sinkiang Provincial Museum in 1957 of some new tenancy agreement documents from a site in the Astana cemetery at Turfan. These documents were published in *Wen-wu* 1960, 6, pp. 13–21, and more fully in

Wu Chen. 'Chieh-shao pa-chien Kao-ch'ang ch'i-yüeh'. *Wen-wu*, 1962, 7/8, pp. 76–82.

They immediately caught the attention of Japanese scholars, in particular Niida Noboru, who dealt with them in two articles later included in his collected studies

Niida Noboru. 'Torohan hakken no Tōdai soden-monjo no ni keitai'. *Chūgoku hōseishi kenkyū: Dorei nōdo hō, Kazoku sonraku hō* (1961), pp. 249–60.

'Torohan hakken no Kōshō-koku oyobi Tōdai soden-monjo'. *Chūgoku hōseishi kenkyū: Hō to dōtoku, Hō to kanshū* (1963), pp. 627–46.

A brilliant summary of recent work on tenancy, superseding several earlier studies by the same author, is

Hori Toshikazu. 'Saiiki monjo yori mitaru Tōdai no soden-sei—toku ni kindensei oyobi sono hōkai-katei to kanren shite'. *Meiji daigaku jimbunkagaku kenkyūjo kiyō*, 5 (1966), pp. 1–47.

This demonstrates clearly that there was a radical change in the form and nature of tenancy contracts between the late seventh and late ninth centuries, reflecting a transition from a form of tenancy which was essentially a short-term purely economic agreement between equals, to semi-permanent contracts on much harsher terms, which imply a measure of personal subordination of the tenant to the land-owner, and thus give a clue to the beginnings of the very harsh semi-servile forms of tenancy characteristic of the Sung period.

A related topic which has been reopened very profitably is that of runaway and vagrant households, and migrant households settled as unregistered squatters or tenants. A well-documented general study of the problem of such '*k'o-hu*', but totally lacking in reference to the many earlier contributions to the subject is

Chang Tse-hsien. 'T'ang-tai ti k'o-hu'. *Li-shih lun-ts'ung*, 1 (1964), pp. 177–94.

The earliest attempts to re-register and resettle such families, put into effect following a memorial by Li Chiao in 703 under the Empress Wu, are discussed in

T'ang Chang-ju. 'Kuan yü Wu Tse-t'ien t'ung-chih mo-nien ti fou-t'ao-hu'. *Li-shih yen-chiu*, 1961, 6, pp. 90–5.

The most important contributions to this subject, however, have been a series of articles by Nakagawa Manabu which deal with every aspect of the *k'o-hu* and of the government policies directed towards them.

Nakagawa Manabu. 'Tōdai ni okeru kinden-hō soyōchō-hō no hampuku kōfu to kakko seisaku'. *Hitotsubashi kenkyū*, 90 (1962), pp. 1–12.

'Tōdai no tōko, fuko, kyakko ni kansuru oboegaki'. *Hitotsubashi ronsō*, 50, III (1963), pp. 339–46.

'Tō Sō no kyakko ni kansuru shokenkyū'. *Tōyō gakuhō*, 46, II (1963), pp. 97–110.

These give an overall view of the problem, which is presented as developing into the *k'o-hu* system of bound tenants as operating in Sung times. The second of these studies makes a very important point in showing how the areas in which the problem of displaced households was most severe changed during the course of the dynasty. In two later articles he deals with the occupation by *k'o-hu* of lands left vacant by refugee households, and with the way in which *k'o-hu* migrant households either became client households under the protection of great families or became tenant farmers, labourers or hired hands on great estates:

Nakagawa Manabu. 'Tōdai no kyakko ni yoru tōkiden no hoyū'. *Hitotsubashi ronsō*, 53, I (1965), pp. 72–90.

'Tōdai no "ryūyō" ni tsuite'. *Tōyōshi kenkyū*, 26, II (1967), pp. 1–19.

II. *Direct Taxation*

A great deal has also appeared in this field. Several substantial studies have dealt with the problem of population registration, which was of fundamental importance as the basis of the early T'ang taxation system.

Pulleyblank E. G. 'Registration of population in China in the Sui and T'ang periods'. *Journal of Economic and Social History of the Orient*, 4 (1961), pp. 289–301

deals with the surviving census figures from early T'ang times. He suggests that the great difference between the 'old' figures from 634–43 included in *Chiu T'ang-shu* and those for 742 are to be attributed to administrative factors, and claims that the 'old' figures for southern China were derived from the household registers of the Southern Ch'en dynasty as taken over by the Sui. He believes that the early T'ang census figures show clearly that the *chün-t'ien* and *tsu-yung-tiao* systems were never put into general effect. He also deals with the regional differences in the rate of increase in registered population between 726 and 742, which he connects with the re-registration begun under Yü-wen Jung after 720. He also denies the extreme theory put forward by Hino Kaisaburō that the T'ang population figures were grossly under-recorded, and that actual population was perhaps some 20,000,000 households or 140,000,000 persons.

Hino has also published regional studies of the population statistics for the 'old' census (which he dates 639) and for 742:

> Hino Kaisaburō. 'Dai-Tō Tempō-gannen no kokō-tōkei no chiiki-teki kōsatsu'. *Shirin*, 42, IV (1959), pp. 61–84.
>
> 'Tō Jōgan jūsannen no kokō-tōkei no chiiki-teki kōsatsu'. *Tōyō shigaku*, 24 (1961), pp. 1–24.

Population statistics and re-registration problems are also dealt with in the studies by Nakagawa Manabu mentioned above.

Two studies have dealt with the quotas of silk and hemp cloth collected under the *tsu-yunh-tiao* tax system:

> Hino Kaisaburō. 'Tōdai yōchō no fuken kachō-kaku to "hiki-tan" sei'. *Hōseishi kenkyū*, 15 (1965), pp. 31–63.
>
> Suzuki Shun. 'Hiki to tan'. *Ishida Hakase kōshu-kinen Tōyōshi ronsō* (1965), pp. 291–6.

A discussion of the various local differences in the medium of payment for the *tiao* tax is in

> Hino Kaisaburō. 'Tō no fuekiryō ni okeru chō no shokumoku'. *Suzuki Shun Kyōju kanreki-kinen Tōyōshi ronsō* (1964), pp. 493–509.

A useful index to the items contributed by each prefecture as tribute (*kung*) as listed in *Hsin T'ang-shu*, with a painstaking attempt to identify each item is in

> Schafer E. H., and Wallacker B. E. 'Local tribute products of the T'ang dynasty'. *Journal of Oriental Studies*, 4, pp. 213–48 (1959).

Two further studies by Hino Kaisaburō set out the basis for graduated tax-assessments on resident households (*t'u-hu*) under the early T'ang system:

> Mino Kaisaburō. 'Tōdai Tempō-izen ni okeru dogo no taishō-shisan'. *Tōhōgaku*, 17 (1958), pp. 52–62

and deal with the supplementary levies collected under the *tsu-yung-tiao* system:

> Hino Kaisaburō. 'Tōdai soyōchō-sei ka no kōchō ni tsuite'. *Tōyō gakuhō*, 45, II (1962), pp. 1–38.

On the extremely important change from the *tsu-yung-tiao* to the *liang-shui* system there have been a number of studies from different points of view. A general account of the various theories on the problem is to be found in

> Nakagawa Manabu. 'Tōdai gohanki no shomondai'. *Shakai keizai shigaku*, 31, 1/5 (1966), pp.   –   .

Perhaps the most lucid and detailed general statement of the underlying principles of the new system are to be found in two excellent articles by Hino Kaisaburō:

Hino Kaisaburō. 'Ryōzeihō no kihonteki yon gensoku'. *Hōseishi kenkyū*, 11 (1960), pp. 40–77

which stresses the political effects of the new system, and

'Yō En no Ryōzeihō no genkyo gensoku to sensū, sennō gensoku'. *Shien* (Kyūshū), 84 (1961), pp. 1–37

which deals with the principle of taxation of all residents and the assessment of taxes in cash.

A further detailed study by the same author

'Tōdai ryōzeihō ka ni okeru taishō-shisan to fuzei no keiretsu' *Tōyō gakuhō*, 41, IV (1959), pp. 1–40

deals in detail with the new basis for tax assessments on property, and particularly with the differences between the assessments on those owning land and those on merchants and city dwellers. He shows how under the Wu-tai and Sung the taxation of merchants and urban dwellers was gradually taken out of the *liang-shui* system, which became the standard system of taxation only for the rural population.

Hino Kaisaburō. 'Ryōzeihō seiritsu no yurai to Taireki no kazei, shūzei'. *Tōyōshigaku*, 29 (1966)

deals with the origins of the *Liang-shui* system in the summer and autumn taxes imposed in the metropolitan district during Tai-tsung's reign. Nakagawa Manabu has also dealt with the origins of the *liang-shui* and the role played in this by the need to regularise the taxable position of the *k'o-hu*:

Nakagawa Manabu. 'So yōchō-hō kara ryōzeihō e no tenkanki ni okeru seidoteki kyakko no sozei-futan'. *Hitotsubashi kenkyū nempō*; '*Keizaigaku kenkyū*', 10 (1965).

'Yō En no zaisei-kaikaku no kichō ni tsuite'. *Hitotsubashi ronsō*, 53, V (1965), pp. 52–72.

From a quite different viewpoint, Koga Noboru continued with his interesting attempt to define regional variations in the system of taxation related to economic conditions. This has led him to the belief that the *Liang-shui* system was essentially a scheme designed to be applicable to the conditions of the rice and wheat producing areas of the Yangtse and Huai valleys.

Koga Noboru. 'Kazei shūzei no genryū'. *Tōyōshi kenkyū*, 19, III (1960), pp. 53–76

shows the intimate connection between the twice yearly pattern of tax collection and the harvest periods of various crops, and points out similarities with the practise under the pre-T'ang southern dynasties. This article also contains some very interesting suggestions about the changes in crops, in particular about the spread of sericulture to southern and central China during the early ninth century. His earlier study

'Chūgoku tamosaku nōhō no seiritsu'. *Kodaigaku*, 8, III (1959), pp. 240–57

dealt with another aspect of this general development of agrarian technique, the origin of multiple cropping of grain crops. Casting some doubts on the theory that during the T'ang it was common in northern China to get three crops of millet and wheat from a field in three years, he sees the origin of multiple cropping in the growth of wheat and rice on the same lands in the Yangtse valley, a technique which he considers to have been the foundation of the region's prosperity in late T'ang times. In a later study,

Koga Noboru. 'Tōdai ryōzei sangen kō'. *Tōyō gakuhō*, 44, I (1961), pp. 77–94,

he draws attention to the very wide variation in the actual system of tax collection in different regions under the *liang-shui* system, and claims that in northern China there were in fact three annual collections, in the sixth, ninth and eleventh months, as against the standard two annual collections in southern and central China.

III. *State Monopolies and Taxes on Trade*

Little new work has appeared on state monopolies. An excellent and extremely detailed account in English of the salt monopoly down to 780 is to be found in

Hino Kaisaburō. 'Government Monopoly on Salt in T'ang in the period before the enforcement of the Liang-shui fa'. *Memoirs of the Research Department of the Toyo Bunko*, 22 (1963), pp. 1–55

which is much fuller and more helpful than the Japanese article by the author published previously:

'Ryōzeihō-izen ni okeru Tō no kakuen hō'. *Shakai keizai shigaku*, 26, II (1960), pp. 171–98.

The production of salt from salt-wells in T'ang times is discussed in

Koga Noboru. 'Tōdai sei-en kō'. *Shikan*, 53 (1958), pp. 35–46

'Zoku Tōdai sei-en kō—futatabi Shin Tōsho "Shokkashi" no kiji ni tsuite'. *Shikan*, 57/58 (1960), pp. 117–29

which includes a discussion of the material translated above in Appendix III, 2 (pp. 177 ff.).

On the salt merchants through whom the system was put into effect see

Yokoyama Hiroo. 'Tōdai no enshō'. *Shirin*, 43 (1960), pp. 501–18.

On the liquor monopoly, I should mention a useful study which I omitted from my bibliography:

Marugame Kinsaku. 'Tōdai no sake no sembai'. *Tōyō gakuhō*, 40 (1957), pp. 286–332.

Much more important than the work on monopolies have been several recent studies on merchants, trade and state taxation of and intervention in trade, which have revived interest in a field where virtually nothing had appeared since the classic studies of Katō Shigeru in the pre-war period. I myself have published two studies which give a general survey of these fields:

Twitchett, Denis. 'The T'ang market system'. *Asia Major* (n.s.), 12, II (1966), pp. 202-48

'Merchant, Trade and Government in Late T'ang'. *Asia Major* (n.s.),

14, I (1968), pp. 63–95.

The question of the market system has also been dealt with by Satō Taketoshi, in an article which also attempts to revise the conception of the 'guilds' (*hang*) in this period:

Satō Taketoshi. 'Tōdai no shi-sei to "kō"—toku ni Chōan wo chūshin to shite'. *Tōyōshi kenkyū*, 25, III (1967), pp. 32–59.

A brief study on rural periodical markets established at canal haulovers and river crossings has also appeared:

Hino Kaisaburō. 'Tōdai entai-sōshi no hattatsu'. *Tōhōgaku*, 33 (1967), pp. 44–53

and a great deal of material relevant to the T'ang is included in the brilliant new book on Sung trade

Shiba Yoshinobu. *Sōdai shōgyōshi kenkyū* (Tokyo, 1968).

The related question of government regulation of prices has been dealt with, largely on the basis of fragmentary price lists among the Otani manuscripts, first by Niida, and more recently in a most important study

Ikeda On. 'Chūgoku kodai bukka no ichi kōsatsu'. *Shigaku zasshi*, 77, I (1968), pp. 1–45; 77, II (1968), pp. 45–64.

Taxes on commerce have been dealt with by

Hino Kaisaburō. 'Tōdai shōzei kō'. *Shakai keizai shigaku*, 31 (1965), pp. 1–28

and in a broader context, taking in a very lucid description of the system of customs barriers (*kuan*), restrictions upon travel, and transit tolls in

Aoyama Sadao. '*Tō-Sō jidai no kōtsū to chishi chizu no kenkyū* (Tokyo, 1963).

IV. Currency and Credit

In the field of monetary policy I should draw attention to two important omissions from my bibliography,

P'eng Hsin-wei. *Chung-kuo huo-pi shih* (Shanghai, 1958)

now the standard work on the history of the Chinese coinage, which deals at length with the T'ang, and

Ch'üan Han-sheng. 'Chung-ku tzu-jan ching-chi'. *CYYY*, 10 (1948), pp. 75–176

which remains the standard account of the development towards a more widespread use of money in place of cloth and other forms of 'commodity money'. I myself have also studied the changes in government monetary policy necessitated by the virtual independence of the north-eastern provinces after 755, and the consequent loss of revenues previously paid in silk cloth in

Twitchett, Denis. 'Provincial Autonomy and Central Finance in Late T'ang'. *Asia Major* (n.s.), 11, II (1965), pp. 211–32.

Recently two articles have appeared dealing with the use of Uighur and Persian coinage during the T'ang, ample evidence of which has been produced in recent years by Chinese excavations both in Ch'ang-an and in Central Asia:

Hino Kaisaburō. 'Tōdai no Kaikotsu-sen'. *Tōhōgaku*, 30 (1965), pp. 38–49

'Tōdai no Hashi-sen ni tsuite'. *Ishida Hakase Koshu kinen Tōyōshi ronsō* (1965), pp. 367–81.

The same author has also published a new study of the *kuei-fang*, proto-banks, of Ch'ang-an:

'Tōdai no "kifuho" to "kibō"—Tōdai miyako Chōan no kinyūgyōsha'. *Tōyō shigaku*, 23 (1961), pp. 1–40.

v. *The Transportation System*

In the field of transportation and communications, by far the most important work is the excellent volume

Aoyama Sadao. '*Tō-Sō jidai no kōtsū to chishi chizu no kenkyū* (Tokyo, 1963)

which reprints, with extensive revisions, the author's earlier works on the canal system, and also includes the first adequate account of the T'ang road network and a very good study of the postal relay system.

Hino Kaisaburō. 'Tōdai entai-sōshi no hattatsu'. *Tōhōgaku*, 33 (1967), pp. 44–53

gives some additional details on the haulovers used on the canals before the development of locks, and on their importance as minor centres of trade.

A number of studies have developed the related field of grain supplies for the armed forces:

Kikuno Kyōko. 'Tōdai no wa-chō'. *Ochanomizu shigaku*, 1 (1957), pp. 1–15

deals somewhat summarily with the 'harmonious procurement' of grain (*ho-ti*), while

Hino Kaisaburō. 'Sozoku to gunryō'. *Tōyō shigaku*, 25 (1962), pp. 1–30
'Tempō-matsu izen ni okeru Tō no gunryō-den'. *Tōyōshi kenkyū*, 21 (1962), pp. 27–53

deal with the supply of grain to the forces in the early T'ang period through taxation in grain, and through direct cultivation on special lands, especially military colonies (*t'un-t'ien*, *ying-t'ien*).

vi. *The Financial Administration*

This field has attracted comparatively little detailed attention, although it is in fact here, in the placing of financial policy in a close and meaningful relationship with government as a whole, and with the detailed course of political history, that the most solid progress may be expected in the immediate future.

In my original account of the financial machinery of early T'ang times I should have drawn attention to the fact that my interpretation of the inter-relationships between the various offices concerned differs somewhat from that given by Yen Keng-wang in an excellent and perceptive study on the central ministries of early T'ang:

Yen Keng-wang. 'Lun T'ang-tai Shang-shu-sheng chih chih-ch'üan yü ti-wei'. *CYYY*, 24 (1953), pp. 1–68.

Yen points out that not only did the Court of Treasury and Court of Agriculture seem to have been more active and more powerful than the comparable sub-sections of the Board of Finance, but that their personnel were also far more numerous. Yen's main contention is that the Six Boards under the Department of State were essentially policy-making offices, while the Nine Courts and the various Directorates also came under the Department of State, but functioned purely as executive organs, implementing policies decided by the Six Boards. I am not entirely convinced by his evidence, and I suspect that the actual situation was far less tidy and more complicated than this. But the subject is obscure, and the scanty evidence admits of varying interpretations.

Yen's other important contribution is his clear demonstration of the changes in the relationships between the Department of State and the other central ministries, the Secretariat and Chancellery, during the course of the T'ang dynasty. This subject is dealt with in more detail in an important study

Sun Kuo-t'ung. 'T'ang-tai San-sheng-chih chih fa-chan yen-chiu'. *Hsin-ya Hsüeh-pao*, 3, 1 (1957/8), pp. 17–121

and also by the general work on T'ang administrative history

Tsuchiyama Jisaburō. *Tōdai sei-ji seido no kenkyū* (Tokyo, 1967)

Most of the studies on the *Chün-t'ien* and taxation systems listed above are concerned with the everyday functioning of local administration, especially as evidenced by the Tunhuang and Turfan manuscripts. In particular the books of Nishimura Genyū and Nishijima Sadao probe more deeply into local administrative procedures than do any studies of a period before the nineteenth century. Very important new material in the shape of registers of official business from the early eighth century preserved in the Otani collection are edited and printed in

Ogasawara Senshū. 'Torohan shutsudo no Tōdai kanchō-kiroku monjo ni shū'. *Ryūkoku Shidan*, 51 (1963), pp. 1–15.

I have myself published a study of local governmental finances based upon this and other Tunhuang and Turfan manuscript material:

Twitchett, Denis. 'Local financial administration in early T'ang'. *Asia Major* (n.s.), 15, 11 (1969).

Two studies of specific aspects of local finance are worth mentioning:

Yokoyama Hiroo. 'Tōdai zokusenko ni tsuite'. *Tōyōshi kenkyū*, 17, 11 (1958), pp. 74–88

which gives a good account of the development of the system of *cho-ch'ien* (funds entrusted to designated households, often merchants, for investment at interest as a source of revenue for local expenditures) and

Okamura Ikuzō. 'Tōdai kōkai no hō to seido.' *Hōgaku Zasshi*, 9, 3/4 (1963), pp. 38–51

which is a somewhat less satisfactory account of the lands and funds known as *kung-chieh-t'ien* and *kung-chieh-ch'ien* which were allocated to every official post as a sort of endowment meant to produce an income to defray office expenses.

On the period after the An Lu-shan rebellion, much attention is paid to the broader implications of the financial reforms of Yang Yen. Much relevant material will be found in the various studies listed above under direct taxation, those of Nakagawa Manabu and Hino Kaisaburō being particularly notable for their attention to the relationship of these reforms with contemporary political and administrative problems.

I have myself dealt with the financial policies of the years following Yang Yen's reform in two studies:

Twitchett, Denis. 'Lu Chih (754-805) Imperial Adviser and Court Official'. In Twitchett and Wright (eds) *Confucian Personalities* (Stanford, 1962), pp. 84–122.

'Provincial Autonomy and Central Finance in Late T'ang'. *Asia Major* (n.s.), 11, II (1965), pp. 211–32.

The latter raises a number of general points connected with the growth of provincial power at the expense of the central government, and in particular attempts to assess the results of the loss of central control over Ho-pei, formerly one of the richest and most productive sources of revenue.

Hino Kaisaburō, in a very important study of this question

Hino Kaisaburō. 'Hanchin taisei to choku-zoku Shū'. *Tōyō gakuhō*, 43, IV (1961), pp. 1–36

recognises the essentially political nature of Yang Yen's reform, and assesses the importance to the central government of those prefectures which remained under their direct administrative control in their struggle with the governors of the semi-autonomous provinces.

Matsui Shūichi. 'Hai ki no zeisei kaikaku ni tsuite'. *Shigaku ɀasshi*, 76, VII (1967), pp. 1–24

also deals with the financial reforms carried out under the Chief Minister P'ei Chi in the early years of Hsien-tsung's reign, in an attempt to reduce the revenues of the provinces and increase those of the central government, and at the same time to solve the problem of increasing incidence of taxation caused by a long period of deflation.

The same author has also made two interesting attempts to deal with the local situation and specific social and administrative problems in two important provinces, Lu-lung (around Peking) in

'Roryū hanchin kō'. *Shigaku ɀasshi*, 68 (1959), pp. 1397–432

and Szechuan where, although local circumstances were just as favourable as in Lu-lung for the development of a powerful autonomous province, in fact the region remained a centre of strong support for the dynasty.

'Tōdai zenhanki no Shisen—ritsuryōsei shihai to gōzoku-sō no kankei wo chūshin to shite'. *Shigaku ɀasshi*, 71, IX (1962), pp. 1–37.

'Tōdai gohanki no Shisen—kanryō shihai to dogō-sō no shutsugen wo chūshin to shite'. *Shigaku ɀasshi*, 73, X (1964), pp. 46–88.

Regarding the changes in the financial organs of the central government, Hino's article on the salt monopoly gives an excellent account of the early stages of the most important of the special commissions which played such an important role.

Tonami Mamoru. 'Sanshishi no seiritsu ni tsuite'. *Shirin*, 44, IV (1961),
   pp. 125–50
gives an extremely lucid account of the development of these special
commissions during the late T'ang, with some useful material on the
recruitment of their personnel, and shows how these new commissions
were combined loosely to form the *San-ssu*, an informal combination of
the Board of Finance, Salt and Iron Commission, and Department of Public
Revenue, which gradually under the Wu-tai and Sung was formalised into
a new-style Finance Ministry.

NOTES

CHAPTER I

PAGE I

1 *Code*, 12, art. 14, quotes as authority for this the well-known *locus classicus* in *Li-chi*, 3: 'The *Rites* say: "Lands are not to be sold", "One receives them from the state and hence one may not sell them privately for oneself".' (In fact the second part of the quotation is not part of the text of the classic at all, but comes from Cheng Hsüan's commentary.) An even more commonly quoted *locus classicus* is the passage in the *Shih-ching* 'Under the whole heaven every spot is the sovereign's ground' (Legge, *Chinese Classics*, 2, p. 228; cf. the quotation of this by *Meng tzu, ibid.* 4, p. 360).

2 The most important account of the influence of the institutions of the Northern Dynasties upon those of the T'ang is that given by Ch'en Yin-k'o, *Sui-T'ang chih-tu yüan-yüan lüeh-lun kao* (1944). The *chün-t'ien* system itself has been the subject of a large and growing literature, the most important items of which are listed in the bibliography. In western languages there is a completely traditional and now obsolete view in Chen Huan-chang, *The economic principles of Confucius and his school* (1911), II, pp. 510–23, and a somewhat more sophisticated account by Maspero, 'Les régimes fonciers en Chine, des origines aux temps modernes', first published in *Recueil de la Société Jean Bodin*, tome 2 (1937), and reprinted in *Mélanges posthumes sur les religions et l'histoire de la Chine* (1950), III, pp. 147–92, and in a revised version of the *Société Jean Bodin* volume (1959) with an additional note by J. Gernet, bringing in some more up-to-date views. In China and more especially Japan there have been two main schools of work on this subject. First and by far the more important is the work done on the evidence from Tun-huang and Turfan which gives a first-hand picture of the system in operation. The main works are listed in the bibliography, but Niida Noboru, *Tō Sō hōritsu monjo no kenkyū* (1937), and the recent volume *Tonkō Torohan shakai-keizai shiryō* (*Monumenta Serindica*, vol. II, 1959) contain the best summaries of results to their respective dates. Second have been the attempts to interpret the relationship between the system and the social structure of medieval China. The earlier works on this line were summarised in Ikeda Makoto, 'Tōdai no henkaku wo dō tenkai suru ka?', *Tōyōshi kenkyū*, 13, III (1954). Since this study, the somewhat controversial interpretation of Sogabe

Shizuo, *Kinden-hō to sono ẕeieki-seido* (1953) has appeared in Japan, while in China a heated controversy raged for a while over the connections between the *chün-t'ien* system and the *tsu-yung-tiao* taxation system. The principal items in this controversy, which was conducted mainly on a theoretical and unhistorical level, are included in the recent volume *Chung-kuo li-tai t'u-ti chih-tu wen-ti t'ao-lun chi* (Peking, 1957). A succinct summary of the main arguments is given by Ts'en Chung-mien, *Sui-T'ang shih*, pp. 243–4. The most recent summary, Han Kuo-p'an, *Sui-T'ang ti chün-t'ien chih-tu*, re-establishes the traditional view that there was a strong connection, and gives some account of the better-known Tun-huang material, but has been rendered completely obsolete by the appearance of the *Tonkō Torohan shakai-keiẕai shiryō*.

3 Li An-shih's memorial is quoted in his biography, *Wei Shu*, 53, pp. 12 *b*– 14 *a*. See note 15 to p. 3 below. The edict enforcing the system is in *Wei-shu*, 7 A, pp. 28 *a–b*, and in a slightly different form in *Wei-shu*, 110, pp. 6 *b*–8 *b*.

4 The idea that the *chün-t'ien* system was derived from the *k'o-t'ien* system imposed under the Chin is suggested by Yang Lien-sheng, 'Notes on the economic history of the Chin dynasty', *Harvard Journal of Asiatic Studies*, 9 (1946). The *k'o-t'ien* system has been as variously interpreted as the *chün-t'ien*, and Sogabe, *Kinden-hō to sono ẕeieki-seido*, summarises seven principal interpretations. On this system see also T'ang Chang-ju, *Wei Chin Nan-pei-ch'ao shih lun-ts'ung* (1955), pp. 43 ff., and Ho Ch'ang-chün, *Han-T'ang chien feng-chien ti kuo-yu t'u-ti yü chün-t'ien chih* (1958).

PAGE 2

5 The *chün-t'ien* system as imposed under the Northern Ch'i is cited from the *Statutes* of 564 by *TT*, 2, p. 15 *a*; *Sui shu*, 24, p. 7 *a–b* (cf. Balázs, 'Le traité économique du Souei-chou' (1953), pp. 143–6). The same sources, pp. 15 *b*, and 9 *a–b* (Balázs, 'Le traité économique du Souei-chou', pp. 148–9) also give an account of the system under the Northern Chou. The Sui's own system, the direct forerunner of that imposed by the T'ang, is described in *TT*, 2, p. 15 *b–c*; *Sui shu*, 24, pp. 10 *b*–11 *a* (Balázs, 'Le traité économique du Souei-chou', pp. 151–3), where the rules are cited from the *New Statutes* (*Hsin Ling*) without a date. These *New Statutes* were in fact promulgated in 582, and were thus formulated by the Sui government while they were still only a succession-state in northern China, and before they had gained control of the whole of China. The best critical accounts of these early versions of the *chün-t'ien* system are in Sogabe, *Kinden-hō to sono Zeieki seido*, and Tamai Zehaku, 'Tō-jidai no tochi-mondai kanken', which first appeared in *Shigaku ẕasshi*, 33, VIII, IX, X (1922), and was reprinted in *Shina shakai-keiẕai shi kenkyū* (1942).

6 Under the Northern Wei, Northern Ch'i, Western Wei, and Northern Chou, a wife received a grant of land separate from that allocated to her husband. For an actual example of this in practice, see the fragment of a tax-register *chi-chang* dated 547 recovered from Tun-huang (S. 613). Under the *Statutes* of the Northern Wei, Northern Ch'i and Sui, the married couple, termed a '*ch'uang*' (bed), were clearly envisaged as the basic unit of taxation. Unmarried males were classified as *pan-ch'uang*, literally 'half-beds', and under the Northern Wei four such persons paid only the same amount of tax as a single married couple. See *TT*, 5, p. 30*a*, also Balázs, 'Le traité économique du Souei-chou', p. 207, note 101. Of course, most unmarried males would have been too young to be fully taxable.

7 This age was fixed at 70 under the Northern Wei, 66 under the Northern Ch'i, and 60 under the Sui. The T'ang followed the Sui, and withdrew part of a person's land grant at 60, when he ceased to be liable for taxation and *corvée*.

8 The principle that land allocation, productive capacity, and tax liability were intimately connected underlay the whole system, and was the reason, for instance, for the reduced grants to the incapacitated and such persons as monks who were neither fully productive, nor liable to full taxation. The Sui statutes made the connection between land allocation and tax liability perfectly explicit, 'No person who has not been allocated lands shall be taxed...'.

9 On the currency used during this period, and especially on the use of commodities as money, see Yang Lien-sheng, *Money and credit in China*, pp. 2, 16, and Ch'üan Han-sheng, 'Chung-ku tzu-jan ching-chi', *CYYY*, 10 (1942), pp. 75–176. Under the Northern Wei, for example, there was no copper currency in circulation prior to 496.

10 The *tsu* tax was the product of the man's labour on the land, and appears to have replaced the double grain taxes levied under the Chin (*tsu* levied *per capita* and *shui* levied on acreage). See Yang Lien-sheng, 'Notes on the economic history of the Chin dynasty', p. 128, and Balázs, 'Le traité économique du Souei-chou', pp. 192–3. The *tiao* tax was the product of the woman's labour at sericulture or weaving. Since both silk and hemp cloth were employed as currency, they were normally made up into standard lengths.

11 The term *lu-t'ien* for arable land persisted down to the Sui *Statutes* of 582, and was replaced by *k'ou-fen*—personal share land—only in T'ang times. The term *yung-ye* first appears in the Northern Ch'i *Statutes* of 564, where it is used to describe the tenure of lands opened up for cultivation by serving officials and commoners (*Sui shu*, 24, p. 7*b*; Balázs, 'Le traité économique du Souei-chou', p. 144) and for the tenure of mulberry fields *sang-t'ien*. In the Sui *Statutes* it has replaced the term *sang-t'ien* entirely. It is probable that the accounts of these earlier dynasties should read *shih-ye* rather than *yung-ye*, *yung* having been a taboo substitute for *shih*, taboo after 627 as part of the personal name of the emperor T'ai-tsung (Li Shih-min). The T'ang *Statutes* of 624, having been compiled before T'ai-tsung's accession, read *shih-ye*, but the later accounts all employ the taboo form *yung-ye*. The editors of *Sui shu*, who were working during T'ai-tsung's own reign, naturally had to comply with this taboo.

12 Fields for hemp (*ma-t'ien*) were granted already under the Northern Wei, but were not hereditary. See *Wei shu*, 110, p. 7*b*; *TT*, 1, p. 13: 'In all areas which produce hempen cloth, when a man reaches taxable age (*chi-k'o*) he shall be given a separate grant of 10 *mou* of hemp land (*ma-t'ien*), and his wife 5 *mou*. Slaves shall receive such land in the same way as free men. All these lands shall be liable to the rule on reversion.' But under the *Statutes* of Northern Ch'i 654 (see *Sui shu*, 24, p. 7*a–b*; *TT*, 2, p. 15*a*): 'In areas not suitable for mulberries, hemp fields shall be granted by the same rule as for mulberry fields.'

An interesting example of the actual granting of such hemp fields under the Western Wei is the Tun-huang tax-register of 547 (S. 613) mentioned above (note 6 to p. 2). This divides land between the categories *ma-t'ien* hemp fields, and *cheng-t'ien* regular fields. It is presumed that the latter were ordinary arable fields under grain crops, destined to produce the *tsu* tax. On this document see Yamamoto Tatsurō, 'Tonkō hakken keichō-yō monjo zankan', *Tōyō gakuhō*, 37, II (1954), III (1954).

13 Balázs, 'Beiträge zur Wirtschaftsgeschichte der T'ang-Zeit', *MSOS*, 36 (1933), p. 43, reckons the T'ang-time *mou* at 5·4 ar., that is 0·133 acres. This size was calculated from the contemporary foot-measures described by Wang Kuo-wei, 'Chinese foot-measures of the past nineteen centuries', *Journal of the North China Branch of the Royal Asiatic Society*, 59 (1928), pp. 114 ff. Pulleyblank gives a slightly higher figure of 0·14 acres (*The background of the rebellion of An Lu-shan*, p. 227). Both figures are slightly less than the modern standard *mou* which is usually reckoned as 0·17 acres. The modern *mou* is subject to quite spectacular local variations in size, however, and there is no reason to assume that it was any more standardised in T'ang times.

According to the estimates of agricultural production published in 1932 by the Nanking government under the direction of C. C. Chang, the average area of arable land for a single farm family was then only 21 *mou*. This is very much smaller than the grant for a married couple under the Northern

Chou (140 *mou*) or that for an adult individual under the T'ang (100 *mou*). The only part of China where holdings of this size have been normal in recent times is the newly settled Manchurian plain. This fact would strengthen my belief that the *chün-t'ien* allotments were designed to encourage the opening of new land and marginal cultivation.

14 The depopulation of the north-west and the drift of population towards the south was a trend which had continued since Han times. See Bielenstein, 'The census of China during the period A.D. 2–742', *Bulletin of the Museum of Far Eastern Antiquities*, 19 (1947), pp. 125–63, which gives the general picture, although the details are in need of considerable revision. See also the materials relevant to this problem collected in Lü Ssu-mien, *Liang Chin Nan-pei-ch'ao shih* (1948), vol. 2, pp. 934ff. The work of Moriya Mitsuo, 'Nanjin to hokujin', *Tōa ronsō*, 6 (1948), pp. 36–60, and *Rikuchō mombatsu no ichi kōsatsu*, makes it clear that this migration was not simply a matter of hard-pressed peasants seeking an easier life in the south, but was a movement involving all classes of society. It also appears that there was not a simple north–south movement, but that there were also some counter-migrations, although the pattern of these is still obscure.

With this background in mind, I find it quite impossible to agree with the view expressed by Maspero, 'Les régimes fonciers en Chine', that the *chün-t'ien* system, from its inception, was designed as a means of limiting the size of holdings. '... Le problème pour les gouvernements de la Chine du Nord, était moins de faire cultiver une superficie donnée que d'employer le plus grand nombre de personnes possible à cette culture...' (p. 166). His general view has recently been adopted by Gernet, in his *Les aspects économiques du Bouddhisme dans la société chinoise du ve au xe siècle*. There seem to me to be insuperable difficulties in the way of such an interpretation. If limitation of holdings was the aim, why were there allowances made for so many slaves? Under the Northern Ch'i a prince could claim lands equal in amount to those allocated to free men on behalf of 300 slaves, while even a commoner could claim lands in respect of up to 60 slaves. Why, moreover, were the concessions made by which newly opened lands were permitted to become hereditary, unless it was to encourage wider cultivation? Above all why were individual grants so large, larger than the area which could normally be worked by a single man? None of these questions can be answered on the basis of Maspero's interpretation.

15 See *Wei shu*, 53, pp. 12*b*–14*a*. The memorial reads: 'In my humble view, the people of the prefectures and commanderies in many cases move their homes because of poor harvests, abandoning or selling their lands and homesteads, and going to live as squatters (*p'iao-hu*) in other localities. This state of affairs has already gone on for several generations. When the system of the

three headmen (*san cheng*) had been established, it was first attempted to make them return to their abandoned former homes. But their cottages and wells had fallen into decay, their mulberry and elm trees had been uprooted or transplanted elsewhere. When this state of affairs had continued for a long while, it came to produce deceits. Powerful clans and influential families wielded their power of intimidation. Those living at a distance laid claim to be members of the royal houses of Wei and Chin, while those near at hand adduced proofs of their being relatives or old allies of the royal house. This too has gone on for many years, and has caused misgivings among the rural elders. Even where evidence has been abundant, it has not been possible to take possession (of property). In all cases personal agreements are made, and mutual concessions, so that when the two sides of the dispute present their evidence, those hearing the case are still undecided. Thus disputed suits are delayed, and no decision given for year after year. Good lands are abandoned and left uncultivated, and the mulberry trees rot unpicked. Those who have been lucky flourish, while the many are involved in court cases. If we wish the families to lay in stocks in years of plenty, and the people to provide revenue for our expenditure, can we possibly do so?

'I humbly submit that now, although it is difficult to restore the mulberry trees and the wells, it would be proper for us to change to a more equitable system, and to examine the possible methods of bringing this about. The division of livelihoods should have a fair level, and labour and land should accord with one another. The populace should be able to reap the profit of their own production, and the powerful and violent will no longer have the abundance of their surplus lands. Thus there will be no enrichment of private persons, but equitable division among the common people, and there will be accumulations of grain like hills and mountains in the village households. Where lands are disputed, the cases should be decided within the year, and where the case is of long standing and difficult to decide, the land should in all cases be given to the present occupier. This having been done, the dissolute and lawless among the people will lose hope of gaining what they covet, and the officers who maintain the correct shares will free the people from usurpation and infringement on their rights for ever.'

This makes it quite clear that Li An-shih's objectives were twofold: prevention of usurpation of lands by the powerful, and prevention of lands falling out of cultivation as the result of migration and of such pressures.

16 That is to say, personal slaves. The T'ang system maintained grants for certain slaves (see appendix 1, 1, art. 25), but these were categories of bondsmen in the state service. The Tun-huang household registers show that the only allowance of land made under the *chün-t'ien* allotment was the extra land for the house and garden mentioned in the *Statutes* (appendix 1, 1, art. 14). Slavery seems to have assumed considerable economic importance under the Toba Wei, and to a lesser degree under the Northern Ch'i. Lü Ssu-mien, *Liang Chin Nan-pei-ch'ao shih*, pp. 1009–23, collects a great amount of material on slavery under the Nan-pei-ch'ao. An excellent study of the situation in northern China at this period is Wang Yi-t'ong, 'Slaves and ȯther comparable social groups during the Northern Dynasties', *Harvard Journal of Asiatic Studies*, I, III/IV (1953). On slavery in general see also Pulleyblank, 'The origins and nature of chattel slavery in China', *Journal of Economic and Social History of the Orient*, I, II (1958), pp. 185–220.

17 These lands were very limited in extent, and the allowance was almost certainly made in respect of draught animals, and not for pasture for large herds, which would in any case have occupied marginal lands. What is significant is that the dynasties of pastoral-nomadic origin should have had an awareness of the importance of animals in husbandry.

18 See appendix I, 2; *Code*, 12, art. 14; 13, *Code*, arts. 1–4.

19 See *Code*, 27, art. 27. This specified a beating of 50 strokes for offences against rulings in the *Statutes* not covered by a specific clause in the *Code*, except in cases where the offence was a purely ritual one.

PAGE 4

20 See appendix I, 1, arts. 3 A, 3 B, 3 C, and the sources there cited.

21 See appendix I, 1, art. 3. The grants for old men are not included in the surviving portions of the 624 *Statutes*. On the formal definition of the categories of disability see the passages from the *Household Statutes* (*Hu-ling*) quoted by *Code*, 22, art. 13; 29, art. 6, and *PSLT*, 9, p. 19 a. These are collected in Niida, *Tōryō shūi*, p. 228. 'All such persons as are blind in one eye, deaf in both ears, lacking two fingers on one hand or three toes from one foot, who have lost either their big toe or thumb, who are bald-headed and without hair, have a chronic discharge, dropsy, or any large tumours, shall be considered partially disabled (*ts'an-chi*). Such persons as are idiots or dumb, dwarfed, with deformed spines, or lacking one limb, shall be considered seriously disabled (*fei-chi*). Such persons as are completely insane, lacking two limbs, or blind in both eyes, shall be considered totally disabled (*tu-chi*).'

22 A further ambiguity is introduced into this clause by *TT*, 2, p. 65 c, which has wrongly interpolated *chung-ting* into the list of personal categories of persons acting as head of household, thus making it appear that the head of household *always* received an additional allocation of 20 *mou*, even if he was a taxable person entitled to a full personal grant. The Sung print of *TT* does not have the two characters, although they are included in the palace edition, and in editions taken from this, such as the Shih t'ung edition. The assessments of land entitlements given in the Tun-huang household registers clearly show that *TT* is incorrect here, and on the basis of these documents Suzuki Shun and Niida Noboru have suggested emendations of the text which are summarised in Niida, *Tō-Sō hōritsu monjo no kenkyū*, pp. 769–72.

23　See appendix 1, 1, art. 3 A. The precise sense of the 737 *Statutes* has been the centre of controversy, the arguments on both sides being summarised in Niida, *Tō-Sō hōritsu monjo no kenkyū*, pp. 776 ff. My own interpretation is that the rule probably applied to cases where a son inherited from his father more land in perpetuity than the quota which he was himself entitled to possess. In such cases he was permitted to retain this surplus land in the possession of the household, but it was transferred to personal share tenure. On this point the *Statutes* of 624 are also vague, the preserved portions reading as if personal share lands reverted to the state on the death of the occupier, not on his reaching the tax-exempt age of 60. It is just possible that this was the case, since the parts of the 624 *Statutes* which we possess contain no provision for grants to old persons (which would of course have been made only after the reversion of the full adult allotment), but I consider this highly unlikely.

24　See appendix 1, 1, art. 3 C, art. 12. The rules on *k'uan-hsiang* and *hsia-hsiang* are not included in the authentic fragments of the 624 *Statutes*. Niida, *Tōryō shūi*, pp. 609–10, accepts the version in *WHTK*, 2, p. 41 *b*, as a quotation of these *Statutes*, but in fact this text is a direct quotation of the account given in *HTS*, 51. This is a composite account of the *chün-t'ien* rules largely based on the 737 series of *Statutes*, extensively reworked. However, in spite of the lack of reliable textual evidence, there is little doubt that such a rule was already included in the 624 *Statutes*. The Japanese *Yōrō Statutes* contained such a clause (see *RGG*, p. 107), and since these were closely modelled on the *Statutes* promulgated by the T'ang in 651, it is almost certain that the rule was included in the latter series.

25　See *Sui shu*, 24, p. 12 *b* (Balázs, 'Le traité économique du Souei-chou', p. 157): 'Dans la capitale, dans ses alentours et dans les trois (commanderies) Ho, il y avait peu de terres et beaucoup d'hommes, les vêtements et la nourriture étaient insuffisants.... Alors des commissaires furent envoyés dans les quatre directions pour égaliser les terres de tout l'empire. Dans les cantons à forte densité, chaque adulte arrivait à peine à 20 *meou*, les vieillards et les enfants avaient encore moins.' The problem is, however, whether there was any actual administrative distinction made between over-populated and under-populated areas in pre-T'ang times.

26　The problem of over-population was of very long standing. Ts'ui Shih had already raised the question in his *Cheng lun* in the second century. See

Maspero, 'Les régimes fonciers en Chine', p. 163. An interesting point about this over-population is that whereas in the pre-T'ang period it was especially severe in north-eastern China, in T'ang times it seems that the north-west was worst affected. The rules incorporated in the *chün-t'ien* system allowing transfer from restricted to broad localities (appendix 1, 1, art. 13), and permitting persons making such moves greater freedom in the disposal of their landed property (appendix 1, 1, art. 15; appendix 1, 2; *Code*, 12, art. 14), were designed to encourage migration from centres of over-population, and the settlement of undeveloped lands.

27 See appendix 1, 1, art. 18.

28 The amounts of land to which the right of possession was granted to officers of various ranks are laid down in appendix 1, 1, art. 4. The ban on such grants being taken up in restricted localities, *ibid.* art. 7.

29 See Wang Kuo-wei, *Kuan-t'ang chi-lin*, 21, pp. 11 *a*–14 *a* (1959 edition).

30 Maspero, 'Les régimes fonciers en Chine', p. 170: 'Les propriétés que la loi accordait le droit de posséder aux fonctionnaires ne leur étaient pas données, ils avaient à les acheter.' There is no ground for such a statement, save in the case of the restricted localities. The clause (appendix 1, 1, art. 7) clearly distinguishes between grants (*shou*) of ownerless wasteland in broad localities, and purchase (*mai*) in restricted ones. Such grants of ownerless wasteland were an inducement to bring marginal land into cultivation, and since most marginal land was in fact ownerless there could be no question of purchase. The continuation of the same article makes the position perfectly explicit, since it says that officials of the lower grades were to receive lands which had reverted to the state. There can have been no question of the state selling off land which had been handled through the land allocation system, and a *grant* must have been envisaged.

31 On the 'lands of the public administration', see appendix 1, 1, arts. 29, 30. On the 'lands pertaining to office', see *ibid.* arts. 31, 32, 34.

PAGE 5

32 For a good discussion of the management of such lands, see Chü Ch'ing-yüan, *T'ang-tai tsai-cheng shih*, pp. 118–26. See also Osaki Shōji, 'Tōdai kyōkan shikiden kō', *Shichō*, 12, III–IV (1943), pp. 121–38.

33 The subject of lands in the hands of individual monks as opposed to those held by the community (*saṃgha*) as community property *ch'ang-chu-t'ien* is very complicated. See Gernet, *Les aspects économiques du Bouddhisme*, pp. 130–2, who considers that the lands held by individuals were more considerable than those held by monastic communities. See also Twitchett,

'Monastic estates in T'ang China', *Asia Major*, 5, II (1956), pp. 123–46. The lands of monks, apart from the special case of *pai-hsing seng*, were probably administered by the *saṃgha* in periods of good order. Late T'ang documents from Tun-huang and Turfan cited by Gernet, *Les aspects économiques du Bouddhisme*, pp. 128–30, show that at that time individual monks held lands which they and their families farmed themselves with the aid of hired labour.

34 *Kuan-hu* were a special category of official bondsmen. For a detailed discussion of the various types of non-free status under the T'ang, see Tamai Zehaku, 'Tō no semmin-seido to sono yurai', reprinted in *Shina shakai-keizai shi kenkyū* (1942). See also Takigawa Masajirō, 'Tōdai dorei-seido gaisetsu', in his *Shina hōseishi kenkyū* (1940), pp. 57–92, and Niida, *Shina mibunhō shi*, pp. 859–997. *Kuan-hu* were not merely official chattels in the same way as *kuan-nu-pi*, who were slaves in the fullest sense. *Kuan-hu* were not continuously employed by the office to which they belonged as slaves were, but performed turns of duty totalling three months per annum, and for this reason they were also called *fan-hu* (duty households). Another mark of their comparative freedom of status is that, like *corvée* labourers, they could pay a tax instead of performing their turn of duty. Being attached to a specific office, of which they formed a permanent labour force, they also came to be known as *kung-chieh-hu* (households of the public administration). They and their lands did not figure on the ordinary household registers of the county where they lived, but were entered on separate registers held by the office under whom they worked. They were restricted in marriage to partners of the same status.

35 See appendix I, I, art. 25 B.

36 *Tsa-hu* were one degree nearer free status than were *kuan-hu*. Although like the latter they were assigned to a specific government office and registered as such, they also were entered in the ordinary household registers of their county. Their turns of official duty were less than those of *kuan-hu*, amounting only to five months in two years. They were given allocations of land, and exempted from all taxes and labour services at 60, just as were free men. The principal limitations on their liberty were that they were forbidden to marry free persons, and they were subject to special fiscal responsibilities.

37 See appendix I, I, art. 14. This rule was already incorporated in the *chün-t'ien* system under the Toba Wei.

38 See appendix I, I, art. 22.

39 See appendix I, I, art. 16, and *Code*, 13, art. 1. The *Code* provided a penalty of up to a year's hard labour for offences committed in restricted localities.

40   See appendix I, I, art. 17, and *Code*, 13, art. 3 (commentary). 'According to the *Statutes*, where lands are improperly bought or sold without an official report being rendered, the price will be confiscated and be irrecoverable, while the standing crops will revert to the original owner of the land.'

41   See appendix I, I, art. 15 A, 15 B, and *Code*, 12, art. 14 (commentary).

42   See appendix I, I, art. 20. With regard to mortgage (*tien, tien-chih*, etc.) it must be remembered that the Chinese system was different from our own in that the mortgagee had the perpetual right to redeem his property, even after the mortgage had been foreclosed. On this very complicated matter see Katō Shigeshi, 'Tōdai ni okeru fudōsan-shitsu ni tsuite', *Tōyō gakuhō*, 12, I (1922), pp. 80–9, reprinted in *Shina keizaishi kōshō*, I, pp. 283–93 (1952). Also see McAleavy, 'Dien in China and Vietnam', *Journal of Asian Studies*, 17, III (1958), pp. 403–15. Katō makes the point, in the context of the *chün-t'ien* system, that it is reasonable to assume that in cases where outright sale was allowed, mortgage was also permissible.

43   See appendix I, I, art. 16.

44   See *Code*, 12, art. 14; 13, art. 1.

PAGE 6

45   Much the most important of these are the official household registers (*hu-chi*) and tax-lists (*chi-chang*), but there are also many private documents which shed light on the subject. The most convenient collection of such material is in Niida, *Tō-Sō hōritsu monjo no kenkyū*, but since its publication in 1937, many further documents have been published, most important of which are those recently published in *Tonkō Torohan shakai-keizai shiryō* (1959). There still remain many unpublished documents among the von le Coq MSS. from Turfan in Berlin, and among the Stein and Pelliot MSS. from Tun-huang.

46   It is incorrect to hold, as some scholars have done, that the household registers and the population statistics which were eventually compiled from them included only taxable persons. All persons of whom the local authorities had cognisance were included. The real distinction was not between taxable and untaxable individuals but between those persons of whom the local authorities had cognisance and those of whom they had not. The material collected in the household registers was an administrative, not a demographic census. For this reason, certain classes were separately registered; monks and nuns appearing on a *seng-chi*, and official slaves and dependants on departmental lists. Such persons were registered separately because, having no legal status within a household but belonging to independent corporations, they were outside the normal relationship of the individual with the authorities through the head of his household.

A very full account of the registration system is included in Niida, *Tō-Sō hōritsu monjo no kenkyū*, pp. 652–64, which gives all the relevant texts and also repairs some mistakes and omissions in the same author's earlier *Tōryō shūi*, pp. 239–42 where the section of the *Household Statutes* (*hu-ling*) dealing with registration had been reconstructed. The household registers were compiled in the cyclical years *ch'ou, ch'en, wei, hsü*, that is at three-yearly intervals. In the preceding years, *tzu, mao, wu, yu* the authorities performed the allocation (*ting-hu*) of household categories (*hu-teng*) (see *TLT*, 3, p. 30 *a–b*). These were entered in the household registers together with the particulars contained in the annual statements (*shou-shih*), drawn up in the form of a household register annually under the supervision of the sub-bureaucratic administration of the village elders (*li-cheng*). Under the Sung 'according to the *Household Statutes* the *Shou-shih* was a document in which the households of the common people were made to enter the facts about the individual family members and their lands and houses' (see *Hsü Tzu-chih t'ung-chien ch'ang-pien*, 254, pp. 18 *b*–19 *a*). On the basis of these statements made by the heads of households and collected by the village headmen, the annual tax-list (*chi-chang*) was compiled. This was a detailed statement of the taxes to which a household was liable for the coming year, and also included the details on status, special *corvée* responsibilities, and land allotments entered in the *shou-shih*. These tax-lists were submitted annually to the Public Revenue Department (*tu-chih*), the subdivision of the Board of Finance responsible for the annual budget (see *HTS*, 51, p. 2 *a*). The material in these tax-lists was incorporated every third year in the household register (*hu-chi*), which included references back to changes of status, etc., recorded in previous tax-lists.

Besides these specific categories of document, the terms *chang-chi* and *pan-chi* are used generally referring to all registers, including those mentioned above and the various types of nominal rolls (for instance of *corvée* dutymen) compiled locally for administrative convenience. The terms *pu-chang* and *pu-chi* are also used in this general way, and also in the restricted sense of household registers.

47 Not only were the lands actually held under the *chün-t'ien* allocation listed in detail, but so also were the lands to which the household were entitled under the system. Not *all* lands in the possession of a family were listed however. Lands not allocated under the *chün-t'ien* system were commonly held, in many cases under the fiction that they were 'loaned wasteland' (*chieh-huang*). A separate register, the *ch'ing-miao-pu*, listed all cultivated lands held by the family, and differentiated lands allocated (*shou-t'ien*) from 'loaned wasteland' brought under culture by the household.

48 It seems that the tax-lists were sent annually to the Department of Public Revenue, while the household registers went to the Board of Finance (*hu-pu*) itself. However, the sources are by no means consistent, the authority for the tax-list's being sent to the Department of Public Revenue being *HTS*, 51, a particularly unreliable chapter of a generally careless history. Since the population totals recorded in *THY* and *TFYK* are sometimes said to have been based on the tax-lists, and not on the household registers, it seems most probable that both documents were sent to the parent Board in the first instance.

49 The principal studies are listed in the bibliography. The only extended study of such a document in a western language is L. Giles, 'A census of Tun-huang', *T'oung Pao*, 16 (1916), which deals with a special example, the household register compiled in 416 under the Western Liang, i.e. before the introduction of the *chün-t'ien* system, and is purely a nominal list of household-members with their ages and places of residence, with none of the details on land and tax liability contained in the T'ang documents. A single household's entry from a T'ang register is translated by Maspero, 'Les régimes fonciers en Chine', pp. 168–9, but the document is incomplete, lacking the register of lands, while Maspero's translation is incomplete and contains certain errors. (For example, it is incorrect to translate *chung-nü* as 'adolescent de sexe féminin', for a woman remained a *chung-nü* from 15 (not 18 as Maspero says) until marriage. There was no such category as *ting-nü* for an adult woman.)

50 For the purpose of this study I have used the examples reprinted in Niida, *Tō-Sō hōritsu monjo no kenkyū*, pp. 677–721. Another large collection of such texts, edited by T'ao Hsi-sheng, appeared in 'T'ang hu-chi pu ts'ung-chi', *Shih-huo*, 4, v (1935), but this depended very heavily on the texts published by Naba Toshisada, and on the inaccurate transcriptions of the documents included in various collections of Tun-huang MS. material published in China. Although there remain some errors of transcription in Niida, *Tō-Sō hōritsu monjo no kenkyū*, the readings are more dependable than those given by earlier scholars. More recently, further texts have been published, notably by Yamamoto Tatsurō, 'Tonkō hakken keichō-yō monjo zankan', *Tōyō gakuhō*, 37, II, III (1954); 'Tonkō hakken kosei densei kankei monjo jūgo shu', *Tōyōbunka kenkyūjo kiyō*, 10 (1956), and by Ikeda On, 'Tonkō hakken Tō Taireki-yonnen shujitsu zankan ni tsuite', *Tōyō gakuhō*, 40, II, III (1957).

51 See Niida, *Tō-Sō hōritsu monjo no kenkyū*, pp. 723–31. There are also some early Sung registers which are again different in form. The late T'ang examples are simple lists of persons and lands, with no information on personal status, type of land tenure, tax liability, etc., while the Sung examples give only the name of the head of household and his lands. It is in fact doubtful whether these are *hu-chi* at all, but may be some sort of land register, such as was used to assess the *ti-shui* land levy under the *liang-shui* tax system.

52 See Chu Coching, 'Climatic changes during historical times in China', *Journal of the North China Branch of the Royal Asiatic Society*, 62 (1931) and the same author's 'Climatic pulsations during historical times in China', *Geographical Rev.* 56 (1926).

53 See, for example, the register of 747 (P. 2592) where sands form the boundaries of certain properties, and numerous mentions in other MSS. of salt-marsh and rocky lands. It should be noted that the word *huang*, which also appears, stands in the technical sense of 'uncultivated land' and does not here mean 'desert'.

54 Further light is thrown on the dense irrigation network of the area by the local irrigation rules, unfortunately without title, P. 3560 v°, published with a most detailed commentary by Naba Toshisada in 'Tōdai no nōden-suiri ni kansuru kitei ni tsukite', *Shigaku zasshi*, 54, I, pp. 49–51, and 54, II, pp. 48 ff. (1943).

PAGE 7

55 Some of the more common foreign surnames found in the Tun-huang MSS. are An (Bukhara), Ho (Kushānika), K'ang (Samarkand), Shih (Kasha-na), Ts'ao (Kaputana), Mi (Maimurg), Shih (Tashkent), Hu (Sogdia)—all referring to families whose origin was in the Sogdian region. There is a large literature on this topic. See the remarks of Pulleyblank in 'A Sogdian colony in Inner Mongolia', *T'oung Pao*, 41, IV–V (1952), and Kuwabara Jitsuzō, 'Zui-Tō-jidai ni Shina ni raijū shita saiikijin ni tsuite', *Naitō Hakase kanreki shukuga Shinagaku ronsō* (1926), pp. 565 ff.; Ishida Miki-nosuke, 'Tempō-jusai no teiseki ni miyuru Tonkō chihō no seiiki jūmin ni tsuite', *Katō Hakushi Kanreki-kinen Tōyōshi shūsetsu* (1941), pp. 83–91; Hsiang Ta, *T'ang-tai Ch'ang-an yü hsi-yü wen-ming*.

56 No sign of such a process can be detected in the Tun-huang MSS.

57 Effective Chinese rule in eastern Kansu ended in 763–4, the governor of Ho-hsi province moving his capital from Lan-chou first to Liang-chou in 762 and then to Tun-huang (766). *YHCHC*, 40, says that Tun-huang in its turn fell to the Tibetans in 782, but Demiéville, who has dealt with this subject at great length in *Le concile de Lhasa* (1952), pp. 167–78, has concluded that Tun-huang did not fall into Tibetan hands until 787, although contact with China was broken after 784. However, the use of the obsolete *nien-hao*

'*Ta-li*' after 779 shows that even before 784 contact with China can hardly have been very effective, although such a usage is not universal (cf. S. 5867) and some official contact must have been maintained. The Tibetan occupation lasted until 848, and during this period there was certainly some degree of central Tibetan control exercised over the Tun-huang area, for among the MSS. (e.g. P. 3336) are records of large-scale Buddhist ceremonies ordered by the *Tsan-p'u* or high Tibetan dignitaries. Some material on the Tibetan occupation may be found in two very poorly preserved *pien-wen* texts, P. 2962, P. 3451, which are published in Chou Shao-liang, *Tun-huang pien-wen hui-lu* (1954).

58 The only notable divergence is that, whereas in the registers dating from before 735 the years of compilation agree with the years in the sexagenary cycle laid down in *TLT*, 3, in the later examples they seem to have compiled the documents in different years. This may either be the result of local administrative laxity, or possibly, in view of the date, represent a change introduced in Li Lin-fu's Permanently Applicable Directive (*ch'ang-hsing chih-fu*). See chapter VI, note 10 to p. 101. See Suzuki Shun, 'Koseki sakusei no nenji to Tōryō', *Chūō Daigaku kiyō*, 9 (1957).

59 See the analyses of entitlements in Niida, *Tō-Sō hōritsu monjo no kenkyū*, pp. 759–68, and in Suzuki Shun, 'Tonkō hakken Tōdai koseki to kinden-hō', *Shigaku ʒasshi*, 47, VII (1936), pp. 1–61.

60 See Niida, *Tō-Sō hōritsu monjo no kenkyū*, and Suzuki Shun, 'Tōdai teichū-sei no kenkyū', *Shigaku ʒasshi*, 46, XI (1935), pp. 82–106.

61 This was noted already by Tamai Zehaku in his pioneer studies, 'Tonkō koseki-zankan ni tsuite', *Tōyō gakuhō*, 16, II (1927), and 'Futatabi Tonkō koseki-zankan ni tsuite', *Tōyō gakuhō*, 24, IV (1937). Suzuki Shun, in 'Tonkō hakken Tōdai koseki to kinden-hō', *Shigaku ʒasshi*, 47, VII (1936), showed that thirteen of seventeen households whose holdings he analysed held their full quota of land in perpetuity. But this applied only to the lands in perpetuity to which the ordinary individual was entitled, not to the very large amounts to which some were entitled in respect of honorific rank or official title.

62 Only one household in the preserved fragments of the registers held more personal share land than it was entitled to, and no other household held its full quota. The one household concerned was that of Suo Ssu-li, a notable local gentry family, who were also unusual in that they held a number of slaves. Wang Kuo-wei, *Kuan-t'ang chi-lin*, 21, suggests that the surplus personal share land which they held was a grant made in respect of these slaves. But there is no foundation for this opinion, and Suzuki and Niida both reject it. However, they offer no alternative, and I am inclined to bear it in mind, with the reservation that it is only a conjecture.

The average family at Tun-huang held less than half of the personal share land to which they were entitled, and many held none at all.

63 Niida, *Tō-Sō hōritsu monjo no kenkyū*, pp. 774ff.

64 Niida, *ibid.* p. 787, says: 'It is a problem how long the distinction in value between lands in perpetuity and personal share land continued in existence. It is also a question whether there was the same distinction between them in the period 624–741 and in the period 742–79. We ought perhaps to recognise that after the earlier period the distinction gradually diminished until it became practically negligible. Hence there is reason to suppose that, during the later period, the difference was merely one of name.' Balázs, 'Beiträge', 34, p. 50, drew attention to a quotation in *WHTK*, 2, p. 42 *b*, of the Sung author Ye Shih, who held that 'in the T'ang dynasty what was nominally state land became in reality private property'. Thus it was already recognised in Sung times that the recognition of private rights in property grew up already under the *chün-t'ien* system, by the increased proportion of lands held on hereditary tenure.

65 The registers here raise a very complicated question. The fragments discovered at Turfan distinguish between two types of lands in perpetuity (*yung-ye*), one called 'permanent land' (*ch'ang-t'ien*), the other 'department land' (*pu-t'ien*). These sub-categories are never mentioned by the printed sources from T'ang times, and no completely satisfactory explanation of them has yet been given. I take it that *ch'ang-t'ien* was inherited land, or land acquired by purchase (we find, for example, in a document from Turfan quoted by Niida, *Tō-Sō hōritsu monjo no kenkyū*, pp. 686–7, '*ch'ang-t'ien mai-fu*'—i.e. *ch'ang-t'ien* incorporated by purchase). *Pu-t'ien* was presumably extra land in perpetuity allocated by the authorities to bring the holdings up to something like a general level. It has been suggested that these categories represent true *yung-ye* land in perpetuity on the one hand, and land nominally registered as land in perpetuity on the other. However, the distinction of the two is to be found only in documents from Turfan, dating from before 740. As Nishijima Sadao in his 'Torohan shutsudo monjo yori mitaru kindensei no sekō jōtai', *Tonkō Torohan shakai-keizai shiryō*, 1 (1959), pp. 151–292, has pointed out, there was virtually no personal share land in Turfan at all, and the amounts of allocated land were extremely small, less than 10 *mou* per household. He also points out that lands in perpetuity, and even lands received by imperial gift (*tz'u-t'ien*), were reallocated and taken in by the state, and that such a practice is covered by a passage in *Sung hsing-t'ung*, 12, quoting a passage from the *Household Statutes* (*hu-ling*) of T'ang

times regarding the division of property (p. 205): 'The father's and grandfather's lands in perpetuity and lands received by imperial gift should also be
equally divided. But the personal share land shall be disposed of in accordance with the laws governing age-status. If the lands in a locality are few, these
lands (in perpetuity and imperial gift) shall also be disposed of according to
this law.' His demonstration of the actual occurrence of reallocation of such
lands is excellent, but I have serious misgivings about the authority for it
which he finds in the quotation from *Sung hsing-t'ung*. To my mind *jo t'ien*
shao che means 'If the lands in the household's hands fall short, these shall be
disposed of according to the law (of seniority of age-status)', rather than
'if the lands in the locality are few', as Nishijima takes it.

If in fact all lands in perpetuity were subject to reallocation in this way,
the point of the division between *ch'ang-t'ien* and *pu-t'ien* becomes addition-
ally obscure. In the registers of deficient lands (*ch'ien-t'ien*) from Turfan,
each family lists its deficiency in both types. Perhaps in this area of acute
land shortage only a certain very limited quota of land in perpetuity was
allowed to be counted as hereditable, and this was classed as *ch'ang-t'ien*.

66 See Suzuki Shun, *Shigaku zasshi*, 47, VII (cf. note 61 to p. 7).

PAGE 8

67 Until recently we had only limited indications of return and reallocation
of lands. The terms *huan-kung*, *huan-t'ien*, *t'ui-t'ien*, all referring to lands
returned to state ownership, occur in the registers among the indications of
neighbouring properties which define the position of each holding. *Huan-
kung* and *t'ui-t'ien* are both used in this sense in the *Code*, the latter in the
specialised usage of lands returned on decrease of entitlement, such as when
the owner reached the age of 60. Niida, *Tō-Sō hōritsu monjo no kenkyū*,
pp. 780–1, cited a much-mutilated MS. from the Turfan area which appeared
to be a register of lands returned to public ownership in 741, distinguishing
between lands returned as surplus (*sheng-t'ui*) and lands returned after
decease (*ssu-t'ui*). Otherwise, nothing was known.

Since the publication of the MSS. recovered by Count Otani's expeditions
to Turfan, and now stored in the Ryūkoku daigaku, Kyōto, we are much
better informed. In *Tonkō Torohan Shakai-keizai shiryō* (1959), an article by
Nishimura Genyu, 'Tōdai Torohan ni okeru kindensei no igi', pp. 293–366,
introduced for the first time a type of document previously unknown listing
the deficiencies of land (*ch'ien-t'ien*) of each household. These were written
applications by the headman of a locality (*hsiang*) listing the amount of the
deficiency of lands of each farmer. This presupposes that there was a local quota
of lands which the authorities attempted to maintain by systematic allocation.
The applicants are listed in accordance with their household category, and it

thus seems that the poorer ones were dealt with before the richer, as the *Statutes* provided.

At the same time as these *ch'ien-t'ien* documents were compiled, the locality also drew up a document listing lands reverting to the state, and thus becoming available for reallocation. The document cited by Niida (see above) was of this type, but was so mutilated and incomplete that it told us very little. Among the Turfan MSS. in the Ryūkoku daigaku are a great number of fragments of similar documents. These are treated in full by Nishijima Sadao, in his article (see note 65 to p. 7 above). These *t'ui-t'ien* documents list both types of land in perpetuity and also lands received by imperial gift, and specify the following reasons for reversion: reversion after decease (*ssu-t'ui*), lands returned as surplus (*sheng-t'ui*), lands reverting after desertion of the title-holder (*t'ao-tsou ch'u-t'ui*), lands reverting through marriage of head of household when the household head was a woman (*ch'u-chia t'ui*), and lands reverting when a household became extinct on the marriage of a female head of household (*ch'u-chia chüeh t'ui*). Further documents quoted by Nishijima show how a second list was made up from this register of returned lands, with a space for the name of the new grantee. These lists of parcels of land for distribution and the names of the recipients show the allocation in actual practice, and doubtless allocation was made to those figuring with high priority on the *ch'ien-t'ien* register.

Further documents showing how the local government kept its registers up to date are introduced in Huang Wen-pi, *T'u lu-fan k'ao-ku chi*, 3, XII (pp. 42–3, plates 36, 37, 38, 39). These are a series of much-mutilated MS. fragments from Turfan which appear to be lists of absconded families dating from the last decade of the seventh century. Some are listed as 'holding land, but not registered', others as 'registered but not holding land', others as 'unregistered, holding land, with no occupier (*chu*)', others as 'unregistered, no land, no occupier'. It would thus seem that the title to land did not automatically lapse if the grantee absconded, and that such land might be occupied and worked by other persons in the absence of the title-holder.

68   There is a slight doubt about the meaning of *sheng-t'ui* (see note 67 to p. 8). This most probably means surplus reverting to the state at 60 years of age. But theoretically lands in perpetuity, and these were all classed as such, did not revert at 60 years of age. It is possible that it means land surplus to the quota which the heirs were entitled to inherit at death. I have little doubt that the former explanation is the correct one, and both Niida and Nishijima understand the term in this sense. But in this instance again, the treatment of lands in perpetuity in Turfan must have been at variance with the rules laid down in the *Statutes*.

69 All the known *t'ui-t'ien* documents from Turfan date from 741, and *huan-t'ien* are mentioned in a household register dated 747 (P. 3354) from Tun-huang. Thus we may say that, before the An Lu-shan rebellion, re-allocation by the village sub-bureaucratic authorities was still in full vigour. However, there is no single mention of *huan-t'ien* in the long registers from *Ta-li* times. It is reasonable then to assume that reallocation had ceased after the rebellion, but it is unsafe to assume that this state of affairs was common to China as a whole, since Tun-huang was at this time cut off from effective central authority (see note 57 to p. 7 above).

70 The sex-ratio in the registers cited by Niida, *Tō-Sō hōritsu monjo no kenkyū*, is 33 men to 67 women. No convincing explanation of this has yet been suggested, but tax-evasion is an obvious solution. One or more registered males would have been sufficient to establish a household's title to its lands, and omission of the other males would have reduced the tax-assessment. This is presumably a case in practice of what the *Code*, 12, art. 4, calls *lou-k'ou* 'omission of individuals'. The term for complete omission of a family from the register was *t'o-hu*.

71 Shortage of land and small average holdings were not universal, since the total of cultivated land in the empire in 755 was 14,303,862 *ch'ing* and 13 *mou* (see *TFYK*, 495, p. 26*a*), which would give an average per registered household (at this date totalling 8,900,000) of over 160 *mou* as against 20 or 30 *mou* at Tun-huang and even less at Turfan. It has been suggested that there was a special category of land which was completely beyond the *chün-t'ien* allocation, known as *tzu-t'ien*. This term is commonly found in the Tun-huang tax registers, and Nishikawa Masao, in 'Tonkō hakken no Tōdai koseki-zankan ni arawareta "jiden" ni tsuite', *Shigaku zasshi*, 64, x (1955), pp. 38–60, advanced a highly ingenious argument that it cannot be explained as meaning 'own property'—the traditional explanation—since if 'own land' appears among the neighbours in one plot among a family's holdings, it should appear again as the neighbour in another plot. He thus assumes that *tzu-t'ien* should be read as meaning 'own land' in the sense of true private property. Quite apart from the linguistic difficulty of taking *tzu* in this way—one would expect perhaps *ssu*—the author's argument is based on a mis-understanding of the nature of these *ssu-chih* boundaries. He assumes a pattern of land division in neat rectangles, in which any given plot would have *only* four neighbours. This is in fact far from the case, especially in areas such as Tun-huang, which are completely dependent on irrigation, and where field boundaries must follow contour lines. The very term for a large-scale cadastral plan in medieval China, *yü-lin t'u* (i.e. fish-scale map), describes admirably the pattern of the boundaries of irrigated fields. Moreover, the *ssu-chih* were not an exhaustive list of neighbours, but four selected to give the relative position of a field, and in any case, as Nishijima, 'Torohan shutsuto monjo yori mitaru kindensei no sekō jōtai', pp. 229–46, has clearly demonstrated, the way in which the reallocation documents were drawn up meant that the *ssu-chih* of a plot were not revised regularly and brought into line with the current changes of ownership of the neighbouring plots concerned. Finally, Nishikawa's hypothesis does not take into account the synonymous term *tzu-chih* 'reaches its own property', which occurs constantly in inscriptions and elsewhere, and which cannot be explained away as a special type of tenure. Such personal lands then cannot explain why the individual holdings at Tun-huang as noted in the registers are so small. A more probable explanation is that many of the residents not only farmed allocated lands held in their own names, but also worked as tenants on government lands at the same time. There seem to have been extensive lands of this type at Tun-huang, and it is important to remember that a person could be both a tenant-farmer and the cultivator of lands held in his own name. It would also appear from the position of the allocated lands that some plots in the possession of a family might be so far away from the homestead that in all probability the plots—although allocated under the *chün-t'ien*— were rented out to tenant farmers in their vicinity.

72 See Niida, *Tō-Sō hōritsu monjo no kenkyū, passim.* See also P. 3018 v°; P. 3559 v°; P. 2657; P. 2803.

73 The rules governing entitlement to honorific rank (*hsün*) are given in des Rotours, *Traité des fonctionnaires et traité de l'armée*, I, pp. 50–9. On the cheapening of these ranks during Hsüan-tsung's reign see *TT*, 148, p. 773.

74 Both Niida and Suzuki have suggested this. It is worth bearing in mind in this connection that among the abuses of the *chün-t'ien* system mentioned at the time of Yü-wen Jung's reform in 723–5 was that of fraudulent honorific rank. See *TT*, 7, p. 41 *a–b*. Possibly to avoid the risk of such abuse, on the household register not only was the honorific title entered, but a note was appended to it giving the date and occasion of its award, with the name of the commanding officer.

75 See appendix I, 1, art. 4.

76 In the case of 'fiefs of maintenance' (*shih-shih-feng*) it was customary to grant the income from only a fraction of the households to whose revenue the noble was theoretically entitled. On this subject see Niida, 'Tōdai no hōshaku oyobi shokuhō-sei', *Tōhō gakuhō* (Tokyo), 10, 1 (1939).

77 Under *Code*, 13, art. 8, the village headmen (*li-cheng*) were supposed annually to prepare lists of lands which ought to revert to the state or to be allocated. The documents from Turfan (see notes 65, 67 to pp. 7, 8) were prepared however by the *hsiang*, the administrative division directly above the village (*li*). In either case, the business was done not by members of the local bureaucracy under the county magistrate, but by members of the sub-bureaucratic rural administration drawn from local families. It would be surprising if an administration of this sort, where the authorities were themselves often interested parties and were always intimately connected with the persons involved, did not show some irregularities. The magistrate, as representative of the central power, could only intervene in case of unsettled disputes, or of flagrant abuse.

PAGE 9

78 *Code*, 25, art. 13 (commentary), specifically mentions the registers and similar documents, making false entries in them punishable under *Code*, 25, art. 8, covering the falsification of official documents, the minimum penalty being a flogging of 100 strokes. *Code*, 12, arts. 1–4, prescribe heavy penalties for non-entry of persons or households in registers or tax lists, and for fraudulent entry of persons in the wrong age-category. Not only were the heads of households involved considered culpable, but the village headman and county and prefectural authorities were held to be responsible, even where they were not privy to the offence. Where the authorities wilfully made such omissions, the penalty was very severe, the minimum being a year's hard labour. Even if the principle of *tang-kuan* were invoked, this would have caused a serious setback in an official's career.

79 Both types of tenure are mentioned in inscriptions recording donations of land, *pia causa*, to Buddhist foundations. Some of these (see Twitchett, 'Monastic estates in T'ang China', *Asia Major*, 5, 11 (1956), p. 128) date from periods long after the decay of the land-allotment system, when the type of tenure was no longer recorded in the household register. In such cases the name *K'ou-fen-t'ien* may be little more than a local place-name. In Japan, after the decay of the *handen* system, 'Kubunden' (i.e. *k'ou-fen t'ien*) survived as a place-name in some places. In the written sources, there are only a handful of mentions of the land categories.

80 This is also the view of Suzuki Shun, 'Tōdai kindenhō sekō no igi ni tsuite', *Shien* (Kyūshū), 50 (1951), pp. 117–26. The complete divorce of the type of tenure and the type of culture is demonstrated from the Turfan by Nishimura, 'Torohan shutsudo monjo yori mitaru kindensei no sekō jōtai', pp. 332–4. Turfan, with its extreme land shortage, may not, however, have been typical. However, *TTCLC*, 73, p. 408, contains an edict dated 738 which clearly shows that lands in perpetuity destined for arable use were accepted as a normal thing in the vicinity of the capital. '. . . Recently in the counties of

Li-yang, etc., there has been a great deal of alkali land which has not been cultivated and allowed to revert to waste. Lately this land has been opened up and made into rice fields. Now that this has already been accomplished, how should its benefits be monopolised by anybody? All land within the jurisdiction of the metropolitan district which is brought into cultivation for use as rice fields ought to be granted to the poor and to those of the common people who have left their homes and subsequently returned, to form their lands in perpetuity....'

81 See *Sui shu*, 24 (note 25 to p. 4). It is very doubtful whether the Sui actually imposed a general system of this type.

82 See *TFYK*, 113, p. 11*b*; *TFYK*, 105, p. 17*a*; *TCTC*, 197, pp. 6207–8. 'The Emperor visited Ling-k'ou. The village was cramped and mean. His Majesty asked what land [the villagers] had received. An adult had only 30 *mou*. At midnight he went to sleep but was troubled about their not being granted their entitlements. He gave orders that the prefecture of Yung-chou (i.e. Ch'ang-an) should record those with little land, grant them remission of taxes, and transfer them to broad localities.' See the comments of Suzuki (note 80 to p. 9 above) and Hamaguchi Shigekuni, 'Fuhei-seido yori shinhei-sei e', *Shigaku zasshi*, 41, XII (1930), p. 69.

83 In early T'ang times Kuan-chung contained somewhat more than four and a half million persons, or 10 per cent of the total population of the empire. The concentration of high-ranking officials in the capital is obvious from a superficial examination of the ranks listed in *TLT*. Moreover, local administration was also much denser in this region, as a glance at the maps in *Li-tai yü-ti t'u* showing all the county towns will show. Each office had attached to it lands pertaining to office (*chih-fen t'ien*) and lands of the public administration (*kung-chieh t'ien*), all of which were rented to tenant-farmers. Moreover, each of the high officials was entitled to possess large quantities of land. All these public lands were concentrated close to the capital, since they were to be granted within 100 *li* of the city (see appendix 1, 1, art. 31). At the same time, a very high proportion of the military forces of the empire was either quartered in Kuan-chung or supplied from Kuan-chung.

84 See *THY*, 92, p. 1669; *TFYK*, 505, p. 19*a–b*; *HTS*, 55, p. 2*a*. The produce of these lands, which formed a part of officials' salaries, was replaced by a grant of 2 *sheng* of grain for each *mou* of land lost. This meant a very considerable reduction in official incomes. On the whole subject of such *chih-fen t'ien* see Osaki Shōji, 'Tōdai kyōkan shikiden kō', *Shichō*, 12, III/IV (1943), pp. 121–38.

85   See *THY*, 93, p. 1676; *TFYK*, 505, pp. 19*b*–20*b*; *TFYK*, 506, p. 2*b*. This revival of the system applied only to lands appertaining to posts in the capital. The similar lands in the provinces, which had also been abolished in 636 were later revived. In 722 they were once again abolished.

86   See *CTS*, 64, p. 3*a*. See also the interesting case quoted by Sudō Yoshiyuki, 'Tōmatsu Godai no shōen-sei', *Tōyō bunka*, 12 (1953), pp. 1–41 (corrected version included in *Chūgoku tochi-seido shi kenkyū*, 1955), from the biography of Wang Fang-i, *CTS*, 185 A, p. 12*a*–*b*, which tells how during the reign of T'ai-tsung, when Fang-i's father Wang Jen-piao died, his widow *née* Li retired to his country seat (*pieh-ye*). Here Fang-i, although he was still very young, built up an estate of several thousand *mou* within a few years. This estate seems to have been in the foothills south of the Wei river, for he planted bamboo and timber on his lands.

87   See *CTS*, 64, p. 3*a*.

88   The Buddhist monasteries had built up extensive estates during the Northern Dynasties, especially under the Northern Wei. See Gernet, *Les aspects économiques du Bouddhisme*, p. 118, for an interesting case of monastic estate building during the early years of the T'ang (see *Hsü kao-seng chuan*, 25, p. 654*b*). He suggests that the monasteries were above all desirous of acquiring marginal lands, upland, etc., where there was no danger of disputes with the local population, and where the large labour force available to a monastic community could be deployed to advantage in clearing forested land, etc. For further examples of presentation of lands to monasteries in early T'ang, see Tamai, *op. cit.* (note 4 to p. 1 above) and Niida, *Tō-Sō hōritsu bunsho no kenkyū*, pp. 200–24.

89   See *CTS*, 185 A, p. 5*a*: 'In 654 Chia Tun-i was promoted prefect of Lo-chou.' At that time the rich and powerful families all held lands in addition to those on their registers. Tun-i brought these into account, and confiscated more than 3000 *ch'ing*, which he granted to the poor and distressed.

90   See the accounts of legislative activity in Bünger, *Quellen zur Rechtsgeschichte der T'ang-Zeit* (1946); Yang Hung-lieh, *Chung-kuo fa-lü fa-ta shih* (1930), I, pp. 343 ff.; Niida, *Tōryō shūi*, pp. 1–59, of which the last is far the most reliable.

91   See the fragments collected in appendix I, 1.

92   In *TLT*, 3 (see appendix I, 1).

93 See *TT*, 2; *TFYK*, 495 (see appendix 1, 1). A further version of these same *Statutes*, almost certainly deriving from *TT*, 2, is to be found in *STCSKS*, 65 (Ming recension).

94 On the use of these *Statutes* of the Chinese series of 651, see Takigawa Masajirō, *Nihon hōseishi* (1928), pp. 90ff.

95 Compare the various articles in appendix 1, 1 which are preserved in more than one version.

96 See *Sung Hsing-t'ung*, 12, pp. 16*b*–17*a*; 13, pp. 1*b*–4*a*.

97 In China, although there was no formal abolition, the *chün-t'ien* system can have had no effect after 780. By 891 even the formal terminology connected with it had disappeared from the household registers.

PAGE 11

98 On the classes of legal privilege see Hulsewé, *The remnants of Han law* (1956), pp. 285–6. Balázs, in the introduction to his *Le traité juridique du Souei-chou* (1954), makes some very relevant remarks on the limits placed in practice on the application of the letter of the *Code* to members of the official class. In general, the *Code* does not seem to have been rigidly imposed under the T'ang, in contrast to the state of affairs under Han described by Hulsewé, *op. cit.*

99 See *Code*, 9, art. 22, which provided a punishment of two years' hard labour for disobeying edicts (*chih*), the commentary extending its application to cases of disobeying edicts (*chih*) which are here in question.

100 The staff of a county depended upon its status, which in turn was determined by its population. If it contained more than 5000 households it ranked as a superior county (*shang-hsien*). Since the average household contained between 5·5 and 5·7 persons, a superior county would have a population of at least 27,000. To administer a district of this size, the magistrate (*ling*) had a staff of only fifty-seven men, only four of whom were members of the ranking civil service. Of the total of fifty-seven, the legal department, with its satellite jailers and lictors, accounted for twenty-six. The registration department, which was responsible for the census and finance, employed only eleven assistants and clerks. Even if the county had a population exceeding 10,000 households (i.e. 55,000–57,000 persons), only ten additional subordinate staff were allowed, three to reinforce the legal department, and seven to assist the registration department (see *TLT*, 30, p. 14*a–b*).

101 See note 100 to p. 11 above. The large proportion of a magistrate's time which was occupied with hearing legal cases may be gauged by the various magistrate's handbooks surviving from Sung times, such as the anonymous *Chou-hsien ti-kang* or Lü Pen-chung's *Kuan chen*, and from the judgements (*p'an*) surviving from T'ang times in *WYYH* and *CTW*. The administration of fiscal policy was the next most important part of a magistrate's work.

102 On the duties and powers of the village headmen (*li-cheng*), see *TLT*, 30, p. 35 *a*; *Code*, 13, art. 8; *TT*, 3, p. 23 *b–c*. According to the latter he was to 'take charge of registering the population, allotting the tasks in agriculture and sericulture, investigate wrongs and crimes, and press the people for the payment of taxes'. The subject of rural administration is discussed in Matsumoto Yoshiumi, 'Rimpo-soshiki wo chūshin toshitaru Tōdai no sonsei', *Shigaku zasshi*, 53, III (1942); Naba Toshisada, 'Tōdai rimpo-seido shakugi', *Haneda Hakase shōju-kinen ronsō*. See also Wada Sei (ed.), *Shina chihō-jichi hattatsu shi*, pp. 6–14.

103 See *Code*, 13, art. 8 (commentary). 'Regarding lands which ought to be returned to the state and granted afresh, the village headman should annually, beginning in the 11th month, make preliminary inquiries and compile a register. The county magistrate should then assemble all those who ought to return lands or receive grants, and make the new allocations before them.' According to *TLT*, 30, p. 35 *a*, the village headmen were to make their investigation in the 10th month, and the magistrate himself was to make the allocations in the 11th month. The same source concludes its account of a magistrate's duties by saying that 'even though there shall be special officers in charge of tax lists, household registers...the magistrate himself holds overall responsibility for them'. His personal responsibility was also stressed in the field of taxation as we may see from an edict dated 728 in *THY*, 83, p. 1533; *TFYK*, 487, p. 17 *b*. The procedure laid down in the *Code*, preparation of lists of lands to be returned and persons entitled to new allocations, and eventual distribution, is borne out exactly by the Turfan MSS. introduced in *Tonkō Torohan shakai-keizai shiryō*, although it seems to have been done by the *hsiang* rather than the *li*. The fragments of a *shou-shih* recovered at Tun-huang (see Ikeda On, *op. cit.*, note 50 to p. 6 above), however, seem to have been made up by the *li*, as stipulated by the *Statutes*.

104 According to *TLT*, 30, *loc. cit.*, and *TT*, 3, p. 23 *b*: 'For village headmen the county officials should select honorific officers of the sixth rank or below (i.e. ex-soldiers), or honest and powerful persons with no rank, to fill the post.' The headman was permitted to supervise agricultural work, planting of trees, etc., in accordance with local custom, and custom certainly played a large part in irrigation. *Code*, 11, art. 17, moreover, contains a specific ruling allowing the local discontinuance of administrative rules which had proved inappropriate to local conditions with the prior consent of the central authorities. There can be not the slightest doubt that under the T'ang, as in every later period, customary law, local usage, and low-level arbitration were the dominant influences on law at the sub-county rural level.

105 The best account of irrigation procedures is that given by Naba, *op. cit.* (note 54 to p. 6). On the more general topic of the spread of irrigation in the various regions of China, see Aoyama Sadao, 'Tōdai no chisui-suiri kōji ni tsuite', *Tōhō gakuhō*, 15, I, pp. 1–44; 15, II, pp. 35–70 (1944).

106 See *CTS*, 58, p. 3*a*: 'Chang-sun Shun-te was appointed prefect of Tse-chou.... The former prefects Chang Chang-kuei and Chao Shih-ta had each possessed fertile lands extending to several tens of *ch'ing* within their jurisdiction. Shun-te investigated the matter, confiscated the lands and granted them to the poor and needy.' See also *CTS*, 185 A, *loc. cit.*

PAGE 12

107 In the early years of the dynasty the chief centre of migration was Kuan-chung, and possibly the great pressure of the militia (*fu-ping*) troops and the shortage of land were the main causes. Later, at the end of the seventh century, Ho-pei was very much affected. Here, the severe exactions during the Korean campaigns under T'ai-tsung and Kao-tsung, a series of natural disasters, and the border troubles with the Khitans, brought about a wave of vagrancy from about 680 onwards, which was heightened when the province was overrun by the Khitans in 696–8, and subsequently brutally 'pacified' by the reoccupying Chinese armies.

108 See Bielenstein, *op. cit.* (note 14 to p. 3 above); Pulleyblank, *The background of the rebellion of An Lu-shan*, appendix II, pp. 172–7, and the remarks on the latter in Twitchett, 'The government of T'ang in the early eighth century', *BSOAS*, 18, II (1956), pp. 325–7. Unfortunately, the preserved statistics derive from years so far apart (during the T'ang we have detailed figures from 639 or 642, the reign of Hsüan-tsung, and 812 only, and of these the first and the last were compiled under unfavourable administrative conditions and are thus incomplete) that it is impossible to correlate population changes with specific events except at the most superficial level.

109 It is generally assumed that during the pre-T'ang period the southern dynasties were at a more advanced level of economy than were their northern contemporaries. See Ch'en Yin-k'o, *Sui-T'ang chih-tu yüan-yüan lüeh-lun kao*, pp. 104 ff. See also the description of the ancient province of Yang-chou (i.e. southern China from the modern Kiangsu to Tongking) given in *Sui shu*, 31, pp. 13 a ff. (cf. Balázs, 'Le traité économique du Souei-chou', pp. 316 ff.). Too much weight should not, however, be given to this regional contrast, which applies only to state finance and commerce in the great cities. Throughout China rural society still maintained a predominantly barter economy far beyond the fall of T'ang. For a lively invocation of such small-scale rural trade, see the memorial of Han Yü translated in chapter III, appendix I.

110 For an extremely detailed case-history of such a clan, see Moriya Mitsuo, *Rikuchō mombatsu no ichi kōsatsu.*

PAGE 13

111 See Pulleyblank, *The background of the rebellion of An Lu-shan.*

112 See *THY*, 84, p. 1553; *TFYK*, 486, p. 33*b.*

113 See *Code*, 28, arts. 7, 10, 11.

114 See Osaki Shōji, 'Tōdai kyōkan shikiden kō', *Shichō*, 12, III/IV (1943), pp. 121–38, and sources there cited.

115 For example, in 641 the Hsiang-yang palace was abolished, and the lands under its control distributed to the local farmers. See *TFYK*, 105, p. 17*a.* In 651 the Yü-hua palace was likewise abolished, and its lands returned to the farmers. See *TFYK*, 14, p. 5*a*; *TFYK*, 105, p. 18*b.*

116 For example, during the early 650's P'ei Hsing-fang brought into cultivation several thousand *ch'ing* of rice fields which were granted to poor and landless people (see *TFYK*, 497, p. 8*a*).

117 For details, see chapter V below. The basic reason for such moves was that whereas Ch'ang-an was in an over-populated region whose productivity was declining with the decay of its irrigation network while its population came to include a growing proportion of unproductive persons, Lo-yang was easily supplied by water from the rich grain-growing regions of Ho-nan and southern Ho-pei, and in a crisis could call upon the still greater potential reserves of the Huai and Yangtze valleys through the canal system. This system was generally efficient and economical as far as Lo-yang, but the stretch from Lo-yang to Ch'ang-an was extremely arduous, involving a long land haul.

118 *THY*, 84, p. 1553; *TFYK*, 486, p. 33*b.* The empress Wu had a further motive in moving her government to Lo-yang, for being a usurper she was there better able to avoid pressure from the Kuan-chung aristocracy who supported the T'ang imperial house (see Hu Ju-lei, 'Lun Wu-Chou she-hui ti-ch'u', *Li-shih yen-chiu*, I (1955), pp. 85–96).

119 See *Ch'en Po-yü wen-chi*, 8, pp. 8*a*–9*a.*

120 There is no doubt that Kao-tsung's reign ended in acute economic crisis. It was a period of progressive inflation. Grain prices rose from 5 cash per *tou* in 665–6 to 220 cash or even 400 cash in 682, in which year grain was so scarce that distilling was forbidden. The famine in Kuan-chung forced the emperor to flee to Lo-yang under the most wretched conditions, many of his entourage dying *en route*. At the same time there was an outbreak of vagrancy, and a spate of counterfeiting. There seems little reason to question the traditional view that this crisis was caused by the cumulative expenses of Kao-tsung's military adventures, which burdened the economy with the upkeep of large armies of professional troops.

121 See *THY*, 85, p. 1561; *TFYK*, 486, pp. 12*b*–14*a*. Okazaki Fumio, 'Ubun Yū no kakko-seisaku ni tsuite', *Shinagaku*, 2, v (1939), pp. 42 ff., considers that this memorial had a deep effect on the later policy of Yü-wen Jung.

122 See the biography of Ti Jen-chieh, *CTS*, 85, pp. 3*b* ff.; *HTS*, 115, pp. 3*a* ff.; *TCTC*, 206. The edict issued in 724, imposing Yü-wen Jung's second policy for re-registering vagrants, attributes the situation in the early years of Hsüan-tsung's reign to the aftermath of these wars (see *TFYK*, 70, p. 11*a*; *TTCLC*, 111, p. 577).

123 See, for example, the case of Chang Ch'ang-ch'i whose appointment to office in 703 was opposed on the grounds that 'when formerly he had lived in Ch'i-chou, vagrancy among the local population had reached great proportions' (see *TCTC*, 207, p. 6563).

124 See *HTS*, 128, p. 3*a*, which records that when Li Chieh went as inspecting commissioner to Shan-nan, he discovered that the rich and powerful families were accumulating lands belonging to the poor.

125 See *THY*, 85, pp. 1561–2; *HTS*, 112, pp. 4*a* ff.

126 Li Chiao's memorial had made certain suggestions, but these were never acted upon.

127 On Yü-wen Jung's schemes see Okazaki, 'Ubun Yū no kakko-seisaku ni tsuite'; Suzuki Shun, 'Ubun Yū no kakko ni tsuite', *Wada Hakase kanreki kinen Tōyōshi ronsō*, pp. 329–44, and Pulleyblank, *The background of the rebellion of An Lu-shan*, pp. 29–32.

128 See *THY*, 85, p. 1562; *TT*, 7, p. 41*a*; *TCTC*, 212, p. 6744. The edict issued at this time is in *CTW*, 22, p. 6*b*.

129 See *CTW*, 22, p. 6*b*; *TFYK*, 63, pp. 16*b*–18*a*, summary in *TCTC*, 212, p. 6744. An edict ordering consideration of the scheme is in *TFYK*, 63, p. 16*b*.

130 For the edict appointing the first nineteen officers, see *TFYK*, 162, pp. 7*b*–8*a*; *CTW*, 29, pp. 1*b*–2*a*, dated 723. They were there described as 'Supplementary Examining Censors in charge of taxation, the land levy, and the investigation of lands'.

The character *t'ien* 田 in this title has been corruped into *ch'iu* 囚.

131 This 'light tax' is discussed by Suzuki, 'Ubun Yū no kakko ni tsuite', and Pulleyblank, *The background of the rebellion of An Lu-shan*, p. 125, n. 34. Suzuki objects that the figure 1500 cash given in *CTS*, 48, for the tax is much too high, and suggests that it was fabricated by the compiler to make Yü-wen Jung's scheme appear oppressive. Pulleyblank suggests on the other hand that, at the very low contemporary prices of commodities in which taxes were normally contributed, the tax was still low. However, he seems to base this opinion on the assumption (*The background of the rebellion of An Lu-shan*, pp. 30–1) that the 1500 cash was a down payment covering the whole period of six years (or five years according to *CTS*, 48, p. 1*b*) exemption. I myself would prefer to take it that the 1500 cash was an annual assessment payable during the period of exemption in place of the normal taxes, although admittedly the text can be read in either sense. If in fact it is an annual assessment, it compares rather unfavourably with the normal tax load. Most vagrants would have been in the lowest household category, and their households rather small. A ninth grade household with a single adult member would have paid, taking the contemporary prices of 210 cash per length (40 feet, not 20 as assumed by Pulleyblank, *The background of the rebellion of An Lu-shan*) of silk, and from 5 to 20 cash per *tou* (I assume an average price of 15 cash) for grain, a total of 1242 cash including both land levy on his maximum entitlement of land and household levy. To this would have been added transport charges, miscellaneous *corvée* charges, and payments in lieu of any special duties. As both *CTS*, 48, and *TT*, 7, make a point of the excessive application of special *corvée* duties, exemption from which cost upwards of 1000 cash per annum, the annual tax liability of such a family might easily have been well in excess of 2000 cash, although ninth grade households were not normally assigned special services. Since the contemporary prices on which I base this calculation are certainly abnormally low, for they are cited to show current abundance of commodities, I think we may assume that 1500 cash per annum was a fairly liberal annual charge, payment of which would exempt the settled vagrant not only from his basic taxes, but from extraordinary levies and employment in *corvée* work during his period of exemption.

132 This change of official attitude is clear from a comparison of the two edicts of 721 and 724, translated by Pulleyblank, *The background of the rebellion of An Lu-shan*, pp. 178–82.

133 See *CTS*, 105, p. 2*a*.

134 On Jung's successive appointments, see Suzuki, 'Ubun Yū no kakko ni tsuite'. The ten further assistants were appointed in the 6th month 724 according to *THY*, 85, p. 1562. The edict appointing them is in *TFYK*, 70, p. 11*a*; *TTCLC*, 111, p. 576; *CTW*, 29, pp. 6*a*–7*b*; *TTCLC* gives the date as the 5th month 724.

135 See *CTS*, 48, p. 1*b*; *CTS*, 105, p. 2*a*; *TT*, 7, p. 41*a*; *THY*, 85, p. 1563.

136 See *CTS*, p. 2*a*; *THY*, 85, p. 1563, read: 'The prefectural and county authorities fell in with Jung's intentions, and made it their concern to bring into account a great many. They all falsely exaggerated the numbers, some of them even registering actually resident households (*t'u-hu*) as vagrants (*k'o-hu*).'

PAGE 15

137 For this total, see *CTS*, 8, p. 14*a*; *THY*, 84, p. 1551; *TFYK*, 486, p. 15*a*; *TCTC*, 213, p. 6773. The number of individuals was 41,419,712. This total must include the 800,000 households brought into account under Yü-wen Jung's scheme.

138 The account given in *CTS*, 48, p. 1*b*, is the most forthright in its condemnation, but all the accounts save that in *TT*, 7, p. 41*a*, are antagonistic to Yü-wen Jung. See, for example, the historian's comment at the end of *CTS*, 105, pp. 10*b*–11*a*.

139 See Pulleyblank, *The background of the rebellion of An Lu-shan*, pp. 50 ff. See also *CTS*, 48, pp. 1*b*–2*a*.

140 See Suzuki, 'Ubun Yū no kakko ni tsuite'.

141 See Pulleyblank, *The background of the rebellion of An Lu-shan*, pp. 29 ff.

142 Yü-wen Jung himself was descended from the ruling house of the Northern Chou dynasty.

143 This insoluble problem has received some attention from Chinese Marxist scholars recently. Hu Ju-lei, 'Lun Wu-Chou she-hui ti-ch'u', sees the new bureaucrats as deriving from 'land-owners and merchants'. I can see not the slightest evidence for suggesting that merchants played any significant role in this movement.

144 See *CTS*, 100, p. 10*a*: 'Yü-wen Jung had previously made a secret report to the throne that Lu Ts'ung-yüan had broad possessions of fertile lands amounting to more than 100 *ch'ing*.' Lu Ts'ung-yüan was so notorious a land-grabber that even Hsüan-tsung himself called him *tuo-t'ien weng* 'Old man with many lands'. See *TPKC*, 495, p. 4060; *TPYL*, 821, p. 11*a*; *TFYK*, 522, p. 19*a–b*; *THY*, 81, p. 1502, and the *Ming-huang tsa-lu* of Cheng Ch'u-min.

145 The estates were largely worked by tenant-farmers or by labourers recruited from among those dispossessed of their lands. When such migrant families were settled and given title to their lands, the labour market for the estate owners was certainly affected.

146 However, there is evidence of strong opposition. See the memorials of Huang-fu Chiung, *THY*, 85, p. 1562; Yang Hsiang-ju, *TT*, 7, p. 41*a*, and Yang Ch'ang, *THY*, 85, p. 1562. All of these opponents were demoted to posts in the provinces.

147 *CTS*, 105, p. 3*a*; *TCTC*, 212, p. 6762.

148 See Pulleyblank, *The background of the rebellion of An Lu-shan*, pp. 50–2.

149 See *CTS*, 105, p. 3*b*. The fall of Yü-wen Jung in 727 did not mean an abrupt end of his measures, for one of the chief ministers, Li Yüan-hung, seems to have followed not dissimilar economic policies, and in the 10th month 728, following Jung's recall to the capital as vice-president of the Board of Finance earlier in the same year (*TCTC*, 213, p. 6781) an edict was issued allowing settler households to reside permanently in the place where they were living, if they so wished (see *THY*, 84, p. 1554). There is, moreover, some evidence from a series of fragments of official correspondence from Turfan dated 728–30, and in the possession of the Ryūkoku daigaku, Kyōto, that the re-registration policies (*k'ua-hu*) were still being enforced (see the MSS. quoted by Ogasawara Nobuhide, *Ryūkoku daigaku ronshū*, 349 (1955), pp. 1–15).

150 See *THY*, 85, pp. 1563–4; *TFYK*, 485, pp. 20*a*–21*a*. Both *TT*, 7, p. 41*a–b*, and following it *CTW*, 303, p. 23*a*, attribute it to Yü-wen Jung. This attribution is accepted by Suzuki, 'Ubun Yū no kakko ni tsuite', but I am inclined to agree with Pulleyblank (*The background of the rebellion of An Lu-shan*, p. 126, notes 42–3) that it is more likely to have been the work of P'ei Yao-ch'ing.

151 The plan envisaged the vagrants being settled on the land in 'quarters' (*fang*), each adult being granted 50 *mou* to work on his own account, and having also to perform a fixed quota of labour on public lands attached to the *fang*. The scheme seems in fact to be a compromise between the colony and the traditional *ching-t'ien* land system. On the organisation of colonies, see Twitchett, 'Lands under state cultivation during the T'ang dynasty', *Journal of Economic and Social History of the Orient*, 2, II (1959), pp. 162–203.

152 See *TFYK*, 495, p. 23b. 'The personal share land and lands in perpetuity of the common people of the empire have long had fixed amounts. The lands are not allowed to be sold or mortgaged. Yet we hear that it has not yet been possible to prevent the poor from losing their livelihoods, while the rich and powerful accumulate their lands. Once again the established shares should be clearly made known, and the prohibition made law. If anyone breaks these laws, it shall be considered as a case of disobeying an imperial edict.'

153 See Appendix I, I to this chapter.

154 See *TFYK*, 495, *loc. cit.*

155 See *TFYK*, 495, pp. 24a–26a.

156 The relevant passage reads: 'Now we hear that the princes and dukes, the hundred officials and the rich and powerful families have been setting up great estates (*chuang-t'ien*). Heedlessly they appropriate land, and none of them show any fear of the regulations. Those who "borrow wasteland" (*chieh-huang*) all include fertile lands among them, and then steal these for themselves. Those who establish "pasturages" simply indicate the mountains and valleys in which they are to be set up, without specifying the limits of the lands involved. When we come to the purchase and sale of personal share lands and lands in perpetuity in contravention of the law, some of them simply alter the registers, while others pass the transaction off as a "mortgage". Thus they have come to cause the common people to have no place in which to settle in peace. Further, they keep vagrant households and cause them to live as their own tenants. Thus, having already robbed the resident population of their means of livelihood, they further bring about the evil of vagrancy. This situation is the same far and near, and has been allowed to continue for a long time without there being any measure of reform or any deep consideration of the evil. If the princes, dukes, the families of the officials and of those with honorific rank or hereditary privilege were to be prevented from exceeding the limits laid down in the *Statutes* and *Ordinances* in building up estates, it would be possible to change to a more lenient system. But at present, it is essential to make the system universally accepted . . .' (*TFYK*, 495, p. 24 *a–b*).

157   See appendix I, I, art. 20. For examples of such presentations see Tamai, *Shina shakai-keizai shi kenkyū*, pp. 71–2. For earlier examples, see *CTS*, 78, pp. 4*b*–5*a*; *HTS*, 104, p. 2*b*, recording presentation of estates to Yü Chih-ning, Chang Hsing-ch'eng and Kao Chi-fu. In later times it also became quite a common practice to grant estates to the heirs of persons granted posthumous honours. See, for example, the cases of Tuan Hsiu-shih (see *CTS*, 128, p. 4*a*) and of Li Huai-kuang (see *CTS*, 121, p. 12*a*; *TTCLC*, 65, p. 362), both of which date from Te-tsung's early years.

158   See *TLT*, 3, p. 53 *a–b*. In theory, of course, such lands were marginal lands, and did not include arable fields. But see the quotation from *TFYK*, 495, in note 156 to p. 16 above.

PAGE 17
159   See Gernet, *Les aspects économiques du Bouddhisme*, pp. 126 ff.

160   See Nishikawa, 'Tonkō hakken no Tōdai koseki-zankan ni arawareta "jiden" ni tsuite', *Shigaku zasshi*, 64, X (1955), pp. 38–60. But see also the remarks of Nishijima, 'Torohan shutsudo monjo yori mitaru kindensei no sekō jōtai', *Tonkō Torohan shakai-keizai shiryō*, I (1959), pp. 151–292, on this theory.

161   See, for example, the instances cited in Tamai, *Shina shakai-keizai shi kenkyū*; Sudō Yoshiyuki, *Chūgoku tochi-seido shi kenkyū* and by Katō in his two classic studies of the *chuang-yüan*, 'Tō no shōen no seishitsu oyobi sono yurai ni tsukite', and 'To-Sō-jidai no shōen soskihi narabi ni sono shūraku to shite hattatsu ni tsukite', both of which are reprinted in *Shina keizai shi kōshō* (1952), vol. I.

162   See Katō, 'Tō no shōen no seishitsu oyobi sono yurai ni tsukite', pp. 208–14.

163   The two are frequently referred to as parallel institutions.

164   For a typical example in Ho-pei see *CTW*, 353, pp. 6*b*–7*a*, and *Chin-shih ts'ui-pien*, 83, pp. 27*a* ff. This estate, belonging to the Chin-hsien princess, included not only grain fields but orchards and hill-land with stands of timber.

165   On this problem, see chapter II.

166 See the figures preserved in *THY*, 84, p. 1551; *TFYK*, 486, pp. 17*a*–19*a*. 742, 8,535763; 754, 9,069,154; 756, 8,018,710; 760, 1,931,145; 764, 2,933,125; 766–79, 1,200,000 (see *TT*, 7, p. 41*c*).

167 See Liu Yen's letter to Yüan Tsai, *THY*, 87, pp. 1588–90; *TFYK*, 498, pp. 20*a*–22*b*; *CTW*, 370, pp. 14*a*–16*a*; *CTS*, 123, pp. 1*b*–2*b*. See also chapter v, notes 57, 58 to p. 92.

168 This can be easily demonstrated by the population statistics for 812 preserved in *YHCHC*. In many parts of the Yangtze valley, these show increases of up to 300 per cent over the figures for 742. It is out of the question that such large increases could be the result of more efficient registration, since the registration machinery was in a state of decline. Nor is it likely to be the result of natural increase alone.

168*a* See *THY*, 85, p. 1565. Similar edicts appeared in 760 and 762 (*ibid.*).

169 See *THY*, 85, p. 1565; *TFYK*, 495, p. 26*a*.

170 See *TFYK*, 495, p. 26*b*.

171 That is they were essentially representative of local autonomy as against the central government, of military rule as against civil government, and had a strong emphasis on personal relationships in their administration as against bureaucratic status.

172 See *Yüan-shih Ch'ang-ch'ing chi*, 37, pp. 1*a*–5*b*. The estates were scattered all over his province.

173 See, for example, the case of Yüan Tsai (*CTS*, 118, p. 2*b*).

174 See Sudō, *Chūgoku tochi-seido shi kenkyū*, pp. 13–23 for examples.

175 See the case of Yü Ch'ao-en, *CTS*, 184, p. 7*b*, which records the gift of his estate to be used as a monastery.

176 See Sudō, *Chūgoku tochi-seido shi kenkyū*, pp. 23–34.

177 See Twitchett, 'Monastic estates in T'ang China', *Asia Major*, 5, II, and sources there cited.

178 See Katō, 'Tō no shōen no seishitsu oyobi sono yurai ni tsukite'. Most common of these names were *chuang-t'ien, chuang-yüan, chuang-chai, pieh-ye, pieh-shu, pieh-chuang, shu,* and *chuang-chü*.

179 See the examples cited by Katō, 'Tō no shōen no seishitsu oyobi sono yurai ni tsukite'.

180 Two of the most famous examples were the Wang-ch'uan chuang belonging to the poet Wang Wei (see *CTS*, 190B, p. 3*b*; *Wang Yu-ch'eng chi*, 17, pp. 368–9; *CTW*, 324, p. 16*a–b*), and the P'ing-ch'üan chuang belonging to Li Te-yü (see *CTS*, 170, p. 12*b*). Many famous estates of this type were in the area around Lo-yang, as was, for example, the famous Wu-ch'iao chuang belonging to P'ei Tu (*CTS*, 170, *loc. cit.*). Many of these estates are described by the Sung writer Chou K'o-fei in his *Lo-yang ming-yüan chi*.

PAGE 19

181 Katō, *Shina keizai shi kōshō*.

182 Tamai, *Shina shakai-keizai shi kenkyū*.

183 Sudō, *Chūgoku tochi-seido shi kenkyū*, pp. 41–57.

184 The best example of such an estate is that of the Ta-hsiang ssu at Lung-chou. See Twitchett, 'Monastic estates in T'ang China', *Asia Major*, 5, II, pp. 138–9, and 'The monasteries and China's economy in medieval times', *BSOAS*, 19, III, pp. 538–9. It is clear that not only were *chuang* normally composed of many small fragments of land, but that many of them were very small. It is quite misleading to think of the average estates of this type as similar to the *latifundia*. They were rather a series of plots linked under a unified management.

185 This was not always the case with monastic holdings. See the account given by Gernet, *Les aspects économiques du Bouddhisme*, pp. 114–15, of the properties of the A-yü-wang ssu near Ningpo.

186 See one of the estates under the Ta-hsiang ssu (Twitchett, 'Monastic estates in T'ang China') called the Hu-t'ao ku lien-chuang ti, 'continuous estate lands of the Hu-t'ao valley', the boundaries of which were watersheds, and which was partly cultivated land (*shu-ti*) and partly scrub and wasteland. See *Chin-shih ts'ui pien*, 113. See also the account of the A-yü-wang ssu in *Chin-shih ts'ui-pien*, 108; *Liang-Che chin-shih chih*, 1, and that of the estate given to the Nan-shih ssu in Jao-chou by Liu Fen in 892, see *CTW*, 793, pp. 15*b*–18*b*. See also Sudō, *Chūgoku tochi-seido shi kenkyū*, pp. 41–3.

187 All the above cited cases date from the ninth century. It is possible that the land which came on the market with the dissolution of the Buddhist communities in 843–6 also provided the opportunity for private persons to buy up large tracts of monastic land, and thus found large estates. See Katō, *Shina keizai shi kōshō*, pp. 245–54.

188 See Katō, *ibid.*; Sudō, *Chūgoku tochi-seido shi kenkyū*. This type of enterprise was common on the estates of the monasteries in the Tun-huang area, which also had large flocks of sheep. On mills and oil-presses held as part of monastic properties see Naba, 'Chūban Tōdai ni okeru Tonkō-chihō Bukkyōjiin no tengai-keiei ni tsukite', *Tōa keizai ronsō*, I, III, IV, 2, II (1941), and 'Ryōgo kō', *Shina Bukkyō shigaku*, 2, I, II, IV (1938), and 'Ryōgo kō', *Shirin*, 23, I (1938). See also Gernet, *Les aspects économiques du Bouddhisme*, pp. 138–40, and the remarks on this passage in Twitchett, 'The monasteries and China's economy in medieval times', *BSOAS*, 19, III, pp. 533–5. Mills were also found on the estates of laymen, see for examples Sudō, *Chūgoku tochi-seido shi kenkyū*, pp. 42–3.

189 See Naba, 'Ryōgo kō'.

190 See Katō, *Shina keizaishi kōshō*, pp. 234–5; Sudō, *Chūgoku tochi-seido shi kenkyū*, pp. 48–56. The terms most commonly used for such persons were *chuang-k'o*, *chuang-hu*, *fou-k'o*, *k'o-hu*, *tien-k'o*, *tien-hu*, *tien-chia*, or simply *k'o*. A similar type of tenant-farmer attached to the monastic estates was called *ssu-hu*. Tenant-farmers working official lands were known as *tien-hu* for the most part.

191 Hired hands are frequently mentioned in later T'ang sources not only in connection with privately owned estates, but also as the labour force on official lands. See Twitchett, *Journal of the Economic and Social History of the Orient*, 2, II, pp. 185, 200–1. They are normally referred to as *ku-min*, *ku-yung*, *yung-chü*, *ku-yung*, or *liu-yung*. It is almost impossible in the case of private estates to distinguish between permanently employed hands and casually hired labour. In official contexts, it is possible that the term *chieh-yung* may be read in this latter sense (see Twitchett, *ibid.*, p. 185). See also Niida, *Tō-Sō hōritsu bunsho no kenkyū*, pp. 422–47 for a full discussion of the nature of such employment.

192 There is a great deal of evidence of employment of slaves on the land during T'ang times. See Sudō, *Chūgoku tochi-seido shi kenkyū*, pp. 48–9, for examples.

193 See *Fou-tsu t'ung chi*, 9, p. 199*b*, and Sudō, *Chūgoku tochi-seido shi kenkyū*.

194 See Sudō, *Chūgoku tochi-seido shi kenkyū*; T'ao Hsi-sheng and Chü Ch'ing-yüan, *T'ang-tai ching-chi shih*, pp. 49 ff. Sudō goes into great detail on the status of tenants (*tien-hu*) under the Sung, pointing out that they came to be attached to the land which they worked by strict legal limitation on their freedom of movement. On tenancy under the T'ang there is a rather limited body of material. Sudō has worked over the MS. material from Turfan and Tun-huang, most of it dealing with tenants of official or monastic lands, in 'Dennin bunsho no kenkyū', *Tonkō Torohan shakai-keizai shiryō*, pp. 91–150, while Niida has devoted a long study to the records of monastic tenants in the same area, 'Tōmatsu Godai no Tonkō jiin-dengo kankei bunsho', *ibid.* pp. 69–90. Both of these articles clearly demonstrate that the status relationships of tenants were by no means straightforward. Although monastic tenants were attached to the monasteries' lands and allowed to marry only within their own group, there are cases where they themselves possessed slaves, who worked on the land for them. In other cases slaves are found working as tenants the lands of persons other than their owner. Moreover, it is quite clear that being a tenant and a farmer of one's own lands, received under the *chün-t'ien* allotment, were not mutually exclusive categories. This in itself seems clear proof of the lack of formal restriction on the status of tenants, apart from the special case of the *ssu-hu* under the monasteries. A further complication of this picture is that some lands received under the *chün-t'ien* system were almost certainly let out to tenant-farmers, since some of the plots recorded in the Tun-huang household registers are so far from the bulk of the family holdings that they would have been quite uneconomical to work.

195 See Sudō, *Chūgoku tochi-seido shi kenkyū*, pp. 52–6, and the examples there quoted.

196 See Katō, *Shina keizaishi kōshō*, pp. 240–3; Sudō, *Chūgoku tochi-seido shi kenkyū*; T'ao Hsi-sheng and Chü Ch'ing-yüan, *T'ang-tai ching-chi shih*; Niida, 'Tōmatsu Godai no Tonkō jiin-dengo kankei bunsho'. The latter has shown how such indebtedness often led to the drawing of a contract under which the debtor became a bondsman of the creditor-landlord until the debt was repayed (see P. 3150). Interest on such loans of grain sometimes reached 100 per cent.

197 See Katō, *Shina keizaishi kōshō*, pp. 234–6. Such quarters were known as *k'o-fang*.

198 Katō, *Shina keizaishi kōshō*, p. 235, cites one example of such a settlement with over 200 households (*TPKC*, 165), and another of 100 families (*Tung-hsüan pi-lu*, 8).

199 See Katō, *Shina keizaishi kōshō*, pp. 245–58.

200 See Katō, *Shina keizaishi kōshō*; Sudō, *Chūgoku tochi-seido shi kenkyū*, p. 57.

201 See *Ennin's Diary*, 840, IV, 21 (Reischauer, p. 210).

202 These bailiffs were normally called *chuang-li* or *chien-chuang*. See Sudō, *Chūgoku tochi-seido shi kenkyū*, pp. 43–7. Monk-bailiffs on monastic estates were known as *chih-chuang, chih-shu,* or *chih-shu-seng.*

203 See Katō, Sudō, T'ao and Chü. Rent was also sometimes known as *tsu-shui, tsu-k'o,* and simply *tsu.* Lu Chih reckoned that in the area around Ch'ang-an the rents rose to 1 *shih* per *mou,* which was twenty times the official taxes in grain due from 1 *mou.* Even the lower grades of rent were ten times the tax assessment (see *Lu Hsüan-kung Han-yüan chi,* 22, pp. 27 *a*–30 *a*; *CTW,* 465, p. 25 *a*).

204 See Katō, *Shina keizaishi kōshō*; Sudō, *Chūgoku tochi-seido shi kenkyū,* pp. 50–2.

205 See *Yu-yang tsa-tsu,* 8, p. 7*b*, which mentions tenants employed in building walls and bridges, and *ibid.* 15, p. 6*a*, which also mentions building operations.

206 See chapter II below.

207 See Tamai, *Shina shakai-keizai shi kenkyū,* p. 69. He cites the case of Cheng Kuang, which occurred in 852. In that year the emperor issued an edict giving remission of taxes in respect of two estates which he had presented to Kuang, who was his uncle. Nevertheless, the secretariat and chancellery memorialised the throne that it was not permissible to make such exceptions to the general rule (see *THY,* 84, pp. 1544–5). Tamai cites a further passage from *T'ang yü-lin,* 2, pp. 37–8, which tells how subsequently the bailiffs of Cheng Kuang's estates were arrested by the local authorities for not paying the taxes due on the estates. This clearly shows both that estates, even imperial donations, were liable to tax, and also that powerful owners could resist taxation.

208 See *TFYK,* 491, p. 6*a*, which quotes an Act of Grace of 805 remitting the tax arrears owing from the estates administered by the Household Commissioners for Estates (*nei chuang-chai-shih*).

209 *HTS,* 52, p. 7*b*; *CTS,* 18A, p. 14*a*–*b*; *Li Wei-kung wen chi,* 20, pp. 3*a*–4*b*; *Fou-tsu t'ung-chi,* 42, p. 386*a*. See Twitchett, *Asia Major,* 5, II, pp. 141–2.

210 See *TFYK,* 495, p. 26*a*, which gives the total of lands granted in the whole empire for 755 as 14,303,862 *ch'ing* 13 *mou.* Even this figure is suspiciously large (see note 13 to p. 3 above and note 71 to p. 8).

211 See *TTCLC,* 110, pp. 570–1; *CTW,* 19, p. 3*a*–*b*; *WYYH,* 465, p. 6*b*.

212 See *THY*, 89, p. 1622; *CTS*, 148, p. 4*a*.

213 See Niida, *Tō-Sō hōritsu monjo no kenkyū*, pp. 205–6.

214 See the cases cited in Twitchett, *Asia Major*, 5, II, p. 141, note 98.

215 See Yang Lien-sheng, *Money and credit in China*, p. 71, and the same author's 'Buddhist monasteries and four money-raising institutions in Chinese history', *Harvard Journal of Asiatic Studies*, 13 (1950). See also Michihata, *Tōdai Bukkyōshi no kenkyū* (1957), pp. 514–45.

216 See Naba, 'Ryōko kō'; Nishijima, 'Tengai no kanata', *Rekishigaku kenkyū*, 125, pp. 38–46.

PAGE 21

217 This is very much a matter of conjecture. For a suggestive case of a person setting up an estate out of monastic land, see the example of Li Pin's redemption of the estates of the Shan-ch'üan ssu at Ch'ang-chou during the *Hsien-t'ung* period (860–74) which had been bought up at the dissolution by an officer in the Salt and Iron Commission (see *CTW*, 788).

218 See *THY*, 48, pp. 854–5, which cites edicts dated 847, 848 and 851 relaxing the legislation against the monastic communities. A reaction set in in 851. In that year memorials attacking the Buddhists were presented by Sun Ch'iao (see *TCTC*, 249, p. 8047) and by the secretariat and chancellery (*TCTC*, *loc. cit.*). In 852 the secretariat again protested against the growing power of the monasteries (*THY*, 48, p. 844). See also *Fou-tsu t'ung-chi*, 42, pp. 386*b*ff.

219 Beside these lands which came into the hands of the state casually, and which normally seem to have been disposed of rather rapidly, the state also possessed large tracts of land both on the frontiers and in central China which were cultivated under state control, either as military colonies (*t'un-t'ien*) or agricultural colonies (*ying-t'ien*). On this question see Twitchett, 'Lands under state cultivation during the T'ang dynasty', *Journal of Economic and Social History of the Orient*, 2, II (1959), pp. 162–203, and Aoyama Sadao, 'Tōdai no tonden to eiden', *Shigaku zasshi*, 63, I (1954).

220 See Katō, 'Nai-sōtaku-shi kō', *Shina keizaishi kōshō*, I, pp. 261–82; T'ao Hsi-sheng and Chü Ch'ing-yüan, *T'ang-tai ching-chi shih*, pp. 38–47. There seem to have been in fact three separate commissioners, according to a quotation of the lost *Po-ssu shu-yao* of Li Chi-fu preserved in *Shih-wu chi yüan*, 6. One, the *chuang-chai-shih* came under the Court of Agriculture (*ssu-nung ssu*). A companion office *Tung-tu chuang-chai-shih* dealt with the estates around Lo-yang. By far the most important was the *Nei chuang-chai-shih*, attached to the palace administration and staffed by eunuchs. This

body is the only one of the three encountered in the sources with any frequency. It seems to have been concerned with the properties of the imperial clan themselves.

221 See the Act of Grace of 821, in *TTCLC*, 10, pp. 60–2.

222 T'ao and Chü, *T'ang-tai ching-chi shih*.

223 See Katō, 'Nai-sōtaku-shi kō', *T'ang-tai ching-chi shih*, pp. 268 ff. See also Tamai, *Shina shakai-keizai shi kenkyū*, pp. 78 ff.

224 See *Chin-shih ts'ui-pien*, 114; *Ch'ih Nei chuang-chai-shih t'ieh*.

225 See *TFYK*, 491, p. 6 b.

226 See Katō, 'Nai-sōtaku-shi kō', *T'ang-tai ching-chi shih*.

227 See Sudō, *Chūgoku tochi-seido shi kenkyū*, pp. 23–34. There seems little doubt that the breakdown of the land-allotment system led to the building of landed properties in a wider social range than had previously been possible. Before the breakdown of the *chün-t'ien* system, it was risky for a person without rank to attempt the illegal acquisition of large quantities of land, since he could receive no legal title to it. With the abandonment of the *chün-t'ien* and its limitation of holdings, it became possible for anybody sufficiently wealthy to acquire estates and remain confident of being able to retain and dispose of them freely.

228 The holder of a *chuang-yüan* had neither any special form of title to his property, save the customary acceptance by the authorities of the rights of possession and disposal of lands, nor any fiscal privilege in respect of his holdings, nor any special jurisdiction within his estates. But the comparative weakness of the central administration meant that although none of these rights was accepted by law, in practice the owner's rights were considerable, and he was able to enforce his control through his bailiffs, and either defy or come to terms with the tax-collector.

PAGE 22

229 See the *Sung hsing-t'ung*, 12, pp 16 b–17 a; 13, pp. 1 b–4 a.

230 See *CTS*, 49, p. 9 b; *THY*, 84, p. 1545; *TFYK*, 495, pp. 26 b–27 a.

231 See chapter II and chapter IV below.

232 The statistics preserved in *YHCHC* show large increases in south-eastern China, which probably represent real growth, but also tremendous decreases in the north, which are certainly the result of lack of administrative control in the north-east.

233 See chapter II.

PAGE 23

234 See *THY*, 85, p. 1566; *TFYK*, 495, p. 30*b*. As the troops concerned were long-service troops (*kuan-chien*) who had normally to be provisioned and clothed at state expense, this measure was probably designed to reduce provincial expenditure.

235 See *THY*, 85, p. 1566; *TFYK*, 495, p. 31*a–b*.

236 See sources cited above, note 209 to p. 20.

237 *Ibid.* See also the account by Tu Mu, *Fan-ch'uan wen-chi*, 10, pp. 7*b*–10*b*.

238 See *THY*, 85, p. 1567; *TFYK*, 495, p. 31*b*.

239 See *THY*, 85, p. 1567; *TFYK*, 495, p. 31*a*.

CHAPTER II

PAGE 24

1 On the *I-t'iao pien fa* reform see Liang Fang-chung, *The single-whip method of taxation in China* (Cambridge, Mass., 1956), and the Chinese article, 'I-t'iao pien fa', *Chung-kuo chin-tai ching-chi-shih yen-chiu chi-k'an*, 3, 1 (1936), from which this was translated. Further very important material is collected by the same author in 'Ming-tai I-t'iao pien fa nien-piao', *Ling-nan ta-hsüeh*, 12, 1 (1952). Needless to say, the new tax system developed under the T'ang (the *liang-shui* system) was much modified under the subsequent dynasties.

2 There has recently been a sharp controversy among Chinese Marxist historians as to whether this connection existed. Both Teng Kuang-ming, 'T'ang-tai tsu-yung-tiao-fa yen-chiu', *Li-shih Yen-chiu*, IV (1954), and Chang Po-ch'üan, 'Shih-t'an tui tsu-yung-tiao ti k'an-fa', *Hsin-shih-hsüeh t'ung-hsün*, VI (1955), strenuously deny any connection on purely theoretical grounds. However, their views were met with irrefutable criticisms from more competent historians, for example in Ts'en Chung-mien, 'Tsu-yung-tiao yü chün-t'ien yu wu kuan-hsi?', *Li-shih Yen-chiu*, V (1955), pp. 65–78, and Han Kuo-p'an, 'T'ang-tai-ti chün-t'ien-chih yü tsu-yung-tiao', *Li-shih Yen-chiu*, V (1955), pp. 79–90. A succinct summary of the evidence is given by Ts'en Chung-mien, *Sui T'ang shih* (1957), pp. 243–4.

3 See *THY*, 83, p. 1530; *TFYK*, 487, p. 16*a*. 'On the 14th day of the second month of the second year *Wu-te* (619) an edict was issued: the grain tax (*tsu*) of each adult male should be 2 *shih*. They shall also contribute 2 *chang* of silk and 3 *liang* of silk floss. Apart from these there should be no irregular levies.'

4 For versions deriving from this series of *Statutes*, see *THY*, 83, pp. 1530–1; *TFYK*, 487, p. 16*b*; *CTS*, 48, p. 3*a*, and *TFYK*, 504, p. 33*b*, for the section on *tiao* alone. Secondary accounts deriving from these and other sources may be found in *HTS*, 51, p. 2*a–b* and *WHTK*, 2, p. 41*b–c*. For translations see appendix 1 to chapter II.

5 Comparison of the versions of the 624 *Statutes* mentioned in note 4 to p. 24 with the parallel rules in the Japanese *Yōrō-ryō* (which almost certainly derive from the Chinese *Statutes* of 651), with the digest of the *Statutes* of 719 preserved in *TLT*, 3, pp. 35*a*–36*a*, and with the quotations of the 737 *Statutes* in the *Code* and in *TT*, 6, p. 33*a–c*, etc., will show at a glance how little modification was made to the rules. Like the material on the *chün-t'ien*, the rulings in the T'ang *Code* on the *tsu-yung-tiao* taxes were reproduced in *Sung hsing-t'ung* of 963, although the whole system had been abandoned in 780.

6 See *Code*, 13, arts. 8–11; *Code*, 15, arts. 19–28. Many other articles are relevant to specific points connected with the collection of taxes.

PAGE 25

7 The vast bulk of these *Ordinances* are irretrievably lost. However, some fragments survive and these are translated in appendix 2 to chapter II. The most important of these fragments are those cited by *RSG*, 13, pp. 406–7, from the *Ko-ki*, a private commentary on the Japanese *Statutes* probably completed between 737 and 740. This cites a number of articles from the *Statutes* of *K'ai-yüan* times together with the relevant *Ordinances* giving more detailed rulings on specific points. Such *Ordinances* were known as *pieh-shih*. On this very important passage see Niida, 'Tō Gumbōryō to hōsui-seido', *Hōseishi kenkyū*, 4 (1953), pp. 207–9; Twitchett, 'The fragment of the T'ang ordinances of the Department of Waterways discovered at Tun-huang', *Asia Major*, 6, 1 (1957), p. 32, note 37*a*. For translation see appendix II, 2, arts. A, 5*a–c*. Beside the *Ordinances*, which contained detailed rules supplementing the general provisions of the *Statutes*, the *Regulations* (*ko*) codified modifications and amendments to these provisions made by edicts (see appendix II, 3).

8 See *THY*, 83, p. 1530; *TLT*, 3, p. 35*a*. In *CTS*, 43, p. 7*b*, the fourth item is written not *tsa-yao* but *k'o*. This is one of the arguments which have led Sogabe Shizuo to the belief that *k'o* is always employed in this technical sense even in such terms as *k'o-i* (see note 15 to p. 25 below). However, *CTS*, 43, is merely a summary of *TLT*, and since the earliest text of the latter (a Sung print) writes *tsa-yao*, as does *THY*, it is hardly possible to postulate an original reading *k'o* preserved in *CTS* but corrupted in all known versions of *TLT* itself. It seems more likely to be an error. *K'o* could certainly be used to mean *tsa-yao* but did not always have this sense.

During the T'ang the *tsa-yao* were always considered separate from the *tsu-yung-tiao*, which are commonly referred to as a unified system of taxes.

9 The length of hemp cloth required was increased from 24 to 25 ft. between the 719 and 737 *Statutes*. See Niida, *Tōryō shū-i*, p. 662. This was one of the very few modifications made in the system.

10 See appendix II, I, art. I. It is possible that the tax in kind (*tiao*) and the supplementary tax in kind (*chien-tiao*) were payable in rather more varied commodities. The corresponding Japanese *Statute* (*RSG*, 13, pp. 382–6) lists an extraordinary medley of products which might be contributed, both as *chō* (*tiao*) and *chōfukusei* (supplementary *tiao*).

11 Presumably *yung* stands for the homophone word meaning 'to hire' or 'to employ' (see appendix II, I, art. 4).

12 *RSG*, 13, p. 392, cites a T'ang *Statute* to this effect (see appendix II, I, art. 4, note 5). The commentator Ato (Ato Ren or Ato no Sukune: his commentary dates from between 791 and 812) dealing with this passage gives it as his opinion that not only retainers (*pu-ch'ü*) but also slaves (*nu-pi*) might be thus employed. The Japanese *Statute* also permitted the hire (*ku*) of substitutes, and this too may well have copied a Chinese ruling which has not survived.

13 On this subject see Hamaguchi, 'Tō ni okeru ryōzeihō-izen no yōeki rōdō', *Tōyō gakuhō*, 20, IV, pp. 567–88, and 21, I, pp. 66–90 (1933); Sogabe, *Kinden-hō to sono ẕeieki seido*, pp. 221ff.; Miyazaki Ichisada, 'Tōdai fueki-seido shinkō', *Tōyōshi kènkyū*, 14, IV (1955), pp. 1–24.

14 See the works cited in note 13 to p. 25 above. Unlike the other taxes the miscellaneous *corvée* was levied not only on adult males (*ting*), but on adolescent males (*chung-nan*) aged 16 and above. Clear proof of this is to be found in the *corvée* registers recovered from Tun-huang (P. 2657, P. 2803, P. 3018 v°, P. 3559 v°). See Naba, 'Seishi ni kisai saretaru Dai Tō Tempō-jidai no kosū to kōsū to no kankei ni tsukite', *Rekishi to chiri*, 33, I, pp. 47–82; II, pp. 10–40; III, pp. 16–50; IV, pp. 25–57 (1934), also Wang Yung-hsing, 'Tun-huang T'ang-tai ch'ai-k'o-pu k'ao-shih', *Li-shih Yen-chiu*, XII (1957), pp. 71–100. This series of documents includes not only adults (*pai-ting*) but also adolescent males (*chung-nan*), old men (*lao-nan*), partially disabled men (*tsan-chi*, see note 21 to p. 4 above), and even one boy (*hsiao-nan*), although the latter was incorrectly registered, since he was 17 years old. Besides the MSS. cited by Naba and Wang a very badly mutilated MS. in the Stein collection (S. 543) of some 84 lines clearly belongs to the same general category of documents, although it does not list special *corvée* duties. This list also includes boys (*hsiao-nan*) aged 15 and 16.

15 There has been a spirited controversy for some years over the precise meaning of the terms *k'o-k'ou* and *k'o-hu*. Most scholars take *k'o* in these terms as a general term for fiscal impositions, and translate them as 'taxable individual' and 'taxable household'. However, Sogabe Shizuo, in a series of articles, has insisted that *k'o* in this context means miscellaneous *corvée* (*tsa-yao*). This view has been vigorously opposed by Niida Noboru, Yang Lien-sheng and others, and there is no doubt that for the T'ang period Sogabe's theory is wrong. But his detractors have not yet satisfactorily answered Sogabe's case for the pre-Sui period. The Western Wei tax register from Tun-huang (S. 613) has a clear case of a *pu-k'o-hu*, which was assessed tax. See Sogabe, 'Hoku-Gi Tō-Gi Hoku-Sei Zui jidai no kakō to fukakō', *Tōhōgaku*, 11 (1955), pp. 59–70, and 'Sono go no kaeki no kaishaku mondai', *Shirin*, 38 (1955), pp. 288–303.

The basic problem is that Sogabe tries to force a generally applicable single technical meaning upon *k'o*, in whatever context it occurs. A very sensible article by Matsunaga, 'Tōdai no "ka" ni tsuite', *Shien*, 55 (1953), pp. 71–96, shows clearly what a wide range of meanings *k'o* had in different contexts. Although the word was used for '*corvée* labour', it was also used for various other types of imposition, and as a general term covering all types of tax and service.

16 For details of these categories, see Niida, *Tōryō shū-i*, p. 228, and note 21 to p. 4 above.

PAGE 26

17 The precise limits of the age categories changed at various times during the course of the dynasty. The best study of this question is in Suzuki, 'Tōdai teichū-sei no kenkyū', *Shigaku zasshi*, 46, XI (1935), pp. 82–106.

18 Lands were not granted to a youth when he became a *chung-nan*, i.e. at 16, but only on attaining 18 years of age. See chapter 1, appendix 1, art. 3.

19 On this question see Wang Yung-hsing, 'Tun-huang T'ang-tai ch'ai-k'o-pu k'ao-shih', and Miyazaki Ichisada, 'Tōdai fueki-seido shinkō', *Tōyōshi kenkyū*, 14, IV, pp. 1–24.

20 See *HTS*, 51, p. 2*a* (and *WHTK*, 2, p. 41*b*, which derives from this passage): 'Every adult male who had received a grant of land was to contribute 2 *shih* of grain per annum....' This is not paralleled by any of the direct quotations of the *Statutes*, but compare a parallel rule in force under the Sui (see *Sui shu*, 24, p. 11*a*). (Balázs, 'Le traité économique du Souei-chou,' p. 152: 'Tous ceux qui n'avaient pas encore reçu de terres ne payaient pas de redevances.')

21   See *Sui shu*, 24, pp. 4*b*, 7*a*–8*a*, etc.; *TT*, 5, pp. 29*c*–31*b*.

22   See above, note 6 to p. 2.

23   See *Lu Hsüan-kung Han-yüan chi*, 22, p. 1*a*–*b*, translated by Balázs, 'Beiträge', *MSOS*, 36, p. 3: 'Weil diese Abgabe auf Grund der Familie berechnet und eingezogen wurde, heiß sie "Abgabe" (*tiao*).' See also the remarks of Chü Ch'ing-yüan, *T'ang-tai tsai-cheng shih*, p. 1, on this passage.

24   See appendix II, 1, art. 20, and sources there cited.

25   See appendix II, 1, arts. 20, 21.

26   *Ibid.* arts. 13, 21.

27   See *Code*, 12, art. 5. The article of the *Statutes* containing this rule have not survived.

28   See *Code, loc. cit.*

29   See appendix II, 1, art. 19; appendix II, 2, art. A, 5 A; appendix II, 3, art. D, for relevant passages from the *Statutes, Ordinances* and *Regulations*.

PAGE 27

30   See appendix II, 1, art. 4.

31   *Ibid.* art. 15.

32   *Ibid.* art. 11.

33   *Ibid.* art. 18.

34   *Ibid.* art. 16.

35   *Ibid.* art. 17.

36   See the fragment of the *Ordinances of the Department of Waterways* (P. 2507; Twitchett, *Asia Major*, 6, 1) for a number of specific examples.

37   See Hino Kaisaburō, 'Tōdai katei no yōchō menjo to soyō menjo', *Hōseishi kenkyū*, 8 (1957), pp. 226–36. Numerous examples of such households may be found in the Tun-huang registers (see next note).

38   Of the households whose registers are cited by Niida, *Tō-Sō hōritsu monjo no kenkyū*, pp. 677–721 (admittedly a very small sample), 41 per cent were non-taxable households. Of the taxable households, 44 per cent

(26 per cent of the whole) were non-contributing, and ot the total only one-third were taxable and actually contributing. It is interesting to note that Tu Yu, in his assessment of the national revenue (see appendix II, 4) makes no allowance for taxable households which did not in fact contribute taxes, but assumes that all taxable households contributed. Further evidence on this question is contained in the *corvée* registers cited in note 14 to p. 25 above. The percentage of persons listed who had special duties is a very high one. For example, of 391 individuals mentioned in P. 3559 v°, only 143 (36·6 per cent) had no special duty allocated them. These same lists, however, suggest that this may well have been a localised phenomenon, since a large proportion of the special duties specified were either military or semi-military, and would only have been necessary in a frontier region.

39 That is *t'u-hu* or *chu-hu*. Such persons were not necessarily actually resident in the locality in which they were registered. The household registers continued to list families which had left the locality, or even become extinct, while the *corvée* lists register under each *hsiang* considerable numbers of persons who had absconded, been captured by the enemy, conscripted for military service elsewhere, or who were otherwise absent and unavailable for services.

40 See chapter I above.

41 See chapter I, note 137 to p. 15.

42 See Liu Fang's *Shih-huo lun* (*WYYH*, 747, pp. 10b–12a), a document probably written towards the end of Hsüan-tsung's reign. '...Those who are known as vagrants (*k'o-hu*) live indiscriminately among the resident population, and amount to one or two out of every ten families. They are the same sort of people as the *fou-hu* and *liu-jen* who have existed since Han and Wei times....'

43 An extreme view is presented in Hino, 'Tempō-izen ni okeru Tō no kokō-tōkei ni tsuite', *Shigematsu sensei koki kinen Kyūshū daigaku Tōyōshi ronsō* (1957), pp. 229–72. The author estimates the population shortly before the An Lu-shan rising at something over 20,000,000 households, against a total of only 9,000,000 registered households, and by comparing the size of registered families under other dynasties also concludes that the number of individual family members was systematically understated. The estimated totals at which he arrives are purely hypothetical, but the author has done a valuable work in pointing out the various ways in which the authorities failed to take full account of the population, even during a reign which was a highpoint of administrative efficiency.

44 See the remarks in Hino, 'Tempō-izen ni okeru Tō no kokō-tōkei ni tsuite', and in chapter I above, notes 70, 74 to p. 8, etc.

PAGE 28

45 See chapter I, and notes 100–4 to p. 11.

46 See chapter I. We may gain a further insight into the status of the village headmen (*li-cheng*) and hamlet headmen (*ts'un-cheng*) from the Tun-huang *corvée* registers. These documents, P. 3559 v°, P. 3018 v°, P. 2657, and P. 2803, list several persons holding these posts. There are eight *li-cheng* all aged between 29 and 46, four of them sons of officials, and four commoners, one of whom was partially disabled. There are also eight *ts'un-cheng* all of whom were youths aged between 17 and 22. There can be no doubt that the *ts'un-cheng* was an office of comparatively minor significance (see *TLT*, 30, p. 35 *a*; *TT*, 3, p. 23 *b–c*).

47 There is no adequate account of such subaltern officials under the T'ang. In general they could be divided into two classes, some who became part of an official's permanent entourage, and who followed him from one provincial post to another, and others who were more or less permanent employees in a district yamen. For a brief account of such staff in early Sung times, see J. T. C. Liu, *Reform in Sung China*, pp. 80 ff.

48 See *Code*, 13, art. 8; *TLT*, 30, p. 35 *a*.

49 See Koga, 'Tōdai kinden-seido no chiiku sei', *Shikan*, 46, pp. 42–54, and 'Tōdai ryōzeihō no chiiku sei', *Tōhōgaku*, 17, pp. 63–81. Koga denies that the *chün-t'ien* system or the *tsu-yung-tiao* taxation system were ever enforced in southern China. However, his evidence is for the most part negative, and even if actual administrative practice differed in north and south, the *legal* enactments embodied in the *Statutes* certainly covered the whole country.

PAGE 29

50 See appendix II, 1, art. 6.

51 *Ibid.* art. 7.

52 See *TT*, 6, p. 33 *c* (see appendix II, 1, art. 1 and note 5 to p. 24). See also *TT*, 6, p. 34 *a–b* (see appendix II, 4) according to which 1,900,000 households paid the tax in this form.

53 See Niida, 'Torohan hakken Tōdai no yōchōfu to sofu ni tsuite', *Tōhō gakuhō*, 11, 1 (1939), pp. 243–259. These cloths are reproduced in Stein, *Innermost Asia*, vol. III, plate CXXVII.

54 See Ch'en Yin-k'o, *Sui T'ang chih-tu yüan-yüan lüeh-lun kao*, p. 114.

55 See *HTS*, 51, p. 3 *b*.

56 *Ibid.* p. 3 *b*.

57 See appendix II, 1, art. 8. See also *RSG*, 13, pp. 382–6, which may derive from a Chinese original (cf. note 10 to p. 25 above).

58 See *TT*, 6, p. 34a (transl. appendix II, 4), which gives the rates for eighth grade households as 452 cash per annum, and for ninth grade households as 222 cash. Nothing is known of the rates for households of higher grades during this early period.

59 According to *Sui shu*, 24, p. 6a–b; *TT*, 5, p. 30c, such a classification had been imposed for the first time under the Northern Ch'i, and the rich made to pay money taxes while the poor were made to contribute labour services. Under the T'ang, at first a threefold classification of grades was imposed in the 623 Statutes. See *THY*, 85, p. 1557; *TFYK*, 486, p. 11a. Such a classification of wealth was found to be insufficiently precise, and in 626 a nine-grade classification was adopted, as had been used under the Northern Ch'i, and this was maintained throughout the dynasty.

60 See above, chapter 1, note 46 to p. 6. In 654 it was ordered that the new classification (*ting-hu*) should be made every other year (see *THY*, 85, p. 1557; *TFYK*, 486, p. 12a), but the triennial assessment was soon restored.

61 This is clear from *TT*, 6, p. 34a–b. The rate for ninth grade households was 222 cash per annum, that for eighth grade households 452 cash, and the average rate for the empire as a whole only 250 cash. Thus ninth grade households must have held a great predominance. On the role of these lower grades, who represented for the most part the small peasantry, see Hino, 'Genshū-jidai wo chūshin toshite mitaru Tōdai Hokushi kaden-chiiki no hachi-kyū-tō ko ni tsuite?', *Shakai keizai shigaku*, 21, v–vi (1957), pp. 441–68. Of the households included among the household registers reprinted by Niida, *Tō-Sō hōritsu monjo no kenkyū*, pp. 677–721, are thirteen specified as of the ninth grade, and twelve of the eighth grade, and none of any higher grade. The *corvée* list P. 3559 vº gives a rather more complete picture of two *hsiang*. The first (possibly Tz'u-hui hsiang) lists persons liable to service from one sixth grade household, twenty seventh grade households, forty-four eighth grade households, and ninety-two ninth grade households. Under Ts'ung-hua hsiang the register lists persons from three sixth grade households, six seventh grade households, twelve eighth grade households, and forty-three ninth grade households. The last figure is incomplete as the end of the MS. is missing. The fragmentary list P. 3018 vº also lists persons from seventh, eighth, and ninth grade households belonging to another unidentifiable *hsiang* in which there were more than five seventh grade households, nineteen eighth grade households, and more than eighteen ninth grade households. See Nishimura, 'Tōdai Tonkō saka-bo no kenkyū', *Tonkō Torohan shakai-keizai shiryō*, II (Kyoto, 1960), pp. 377–464.

62   See also Hino, 'Gensō-jidai wo chūshin toshite mitaru Tōdai Hokushi kaden-chiiki no hachi-kyū-tō ko no tsuite', and Matsunaga, 'Kindensei ka ni okeru Tōdai kotō no igi', *Tōyō shigaku*, 12 (1956), pp. 81–112, together with the later studies of the latter author (see note 71 to p. 30 below).

PAGE 30

63   See Hino, 'Tōdai katei no yōchō menjo to soyō menjo', *Hōseishi kenkyū*, 8, pp. 226–36.

64 . Hino, *ibid.* The evidence for this is contained in two fragments, P. 3557 and P. 2684, both comprising only a few lines, and I feel hesitant to deduce any general rule from them.

65   See the edict of 746 in *WYYH*, 433, p. 2*a*, which says that under the 'permanent practice' (*ch'ang-hsing*), ten adults in each *hsiang* had been given exemption. It is possible that *ch'ang-hsing* may here refer to the 'Permanently applicable directive' of Li Lin-fu, in which case the exemption of a regular quota of adults from poor families would date only from 736.

66   See *TT*, 6, pp. 33*c*–34*a*; *WYYH*, 433, p. 2*a*. The number was increased to thirty adults in each *hsiang*.

67   See *WYYH*, 425, p. 2*a*, Act of Grace of 744. Under the same Act of Grace an adjustment was made of the ages of the personal-status categories, a measure which freed still more persons from fiscal obligations, since they now became adults (*ting*) at 23 instead of 21, and adolescents (*chung-nan*) at 18 instead of 16 years of age (see also *THY*, 85, p. 1555; *TFYK*, 486, p. 14*b*; *TT*, 7, p. 42*a*; *CTS*, 48, p. 3*b*).

68   See Hino, 'Tōdai katei no yōchō-menjo to soyō-menjo', pp. 234–6. The author develops this same theme in his 'Tempō-izen ni okeru Tō no kokō-tōkei ni tsuite' (see note 43 to p. 27 above).

69   See *WYYH*, 425, p. 2*a*.

70   *Ibid.*

71   Much the best discussion of this problem in general terms is that by Matsunaga, 'Ryōzeihō-izen ni okeru Tōdai no saka', (i) in *Shigematsu sensei koki kinen Kyūshū Daigaku Tōyōshi ronsō* (1957), pp. 295–315, and (ii) in *Toyō shigaku*, 18 (1957), pp. 1–41. This study supersedes the same author's earlier 'Kindensei-ka ni okeru Tōdai kotō no igi', *Tōyō shigaku*, 12 (1955), pp. 81–112.

72   For details of such duties, see Chü Ch'ing-yüan, *T'ang-tai tsai-cheng shih*, pp. 102–18; Matsunaga, 'Ryōzeihō-izen ni okeru Tōdai no saka', and

'Tōdai saeki kō', *Tōyō shigaku*, 15 (1956), pp. 17–41; Wang Yung-hsing, 'Tun-huang T'ang-tai ch'ai-k'o-pu k'ao-shih', *Li-shih Yen-chiu*, XII (1957), pp. 71–100; Nishimura, 'Tōdai Tonkō saka-bo no kenkyū', *Tonkō Torohan shakai-keiₐai shiryō*, II (Kyoto, 1960), pp. 377–464; Hamaguchi, 'Tō ni okeru ryōzeihō-izen no yōeki rōdō', *Tōyō gakuhō*, 20, IV, pp. 567–98; 21, I, pp. 66–90 (1933).

73   See, for example, Ts'en Chung-mien, *Sui-T'ang shih* (1957), pp. 340–46, where the author fails completely to appreciate the distinction. The situation is clearly stated by Miyazaki Ichisada, 'Tōdai fueki-seido shinkō', *Tōyōshi kenkyū*, 14, IV (1955), pp. 1–24, and by Sogabe, *Kinden-hō to sono ₐeieki seido* (1953), pp. 221 ff.

PAGE 31

74   See Chü Ch'ing-yüan, *T'ang-tai tsai-cheng shih*, etc.

75   See *TLT*, 3, p. 35 a, which records that in 734 no less than 220,294 superfluous special duties were abolished.

76   See note 38 to p. 27 above, and the *corvée* registers cited by Wang Yung-hsing, 'Tun-huang T'ang-tai ch'ai-k'o-pu k'ao-shih'.

77   See on the general problem of *tₐu-k'o*, Chü Ch'ing-yüan, *T'ang-tai tsai-cheng shih* and Miyazaki, 'Tōdai fueki-seido shinkō'. That most special duties gave exemption from military service as well as *corvée* is clear from the *Ordinances of the Department of Waterways* (P. 2507). See Twitchett, 'The fragment of the T'ang ordinances of the Department of Waterways discovered at Tun-huang', *Asia Major*, 6, 1 (1957), pp. 50–5, 57.

78   The only evidence for this practice, which was used for providing professional seamen for canal and sea transport and for personnel serving in military colonies, comes from the *Ordinances of the Department of Waterways*. See Twitchett, *Asia Major*, pp. 50–3 and notes 65, 69 thereon. The institution is also noted by Chü Ch'ing-yüan, *T'ang-tai tsai-cheng shih*, pp. 109–10.

79   See Matsunaga, 'Ryōzeiho-izen ni okeru Tōdai no saka' (II), *Tōyō shigaku*, 18, pp. 1–41.

80   *TT*, 6, p. 34a (see appendix II, 4).

PAGE 32

81   See *TLT*, 3, p. 37a: 'The household levy (*shui-ch'ien*) for the prefectures of the empire has a fixed standard. Every third year there is a heavy tax (*ta-shui*) which brings in 1,500,000 strings of cash. Every year there is a

light tax which brings in 400,000 strings which provides for the armies and postal and relay services. Every year there is also a separate levy (*pieh-shui*) of 800,000 strings, which provides for the expenses of provincial officers' salaries, and funds for the public administration.' I have found no textual reference to this threefold division of the household levy in other T'ang works, but recently Ogasawara Nobuhide, in an article in *Ryūkoku daigaku ronshū*, 349 (1955), pp. 1–15, reprints some fragmentary documents recovered from Turfan by the Ōtani expedition, among which is a fragmentary register of official correspondence from the yamen of the *Tu-tu fu* governor-general of Hsi-chou dating from 729–31. One of the items recorded is a report of the payment of 35,635 cash for the 'heavy tax' (*ta-shui*) from one of the subordinate districts of Hsi-chou (*loc. cit.* p. 9). There can thus be no doubt that the system represented in *TLT*, 3 was in fact enforced.

82   See *TT*, 6, p. 34*a*.

83   See chapter I, note 131 to p. 14.

84   See *TT*, 6, p. 34*a*.

85   For the edict of 696, see *THY*, 85, p. 1557; *TFYK*, 486, pp. 12*b*–14*a*. 'The household categories of those households of the common people which have split off from the families of their parents during the lifetime of the latter, shall in all cases be the same as those of their original household and may not be reduced. Where the persons are due for labour service, they shall be counted together with the adults and adolescents of the original household to arrive at their grade. They may not give rise to any exemption by splitting the household. Their selective impositions (*ch'ai-k'o*) may be made in accordance with the divided households, but they may not protect one another in any way.' The Act of Grace of 742 is cited in *THY*, 83, p. 1534; *THY*, 85, 1559; *CTS*, 48, p. 4*b*; *TFYK*, 486, p. 19*a*; *TT*, 6, p. 33*c*. 'It has come to our notice that among the common people there are cases where, the household being of high rank and its adult male members numerous, they have illicitly divided their register and live apart, their parents still being alive, in order to evade the law....' For the edict of 744 see *WYYH*, 425, p. 2*a*; *TTCLC*, 74, pp. 417–18, which prohibits the practice in severe moralistic terms. For a detailed discussion of the legal consequences of such division of households, see Niida, *Shina mibunhō shi*, pp. 435–89, and 'Tō-Sō-jidai no kazoku kyōsan to yuigon hō', in *Ichimura Hakase koki kinen Tōyō-shi ronsō* (1933), pp. 885 ff.

86   See *THY*, 85, p. 1557; *TFYK*, 486, p. 15*a*.

87   The edict of 741 is in *THY*, 85, p. 1555; *TFYK*, 486, p. 16*a*–*b*. That of 745 is in *THY*, 85, p. 1557; *WYYH*, 425, p. 2*a*–*b*; *TTCLC*, 74, pp. 417–18.

88 T'ai Chou's memorial is in *THY*, 88, pp. 1611–12; *CTS*, 49, p. 6*b*–7*a*; *TFYK*, 502, pp. 21*b*–22*b*; *TT*, 12, p. 70*b–c*. This suggested the scheme in very general terms, which the emperor approved. The rate of the levy and other arrangements were then set out in a further memorial from Han Chung-liang, see *THY*, 88, p. 1612; *CTS*, 49, p. 7*a*; *TT*, 12, p. 70*c*.

PAGE 33

89 See *TLT*, 3, p. 53*a–b*: 'All persons from princes and dukes downwards shall annually draw up a schedule of lands under cultivation for each separate household, in accordance with the lands actually received (under the *chün-t'ien* allocation) and wasteland in temporary cultivation (*chieh-huang*), etc., to make a register of cultivated land (*ch'ing-miao pu*). Every prefecture shall forward these to the Department of State before the 7th month. When the time for collection of taxes comes, they shall make a surcharge (*pieh-na*) of 2 *sheng* on each *mou* to provide for the relief granaries.'

90 See *THY*, 88, p. 1612; *CTS*, 49, p. 7*a*; *TFYK*, 502, p. 22*b*. According to *TT*, 12, p. 70*c*, this change was made under the New Regulations (*hsin-ko*) promulgated in 651.

91 See *TLT*, 3, p. 53*b*. The rate of contribution was not very high. A merchant household of the fourth grade paid 2 *shih*, the equivalent of the tax on the 100 *mou* allocation under the *chün-t'ien* system, and merchant households of lower grades paid still less, those of the ninth grade being exempted altogether.

92 See *TTCLC*, 2, p. 7.

93 See *TFYK*, 502, p. 23*b*; *THY*, 88, p. 1613; *CTS*, 49, p. 7*b*. The latter describes the increasing misapplication of these funds as follows: 'During the decades of the empress Wu's reign the grain for the relief granaries was not permitted to be used for miscellaneous expenditure. But thereafter, when both public and private finances fell into dire straits, these funds were gradually borrowed from the relief granaries to provide for expenditure. In the Shen-lung period and after, these granaries came to be almost exhausted.'

94 *TLT*, 3, p. 54*a*.

95 *TT*, 6, p. 34*a*, see appendix II, 4.

96 All these dates refer to Acts of Grace mentioned in *TFYK*, 490. Unfortunately, the text of this chapter in current editions is out of order, and material relating to 640–75 is lacking, being replaced by material on the Northern Chou and Sui dynasties belonging elsewhere. *TTCLC*, 79, p. 450, also mentions what may be a similar exemption dated 677, while *TTCLC*, 2, p. 7, and *WYYH*, 463, p. 14*a*, mention exemption under 705.

97 See Hamaguchi, 'Tō no Gensōchō ni okeru Kōwai jōkyō bei to chizei to no kankei', *Shigaku ẓasshi*, 45, I, pp. 78–97; 45, II, pp. 221–54 (1934).

98 See *TT*, 6, p. 34*a* (appendix II, 4).

99 See the table of grain reserves in appendix V, 2, based on material in *TT*, 12.

PAGE 34

100 See *WYYH*, 747, pp. 10*b*–12*a*, which estimates that between 10 and 20 per cent of the population were still unregistered.

101 See *TLT*, 3, p. 43*b*; *THY*, 59, p. 1020; *TT*, 23, p. 136*c*. These quotas were probably envisaged as subject to periodical revision, but they nevertheless made the annual estimate of income from each county less urgent, and thus helped slacken the administration of the system.

102 See *TT*, 6, p. 34*a*; *TT*, 7; *WHTK*, 10, give the empire's population as 8,914,709 households and 52,919,309 persons in 755. Of these persons 8,208,321 were taxable (15·5 per cent) and 44,700,988 untaxable (84·5 per cent). Of the households 5,349,208 (60 per cent) were taxable and 3,565,501 (40 per cent) untaxable. Balázs, 'Beiträge', *MSOS*, 34, p. 15, has mistakenly assumed that all the untaxable individuals were in untaxed households. This was of course far from the case, since any household was likely to contain a number of untaxable persons, women, children, and old persons. Nevertheless, it seems quite inconceivable that 40 per cent of all households should contain no taxable member.

103 Even if we allow 3,000,000 persons among the registered population as exempt under the *Statutes*, if we assume the expectation of life as 40 years we should expect 23 per cent of the population, that is, some 12,000,000 persons, to have fallen within the taxable limit. To bring the figure so low as 15·5 per cent we must assume an expectation of life well below 30 years. This expectation of life moreover applies to those reaching three or four years of age, since it seems unlikely that children were commonly registered before this age, and thus cannot be accounted for by a high infant mortality rate.

104 Compare the study of Hino cited in note 43 to p. 27 above. The reasons given in the previous note for considering there were many unregistered individuals are concerned only with the registered households who figured in the population statistics. The unregistered squatters are a separate problem.

105 See note 167 to p. 17, notes 57 and 58 to p. 92.

106 See *CTS*, 48, p. 2*a*; *HTS*, 51, p. 4*b*.

107 See *CTS*, 48, p. 2*a*; *HTS*, 51, p. 4*b*. *CTS* gives the name of Cheng Shu-ch'ing's collaborator as K'ang Yün-chien.

108 See *CTS*, 48, p. 2*a*; *HTS*, 51, p. 4*b*. *CTS* ascribes this scheme to Cheng Fang, and *HTS* to Ti-wu Ch'i. Unfortunately, the information regarding all these schemes is in the introductory sections of the *Financial Monographs* of the two histories, and is only vaguely dated.

109 See *CTS*, 48, p. 2*a*; *HTS*, 51, p. 4*b*. The latter tells us that the forced loan (*shuai-tai*) levied on merchants amounted to 20 per cent of their property.

110 See *CTS*, 48, p. 2*a*.

111 See below, chapter IV.

112 See below, chapter III.

113 In 764 an edict ordered that vagrants who wished to be re-registered might be given a fresh grant of land in accordance with the *Ordinances* (see *THY*, 85, p. 1565; *TFYK*, 495, p. 26*b*). A subsequent edict of 766 allowed such persons two years' exemption from taxation, and exemption from selection for special duties (see *THY*, 85, p. 1565; *TFYK*, 495, p. 26*b*).

114 See the edict of 762 cited in *TFYK*, 495, p. 26*a*: 'Recently many of the lands of the common people have been accumulated in the hands of rich and powerful families. This is the only reason for which people abscond from their homes. We should therefore depute the county authorities to prohibit this, and if they themselves offend against the law (in this respect) within the area under their jurisdiction, they shall be punished doubly.'

115 Edicts forbidding the collection of taxes due from households who had run away from their neighbours were promulgated in 757 (see *THY*, 85, p. 1565), in 760 (*ibid.*), and in 762 (*THY*, *loc. cit.*; *TFYK*, 495, p. 26*a*). The second of these was specially designed to ease the burden caused by the re-allocation of 'special labour services' (*se-i*) on the minority of taxpayers remaining in their registered residence.

116 See *THY*, 85, p. 1565, edict of 760: '...From this time onwards, where there are lands and homesteads (left vacant) belonging to persons who have run away, these should be rented out by the authorities, who should take the rents to provide the taxes due. If the persons who had run away return, their lands should be given back to them, and the authorities must not claim that they still owe arrears of taxes and thus collect (the money) a second time.'

117 The clearest example of this is to be found in two memorials written by Yüan Chieh in 764 and 765 requesting remissions of taxation with reference to the prefectures in which he was serving (see *T'ang Yüan Tz'u-shan wen-chi*, 10, pp. 9*a*–11*a*). For an example of the extent of local depletion of registered population see *ibid*. 10, p. 7*a*–*b*, where in a memorial dated 760 Yüan Chieh tells how the population of the county of Fang-ch'eng had fallen from more than 10,000 to 200 households (for these documents, see also *CTW*, 370).

PAGE 36

118 See the memorial of Yang Yen translated in appendix II, 5, and the memorials of Yüan Chieh mentioned in the previous note. Such additional impositions were commonly known as *pei-shuai*. On the growth of provincial influence on taxation, see chapter VI below.

119 See *CTS*, 48, p. 4*b*; *THY*, 83, p. 1534; *TFYK*, 487, pp. 20*b*–21*a*. The last of these sources further prescribes that this tax may be levied only on families actually in residence, and may not be 'apportioned' (*hsü-t'an*) on members of their security groups (*pao*) or on their neighbours. On the land levy during this period, see Chü Ch'ing-yüan, *T'ang-tai tsai-sheng shih*, pp. 17–27; Hamaguchi, 'Tō no chizei ni tsuite', *Tōyō gakuhō*, 20, 1 (1932), pp. 138–48.

120 See *CTS*, 48, p. 4*b*; *THY*, 84, p. 1549; *TFYK*, 487, p. 21*a*. This was certainly an extraordinary measure, since special commissioners (*tsu-yung-shih*) were appointed to enforce it. The scheme seems to have been based on the tax of one-tenth said to have been imposed under the Chou (see *Meng-tzu*, Legge, 3A, 3, VI). It was rescinded by an Act of Grace in 766 (see *TFYK*, 88, pp. 4*b*–5*a*; *TTCLC*, 4, p. 25), which specifically attacks the measure as being inappropriately modelled on a classical system.

121 See, for example, Tamai, 'Tō-jidai tochi-mondai kanken', *Shina shakai-keizai shi kenkyū*, p. 62.

122 See Chü Ch'ing-yüan, *T'ang-tai tsai-cheng shih*, pp. 17–19, and Suzuki, 'Tō no kazei, shuzei ni tsuite', *Katō Hakase kanreki kinen Tōyōshi shūsetsu*, pp. 435–45.

123 See *CTS*, 48, p. 5*b*; *CTS*, 11, p. 15*b*; *TFYK*, 487, p. 23*a*–*b*. *HTS*, 51, p. 5*a*, mentions the measure without date in a context which would suggest that it was introduced in 766.

124 *CTS*, 48; *TFYK*, 487, *loc. cit.* The rate for superior land was rather high, since the average grain crop per *mou* was from 1 to 1·5 *shih* per *mou*, and the tax thus represented from 7 to 10 per cent of the crop.

125   See *TFYK*, 487, p. 23 *b*.

126   See Katō, *Ku Tōjo shokkashi, Ku Godaishi shokkashi*, p. 47, note 170.

127   See *CTS*, 48, p. 5 *b*; *CTS*, 11, p. 17 *a–b* (which mistakenly refers to the tax as the 'household levy'), *TFYK*, 487, p. 23 *b*.

PAGE 37

128   For general discussion of these money taxes on land see Chü Ch'ing-yüan, *T'ang-tai tsai-cheng shih*; Suzuki, 'Tō no kozei to seibyōsen to no kankei ni tsuite', *Ikeuchi Hakase kanreki kinen Tōyōshi ronsō*, pp. 375–96; Sogabe, 'Tō no kozei to chitōsen to seibyōsen no honshitsu', *Bunka*, 19 (1955), pp. 91–102, and Hino, 'Ryōzeihō-izen ni okeru seibyōsen chitōsen ni tsuite no shiken', *Tōyō shigaku*, 20 (1958), pp. 1–18; 21 (1959), pp. 1–15. A further study by Kanei Yukitada, 'Tō no seibyō-chitōsen', *Bunka*, 9, VII (1942), has not been available to me. On the first levying of this tax see *CTS*, 48, p. 4 *b*; *TFYK*, 487, p. 21 *a*. Sogabe suggests that these taxes, being supplementary sources of revenue for official salaries, were essentially local in character, as were miscellaneous *corvées* (*tsa-yao*).

129   See *TT*, 11, p. 63 *a*.

130   See *TFYK*, 506, p. 9 *a*.

131   See *TCTC*, 223, pp. 7165–6, and Hu San-hsing's commentary which cites the edict of 700 from Sung Pai, one of the editors of *WYYH* at the end of the tenth century. I have found no trace of this edict elsewhere.

132   *Ibid.*

133   See *CTS*, 48, p. 5 *b*; *CTS*, 11, p. 20 *b*; *THY*, 83, p. 1535; *TFYK*, 487, p. 23 *b*; *TCTC*, 233, p. 7165; *TTCLC*, 111, p. 579; *WYYH*, 434, p. 6 *a–b*.

134   See Ch'üan Han-sheng, 'T'ang-tai wu-chia ti pien-tung', *CYYY*, 11 (1947), and chapter IV below.

135   See *CTS*, 48, p. 5 *b*; *TFYK*, 487, p. 23 *a*. The censors are said to have been despatched throughout the empire, but the date is left vague. *TCTC*, 233, p. 7165, gives 764 as the date when the tax was enforced in the empire as a whole rather than in the metropolitan district alone. The president of the censorate was given the special title of Commissioner for Money and Commodity Taxes on Land (*shui-ti ch'ien-wu shih*) to formalise his authority in this matter.

136 See *CTS*, 48; *TFYK*, 487, *loc. cit.*

137 See Tu-ku Chi's letter to Yang Pen, *Pi-ling chi*, 18, pp. 7*a*–9*a*, the memorial of Yüan Chieh dated 764 in *Yüan Tzu-shan wen-chi*, 10, pp. 9*a*–10*a*, and another dated 765, *ibid.* pp. 10*a*–11*a*.

138 Some idea of the great increase in population in southern and central China may be gained from a comparison of the prefectural population figures recorded for 742 and for 812. The later census, which is manifestly incomplete, especially for northern China, shows increases of *registered* population of upwards of 300 per cent in some parts of the Yangtze valley.

139 See chapter I.

140 See *CTS*, 48, p. 5*a*–*b*; *THY*, 83, pp. 1534–5; *TFYK*, 487, p. 22*a*. The document reads as follows: Edict of 769, I, 18.

'Those in office shall divide the (household) levy which is to be paid annually by the common people of the empire and by the princes, dukes and below into nine grades. Households of the first grade shall pay 4000 cash; second grade, 3500 cash; third grade, 3000 cash; fourth grade, 2500 cash; fifth grade, 2000 cash; sixth grade, 1500 cash, seventh grade, 1000 cash; eighth grade, 700 cash; ninth grade, 500 cash. Those holding office of the first rank (*p'in*) shall contribute as a household of the first grade, those holding office of the ninth rank as a household of the ninth grade and those holding intermediate ranks shall pay in accordance with this. Where members of a single household are employed as officials in several different places, they shall each pay the tax in accordance with their rank in their place of residence. Both metropolitan and provincial officials shall contribute tax in accordance with their established rank or with the ranking of the vacancy in the establishment which they fill. Supplementary and supernumerary officials, both civil and military, shall not come within the scope of this rule.

'The amount of tax which should be contributed by those of the common people who possess store-houses and inns, shops or foundries, and who should thus, in accordance with the *Ordinances*, pay tax two grades higher than their household assessment, should be rectified and levied in accordance with this rule.

'Households of officials residing on their own estates were under the former rule taxed as households of the eighth grade, while those resident other than on estates were taxed as households of the ninth grade. In comparison with the case of the common people this was perhaps inequitable, and they should be taxed one grade higher.

'The various categories of migrants (*fou-k'o*), and temporarily resident households, whether they are officials or not, should be divided into two grades and taxed in their actual place of residence. Those with comparatively large possessions should be taxed as households of the eighth grade, the others as ninth grade households.

'Any person holding estates in a number of places shall pay tax in each place. The estates of military officers in the provinces may not be classed with those of the common people, since they already bear the arduous duties of defence. They shall all pay tax as households of the ninth grade.'

141 See the assessments mentioned in Yüan Chieh's memorials. See also the letter of Tu-ku Chi to Yang Pen, written about 768–70, while the former was prefect of Shu-chou (*Pi-ling chi*, 18, pp. 7*a*–9*a*): '...Recently, according to the registers of the neighbourhood groups (*pao-pu*), there have been 33,000 households of commoners and settlers from elsewhere, but those liable for selective service have numbered only 3500. The other 29,500 families rear silkworms for clothing, and plough to produce food, but bear the responsibility for paying not a single cash in state taxes....Each year 310,000 strings of taxes are laid solely on 3500 families of the common people. Those who are known as high-ranking households pay 1000 strings, the next in rank 900 or 800, the next 700 or 600. The grades are thus discriminated, and even the very lowest of the nine grades of household contribute, together with the *tsu* and *yung* taxes on their adult members, 40 or 50 strings. Things being thus, how can the people avoid falling daily deeper into distress, and how can affairs escape becoming daily more grievous? How can those among the people who cannot fulfil their obligations avoid running away bearing their children on their backs?...'

PAGE 39

142 See *CTS*, 49, p. 4*a*; *THY*, 1588; *TT*, 10, p. 57*c*, and chapter III below. Probably the heaviest burden on the ordinary taxpayer during this period was the great variety of irregular taxes and levies collected by the provincial authorities. See Yüan Chieh, *loc. cit.*, and Yang Yen's memorial translated in appendix II, 5.

143 See *TCTC*, 226, pp. 7267 ff., etc.

144 On Liu Yen's administration see Chü Ch'ing-yüan, *Liu Yen P'ing-chuan*.

145 See Yang Yen's memorial in appendix II, 5. See also Twitchett, 'The salt commissioners after An Lu-shan's rebellion', *Asia Major*, 4, 1, pp. 60–9, for the place of the reforms in their administrative context.

146 See chapter VI below, pp. 112–14.

147 *Liang-shui*, literally 'two taxes', refers to the collection of taxes in two annual instalments in summer and autumn. The term had been used before Yang Yen's reform referring to the collection of the land levy alone.

148 There is a very large secondary literature on the *liang-shui* reform. Traditional accounts, such as that given in Ch'en Teng-yüan, *Chung-kuo t'ien-fu shih* (1931), present it as a revolutionary new system. Balázs, 'Beiträge', *MSOS*, 34, also exaggerates the actual changes introduced by the reform. These changes were of course extremely important, but they had already been effected on a limited scale before 780. The reform is seen then as a formalisation of the new methods of taxation introduced during the preceding century, to replace the old system inherited from the northern dynasties. The most important account of the reform, in this light, is that in Chü Ch'ing-yüan, *T'ang-tai tsai-cheng shih*, which replaced and rendered obsolete all previous studies. Recently, in a long series of articles, Hino Kaisaburō has explored the effects of the reform in great detail. See the bibliography (pp. 348–9) for his principal studies.

PAGE 40

149 See appendix II, 5 and note 50 to p. 157 thereto.

150 See appendix II, 5, 2.

151 See appendix II, 5, 4.

152 See the commentary to the memorial of Yang Yen in *TFYK*, 488, p. 2*a*: 'Te-tsung approved of the scheme, and was going to enforce it, ordering those in control of taxation to cease their unprofitable methods. But they said that the system of the *tsu* and *yung* taxes had been in force for four centuries, and might not be lightly altered....'

153 Under the new tax system the individual did not come into account at all, save that the number of adults of taxable age affected the assessment of the household grade. The age-category system thus ceased to have any effect on taxation after 780. However, it continued to be the basis upon which labour services, which were retained, were allocated.

154 See appendix II, 5, 1, and appendix II, 5, 4. In fact the government was powerless to prevent provincial governors continuing to levy irregular taxes, and the central government themselves retained the *ch'ing-miao ch'ien* as a supplementary tax.

PAGE 41

155 It would appear from later documents that there were local quotas down to the level of the localities (*hsiang*). These, however, were probably fixed, for the sake of convenience, by the prefects as a guide for the actual levying of tax. It is improbable that the commissioners sent to the provinces were concerned with such low-grade quotas.

156 On this practice see Hino, 'Hanchin-jidai no shuzei sambunsei ni tsuite', *Shigaku zasshi*, 65, VII (1956), pp. 646–66; and the same author's 'Tōdai ryōzei no bunshūsei', *Tōyō shigaku*, 16 (1956), pp. 37–52; 17 (1957), pp. 1–31, and 'Hanchin taisei ka ni okeru Tōchō no shinkō to ryōzei jōkyō', *Tōyō gakuhō*, 40 (1957), pp. 223–61. An actual example of the threefold assessment for a prefecture is preserved in the *Wu-ti chi* (see appendix II, 6).

PAGE 42

157 See Hino, 'Yō En no ryōzeihō ni okeru zeigaku no mondai', *Tōyō gakuhō*, 38, IV (1956), pp. 370–410. The freedom to make local tax assessments led in later times to an immensely complicated local tax structure, in which there might be upwards of a hundred separate rates applicable within a single county (see Liang Fang-chung, *The single-whip method of taxation in China*, pp. 2–4).

158 This is quite clear from the deflationary problem which arose at the end of the eighth century. For a vivid picture of the limited role of money in rural economy, see the memorial of Han Yü in appendix III, 1.

159 See, for example, Balázs, 'Beiträge', *MSOS*, 34 (1931), pp. 86–9.

160 It meant also that government accounting could now be carried out in terms of cash, rather than in the mixture of cash and commodities shown for example in Tu Yu's account of the finances of the *T'ien-pao* period (see appendix II, 4). The cash assessments did not of course apply to the land levy itself, which was still assessed and collected in grain.

161 See appendix II, 5, 2.

162 See Matsunaga, 'Ryōzeihō-izen ni okeru Tōdai no saka' (II), *Tōyō shigaku*, 18 (1957), for some remarks on this. Nobody has yet assembled the fragmentary information on this important topic.

163 Matsunaga, *ibid.*

164 See Chü Ch'ing-yüan, *T'ang-tai tsai-cheng shih*; Acts of Grace dated 805 (see *TFYK*, 491, p. 5b), 806 (*TFYK*, 491, p. 6a; *TTCLC*, 5, p. 29), 807 (*TFYK*, 491, pp. 6b–7a), 811 (*TFYK*, 491, p. 9b), 812 (*TFYK*, 491, pp. 9b–10a), 814 (*TFYK*, 491, p. 10a), 816 (*TFYK*, 491, p. 10b), 819 (*TFYK*, 491, p. 11b); *TTCLC*, 10, p. 59; *WYYH*, 422, p. 10a), 824 (*TFYK*, 491, p. 13b), 829 (*TTCLC*, 71, p. 397; *WYYH*, 428, p. 2b), 833

(*TFYK*, 491, p. 15*a*), 836 (*TFYK*, 491, p. 15*b*), 843 (*WYYH*, 434, p. 11*b*) and 851 (*TTCLC*, 130, p. 710; *WYYH*, 439, p. 2*b*) all mention *ch'ing-miao-ch'ien*, and that of 843 *ti-t'ou-ch'ien* as well. There can be no doubt that the tax was regularly collected as a supplementary tax.

165   See chapter III below. The wine-monopoly money and the *ch'ing-miao-ch'ien* are coupled together as supplementary money taxes in several of the Acts of Grace mentioned in note 164.

PAGE 43

166   The wine-monopoly money, when collected as an item of direct taxation, was levied 'according to the contribution of the *liang-shui* taxes'—that is, in accordance with the household categories.

167   See *TFYK*, 488, pp. 1*b*–2*a*: 'In this year the households in the empire contributing the *liang-shui* numbered 3,085,070. The tax income was 13,056,070 strings of cash and *hu* of grain. The profits from salt are not included in these figures.' *HTS*, 52, p. 1*a–b*, tells us that 'annually more than 20,500,000 strings of cash and 4,000,000 *hu* of grain were collected to provide for the needs of the provinces, and 9,500,000 strings and over 16,000,000 *hu* of grain to supply the capital'. The income from salt had been something over 6,000,000 strings, and the total revenue in 779 only 12,000,000 strings of cash.

168   See chapter VI below.

169   There is no really satisfactory account of these risings. For a general picture see Hino, *Shina chūsei no gumbatsu*.

170   This led to a general increase in the tax quotas. The loss of Ho-pei also meant the defection of an area which had been a major source of revenue.

171   See the account of the measures introduced by Chao Tsan in *CTS*, 49, pp. 9*b*, 11*b*; *THY*, 84, pp. 1545–6; *TFYK*, 502, p. 26*a–b*; *ibid*. 501, p. 12*a*; *ibid*. 510, p. 7*a–b*. The principal measures were taxes on commodities, including tea, bamboo, timber and lacquer, a house tax, based on the size of buildings, and a levy on all market transactions of 5 per cent. All these measures were speedily abandoned. The only abiding innovation introduced at this time was the liquor monopoly tax (see chapter III below). Chao Tsan also suggested a land reform, but this was never enforced. On the revival of the salt administration, see chapter VI below and Twitchett, 'The salt commissioners after An Lu-shan's rebellion', *Asia Major*, 4, 1 (1954), pp. 70ff.

172   See *TCTC*, 237, pp. 7647–8; *THY*, 84, pp. 1552–3, and chapter VI below. On the ineffectiveness of the *liang-shui* system in providing the central authorities with an adequate regular revenue, see Hino, 'Hanchin taisei-ka ni okeru Tōchō no shinkō to ryōzei jōkyō', *Tōyō gakuhō*, 40 (1957), pp. 223–61.

173   On these irregular tributes, see *CTS*, 48, p. 2 *a–b*; *HTS*, 52, p. 5 *a–b*, for general accounts.

174   See the Act of Grace of 785 composed by Lu Chih, *TTCLC*, 69, pp. 386–8, and a slightly fuller version in *Lu Hsüan-kung Han-yüan chi*, 2, pp. 5 *b–*13 *b* (at p. 12 *a*).

PAGE 44

175   See chapter III and below, Twitchett, *Asia Major*, 4, 1.

176   See chapter VI below.

177   See *CTS*, 139, Lu Chih's biography. His criticisms may be found in the various Acts of Grace composed by him when he was employed as a Han-lin scholar, but are set out in full in the famous six-part memorial entitled 'Chün-chieh fu-shui hsü pai-hsing liu-t'iao' (see *Lu Hsüan-kung Han-yüan chi*, 22, pp. 1 *a–*30 *a*. Translated in full by Balázs, 'Beiträge', *MSOS*, 36 (1933), pp. 3–41).

178   Lu Chih became chief minister in the 4th month 792 on the dismissal of Tou Shen. In the field of finance he was increasingly at loggerheads with P'ei Yen-ling, who had been placed in control of the Public Revenue Department in the 7th month of the same year, in spite of Lu Chih's opposition to the appointment. In 794 their opposition came to a head, as it became obvious that P'ei was gaining favour at court. In the 11th month of this year Lu Chih presented a detailed and forceful denunciation of P'ei Yen-ling (see *Lu Hsüan-kung Han-yüan chi*, 20, pp. 1 *a–*20 *a*), which angered the emperor, and in any case forced him to choose between the two ministers. In the next month Lu Chih was demoted.

179   See *Lu Hsüan-kung Han-yüan chi*, 22, p. 22 *a–b*; Balázs, 'Beiträge', *MSOS*, 36 (1933), p. 31.

180   See the Act of Grace of 845 cited in *WYYH*, 429, pp. 1 *a–*11 *b*. (The relevant passage is omitted by the version of this document in *TTCLC*, 71, pp. 398–9.) This passage (p. 7 *a*) reads as follows: 'Sometimes as a result of inspecting officials seeking to lighten the load imposed on resident households, the household registers have been reduced, and the lost labour services (*cheng-yao*) are difficult to reallocate. The settlers (*k'o-hu*) of the Yangtze–Huai region, and those persons who have absconded to evade the household tax, etc., although they have recently been made liable for the *liang-shui* taxes, still remain exempt from *corvée* imposition (*ch'ai-i*)....'

On this problem see Matsunaga, 'Ryōzeihō-izen ni okeru Tōdai no saka', and Hino, 'Yō En no ryōzeihō-jisshi to doko kakuko', *Takikawa Hakase kanreki kinen rombunshū*, I, pp. 27–50.

181 See the following passage from the same document as quoted in the previous note (*WYYH*, 429): 'In other cases commoners of a given prefecture, one of their junior members having been given a single office, will, after the expiration of his term in office, move to a neighbouring prefecture or attach themselves to one of the armies or a provincial administration and claiming to be "employed", call themselves gentry families (*i-kuan hu*). They establish broad properties, but pay the lowest possible taxes, and gain exemption from every sort of *corvée* imposition (*chu-se ch'ai-i*). By degrees they will sell or let out on mortgage their family property in their place of origin, and break up their official registration. In this way the numbers of commoners paying full taxes daily decrease, and the special servicemen available to the prefectural and county authorities become fewer by degrees. From this time onwards, the common people of the Yangtze–Huai region, unless they are former *chin-shih* or persons who have gained renown in the state examinations, who, after they are no longer employed in office, divide their households to reside in other prefectures, may not style themselves "gentry", and their liability to *corvée* imposition and special services shall remain exactly the same as those of the local commoners.'

182 See *THY*, 85, p. 1558; *TFYK*, 488, p. 2*b*; *TCTC*, 233, p. 7509, and the note to the latter in the *K'ao-i*, which cites the Act of Grace after the *Shih-lu*.

183 See *TTCLC*, 70, p. 391, which cites as its authority the edict (Act of Grace) of 788.

184 See *WYYH*, 422, pp. 8*a*–13*b*, especially p. 11*a*.

185 See *THY*, 85, p. 1558; *TFYK*, 488, p. 8*a*; *TTCLC*, 2, pp. 10–12.

186 See, for example, the Act of Grace of 785 composed by Lu Chih, *TTCLC*, 69, pp. 386–8, and *Lu Hsüan-kung Han-yüan chi*, 2, pp. 5*b*–13*b*. For a more detailed exposition of the problem, compiled in the early years of Hsien-tsung's reign, see Tu-ku Yü, 'Tui tsai-shih chien mao-ming yü t'i-yung ts'e', *CTW*, 683, pp. 5*a*–12*b*. See also the examples cited by Chü Ch'ing-yüan, *T'ang-tai tsai-cheng shih*, pp. 41–2.

187 See the following memorial of Lü Wen, prefect of Heng-chou (Hu-nan), submitted in 811 (see *THY*, 85, p. 1558; *TFYK*, 486, p. 20*a*–*b*): 'The former quota of households for this prefecture was 18,407, and, setting aside the poor and distressed, families which have become extinct, the old and the young, orphans and persons unable to support themselves, the households liable to selective impositions (*ch'ai-k'o*) number 8257. After my arrival, I fixed the order for the collection of the household levy, and by inquiry elicited from the petty officials (*so-yu*) that there were a further 16,007 households which were concealed and did not pay taxes. Since I have humbly followed the divine grace which has taken note of my meagre achievements while in office in Tao-chou, and appointed me to a superior commandery, ordering me to give succour to its sufferings, I have lately searched the old official records (*an*), and interrogated the villagers. The levying of taxes, as previously conducted, has been totally lacking in proper gradation. Moreover, there has been no reclassification of households for more than twenty years. Nobody was aware who had died and who survived. The rich and poor were not equitably (classified). I dared not allow this state of affairs to continue, and established rules for reclassification of households, and made inquiries to bring into account the concealed households, whose numbers amounted to more than ten thousand. Although the prefectural and county authorities have not collected taxes (from these), the petty officials (*suo-yu*) have already been making levies from them on their own account, and granting their secret profits to corrupt underlings (*li*). How can this be like giving equitable assistance to the exhausted population? I therefore request that I may make a detailed plan to succour the exhausted and distressed. Thus the masses will manage to escape inequitable treatment, and yet there will be no deficiency in the income which they provide.'

PAGE 45

188 See the document of Tu-ku Yü cited in note 186 to p. 44. 'In former times, if a man had possession of not less than 1000 *mou* of fertile land, 1000 stems of good tender mulberry trees, a residence of a hundred *tu* in size, a thousand feet (250 head) of cattle and sheep, and a thousand fingers (100) of slaves, his taxes would not have been less than 70,000 cash. However, if after three or four years or more his mulberries and fields were laid waste, his residence destroyed, and not more than one in ten of his beasts and slaves survived, the taxes of the owner's family were still neither reduced nor remitted, and he himself would be reproved, questioned and beaten until he himself died, and all was finished. Thereupon, the prefects and magistrates, just in order that the people shall be at peace and taxes accumulated, bare their arms among the people, and hasten to act so that the court will improve their merit rating. They take the deficiencies of those who have absconded and are in debt [to the authorities] and allocate what they owe upon those who remain. This leads to still further persons running away, and to further registration of families [elsewhere]. Thus taxes become more onerous, and the people become daily more impoverished, and extreme inequity is universal.'

189 See *TFYK*, 488, pp. 8 *b*–9 *a*.

190 See *HTS*, 177, p. 7 *a*, which describes how Li Ao, when he became prefect of Lu-chou, was faced with a situation in which, as the result of a severe drought, many of the poor had sold up their lands and houses to rich and influential families at low prices. The former, however, still remained liable to contribute taxes on their former property. Li Ao gave instructions that land tax should be collected from the actual landholders, and levied 12,000 strings in tax from the rich and thereby eased the burden on the poor.

A later edict of 850 (see *THY*, 84, p. 1544) again raises this problem: 'Moreover, the *ch'ing-miao* and *liang-shui* taxes were originally linked to the land, and when the land passed into the possession of another person, the responsibility to contribute taxes on it should also pass with it [to the new owner]. However, since the former Act of Grace there have been continual reports that rich and powerful families are not respecting this rule. They take advantage of pressing situations privately to force deeds of sale on the sellers. . . .'

For an example of a deed of mortgage incorporating a clause covering taxation of the type envisaged in this edict, see P. 3155. (This MS. is translated inaccurately by Gernet, *Les aspects économiques du Bouddhisme*, pp. 183–4. For the relevant passage see Twitchett, 'The monasteries and China's economy in medieval times', *BSOAS*, 19, III, pp. 548–9.)

191 See *Yüan-shih Ch'ang-ch'ing chi*, 38, pp. 4 *a*–5 *b*, 'T'ung-chou tsou chün t'ien chuang'.

192 According to an edict of 811, promotion based on the increase in the number of households dated back to 780 (see *THY*, 84, p. 1553; *TFYK*, 486, p. 19 *b*; *WYYH*, 435, p. 8 *b*). The rule making merit ratings dependent also upon land brought into cultivation is first promulgated in an Act of Grace of 785, 11th month. See *Lu Hsüan-kung Han-yüan chi*, 2, pp. 5 *a*–13 *b* (at p. 11 *b*). The same Act of Grace allowed exemption of taxation to such newly opened lands.

193 This problem is raised by Lu Chih in his six-part memorial of 794 (see note 177 to p. 44). The relevant passage is on pp. 20 *a*–21 *b*; Balázs's translation, pp. 28–31.

194 After 821 soldiers who were willing to bring back into cultivation lands abandoned by their owners were granted three years' exemption of land taxes. See *TFYK*, 495, p. 30 *b*. Possibly the same rule was applied to newly cultivated land, much of which was certainly abandoned farmland rather than virgin waste.

195 See *THY*, 84, pp. 1543–4. It was forbidden for the local authorities to increase the overall quota for the land levy in proportion with this land newly brought into cultivation.

196 This is clear for instance from *Yüan-shih Ch'ang-ch'ing chi*, 39, pp. 1a–2a: 'Lun tang-chou Ch'ao-i teng san hsien tai-na Hsia-yang Han-ch'eng liang hsien shuai-ch'ien chuang', dated 818.

197 This is obvious from the way in which such local readjustments of taxes are mentioned as matters worthy of special note in contemporary biographies and accounts of conduct.

198 See the memorial of Lü Wen translated in note 187 to p. 44.

199 *Ibid.* Irregular taxation was also widely practised by the officials themselves. One widely imposed irregular levy was a contribution of fodder for the provincial armies. For a very detailed example of this type of malpractice see the two memorials of Yüan Chen impeaching the governors of Chien-nan tung-ch'uan and Shan-nan hsi, *Yüan-shih Ch'ang-ch'ing chi*, 37.

PAGE 46

200 See *CTS*, 171, p. 3a; *THY*, 84, pp. 1541–2; *TFYK*, 488, p. 7b.

201 See *Yüan-shih Ch'ang-ch'ing chi*, 39, pp. 1aff.

202 See *CTS*, 171, pp. 1b, 3a, which refers to a redistribution of quotas between localities (*hsiang*). Such small-scale reallocations were described as *t'an-pei* or *chün-t'an*.

203 This is obvious from the large sums of arrears which were constantly cancelled in Acts of Grace, usually described as 'deficient and consumed by the people'. The cancellations of such debts often specify that the deficiency is in the quota due for despatch to the capital (*shang-kung*).

204 See chapter IV below, and sources there cited.

205 *Ibid.*

206 The detailed orders given to the commissioners sent to assess the provinces in 780 say: '...They should report to the throne together with... what should be paid in money in grain and in cloth....'

207 See *THY*, 83, p. 1537; *TFYK*, 488, pp. 2b–3a; *TFYK*, 510, p. 7a; *CTS*, 48, p. 6a.

208 See *THY*, 83, p. 1537; *TFYK*, 488, pp. 2*b*–3*a*; *CTS*, 48, p. 6*a*.

209 See, for example, the document quoted in note 187 to p. 44.

210 See the six-part memorial of Lu Chih, *T'ang Lu Hsüan-kung Han-yüan chi*, 22, pp. 5*b*–6*a*; Balázs's translation, pp. 8–9.

211 Lu Chih's memorial was not the solitary note of protest in the 790's. In 796 Ch'i Kang made a memorial in the same vein (see *HTS*, 52, p. 5*a*). See, for example, the essay *Hsi-yu ch'ing* among Po Chü-i's model examination essays 'Ts'e-lin', *Po-shih Ch'ang-ch'ing chi*, 62, pp. 31*a*–33*a*.

PAGE 47

212 See Li Ao, 'Shu k'ai shui-fa', *Li Wen-kung chi*, 9, p. 71.

213 See chapter IV below. The shortage of currency was of course aggravated by the increasing use of money in revenue transactions, and it is clear that many tax-collecting authorities demanded payment in cash, since this practice was later forbidden. The demand for money was also very considerably increased by the rapid growth of internal and external trade.

214 See *THY*, 83, p. 1537–8; *TFYK*, 488, pp. 3*b*–5*a*. The same edict prohibits the compulsory contribution of cash for taxes assessed in terms of cloth.

215 See *THY*, 83, pp. 1538–9; *CTS*, 48, pp. 10*b*–11*a*; *TFYK*, 488, pp. 5*b*–6*a*.

216 See *TFYK*, 501, p. 15*a*–*b*; *CTS*, 48, p. 12*a*; *THY*, 89, p. 1630. A further measure which was widely used in official accounting at this period was the employment of token accounting values for commodities, much higher in terms of cash than the market prices. Such token values were called *hsü-ku* in opposition to the full price *shih-ku*.

217 See *Li Wen-kung chi*, 9, p. 71; *Han Ch'ang-li chi*, 37; Ch'ien chung huo ch'ing chuang, *Yüan-shih Ch'ang-ch'ing chi*, 34, pp. 4*b*–5*b*, for memorials drawn up by Li Ao, Han Yü and Yüan Chen at this time. The latter is almost certainly a draft of the memorial from the secretariat and chancellery cited in *THY*, 84, p. 1541; *CTS*, 48, p. 6*a*–*b*.

218 See *TTCLC*, 70, pp. 392–3; *WYYH*, 426, pp. 10*b*ff. *TFYK*, 488, pp. 7*a*–*b*, gives a summary of this.

219 See, for instance, the edict of 844 in *THY*, 84, p. 1544; *TFYK*, 488, p. 12*b*.

220 See, for instance, the memorial from the secretariat and chancellery of 872, sixth month in *CTS*, 19A, pp. 19*b*–20*a*. This memorial, dealing with the reallocation of taxes and labour dues owed by runaway families, concludes that such problems can be decided only by the local prefects and magistrates, and not by general orders issued from the capital.

<h3 style="text-align:center">CHAPTER III</h3>

PAGE 50

1 See *HTS*, 54, p. 1*a*: 'The grain tax (*tsu*) of the coastal prefectures is annually remitted. They should manufacture 20,000 *hu* of salt which should be sent to the Court of Agriculture. The prefectures of Ch'ing-chou, Ch'u-chou, Ts'ang-chou, Ti-chou, Hang-chou and Su-chou should purchase light commodities of high value with the price of their salt, and pay these in to the Court of Agriculture.'

2 See *HTS*, 48, p. 13*b*, translated by des Rotours, *Traité des fonctionnaires et traité de l'armée*, p. 433, where they are described as subordinate to the Court of Agriculture. At the same time *HTS*, 54, p. 1*a*, specifically states that the salt pools in Ho-tung came under the control of the Public Revenue Department.

3 *CTS*, 48, p. 16*b*; *THY*, 88, p. 1608, give this date as *Ching-yün* 4th year. There was no such year under the T'ang, and I assume that *Ching-yün* is simply an error for *Ching-lung* 4th year, i.e. 710. At that time the prefect of P'u-chou, within whose boundaries the important twin pools (*liang-ch'ih*) were situated, was made concurrently commissioner for the salt pools of Kuan-nei (*Kuan-nei yen-ch'ih shih*).

4 *CTS*, 48, p. 14*a*–*b*; *THY*, 88, p. 1608, which tells us that Chiang Hsün was appointed prefect of Pin-chou, and concurrent commissioner for the salt pools (*yen-ch'ih shih*), a note being added that the pools were those under Yen-chou in north-western Kuan-nei, where, according to *HTS*, 54, p. 1*a*, there were four important salt pools. These were so important that seven military colonies (*t'un-t'ien*) were attached to them (see *TLT*, 7, Sung print only; text cited in Tamai, *Shina shakai-keizai shi kenkyū*, pp. 512–13), presumably to provide food for the people working the salt pans.

5 See *CTS*, 48, p. 16*b*; *THY*, 88, p. 1608: 'In the 5th month of 727, Hsiao Sung, president of the Board of War, was appointed commissioner for the salt pools of Kuan-nei (*Kuan-nei yen-ch'ih shih*). From that time onwards the military governors of Shuo-fang have regularly been invested with the title of Commissioner for the Salt Pools.'

6 See *CTS*, 48, p. 14*a*; *THY*, 88, p. 1603; *TFYK*, 493, p. 14*a*. All date this wrongly. Kanei, 'Tō no empō', *Bunka*, 5, v (1938), pp. 491–529, points out that the date 713 given by all the texts does not coincide with the title Governor of Ho-chung given to Chiang Shih-tu, since that title was created for the first time in 721 1st month, Chiang being its first holder. He therefore postulates, and I concur in this suggestion, that the character *chiu* (nine) has been corrupted into *yüan* (1st year), as not infrequently happens. Historically, too, the later date makes better sense, as the move would then become a part of the series of fiscal reforms begun in 721, of which Yü-wen Jung's first scheme to register the population is the most important. It would also be seen to be closely connected with the attempt to impose a salt monopoly later in the same year.

7 We know, from *HTS*, 54, p. 1*a*, and from the *Regulations for Military Colonies* (*t'un-t'ien ko*) cited in *TT*, 10, p. 59*b*; *TFYK*, 493, p. 15*a–b*, that there were salt colonies in Yu-chou and under the Ta-t'ung and Heng-ye armies, all in northern Ho-pei. The passage quoted from the *Regulations for Military Colonies* reads: 'Regarding the salt colonies of Yu-chou, 50 adults (*ting*) shall be assigned to each colony. Those whose annual rate of production is more than 2800 *shih* shall be treated as an agricultural colony (*ying-t'ien*) of the second grade, those whose production is more than 2400 *shih* as one of the third grade, and those whose production is more than 2000 *shih* as one of the fourth grade. Regarding the salt colonies under the Ta-t'ung and Heng-ye armies, 50 men shall be assigned to each colony. Those whose annual rate of production exceeds 1500 *shih* shall be treated as an agricultural colony of the second grade, those whose production exceeds 1200 *shih* as one of the third grade, and those whose production exceeds 900 *shih* as one of the fourth grade.'

By 737 the original colonies at P'u-chou seem to have been abandoned, since the pools there were dealt with under the *Regulations of the Department of Granaries* (*ts'ang-pu ko*), which would suggest that they remained under the control of the Board of Finance. The fragment of the *Regulations* (*TT*, 10; *TFYK*, 493, *loc. cit.*) reads: 'Regarding the salt pools in P'u-chou, the prefectural services shall superintend them. They shall rent them out to families with the necessary ability to manage and tend them, and tax the salt which they produce. Each year the inferior, medium, and superior salt pans (*hsi*) shall produce on average 10,000 *shih*. Officers should also be deputed to inspect them. If any labour is required for diking the channels or digging the salterns, this should in the first place be provided from the adult members of the producing families. If the damage is very great, and they estimate that the labour of these families will not be adequate to make the repairs, it is permitted to employ the persons liable for *corvée* among the nearby population.'

Kanei, 'Tō no Empō', has pointed out that *HTS*, 54, has mistaken the 10,000 *shih* average annual production of a single saltern as the annual total for the two pools. This is obviously nonsense, since the unimportant Hu-lo ch'ih pool in Kuan-nei had an annual output of 14,000 *shih* (see *HTS*, 54, p. 1*a*), and it is probable that the output of the P'u-chou pools in the early eighth century was something over 200,000 *shih*.

8 See *HTS*, 54, p. 1*a*; *TT*, 10, p. 59*b–c*; *TFYK*, 493, p. 15*b*. The two latter sources, dating from 737, give the total number of wells as 90, a much lower figure than that given by *HTS*, whose account clearly refers to the early years of the ninth century, of 639 wells. This great increase in production may be the reason underlying the struggle between the Public Revenue Department and the Salt and Iron Commission over control of the Szechuan salt industry in the last decades of the eighth century.

9 See *TT*, 10, p. 59*b–c* (cf. appendix III, 3, 3). The imposition was a quota tax assessed in cash terms on each producing prefecture. It was payable in monthly instalments, and the regulations allowed for its payment either in cash, grain, or silver. All deficiencies, and so presumably the tax itself, were to be levied on the producer households (*tsao-hu*).

10 See *CTS*, 48, p. 14*b*; *THY*, 88, p. 1603; *TFYK*, 493, p. 14*a–b*; *TT*, 10, p. 59*a–b*.

PAGE 51

11 See *CTS*, 48, pp. 14*b*–15*a*; *THY*, 88, pp. 1604–3; *TFYK*, 493, p. 14*b*. Both *CTS* and *TFYK* lack the date and beginning of the edict. The edict not only in effect suspended the monopoly and ordered 'the prefect and his chief administrator in each prefecture to investigate the circumstances and to collect the tax in accordance with the *Statutes* and *Ordinances*'; it also restricted Chiang Shih-tu's authority to P'u-chou, and thus prevented the development of a general monopoly system. Chiang remained commissioner for the salt pools in P'u-chou.

12 See *TLT*, 30, p. 25*b*, and Niida, *Tōryō shūi*, pp. 848–9. This article is mainly concerned with mining, and ends 'The profits coming from the hills, rivers, and marshes, apart from these specific things, are to be shared between public and private interests...'. Cf. also *RGG*, 10, p. 334, which contains an analogous rule.

13 In the *hsing-chuang* of Yen Chen-ch'ing composed by Yin Liang (*CTW*, 514, pp. 9*a*–26*a*), and appended to his collected works (*Yen Lu-kung chi*), it is claimed that a scheme for a salt monopoly tax was worked out by Yen Chen-ch'ing and Li Hua at Ching-chou in Ho-pei during the opening phase of the An Lu-shan rebellion. Ti-wu Ch'i was at the time employed in the vicinity of Ching-chou, and is said to have observed their method, and when sent to report some local successes to the throne, to have memorialised the scheme as his own invention.

14 What, for instance, is the connection between Ti-wu Ch'i's scheme and the mission of Cheng Fang, who in 756 had been sent to Chiang-ling to impose taxes on salt and hemp? (See *CTS*, 48, p. 1*b*.)

15 This question is discussed in detail by Kanei, 'Tō no empō', and by Yen Keng-wang, *T'ang p'u-shang-ch'eng-lang piao*, pp. 787–8.

16 See *CTS*, 49, p. 3*a*; *THY*, 87, p. 1588; *TFYK*, 493, pp. 15*b*–16*a*; *CTS*, 123, p. 2*b*. Also see the account in *HTS*, 54, p. 1*a–b*, which gives the details on the increase of prices.

PAGE 52

17 *HTS*, 54, p. 1*b*, gives the annual figure of revenue from salt in 762–3 as 400,000 strings. *CTS*, 49, p. 4*a*; *THY*, 87, p. 1590; *CTS*, 123, p. 2*b*, give the figure as 600,000. But in either case, it represented a very small item among the total revenues.

18 For the details of Liu Yen's career in the Salt and Iron Commission, see Chü Ch'ing-yüan, *Liu Yen p'ing-chuan* (1937); Twitchett, 'The salt commissioners after the rebellion of An Lu-shan', *Asia Major*, 4, 1 (1954), pp. 60–89, and Yen Keng-wang, *T'ang p'u-shang-ch'eng-lang piao*, pp. 788–95.

19 See Twitchett, *Asia Major*, 4, 1, pp. 64–76, and chapter VI below.

20 According to *CTS*, 49, p. 4*a*; *THY*, 87, p. 1588; *CTS*, 123, p. 2*b*, in 779 the total annual revenue of the empire was 12,000,000 strings of which salt revenue accounted for more than half. *HTS*, 54, p. 1*b*, gives a figure of 6,000,000 strings. *TT*, 10, p. 57*c*, cites a total of 9,000,000 strings, and *Yü-hai*, 181, p. 20*a*, cites an identical figure from another work by Tu Yu, the lost *Li-tao yao-chüeh*.

21 See *HTS*, 54, p. 1*b*: 'In the localities producing salt offices were established corresponding with the old directorates. The producers (*ting-hu*) sold to the merchants, who were free to go wherever they wished (to sell the salt). . . .'

Similarly, *CTS*, 49, p. 3*a*; *THY*, 87, p. 1588; *TFYK*, 493, p. 16*a*: 'He established the salt laws. They went to the mountains and seas, the wells and the furnaces, and collected a monopoly tax upon the salt which they produced. Salt directorates (*chien*) and branches (*yüan*) with officials and subordinates (*li*) were set up to sell the salt. . . .'

22 *HTS*, 54, p. 1*b*.

23 See accounts in *CTS*, 49, p. 3*a*; *THY*, 87, p. 1588; *TFYK*, 493, p. 16*a*, and *TCTC*, 226, p. 7286: 'Yen considered that if the officials were numerous the people would be oppressed, and thus he only set up salt offices in the localities producing salt, who collected in the salt refined by the salt-pro-ducing households and sold it off to the merchants, who were permitted to go where they wished with it. No further salt offices were established elsewhere . . . .'

24 See *HTS*, 54, p. 1*b*: 'Taxes were levied wherever the ships of the merchants passed. Liu Yen memorialised the throne to abolish the taxes imposed by prefectural and county authorities, and to prohibit the inter-ception of merchants at haul-overs on the canals for gain.'

25 See *HTS*, 54; *TCTC*, 226, p. 7286, which tell us that he made special orders in accordance with whether the season was wet or dry.

26 See chapters v and vi below. See also the accounts in *HTS*, 54, p. 1*b*; *CTS*, 49, p. 3*a*; *THY*, 87, p. 1588; *TCTC*, 226, p. 7286. The branch establish-ments (*hsün-yüan*) established by Liu Yen on the route to the north seem all to have been shared by the Commissions for Salt and Iron and for Trans-portation, although Aoyama, 'Tō-Sōjidai no denunshi to hatsuunshi ni tsuite', *Shigaku zasshi*, 44, IX (1933), pp. 1105–29, does not agree with this view.

27 See *HTS*, 54, p. 1*b*; *TCTC*, 226, p. 7286.

PAGE 53

28 On the organisation of the Salt Commission, see Twitchett, *Asia Major*, 4, I, pp. 64 ff.; Chü Ch'ing-yüan, *Liu Yen p'ing-chuan*, pp. 15–32, and chapter vi below. *HTS*, 54, p. 1*b*; *TCTC*, 226, p. 7286, also inform us that there was an extensive chain of local salt stores in the coastal districts, with stocks of upwards of 20,000 *shih* of salt. Details about the subordinate personnel are preserved in a memorial on official dress in *THY*, 31, pp. 576–7.

29 See Twitchett, *Asia Major*, 4, I, pp. 65–7. See also *CTS*, 49, p. 3*b*; *THY*, 87, p. 1590; *THY*, 88, p. 1609; *CTS*, 11, p. 10*a*; *CTS*, 123, p. 1*a*.

30 The title of his successor Han Huang included the provinces Shan-chien (i.e. Shan-nan and Chien-nan), but he no longer held the title of Commissioner for Salt and Iron. *CTS*, 49, p. 4*b*, mentions the resumption by the Public Revenue Department of authority over salt administration in Szechuan in 792.

31 See Twitchett, *Asia Major*, 4, I, pp. 67–77; *CTS*, 49, p. 4*b*; *THY*, 87, p. 1591.

32 See *TCTC*, 226, p. 7286: 'From Hsü-chou, Ju-chou, Cheng-chou, and Teng-chou to the west, all consume salt from the pools of Ho-tung (i.e. P'u-chou), and the Department of Public Revenue is in control of it. From Pien-chou, Hua-chou, T'ang-chou, and Ts'ai-chou to the east all consume sea salt, and Liu Yen controls it.' It is clear from the edict raising the mono-poly prices in 782 that different tax rates were imposed in the two regions (see *HTS*, 54, p. 2*a*).

33 See the table in Kanei, 'Tō no empō', p. 40. After 780 the price in Ho-chung was roughly 50 cash per *tou* above that in the coastal region.

34 In 780 the income was only 800,000 strings compared with 6,000,000 strings produced by the Salt Commission.

PAGE 55

35 This edict (see *TFYK*, 494, p. 2*a*; *CTS*, 49, p. 4*a*; *THY*, 87, p. 1591: the two latter do not date it, but *TFYK* cites it as quoted in a much later memorial, with date of promulgation) was promulgated following a memorial from Han Hui which is quoted in *CTS*, 129, p. 5*b*; *HTS*, 126, p. 17*a*.

36 At the same time the government were forced to increase the rate of the newly imposed *liang-shui* taxes (see chapter II above). The income from the *liang-shui* in its first year of operation amounted only to 13,000,000 strings—little more than the total revenue for 779 including income from salt.

37 See *HTS*, 54, p. 2*a*; *TFYK*, 483, p. 16*b*.

38 See *TFYK*, 493, p. 17*a*.

39 We know that the price was raised to 360 cash, since it stood at that figure in 805, at which time the rate in Ho-tung under the Public Revenue Department was 560 cash (see *TFYK*, 493, pp. 17*b*–18*a*). But it has proved impossible to assign dates to these increases (see Kanei, 'Tō no empō', table p. 40).

40 *TFYK*, 492, *loc. cit.*

41 See *HTS*, 54, p. 2*a*: 'When Pao Chi became commissioner (780)...he permitted the payment of lacquer utensils, tortoiseshell or fine silk in return for salt. Even if these things could not be used, they could be sold off at a high price.'

42 See *CTS*, 49, p. 4*b*; *THY*, 87, p. 1591.

43 *Ibid.*, and references to him in *CTS*, 48, p. 2*b*; *HTS*, 52, p. 5*a–b*.

PAGE 56

44 See *HTS*, 54, p. 2*a*: 'At this period Li Ch'i increased his tribute offerings to assure himself of favour. The Great Ministers at court were all placated with lavish gifts of goods. Thus the profits from salt were piled up in private households, while the state's revenues were wasted and misapplied. The laws governing the salt monopoly fell into complete confusion. In many cases fictitious accounting prices were employed, and where the nominal rate was 1000 cash, only 300 and no more were actually collected.'

45 After Li Sun's reform of the salt system in 806–9, the annual revenue ranged between 18,000,000 and 20,000,000 strings of cash, reckoned at token accountancy rates, which represented only about 6,000,000 strings in actual cash. Thus the revenue was roughly the same in terms of cash as before 779, although the purchasing power of the money was very much greater. In 806, before Li Sun's reforms got under way, the income was only a nominal 11,280,000 strings, representing about 4,000,000 strings of actual money. Since even this figure dates from after the reforms effected by Tu Yu, the salt revenue at the end of the eighth century must have fallen to about half of the total for 779.

46 See *HTS*, 54, p. 2*a*.

47 See *HTS*, 54, p. 2*a*: 'The salt-producing families broke the law and made illicit sales without cease, while the soldiers who should have patrolled around and arrested the offenders wandered off to the prefectural and county towns....'

48 Tu Yu was appointed during the administration of Wang Shu-wen. See Twitchett, *Asia Major*, p. 77; Yen Keng-wang, *T'ang p'u-shang-ch'eng-lang piao*, pp. 769, 799, etc. Many authors have drawn attention to the concern shown by Wang Shu-wen for financial reform. It is rather surprising, therefore, that the Act of Grace of the 2nd month 805 (see *TFYK*, 89, p. 17*a*), which set out a great variety of financial measures, makes no mention whatever of the salt administration, although it does expressly forbid the types of irregular tribute offering which Li Ch'i had been making in his capacity of provincial governor. It seems possible, then, that the abuse of the monopoly has been somewhat exaggerated.

49 Li Sun succeeded Tu Yu, at the latter's request, in the 4th month 806. See Twitchett, *Asia Major*, 4, 1; Yen Keng-wang, *T'ang p'u-shang-ch'eng-lang piao*.

50 This was the result of a memorial from Tu Yu in his capacity as commissioner for public revenue (see *TFYK*, 493, pp. 17*b*, 18*a*).

51 See *HTS*, 54, p. 2*b*: 'During the *Chen-yüan* period, anyone stealing a *shih* of salt from the two pools (at P'u-chou) was punished with death. With the beginning of the *Yüan-ho* period, this punishment was reduced to banishment to the five fortresses of T'ien-te.' The T'ien-te fortresses were in the northern bend of the Huang-ho in the Ordos region.

52 See *TFYK*, 493, p. 18*a*. The system was put under the joint control of the salt authorities and the county magistrates.

53 See *CTS*, 49, p. 5*a*; *THY*, 87, p. 1592; *TFYK*, 493, p. 18*a–b*. See also the series of memorials setting out the annual revenue in *TFYK*, 493, pp. 18*b*ff.

54 On the dates of Wang Po's tenure of office see Yen Keng-wang, *T'ang p'u-shang-ch'eng-lang piao*, p. 801.

55 See *CTS*, 49, p. 5*b*; *THY*, 87, pp. 1592–3. The agent (*liu-hou*) of the Salt and Iron Commission at Yang-tzu (*hsien*) became commissioner for the *liang-shui* tax for the Yangtze and Huai region and the south (*Chiang-Huai i-nan liang-shui shih*), the agent at Chiang-ling became commissioner for the *liang-shui* tax from south of Ching and Heng (i.e. Hunan), the eastern parts of the Han and Mien river valleys and south of the P'eng-li (i.e. Poyang) lake (*Ching-Heng-nan Han-Mien-tung-chieh P'eng-li i-nan liang-shui shih*), while the head of the branch establishment of the Public Revenue Commission in western Shan-nan became commissioner for the *liang-shui* tax in the three Ch'uan provinces (i.e. Szechuan) (*San-ch'uan liang-shui shih*).

56 *CTS*, 49; *THY*, 87, *loc. cit.* By the same edict which established the commissioners for the *liang-shui* tax, the Public Revenue Commission's branch in Shan-nan was given control of all salt production in Szechuan. However, *HTS*, 54, p. 1*a*, states that this authority was divided between three branch establishments, one in each of the three provinces (Shan-nan, West; Chien-nan tung-ch'uan; Chien-nan hsi-ch'uan) concerned. During the period 810–17 there seems to have been considerable rivalry between the two offices, which came to a head in 816–17 when Huang-fu Po gained control of the Public Revenue Department (see Twitchett, *Asia Major*, 4, 1, p. 80; Yen Keng-wang, *T'ang p'u-shang-ch'eng-lang piao*, pp. 771–2).

57 The death penalty was imposed upon offenders at the P'u-chou pools (see *HTS*, 54, p. 2*b*).

58 See *HTS*, 54, p. 2*b*: 'Huang-fu Po memorialised the throne that offenders should be liable to death as before. If they stole 1 *tou* of salt they were to be flogged on the back, and their carts and donkeys were to be confiscated. Anyone able to apprehend the thief of 1 *tou* of salt was to be given a reward of 1000 cash. The provincial governors were to make their executive officers (*p'an-kuan*) look into illicit dealings in salt. The prefectures were to make their chief clerks do so. Should more than 1 *shih* be allowed to slip through, the responsible official was to be punished. In the case of illegal sale of salt from the two pools (at P'u-chou), the keepers of stores and brokers involved in the transaction were to be considered guilty as of robbery. Cutting away a *tou* of salt-bearing soil was to be the equivalent of stealing one *sheng* of salt. Within the counties, the mutual security groups (*pao*) were to superintend one another. The tyranny (of the system) was as bad as it had been in the *Chen-yüan* period.'

59 The plant concerned was the *shui-po*, which is identified as *Menianthus trifoliata*, a common swamp weed known as the bog bean, buck bean, etc. This weed was collected and burned, and salt refined from the ashes. A similar method of production by burning seaweed and refining the ashes was employed in ninth-century Japan, the salt being called *mo-shio*. According to the edicts relevant to this practice in T'ang China, this was a more profitable and simple method of extracting salt than extracting it from alkali soil (see *CTS*, 17A, p. 14a; *THY*, 88, p. 1606; *TFYK*, 494, p. 1a–b; *HTS*, 54, pp. 2b–3a).

60 For example, the Hu-lo pool came under the commissioners for provisioning the armies in Ho-tung until in 850 it was overrun by the Tanguts. The Pai-ch'ih pool was also under the jurisdiction and control of the military governor of Ho-tung.

PAGE 57

61 See *HTS*, 54, p. 2b; *TTCLC*, 112, p. 584; *TFYK*, 493, p. 22a. We are told that prior to this memorial the monopoly tax had applied in Ho-pei only to non-Chinese.

62 See *TFYK*, 493, pp. 21b–22a; *THY*, 88, p. 1605; *CTS*, 48, p. 15b. The three branches were set up at Yün-chou, Yen-chou, and Ch'ing-chou.

63 See *TFYK*, 493, p. 27a; *THY*, 88, p. 1605; *CTS*, 48, p. 15b; *CTS*, 16, p. 8b.

64 See *TFYK*, 493, p. 27a; *THY*, 88, p. 1606; *CTS*, 48, pp. 15b–16a; *TTCLC*, 112, p. 584.

65 On Chang P'ing-shu's appointment, see Yen Keng-wang, *T'ang p'u-shang-ch'eng-lang piao*, pp. 708–9.

66 The suggestions of Chang P'ing-shu are preserved in the long memorial on Han Yü opposing the scheme (see appendix III, 1; see also *TCTC*, 242, pp. 7815–16).

67 The memorial of Han Yü, entitled 'Lun pien yen-fa shih-i chuang', translated in appendix III, 1, is in *Han Chang-li chi*, 40, pp. 55–60. Wei Ch'u-hou's equally long and detailed attack is in *TFYK*, 493, pp. 23*b*–26*b*.

68 See *CTS*, 49, p. 6*a*; *THY*, 87, p. 1594.

69 See *TFYK*, 494, p. 4*b*.

70 *Ibid.* pp. 6*b*–9*a*.

71 The chronology of the salt and iron commissioners in the late 840's is obscured by a passage in *CTS*, 49, p. 6*a*, which informs us that in the space of nine years five men, Hsüeh Yüan-shang, Li Chih-fang, Lu Hung-cheng, Ma Chih, and Ching Hui, followed in one another's footsteps in control of the salt administration. Yen Keng-wang, *T'ang p'u-shang-ch'eng-lang piao*, p. 805, has drawn attention to the difficulties caused by this passage, for Lu Hung-cheng (also written Hung-chih) would have to be made commissioner in 847 to fit in at all with the sequence. However, *TCTC*, 248, p. 8029, records Ma Chih's appointment in the 2nd month 847, and since he was concurrently vice-president of the Board of Justice it seems very likely that he was responsible for the new laws, especially for their penal provisions.

72 See *HTS*, 54, p. 3*a*. Neither his biographies in *CTS*, 177; *HTS*, 182, nor the accounts given in *CTS*, 49 and *THY*, 87 of the salt administration, mention his reform of the salt administration, but he may well have done so at the same time as his reforms of transportation and tea taxation.

PAGE 58

73 See *HTS*, 54, p. 3*a*; *THY*, 87, p. 1595.

PAGE 59

74 See Dubs, 'Wang Mang's economic reforms', *T'oung Pao*, 35, IV, pp. 219–65, and vol. III of the same author's *History of the former Han dynasty*, pp. 526ff.; Swann, *Food and money in ancient China*, pp. 344ff.

75 See *TFYK*, 504, which notes such prohibitions imposed in 619 (p. 5*a–b*), 670 (p. 5*b*), 713 (*ibid.*), 758 (*ibid.*), and 759 (p. 6*a*). The prohibition of 758 is recorded in fuller form in *TTCLC*, 112, p. 582.

76 *TFYK*, 504, p. 6*a*, gives the date of this edict as 3rd month of *Pao-ying*, 2 (763). *TT*, 11, p. 62*a*, gives the date as the 12th month of the same year, while *HTS*, 54, p. 3*b*, also gives the same date.

77 See *TT*, 11, p. 62*a*; *WHTK*, 17, p. 168*a*.

78 See *TFYK*, 504, p. 6*a*; *TTCLC*, 119, p. 827; *HTS*, 54, p. 3*b*.

79 *TT*, 11, p. 62*a*, simply says: 'In 782 the people were prohibited from dealing in liquor. The officials established shops, and collected the proceeds to provide for the expenses of the armies.' *CTS*, 49, p. 11*b*; *TFYK*, 504, p. 6*a*; *TPYL*, 828, pp. 3*b*–4*a*; *WHTK*, 17, p. 168*a*, preserve a more detailed version. 'A monopoly tax was first imposed on liquor. Everywhere within the empire officials were ordered to brew wine. On each *hu* they were to collect 3000 cash (1000 *apud TFYK*), and even though grain was cheap this was not to be reduced below 2000 cash. The prefectural and county authorities were given general control of this policy. Varying penalties were specified for diluting wine or for illicit brewing. The capital, being the seat of the ruler, was specially exempted from the monopoly tax.'

80 *TFYK*, 504, p. 6*a*; *THY*, 88, p. 1607; *HTS*, 54, p. 3*a*; *CTS*, 12, p. 23*b*; *WHTK*, 17, p. 168*b*. 'In the 12th month 786, the Department of Public Revenue memorialised the throne requesting that the liquor monopoly tax be imposed in the capital and the metropolitan province. On each *tou* the monopoly tax should be 150 cash. The households engaged in wine-making should be granted exemption from miscellaneous *corvée* duties (*tsa ch'ai-i*).' This was put into effect.

PAGE 60

81 On the manufacture of wines and ferments, see Tenney L. Davis, 'The preparation of wines and ferments', *Harvard Journal of Asiatic Studies*, 9 (1947), pp. 24–44. This article includes a translation of the relevant passages from the *Ch'i-min yao-shu*, which reflects the practice in northern China in the sixth century. See also Shih Sheng-han, *A preliminary survey of the work 'Ch'i-min yao-shu'*, pp. 80 ff.

82 According to *HTS*, 54, p. 3*b*: 'Only in Huai-hsi, Chung-wu, Hsüan-wu and Ho-tung provinces was there simply a monopoly tax on ferments and nothing more.' Regarding its imposition in the form of a supplementary direct tax, see below. This practice must have begun soon after the monopoly was first introduced, since *TFYK*, 491, p. 4*b*, cites an Act of Grace granting exemption from this form of the tax dated 798.

83 See *TFYK*, 504, p. 6*b*, and the text of the edict in *TTCLC*, 70, pp. 391–2.

84 See *THY*, 88, p. 1607.

85 See *THY*, 88, p. 1608; *TFYK*, 504, p. 6*b*; *TPYL*, 828, pp. 3*b*–4*a*. Ts'en Chien-kung in his *Chiu T'ang-shu i-wen*, 7, p. 14*b*, considers that this passage, which is introduced in *TPYL* as from *T'ang shu*, is a lost passage from the *Shih huo-chih* of *CTS*. But *T'ang-shu* here probably referred to the *Shih-lu* of Hsien-tsung's reign.

86 This commentary reads: 'The liquor monopoly tax was formerly always collected from all households together with the *liang-shui* tax. However, from the *Chen-yüan* period onwards, provincial magnates strove with one another to make tribute offerings. For this reason they presented memorials claiming that the common people were in distress and had been unable to fulfil their contribution of taxes, and requesting that they might set up official establishments (*kuan-fang*) to deal in wine to replace [the deficient taxes]. When these requests had been granted, they would enforce the laws on liquor very rigorously, so that the country folk offended against the prohibitions whenever they raised a hand. Thus the officials have made considerable profits, which have gone to provide their personal interests. This abuse has continued for a long while.' (See *TFYK*, *TPYL*, *loc. cit.*)

87 For the memorial see *THY*, 88, p. 1607. *TFYK*, 491, preserves Acts of Grace giving exemption from the liquor monopoly tax as a supplementary direct tax dated 798 (p. 4*b*), 805 (two edicts, p. 5*b*, p. 6*a*), 807 (two edicts, p. 7*a*, p. 7*b*), 819 (p. 11*b*), and 833 (p. 15*a*).

88 See the memorial from the administration of the metropolitan district presented in 811, *TFYK*, 504, p. 6*b*; *CTS*, 49, p. 11*b*; *THY*, 88, p. 1607; *HTS*, 54, p. 3*b*. 'The liquor monopoly tax should be levied equitably as a supplementary tax according to the number of strings paid for the *liang-shui* and *ch'ing-miao* taxes, except in the case of the wine-producing households paying the regular tax.' The meaning of the term *ch'u-cheng chiu-hu* is not certain, but I take it that there was some similar distinction between registered wine-producing shops and unregistered (? non-producers) retailers, as was the case in Sung times when there were wine shops called *cheng-tien* and others called *chüeh-tien*. See Katō's translation of the *Chiu T'ang-shu shih-huo chih*, *Ku Tōjo shokkashi*, *Ku Godaishi shokkashi*, p. 185.

89 See *THY*, 88, p. 1607.

90 See *TFYK*, 504, p. 6*b*; *TPYL*, 828, p. 3*b*; *THY*, 88, p. 1608.

91 See *TFYK*, 504, pp. 6*b*–7*a*, memorial of Tou I-chih.

92 See *Yüan-shih Ch'ang-ch'ing chi*, 36, pp. 3*b*–4*a*: '...When we come to the liquor monopoly tax, although the names and types of levy are not the same, in actual fact all are extracted from the common people. Now at present in nine out of ten prefectures and administrations of the empire, this tax is apportioned together with the *liang-shui* taxes, while in one out of ten places, official shops are established to deal in liquor. However, apart from these sums the insatiable requirements (of provincial officials) lead them on the one hand to make excessive levies and thus exhaust the people, and on the other to impose severe penalties to control their subjects. Since the amount which they have to provide to the central government is already fixed, these surplus profits go to the governors and their officers. The state of affairs is oppressive, and the laws are not uniform. I therefore request that the liquor monopoly tax be equitably apportioned according to the amount paid for the *liang-shui* tax by all households contributing two strings or more. Those who pay less [for the *liang-shui*] should not come within the scope of taxation. Where official shops were formerly established to deal in liquor, we request that they be abolished. If this is done, there will be no confusion in the rates and types of tax, while there will be discrimination made between rich and poor. The people will be aware of the fixed standard, and the officials prevented from causing abuse. We have given consideration to this matter, and think that it would be beneficial.'

93 See *TFYK*, 504, p. 7*a*; *TTCLC*, 70, p. 392; *WYYH*, 426, p. 8*b*. Another edict mentioning a suspension of the monopoly is quoted in the biography of Li Te-yü, *CTS*, 174, p. 2*b*.

94 See *TFYK*, 504, p. 7*a–b*.

95 *Ibid.*

96 *Ibid.* p. 8*a*.

97 *Ibid.* pp. 7*b–8a*.

98 See *THY*, 88, p. 1608, and the longer version of this in *TFYK*, 504, p. 8*a–b*.

PAGE 62

99 See *CTS*, 49, p. 11*b*; *THY*, 88, p. 1608; *TFYK*, 504, p. 8*b*.

100 See *TTCLC*, 5, p. 33.

101 See *HTS*, 54, p. 3*b*. The text reads *chüeh-chiu wei ch'ien*, i.e. the money raised from imposing a monopoly tax on wine, not simply *chüeh-chiu-ch'ien*, i.e. the liquor monopoly tax. It is possible, then, that the figure here refers to profits from official dealings subsequent to the edict of 846, in which context the following sentence 'Of this sum the cost of brewing amounted to one-third' would make sense, whereas if the tax were in question this would be irrelevant.

102 See the figures given above.

103   See *CTS*, 49, p. 9*b*; *THY*, 88, pp. 1614–15; *TFYK*, 502, pp. 26*a*–27*a*. *WHTK*, 18, p. 173*a*, dates this incorrectly as 780.

104   See *CTS*, *THY*, *TFYK*, *locc. cit.* The memorial of Chao Tsan is quoted also in *CTS*, 12, p. 10*b*, and in *WHTK*, 21, p. 205*c*, where it is wrongly dated 780.

105   See *THY*, 84, pp. 1545–6. On the court's flight to Feng-t'ien see *TCTC*, 228, pp. 7350ff.

PAGE 63

106   See *CTS*, 49, pp. 4*b*, 10*a*; *THY*, 84, p. 1546; *TFYK*, 493, p. 17*a*; *WHTK*, 18, p. 173*a*. Brief notices of this development are in *TT*, 11, p. 63*a*; *HTS*, 54, p. 3*b*.

107   See *Lu Hsüan-kung Han-yüan chi*, 22, pp. 23*b*–27*a*. Translated by Balázs, 'Beiträge', *MSOS*, 36, pp. 33–8.

108   See *CTS*, 49, p. 10*a*; *THY*, 84, p. 1546; *TFYK*, 493, p. 17*a*. From a later memorial, *TFYK*, 494, p. 5*a*–*b*, and the subsequent edict, *ibid.* pp. 5*b*–6*b*, it seems the tax was charged on the transaction between the grower and the wholesale merchant, and was actually imposed through the brokers who conducted such sales.

109   See the material on tea production, *Ch'a-ching*, 8, *passim*; *T'ang kuo-shih pu*, 3, p. 60.

110   See the account of varieties of tea in *T'ang kuo-shih pu*, 3, p. 60.

111   See *CTS*, 49, p. 4*b*.

112   See *CTS*, 49, p. 10*a*; *THY*, 84, p. 1546; *TFYK*, 493, p. 17*b*. Kanei, 'Tō no chahō', *Bunka*, 5, VIII (1938), pp. 35–53, calculates that the contemporary revenue from salt was about 3,600,000 strings, and that tea revenue was thus only about one-ninth of that from salt.

113   See *CTS*, 48, p. 15*a*–*b*; *TFYK*, 493, p. 21*a*.

114   See *CTS*, 16, p. 2*b*; *WHTK*, 18, p. 173*b*; *HTS*, 54, pp. 3*b*–4*a*.

115   See *THY*, 84, pp. 1546–7; *TFYK*, 493, pp. 22*b*–23*a*; *CTS*, 173, p. 9*b*.

116   See *THY*, *TFYK*, *loc. cit.*, and *HTS*, 54, p. 4*a*, which puts the blame for the current financial crisis on the expenses of military campaigns and the maintenance of the frontier armies, and on the works carried out by the emperor within the palace precincts.

117 *HTS*, 54, p. 4*a*: 'Ling-hu Ch'u became commissioner for the tea monopoly (*chüeh-ch'a shih*). He once again ordered that a monopoly tax should be paid, increasing the price of it, and that is all.'

118 See *HTS*, 54, p. 4*a*. See also *TFYK*, 494, pp. 5*b*–6*b*.

PAGE 64

119 See *HTS*, 54, p. 4*b*. This increase in the size of the standard catty seems to have been confined to the tea merchants of the Huai–Yangtze region. It was in this region alone that the increase in tax of 840 took effect.

120 See *TFYK*, 493, p. 21*a*. Kanei, 'Tō no chahō', cites many examples of tea being used to buy horses from the Uighurs, to reward ministers and for similar purposes. There are many extant memorials thanking the emperor for gifts of tea.

121 See *TTCLC*, 10, pp. 60–2; *TFYK*, 90, p. 2*b*. In 816 troops had been sent specially to protect the tea plantations in Shou-chou (Anhwei) during the rebellion of Wu Yüan-ch'i. Presumably these were official plantations of some kind. Further official plantations in Kuang-chou in the same vicinity were handed over to the ownership of the common people in 819 (see *TFYK*, 493, p. 21*a–b*).

122 Kanei, 'Tō no chahō', rightly draws a rigid distinction between those regular prefectural tribute offerings of tea, listed, for example, in *YHCHC* and *HTS*, most of which were of comparatively small amounts, and irregular tribute such as that mentioned in 833 (see *CTS*, 17B, p. 8*b*). These irregular tributes were normally made out of season.

123 See *CTS*, 49, p. 6*a*; *ibid.* pp. 10*b*–11*a*; *THY*, 84, p. 1548; *TFYK*, 494, pp. 3*b*–4*a*. See also *CTS*, 172, p. 3*a*; *CTW*, 541, p. 1*a–b*; *CTS*, 169, p. 4*a*; *HTS*, 179, p. 4*b*.

124 Wang Yai's scheme was introduced in the 10th month of 835, and already abolished by the 12th month by Ling-hu Ch'u.

125 Ling-hu Ch'u had the new tea commission and the monopoly production scheme abolished in 835. He also requested that the taxation of tea should revert to the control of the local authorities, who should pay the tax money to the Board of Finance (see *THY*, 87, p. 1593; *CTS*, 49, p. 6*a*). In 836, Li Shih, vice-president of the chancellery, was put in control of tea taxation, and revised the system as operated under Chang P'ang (see *THY*, 87, p. 1593; *CTS*, 49, p. 6*a*; *HTS*, 54, p. 4*a*). *HTS* states specifically that at this time control reverted to the commissioners of salt and iron. But *THY*, 88; *TFYK*, 493, inform us that control by the commissioners of salt and iron was restored only in 840. Kanei, 'Tō no chahō', explains this by the sup-position that Li Shih had transferred control back to the prefectures almost immediately after restoring the authority of the Salt and Iron Commission. His evidence for this is a memorial from Lu Shang dated 839 (see *TFYK*, 494, p. 4*b*) which says 'since the edict of *K'ai-ch'eng* 1 (836) 7th month responsibility for tea in Ch'ang-chou has been deputed to the prefectural and county authorities...'. Li Shih was made commissioner for salt and iron in the 4th month of 836, and this cannot thus refer to the transfer of responsi-bility made under Ling-hu Ch'u. However, as has been seen above, at this period Che-hsi, Lu Shang's province, was subject to special local arrange-ments, even regarding salt revenue, and there is nothing to prove that the edict mentioned in the memorial was applicable throughout the empire. Chü Ch'ing-yüan, *T'ang-tai tsai-cheng shih*, p. 77, suggests that the date for the reversion of authority given by *THY*, 88, is corrupt, *san* (third year) having been corrupted to *wu* (fifth year). This would place the re-establishment of the authority of the Salt and Iron Commission in 838, which would fall within Li Shih's term of office. This hypothesis seems preferable to that of Kanei, but there is no conclusive evidence either way.

126   See *TFYK*, 494, p. 5*a*. The person appointed was the executive officer of the provincial armies of Che-hsi, another evidence of special local control within this province. He was mainly responsible for tribute tea. The appointment provoked a protest from one of the great ministers on the grounds that 'tea production is one of the normal responsibilities of the prefectural and county authorities, and the appointment of such a special commissioner would mean that the local population would not be under the direct control of the local authorities'. The transfer of power to the Salt and Iron Commission must have been subsequent to this appointment, which was made in the 3rd month 838.

127   See *TFYK*, 494, p. 5*a–b*.

PAGE 65

128   *Ibid.* pp. 5*b–6b*.

129   See *WYYH*, 422, pp. 4*a–8a*, especially p. 6*a–b*.

130   See *CTS*, 49, p. 11*a*; *THY*, 84, p. 1548; *WHTK*, 18, p. 173*b–c*.

131   See *CTS*, 49, p. 6*b*; *THY*, 87, p. 1594; *TFYK*, 494, p. 10*a*; *HTS*, 54, p. 4*a*.

132   *HTS*, 54, p. 4*b*, says that the empire's revenue from tea was double what it had been in *Chen-yüan* times; however, Kanei, 'Tō no chachō', quotes a total figure of 603,370 strings quoted in the *T'ang-shu chih-pi hsin-li*. Since the tax rate had at least doubled since 793, this figure would represent revenue from considerably less tea than the 400,000 strings collected annually under Chang P'ang. However, it is misleading to pay too much attention to such figures in view of the confusion over the size of measures used for tea, which would partially offset the effect of the tax increase.

<h2 style="text-align:center">CHAPTER IV</h2>

PAGE 66

1 See *CTS*, 48, pp. 6*b*–7*a*; *THY*, 89, p. 1623; *TPYL*, 836, p. 2*a*–*b*: 'The Prince of Ch'in (i.e. Li Shih-min) and the Prince of Ch'i (i.e. Li Yüan-chi) were each presented with three hearths to cast coin. P'ei Chi, vice-president of the right of the Department of State, was presented with one hearth.'

2 See *An Lu-shan shih-chi*, A, p. 13*a*; *TCTC*, 216, p. 6900, which inform us that An Lu-shan was permitted to operate five hearths in his province.

3 See the arguments used in the various memorials opposing the proposal of Chang Chiu-ling in 734 freely to allow the manufacture of coin, *CTS*, 48, pp. 8*a*–9*b*; *TT*, 9, p. 53*a*–*b*; *THY*, 89, pp. 1625–7; *TFYK*, 501, pp. 4*a*–7*a*. The long memorial of Liu Chih (*loc. cit.*; *WYYH*, 769, pp. 1*a*–3*a*) bases its argument on a passage from *Kuan tzu*, 73—a part of which is not preserved in the current texts—propounding this principle.

4 See the sources cited in note 3 above, also *HTS*, 54, p. 5*b*, which gives Chang Chiu-ling's counsel as follows: 'The ancients were unable to equalise the short lengths and small weights by making use of cloth and grain in exchange, and so they made money to make free exchange of commodities. The (coin) produced by official casting is very little, while the labour and expense involved are great. We ought, therefore, to allow the people to cast coin.'

5 *CTS*, 48, p. 7*a*; *THY*, 89, p. 1623; *TPYL*, 836, p. 2*a*–*b*: 'Those who dared to cast coin illicitly were themselves executed and the members of their households were exiled and enslaved to the state.'

6 See Niida Noboru and Makino Tatsumi, 'Ko Tōritsu-sogi seisaku nendai kō', *Tōhō gakuhō*, 1 and 2 (1931).

7 See *Code*, 26, art. 3: 'All who illicitly cast coin shall be exiled beyond 3000 *li*. If they have already prepared the implements, but have not yet cast any (coin), they shall be sentenced to two years' hard labour. If the implements are not yet ready for casting, they shall be given a flogging of 100 strokes.'

[*Commentary:* . . . If they privately cast coins from gold, silver, etc., and do not put them into circulation, they shall be guilty of no offence.]
If they grind down whole cash, making them thin and small, taking the copper with a view to profit, they shall be given a year's hard labour.'

8 For instance, in 682, when there seems to have been a currency crisis, the following edict was issued: 'In cases of illicit casting of coin, the instigator of the crime and the principals involved with him shall all be punished by strangling, and before execution be given a flogging of 100 strokes. Accomplices, and the master of the premises (where the counterfeiting is done) will be punished with exile and additional hard labour, and each be given summarily a flogging of 60 strokes. Where members of a household are together guilty of such a crime, and the head of the household is both old or infirm and not involved, the punishment (to which he is liable) shall fall on the next in succession. The neighbourhood and joint-responsibility groups (*lin, pao*) of the place where illicit coining is done will be sent to one year's hard labour. The village headman (*li-cheng*) and the headman of the ward (*fang-cheng*) or hamlet (*ts'un-cheng*) shall each be given a summary flogging of 60 strokes. Informers shall be rewarded with the coin which has been cast and broken up, with copper utensils, etc. If an accomplice gives himself up, his punishment shall be remitted, and a reward granted him in accordance with this rule' (see *TT*, 9, pp. 52*b*–52*c*). The provisions of this edict were incorporated in the *Regulations of the Board of Justice* (*hsing-pu ko*) promulgated in 706. See Fonds Pelliot chinois (Touen-houang), P. 3078, lines 40–7. For a reproduction of this MS. see *Sei-kyū gakusō*, 17, pp. 171 ff. The death penalty thus remained in the regulations for over two decades. After the abortive attempt by Ti-wu Ch'i to introduce a new coinage in high denominations in 759 there was a great outbreak of coining, and the governor of the metropolitan district had some 800 persons guilty of the offence flogged to death within a few months (see *CTS*, 48, p. 10*b*; *THY*, 89, p. 1627; *HTS*, 54, p. 7*a*). The death penalty was once more imposed by an edict of 829 not only for illicit coining, but also for casting prohibited articles from bronze (see *HTS*, 54, p. 9*a*; *TFYK*, 501, pp. 20*b*–21*a*).

PAGE 68

9 See *CTS*, 48, pp. 6*b*, 7*a*; *THY*, 89, p. 1623. The sources do not specify whether or not these mints were under the direct control of the Directorate of Imperial Workshops.

10 See *TLT*, 22, p. 29*a*: 'Under the present dynasty, the Directorate of Imperial Workshops established 10 hearths. Those in the prefectures are also all under their control.'

11   See *CTS*, 48, p. 7*b*: 'At that time the price of grain grew higher by degrees, and the counsellors considered that the gradual increase in the amount of money cast was the reason why money was cheap and goods dear. Thereupon the casting of coin by the Directorate of Imperial Workshops was suspended. Subsequently the old system was revived....' *TLT*, 22, p. 29*a*, says: 'When the imperial workshops temporarily ceased casting money, the mints in the prefectures were separated from them.'

12   See *TLT*, 22, pp. 28*b*–29*a*; *CTS*, 44, p. 33*a*. The latter reads 'The directorates for minting (*chu-ch'ien-chien*) shall be controlled by the protector general or prefect of the administration or prefecture in which the mint is situated. The duties of the deputy director (*fu-chien*) shall be performed concurrently by the chief of staff (*shang-tso*). There shall be two assistants, whose duties shall be discharged by the persons in charge of one of the prefectural services (*p'an-ssu*), a supervisor of business (*chien-shih*), whose duties shall be performed by an administrator (*ts'an-chün*) or marshal (*wei*) of one of the subordinate counties, and clerks and scribes who shall be appointed from among the officials.' Cf. *HTS*, 48, p. 17*a* (des Rotours, *Traité des fonctionnaires et traité de l'armée*, I, p. 474).

13   All the officials named in the passages mentioned in the previous note were busy with a multitude of local affairs, and can have exercised only the most general supervision over the minting of coin.

14   See *HTS*, 54, p. 6*b*; *CTS*, 138, p. 6*a*–*b* (biography of Wei Lun): '...Yang Kuo-chung presumed upon his favour and authority and strove after personal fame. He mobilised peasants from the prefectures and counties, and made them cast coin. These farmers were not artisans by origin, but were forced nevertheless by the authorities to go and labour. Many of them suffered thrashings and punishment. The people were without means of livelihood. Wei Lun informed Yang Kuo-chung, "For the casting of coin you should obtain people who are originally of the appropriate profession. Now you are forcing peasants from among the common people to do it. This is a great waste of effort for no result, and the people speak ill of you. I request that you enroll skilful artisans to do it, offering them a generous market wage. By this means the labour services will be reduced, and yet the production of coin will be increased...".'

15   The list of mints in *TLT*, 22, p. 29*a*, lacks the mint at Jun-chou, as does that in *CTS*, 44, p. 33*a*. The latter, however, is not surprising, for it is copied directly from *TLT* and cannot be considered in any way independent evidence. The lists given in *TT*, 9, p. 53*b*–*c*; *TFYK*, 501, p. 8*a*; *HTS*, 54, p. 6*b*, are all dated *T'ien-pao*, and we may suppose that the Jun-chou mint was established between the dates of compilation of *TLT* and T'ien-pao

times. There is evidence for this, as *TFYK*, 501, p. 7*a*; *THY*, 89, p. 1627; *HTS*, 54, p. 6*a*, report that mints were established for the first time at Jun-chou and Hsüan-chou in 738. However, Hsüan-chou is already included in the *TLT* list, which forms part of the *TLT* commentary which is usually held to have been completed in 739. Why was not Jun-chou included also?

PAGE 69

16 See *THY*, 59, p. 1022. The first commissioner, Lo Wen-hsin, was an examining censor. His successor, Yang Shen-chin, was also a censor.

17 See *THY*, 59, p. 1022. Liu Yen was commissioner in 760, and again in 762. In 764 Ti-wu Ch'i also became commissioner, and from 765 the two divided responsibility geographically, as in the case of their other special financial responsibilities (see chapter VI).

18 See *THY*, 59, p. 1022. In 760 Li Fu-kuo became minting commissioner for the metropolitan province (*Ching-chi chu-ch'ien shih*). In 764 Li Hsien was made commissioner for coinage in Chiang-nan West (*Chiang-nan hsi-tao kou-tang chu-ch'ien shih*). He was undoubtedly selected for a special mission, rather than a permanent post as regional commissioner, for the province was not only a most important source of copper and of legitimate coin, but also a hotbed of counterfeiting throughout T'ang times. It is significant that Li Hsien already held high office in the censorate when appointed.

19 See *HTS*, 54, p. 9*a–b*: 'When Wu-tsung abolished Buddhism, Li Yü-yen, an official of the Yung-p'ing mint (at Jao-chou), requested that all the images, bells, chimes, tripods and handbells should be handed in to the branch establishments (*hsün-yüan*) of the Salt and Iron Commission, so as to increase the supply of copper from the prefectures and counties. The Salt and Iron Commission had a regular labour quota for this task, but it was inadequate for the increased amount of casting. The civil governors of provinces were therefore permitted to establish mints (*ch'ien-fang*).'

20 See *HTS*, 54, *loc. cit.*

21 See *HTS*, 54, p. 9*b*: 'Li Shen, military governor of Huai-nan, requested that the empire might cast coins bearing the name of the prefecture in which they were minted, those from the capital being designated *Ching-ch'ien*. Their size and diameter were to be the same as those of the *K'ai-yüan t'ung-pao* coins.' A great quantity of such coin survives and is illustrated in the various numismatic works. In appendix IV, 2, I list all known mint marks. Certain of these mints cast a quantity of iron coin, as well as copper cash, and during the tenth century iron coinage was very widespread in Szechuan

—on this important topic see Miyazaki Ichisada, *Godai Sōsho no tsūka mondai*, especially pp. 61 ff. There is some question whether this iron coinage was simply the result of an abnormal local demand for currency, and Szechuan developed paper currency in the form of *chiao-tzu* for just this reason, or was an attempt to prevent the export of copper cash into the Tibeto-Burmese frontier regions. To judge by the Tun-huang MSS. Ho-hsi (i.e. modern Kansu) was almost completely denuded of coin by the late ninth century.

22 See the rubbings of coins in the *Ch'üan-shih*, 5, of Hsiao Ling-yü, the *Ch'ien-lu* of Liang Shih-cheng, and the recent *Ku-ch'ien Ta-tzu-tien* (1938) of Ting Fu-pao. All accept these signs as mint marks, but find it impossible to identify them.

23 See *Sui shu*, 24, p. 23 a: 'From the *Ta-ye* period (605–16) onwards the authority of the emperor was relaxed, great evils flourished and there was a great deal of illicit coining. The cash became more and more thin and bad. At first each 1000 cash still weighed 2 catties (*chin*), but later they became lighter and lighter until they weighed only one catty. Some people cut out iron sheets, cut up hide, or pasted together layers of paper to make coins, and these were all employed indiscriminately. Money became cheaper and commodities dearer, and this state of affairs continued until the end of the dynasty' (cf. Balázs, 'Le traité économique du Souei-chou', *T'oung Pao*, 42, III–IV, pp. 181).

24 See *CTS*, 24, p. 6 b; *THY*, 89, p. 1622; *TT*, 9, p. 52 b. 'In 621 the *wu-shu* coins of the Sui were abolished, and replaced by the *K'ai-yüan t'ung-pao* as currency.' On this coinage see Yang Lien-sheng, *Money and credit in China*, pp. 24–5.

25 See *CTS*, 48, p. 6 b; *THY*, 89, p. 1622; *TT*, 9, p. 52 b.

26 See *TLT*, 22, p. 28 b.

27 See *TT*, 9, p. 53 b–c; *TFYK*, 501, p. 8 a, which say that during the *T'ien-pao* period each hearth produced 3300 strings annually, and consumed in the process 21,220 catties of copper, 3790 catties (3709 *apud TT*) of white tin (*pai-la*) and 540 of black tin (*hei-hsi*). This would have given an average weight of 7 catties 2 ounces per 1000 cash.

PAGE 70

28 See *TT*, 9, p. 53 c; *TFYK*, 501, p. 8 a. *HTS*, 54, p. 6 b, simply says that it cost 750 cash to mint 1000, and does not specify that this was the cost of the metal alone.

29 See *CTS*, 48, pp. 10*b*–11*a*; *CTS*, 129, p. 8*b*; *HTS*, 126, p. 17*a*. Han Hui estimated the cost of manufacture and transport of cash from the mints in the Yangtze and Huai regions at 2000 cash per 1000. Since he also estimated that the Lo-yüan mint at Shang-chou, close to the capital, could produce and transport cash to Ch'ang-an for 900 cash per 1000, we may assume that a considerable part of the cost of coin from the south was in fact the cost of transport.

30 These attempts were made in 666 and 759. For details see below.

31 As an illustration of the inconvenience of copper coin for very large transactions, when in 817 the hoarding of copper coin above a specified quantity was prohibited, 'those with a great deal tried to buy up whole wards and streets (in the capital), and hired carts to carry the price for them' (see *CTS*, 48, p. 12*b*; *TFYK*, 501, p. 17*b*; *THY*, 89, p. 1631).

32 During the Han dynasty gold was the more important of the precious metals, silver becoming important only at the end of the Later Han. During the Six Dynasties, both metals were to a large extent replaced by silk as the most important medium of exchange. After the sixth century, the precious metals recovered, silver taking the place of gold as the more important one (see Yang Lien-sheng, *Money and credit in China*, p. 43).

33 Katō, *Tō-Sō-jidai ni okeru kingin no kenkyū*.

34 On the 'harmonious purchase' of grain (*ho-ti*) and of other commodities (*ho-shih*), see Ch'en Yin-k'o, *Sui-T'ang chih-tu yüan-yüan lüeh-lun kao*, pp. 148–54. The provincial allocations for such purchases were very considerable (see *TT*, 6, p. 34*a*; Twitchett, 'Lands under state cultivation during the T'ang dynasty', *Journal of Economic and Social History of the Orient*, 2, II, p. 178).

PAGE 71

35 See *TCTC*, 224, p. 7208; *HTS*, 51, p. 5*b*, which give 40 lengths of silk as the standard price paid per horse.

36 See the edict of 720 preserved in *CTS*, 48, p. 4*a*; *THY*, 83, p. 1532: 'Recently there has been no reliance to be placed on the cloth for the *tiao* and *yung* taxes, and there should be a standardisation of their quality. We are therefore sending out model patterns to be promulgated to the various prefectures. It shall be ensured that the good cloth is not exceedingly fine, and the bad not excessively poor.... The width should be 1 foot 8 inches, and the length of each piece 40 feet.... They should have the same pattern, and a common gauge of weaving....'

37 See the commentary to *Code*, 26, art. 3, translated above, note 7 to p. 66.

38 See appendix II, I, *Taxation Statutes*, art. 6; *TLT*, 3, pp. 36*b*–37*a*.

39 See Katō, *Tō-Sō-jidai ni okeru kingin no kenkyū*, pp. 63–4, where the author points out that taxes were collected in silver in Kucha and Hotcho. For examples of such coins recovered in the area of Turfan, see Huang Wen-pi, *T'u lu-fan k'ao-ku chi*, p. 49, and plate 56.

40 See *TCTC*, 216, p. 6903; *An Lu-shan shih-chi*, A, p. 14*b*. Katō, *Tō-Sō-jidai ni okeru kingin no kenkyū*, collects a number of references to similar coins made for ceremonial or other non-currency purposes.

41 See Katō, *Tō-Sō-jidai ni okeru kingin no kenkyū*; Yang Lien-sheng, *Money and credit in China*, pp. 43–4. The latter describes a surviving T'ang example, published by Okutaira, *Tōa senshi*, 9 (1938), pp. 34*a*–36*b*.

42 The Japanese pilgrim Ennin was supplied with gold in the form of dust to pay his travelling expenses. See Yang Lien-sheng, 'Numbers and units in Chinese economic history', *Harvard Journal of Asiatic Studies*, 12 (1949), p. 222; Waley, *The real Tripiṭaka*, p. 143; and Reischauer, *Ennin's Diary*, pp. 33–4, 41, 44, 318, 321, etc. At this time (838–45) gold was valued at 5000 cash per ounce (*liang*).

43 On these institutions, see Katō, *Tō-Sō-jidai ni okeru kingin no kenkyū*, pp. 574–613. Regarding the existence of a silversmith's guild (*yin-hang*) in T'ang times not only in the capital but also in Su-chou, see Katō, 'On the "Hang" or associations of merchants in China, with special reference to the institution in the T'ang and Sung period', *Memoirs of the Research Department of the Tōyō Bunko*, 9 (1936), pp. 45–83, and the Japanese articles from which this was taken, reprinted in *Shina keizaishi kōshō*, I (1953), pp. 422–61.

44 See Katō, *Tō-Sō-jidai ni okeru kingin no kenkyū*, pp. 496–508.

45 For the tax levied on mining operations in general see Katō, *Tō-Sō-jidai ni okeru kingin no kenkyū*, pp. 533–4; Chü Ch'ing-yüan, *T'ang-tai tsai-cheng shih*, pp. 65–6. The figure of 25,000 ounces is given in *HTS*, 54, p. 4*b*.

46 See *THY*, 86, p. 1578. On this ban see also Kuwabara Jitsuzō, 'Tō-Sō-jidai no dōsen', *Rekishi to chiri*, 13, I (1934), pp. 1–8.

47 See *THY*, 86, p. 1581, which cites an edict forbidding the trading of gold or of iron with foreigners.

48 See *TFYK*, 999, p. 3*b*: 'At the beginning of the *Chien-chung* period (i.e. 780) it was forbidden to trade in silver, copper, iron or slaves with foreigners.'

49 See Katō, *Tō-Sō-jidai ni okeru kingin no kenkyū*, pp. 539–46.

PAGE 72

50 Miyazaki Michisaburō, 'Tōdai no chashō to hisen', published in *Tōyō gakuei zasshi*, 15 (1902), and reprinted in *Miyazaki sensei hōseishi ronshū*, is cited by all Japanese historians, but I have had access to neither version.

51 For descriptions of the workings of the *fei-ch'ien* system, see Niida, *Tō-Sō hōritsu monjo no kenkyū* (1937), pp. 454–6; Yang Lien-sheng, *Money and credit in China*, pp. 50–1, and the entry in *Tōyō rekishi daijiten*, 7, p. 288, by Hino Kaisaburō.

52 Compare, for example, the ban on coin being taken from Kuan-chung over the passes south of Ch'ang-an imposed in 785. See *HTS*, 54, p. 8*a*: 'At the beginning of the *Cheng-yüan* period (785) travellers were prohibited from going out over the Lo-k'u and San-kuan passes with a single cash.' On this passage see the article of Ono, 'Tōdai ni okeru ichi kinrei no kaishaku ni tsuite', *Shirin*, 22, 1, p. 87.

53 *CTS*, 48, p. 12*a*; *THY*, 89, p. 1620: 'All credit transfers (*pien-huan*) of ready money by tea merchants, etc., with either private persons or officials, should be prohibited.' A longer version of this edict, dated 811 2nd month, is preserved in *TFYK*, 501, p. 15*a–b*. According to *HTS*, 54, p. 8*a*, this resulted from a request by P'ei Wu, governor of Ch'ang-an, that 'it should be prohibited to engage in the use of *fei-ch'ien* with merchants. In the various wards of the capital ten men were to be sought out to act as guarantors (*pao*).'

54 See *CTS*, 48, p. 12*a*; *THY*, 89, p. 1620; *TFYK*, 501, p. 16*a–b*: '...Recently credit transfer with the merchants has been prohibited, and for this reason there has been the accumulation of cash within the households. This is why the prices of commodities have risen high, and why a great amount of currency does not come into circulation. We have now deliberated about this, and we humbly request that it be permitted for the merchants to make credit transfers through the three offices (*san-ssu*: i.e. the three major finance offices). This memorial was put into effect.' This was a joint memorial from the heads of the Board of Finance, Department of Public Revenue, and Salt and Iron Commission, dated 812 5th month.

55 *HTS*, 54, p. 8*b*, gives a version of the memorial of 812 5th month, which reads: 'Lu Tan, in charge of public revenue, Wang Shao, president of the Board of Finance, and Wang Po, commissioner for salt and iron, requested that merchants might be allowed to make credit transfers through the three offices, the Board of Finance, Department of Public Revenue, and Salt and Iron Commission, and that 100 cash (commission) should be paid in addition on each 1000 cash transferred. But there were no merchants who would arrive (to take advantage of this). Exchanges with the merchants at a string for a string were then permitted.'

56 See *TFYK*, 484, p. 20*a–b*. In the tenth month of 867 Ts'ui Yen-chao, vice-president of the Board of Finance in control of public revenue, memorialised the throne: '...According to the old system, year by year the merchants handed in their statements and made credit transferences. Since the beginning of the wars with the southern Man, commissioners for the provisioning of the armies (*kung-chün-shih*) have been appointed. We still make credit transfers with the merchants with the money from the salt of the various prefectures, administrations, and establishments under our office, and with those offices to which we should offer money. However, when the documents reach the prefectures and local administrations, and it is asked that payment be made on them, the prefectural authorities constantly claim that the money has been impounded and seized by the commissioners for provisioning the armies. Because of this the merchants are dubious of being paid, and when they in turn go to the office in the capital, their payments are not fulfilled. Therefore the branch establishments and directorates of the salt administration in the prefectures and local administrations should be ordered to pay the money over to the returning merchants according to the time limit, and may not falsely claim that it has been impounded.'

57 See the passages from *Hsü tzu-chih t'ung-chien ch'ang-pien*, 85, 88, cited by Niida, *Tō-Sō hōritsu monjo no kenkyū*, pp. 459–60.

58 See Niida, *ibid.* pp. 459–60.

59 See *HTS*, 54, p. 8*a*: 'Prior to this, when the merchants reached the capital they entrusted their money to the memorial-presenting courts (*chin-tsou-yüan*) of the provinces, to the representatives of the armies or of the various commissioners, or to rich persons, and then with light packs hastened off to the four quarters. When their documents were matched, they received their money. This was called *fei-ch'ien*.' Balázs, 'Beiträge', p. 35, takes this quite differently: 'Sie behalten den entsprechenden Schein (Zertifikat), der fliegendes Geld heißt.' I base my own reading on comparison with the *Hsü tzu-chih t'ung-chien ch'ang-pien*, 85: 'The order was sent to the prefecture to await the arrival of the merchant. When he delivered his certificate, payment was made to him of the amount owing....' *WHTK*, 9, p. 94*a*: 'When the merchant arrived and presented his certificate, he was to be paid on the same day.' These passages admittedly refer to early Sung times, but I feel confident that the procedure in T'ang times must have been the same.

60 Yang Lien-sheng, *Money and credit in China*, pp. 78–9.

61 On the *kuei-fang*, see Katō Shigeshi, 'Kihō kō', reprinted in *Shina keizai shi kōshō*, vol. I, pp. 485–509. This article originally appeared in *Tōyō gakuhō*, 12, IV (1936), but the reprinted version is much revised, and incorporates some extra material utilised by T'ao Hsi-sheng and Chü Ch'ing-yüan, *T'ang-tai ching-chi shih*, pp. 107–13.

62 See Katō, *Tō-Sō-jidai ni okeru kingin no kenkyū*, pp. 574–613.

63 Katō's contributions to this subject are collected in vol. II of *Shina keizai shi kōshō*, pp. 1–164. The most important of the articles of Hino are 'Nan-Sō no shihei "Gensen kōkyo" oyobi "Gensen kanshi" no kigen ni tsuite', *Shigaku zasshi*, 48, VII, VIII, IX (1937), and 'Hoku-Sō-jidai no tegata "Gensen kōin" wo ronjite shihei "Senin" no kigen ni oyobu', *Shakai keizai shigaku*, 8, I, II, III (1938).

64 See Yang Lien-sheng, *Money and credit in China*, p. 79; Niida, *Tō-Sō hōritsu monjo no kenkyū*, pp. 470–7.

PAGE 74

65 See Yang Lien-sheng, *Money and credit in China*, pp. 52–4, and the articles of Katō mentioned in note 63 to p. 73.

66 See the extract from *Sui Shu*, 24, quoted in note 23 to p. 69.

67 For an extremely painstaking collection of price data for the T'ang dynasty see Ch'üan Han-sheng, 'T'ang-tai wu-chia ti pien-tung', *CYYY*, 11 (1947), pp. 101–48. Unfortunately, the figures are not interpreted with any imagination. Price data are rarely quoted unless they are either unusually high, as in times of famine, or unusually low. Hence it is dangerous to use these figures as they stand to produce price graphs, for the result is a highly exaggerated curve. It is of course possible to deduce trends from these figures, but very risky to accept them absolutely as they stand. Furthermore, almost all the available data refer to the vicinity of the capital where, owing to the dense population depending heavily on supplies from elsewhere, prices were very sensitive to all kinds of influences. All the prices quoted below must be read with this in mind.

The prices which I quote here are from *Chen-kuan cheng-yao*, I, p. 30*b*, and *TCTC*, 193, pp. 6084–5. *HTS*, 51, p. 3*a*, gives 4 or 5 cash per *tou*, instead of 3 or 4 cash. This probably derives from the six-part memorial of Lu Chih's 'Chün-chieh fu-shui-hsü pai-hsing liu-t'iao', which was widely used in compiling the *Shih-huo chih* of *Hsin T'ang shu*.

68 *TT*, 7, p. 40*c*, says that in 641 the price had dropped to 2 cash per *tou*, and that it was only 5 cash per *tou* in 665–6. This is attested by *TCTC*, 201, p. 6345, which adds that beans were no longer marketable. *CTS*, 4, p. 11*b*, says the same of barley.

69 See *CTS*, 48, p. 7*a*; *THY*, 89, p. 1623; *HTS*, 54, p. 5*a*.

70 See *CTS*, 48, p. 7*a*; *THY*, 89, p. 1623.

71 For instance, grain was sold off in 679 (see *CTS*, 48, p. 7*b*; *THY*, 89, p. 1623) and again in 719 (see *THY*, 89, p. 1624). Good money was again issued in exchange for bad in 752 (see *CTS*, 48, p. *b*; *TFYK*, 501, pp. 7*b*–8*a*).

72 See Kanei, 'Tō no tsūka-mondai', *Bunka*, 4, III (1937), p. 28.

73 He cites as an example the case of the prohibition of certain types of counterfeit coin in 732, described in *HTS*, 54, p. 5*b*. People holding such coin were allowed to give them up to the authorities by weight, and were given 80 good cash for each *chin* of copper. At that time a *chin* of copper was the equivalent in metal of 160 cash.

74 See the passage from *TT*, 9, pp. 52*c*–53*a*, translated in note 8 to p. 66 above.

75 On the continuance of a money economy in southern China during the Six Dynasties, see Yang Lien-sheng, *Money and credit in China*, pp. 16–17; T'ao Hsi-sheng and Wu Hsien-ch'ing, *Nan-pei ch'ao ching-chi shih*, pp. 126–42; Lü Ssu-mien, *Liang-chin nan-pei-ch'ao shih*, pp. 1102–24, etc.

PAGE 75

76 See *CTS*, 48, p. 7*a*; *THY*, 89, p. 1624; *TPYL*, 836, p. 2*a–b*, also *HTS*, 54, p. 5*a*; *TCTC*, 201, p. 6347. The new coins weighed 2 *shu* and 6 tenths against 2 *shu* and 4 tenths for the *K'ai-yüan t'ung-pao* coins. The edict abolishing the new coins is in *TTCLC*, 112, p. 582.

77 On the relations of the Chinese with the western Turks at this period, see Chavannes, *Documents sur les Tou-kiue occidentaux* (1903), pp. 279–81.

78 Ch'üan Han-sheng, 'T'ang-tai wu-chia ti pien-tung', lays the principal blame for this policy of debasement on the campaigns against Korea. But

NOTES

it undoubtedly also had some connection with the rise to ascendancy of the empress Wu, after her successful clash in 664 with Shang-kuan I and Wang Fu-sheng.

79   A memorial from Wei Ch'eng-ch'ing, dated 679, says that '...in recent years there have been successive floods and droughts....This summer has been violently hot, and the price of grain is very high' (see *CTS*, 88, p. 6*a–b*). *HTS*, 3, p. 8*b*, also records that as far back as 670 grain had been so scarce that the distilling of liquor had had to be prohibited (see also *TFYK*, 504, p. 5*b*), while *CTS*, 5, p. 10*b*, records a famine in Kuan-chung and very high grain prices in 682, and *CTS*, 37, p. 5*a–b*, records a serious flood in Ho-nan in the same year. *TCTC*, 203, p. 6410, says that the floods were followed by a drought and a plague of locusts, and the price of grain rose first to 300 and then to 400 cash per *tou*.

80   The vagrancy problem first became a matter of serious official concern in the last two decades of the seventh century. See above, chapter I, pp. 12–16, and the references given in notes 119–25 to pp. 13–14.

81   See *CTS*, 48, p. 7*b*; *TT*, 9, p. 52*b*: 'At the time (679) grain grew increasingly dear, and the counsellors considered that coin was being cast in increasing quantities, and that thus money was cheap and goods dear.' *HTS*, 54, p. 5*a*, also says that at that time a great deal of coin was cast so that money became cheap and grain increased in price.

82   According to *CTS*, 37, p. 5*b*, 1 *tou* of hulled grain cost 220 cash, while *TCTC*, 203, p. 6410; *TT*, 7, p. 40*c*, give a figure of 400 cash.

83   Casting of coin by the Directorate of Imperial Workshops (*shao-fu chien*) was abandoned (see note 22 to p. 69 above). However, casting of coin by prefectural mints not controlled by the Directorate continued.

84   Already in 679 the better types of counterfeit coin were tolerated in circulation. In that year grain which had been in store for a long period was issued in exchange for debased coin, and *CTS*, 48, p. 7*b*; *THY*, 89, p. 1623, tell us that 'those of the debased coin whose weight and diameter agree with the official coins will be allowed to be put into circulation'. The same sort of policy was followed under the empress Wu, when an edict was promulgated that 'all those coins which are not made of iron or tin, whose metal has not been broken, and which have not been drilled out, are allowed to be circulated...' (see *CTS*, 48, p. 7*b*; *TT*, 9, p. 52*b–c*). Types of coin specifically excluded from circulation were the following: *shu-t'ung* (? wrought copper coin), *p'ai-tou* (full peck?), *sha-se* (sand-mixed?), which were banned, even if up to size and weight. The precise meaning of these terms for counterfeit coin is very obscure. *Shu-t'ung* presumably means coin made of copper 'tempered' with some base ingredients. *Sha-se* may mean either coin with sand added to the metal, or more likely coin which is sand-rough—i.e. rough and uneven in casting. The term *p'ai-tou*, which is encountered commonly, is very difficult to explain. Professor Yang Lien-sheng has suggested to me that it may refer to a passage in *HTS*, 54, p. 5 a: 'When Kao-tsu entered Ch'ang-an among the people *hsien-huan* (threaded ring) coins were used, whose manufacture was so light and small that 80,000 or 90,000 would only fill a half *hu* measure', and suggests the tentative translation 'full peck'. However, the context here would seem to rule out a type of coin differentiated by size or weight, as they were banned even if up to size. The term *ch'uan-hsüeh* refers to coins which had had the hole bored out, an alternative method of 'clipping' coin hard to detect when the coins were strung together, and which was forbidden in the *Code*, 26, art. 3. *T'ung-t'ang* in *CTS*, *TT*, and *T'ung-i*, which is used in the same context in *HTS*, probably refers to coin in which the metal had run imperfectly in casting. *T'ieh-hsi* occurs frequently, and may refer to coins of iron or tin, or to coin containing an admixture of iron and tin.

85 See *TFYK*, 501, p. 1 a: 'In the 9th month of 713, the imperial counsellor Yang Hsü-shou memorialised the throne: "In my humble opinion the coin in use in the markets in the capital is intolerably bad. Some of it has iron or tin added, and it is not coin cast officially. This brings the correct way into ruin, and injures and disorders the people. Outside the cities the use of such coin is not permitted, yet in the capital the situation is still like this...".' See also the version of this memorial in *THY*, 89, p. 1623.

86 See *CTS*, 48, p. 8 a; *TT*, 9, p. 52 c; *THY*, 89, p. 1623. The edict of prohibition, which was promulgated in the 2nd month 718, is in *CTS*, 48, p. 8 a; *TT*, 9, p. 52 c; *TFYK*, 501, p. 2 a–b. The result is described as follows by *THY*, *loc. cit.*: 'After the promulgation of the edict, the common people became clamorous, and the prices of goods were disturbed. The merchants were unwilling to make any transactions....' It goes on to record that as a result the government were forced to issue 50,000 strings of good cash, which were exchanged for commodities at equitable prices to restore order and currency circulation to some degree.

87 See *CTS*, 48, p. 8 a, on the despatch of the censor Hsiao Yin-chih and the failure of his mission. *CTS*, 96, p. 9 a, says that Sung Ching 'also prohibited debased coinage, and sent out envoys into the various provinces to search it out and destroy it, melting it down. This aroused great popular resentment.' The state of the coinage in the south at this time is described as follows by *CTS*, 48, pp. 7 b–8 a: 'When it came to the *Shen-lung* and *Hsien-t'ien* periods (707–13) the coinage in use in the capitals grew still worse. Small cash illicitly cast in the prefectures of Ch'en-chou and Heng-chou (in Hu-nan), which consisted only of an outer rim (*lun-kuo*), and such types as iron or tin coin (*t'ieh-hsi*) or *wu-shu* coins also came increasingly into use. Then there were some who bought tin, melted it down and pressed it in the mould of a coin....' *CTS*, 48, p. 8*a*, has a later passage: 'At that time (718) the coinage of the Yangtze and Huai region had become even more debased. There were a great many types of coin such as *kuan-lu* (official hearth), *p'ien-lu* (side hearth), *leng-ch'ien* (rimmed coin), *shih-ch'ien* (provisional coin?), etc.' These terms are also difficult to explain satisfactorily. *Kuan-lu* obviously refers to the official mints. But why are coins minted officially included in such a list? They may of course have been debased coins produced beyond the official quota to satisfy the demands for currency. *P'ien-lu* are 'irregular hearths'—clearly coin manufactured in private establishments. *Leng-ch'ien* is a term used for the heavy rimmed coinage first made officially after the An Lu-shan rising but cannot refer to this coinage here. *Shih-ch'ien* is inexplicable, and it is possible that the text here is corrupt.

PAGE 76

88 See *CTS*, 48, p. 8*a*.

89 See Ch'üan Han-sheng, 'T'ang-tai wu-chia ti pien-tung'. The periods of lowest prices seem to have been 725, when hulled grain fetched only 15 cash per *tou* (*TCTC*, 212, p. 6769), 740 when it was 20 cash (*TCTC*, 214, p. 6843), and 746 when it dropped to 13 cash (*HTS*, 51, p. 4*a*).

90 See *CTS*, 48, p. 8*b*. *HTS*, 54, p. 5*b*, gives a résumé of Chang Chiu-ling's original counsel. The edict requesting the advice of the state counsellors is in *THY*, 89, p. 1625; *TFYK*, 501, p. 4*a*.

91 The advice given by Li Lin-fu, Hsiao Chiung, and P'ei Yao-ch'ing is given in *TFYK*, 501, pp. 5*b*–6*a*; *CTS*, 48, p. 8*a*–*b*; *HTS*, 54, p. 5*b*. The most important memorials, however, were those of Ts'ui Mien (see *THY*, 89, pp. 1625–6; *TFYK*, 501, p. 4*b*) and Liu Chih (see *CTS*, 48, pp. 8*b*–9*b*; *THY*, 89, pp. 1626–7; *TT*, 9, p. 53*a*–*b*; *TFYK*, 501, p. 5*a*–*b*; *WYYH*, 769, pp. 1*a*–3*a*). *HTS*, 54, p. 6*a*, mentions a subsequent attempt to free coinage manufacture by Li Wei, prince of Hsin-an commandery, a younger brother of the emperor. This was opposed by the advice of Wei Po-yang, and was never put into force.

92 See *CTS*, 48, p. 9*b*; *TFYK*, 501, p. 7*a*–*b*. 'At the beginning of the *T'ien-pao* period (742) the coinage in the two capitals was comparatively good, while grain was plentiful and cheap. But after a few years the situation deteriorated by degrees. The authorities of the local administrations and counties did not permit good coin to be exchanged at a higher price than bad, and good and debased coin were used interchangeably. Rich merchants and evildoers gradually collected together the good coin, and then secretly went to the south of the Huai and the Yangtze, where from the metal of each coin they could cast five debased cash. They passed these off as official coin and they were put into private use in the capital. Thus the coinage in the capital became daily more broken and debased. Each string of such types of counterfeit coin as *e-yen* (goose-eye), *t'ieh-hsi* (iron or tin coin), *ku-wen* (old inscription?). and *yen-huan* (strung rings?) weighed no more than three or four *chin*.' The coins referred to here as *yen-huan* are certainly the same as the *hsien-huan* mentioned in HTS, 54, p. 5a (see note 84 to p. 75). The *e-yen*, goose-eye, coins were presumably very small-sized counterfeit cash. I can suggest no explanation for *ku-wen*, unless they were patterned on coins of earlier dynasties, which had incriptions in seal characters. HTS, 54, p. 6a–b, describing the same situation, says that 'illicit coining was increasing. It was worst in Kuang-ling (Yang-chou), Tan-yang (Jun-chou) and Hsüan-ch'eng (Hsüan-chou). The powerful persons in the capital took away (good coin) year after year, boat-loads and cart-loads following after one another. In the Yangtze–Huai region there were several tens of types of counterfeit (*p'ien-lu-ch'ien*) from private hearths, which were used together with iron or tin coins. These were so light and large that they no longer had the appearance of money. Officially cast coin was called *kuan-lu-ch'ien*, and one of these was equivalent to seven or eight *p'ien-lu* coins. Rich merchants gradually stored them up, and changed illicit coin from the Yangtze–Huai region for them. Among the types of cash employed in the capitals were *e-yen*, *ku-wen*, and *hsien-huan*, the weight of each string of which did not exceed three or four *chin*. They even cut out iron (sheet) and made it up into strings.'

It is interesting that all the centres of counterfeiting mentioned here were also centres of official minting. They were also very flourishing centres of trade, especially Yang-chou, which was one of the greatest cities in China outside the capital (see Ch'üan Han-sheng, 'T'ang Sung shih-tai Yang-chou ching-chi ching-k'uang ti fan-jung yü shuai-lo', CYYY, 11 (1947), pp. 149–76). Undoubtedly it was the great demand for currency in these cities which made it all but impossible for the government to take effective steps to prevent the use of sub-standard coin.

Some idea of the large quantities of coin available in Yang-chou at this period is given by the Japanese account of the life of the monk Ganjin, *Tō Daiwa jō Tōseiden* (Dai Nihon Bukkyō Zensho, vol. 113), p. 111. In 743, in preparation for his second attempt to reach Japan, Ganjin took on board ship at Yangchou 25,000 strings of cash. Of this total 10,000 strings were *ch'ing-ch'ien*, 10,000 strings *cheng-lu-ch'ien*, and 5000 strings *tzu-pien-ch'ien*. Andō Kōsei, in his illuminating work on Ganjin, *Ganjin Daiwajō den no kenkyū* (Tokyo, 1960), p. 133, explains *cheng-lu-ch'ien* as officially cast coin (i.e. as equivalent to *kuan-lu-ch'ien* above), and the 'purple-bordered' *tzu-pien-ch'ien* as old coin of the *wu-shu* type still in circulation although no longer officially recognised currency.

93 See *CTS*, 48, p. 9*b*; *TFYK*, 501, pp. 7*b*–8*a*.

94 See *CTS*, 48, pp. 9*b*–10*a*; *TFYK*, 501, p. 8*a*. An edict was promulgated shortly afterwards allowing all coin to circulate as before apart from iron or tin coin, *t'ung-sha* (coin with sand mixed in the copper, cf. *sha-se*), *ch'uan-chüeh* (drilled coin) and *ku-wen* (old inscription) coins. This was done at the instance of Yang Kuo-chung, who held office as coinage commissioner (see *HTS*, 54, p. 7*a*).

95 See *CTS*, 48, p. 9*b*; *TFYK*, 501, p. 7*a*, translated at note 92 to p. 76. Interchangeability at varied rates must have been very desirable, since *p'ien-lu* coin were worth only one-fifth of an official cash (*CTS*, *TFYK*, loc. cit.) or even as little as a seventh or an eighth (*HTS*, 54, p. 6*b*). The weight of a string of the debased cash used in the capital (*e-yen*, etc.) at 3 or 4 *chin* per string was about half that of a string of official coin, which at this period weighed 7 catties or more.

96 On the new coinage, see *CTS*, 48, p. 10*a*; *THY*, 89, p. 1627; *TFYK*, 501, p. 8*a*; *CTS*, 123, pp. 4*b*–5*a*. The edict for casting the coins valued at 10 cash *Ch'ien-yüan chung-pao* was issued in the 7th month 758 (see *TTCLC*, 112, p. 582), that permitting the issue of coins valued at 50 cash *Chung-lun Ch'ien-yüan ch'ien* was issued in the 3rd month 759 (see *TTCLC*, 112, pp. 582–3; *TFYK*, 501, pp. 8*b*–9*b*—in the latter it is wrongly dated in the 8th month) following a request from Ti-wu Ch'i. Illustrations of these coins may be found in all the numismatic works mentioned in note 21 to p. 69 above.

97 On the outbreak of counterfeiting, see *CTS*, 48, p. 10*a*–*b*; *THY*, 89, p. 1627; *TFYK*, 501, p. 9*b*; *CTS*, 123, p. 5*a*; *HTS*, 54, pp. 6*b*–7*a*. But *HTS*, 54, p. 7*a*, mentions that counterfeiting was rife already before the new coinage was issued.

98 See *HTS*, 54, p. 7*a*; *CTS*, 48, p. 10*a*; *TFYK*, 501, p. 9*b*.

99 See Ch'uan Han-sheng, 'T'ang-tai wu-chia-ti pien-tung'.

100 See *CTS*, 123, p. 5*a*; *THY*, 89, p. 1627: 'The courtiers all considered that Ti-wu Ch'i's changing the law was an abuse, and sealed memorials were heard by the emperor daily. Chi was thereupon demoted to be prefect of Chung-chou.' The edict requesting counsel on the new coinage is in *TTCLC*, 12, p. 583.

101 See the edict of the 6th month 760 cited in *THY*, 89, p. 1625; *CTS*, 48, p. 10*b*; *TFYK*, 501, p. 10*b*; *TTCLC*, 112, p. 582. The revaluation was at first confined to Ch'ang-an, but extended to the empire as a whole by a further edict issued in the next month. See *CTS*, 48; *THY*, 89; *TFYK*, 501, *locc. cit.*

PAGE 77

102 See edict of 4th month 762 cited in *CTS*, 48, p. 10*b*.

103 See the Act of Grace of the 5th month 762 cited in *THY*, 89, p. 1625; *TFYK*, 501, p. 11*a*. This same fact is given with no date in *CTS*, 48, p. 10*b*.

104 See *THY*, 89, p. 1625, *loc. cit.*: 'reckonings may not be made at token prices....'. The use of money at a token value (*hsü-ku*) as well as at its normal value (*shih-ku*) is also mentioned by *CTS*, 48, p. 10*b*, at this period. A sidelight is thrown on this practice by the following edict dated 29th day of the 12th month 760, which is cited in *THY*, 89, p. 1625; *TFYK*, 501, pp. 10*b*–11*a*: 'in all cases of the mortgage (*tien*) of estates, shops, lands, mills, etc.,...where they have previously been mortgaged for money reckoned at its actual value, repayment of the amount loaned shall be made in money reckoned at its actual value. If they were previously mortgaged for a sum reckoned at token values (*hsü-ku*), they shall also be redeemed in money reckoned at token values. In all other transactions cash should, as previously, be used as the equivalent of 10 cash. From this time onwards, money was known either as "actual value" (*shih*) or "token value".' The use of token value cash for official accountancy has already been discussed in chapter II above.

105 See *HTS*, 54, p. 7*a*: 'From the time when Ti-wu Ch'i changed the coinage, those who offended against the law numbered hundreds daily, and the prefectural and county authorities could not stop them. When the [coinage was again unified] the people thought it very convenient. Afterwards the two types of *Ch'ien-yüan* coins were cast into implements by the people and no longer circulated.' *CTS*, 48, p. 10*b*, reads: 'In the city of Ch'ang-an the people strove to carry on illicit coining. Bells and bronze images from the Buddhist and Taoist temples were destroyed and used to make cash in large numbers. Evildoers and members of the powerful clans unceasingly offended against the prohibitions. Cheng Shu-ch'ing, governor of the metropolitan district, arrested them, and they were sure not to be treated leniently. In the space of a few months more than 800 persons were flogged to death.'

106 See *HTS*, 54, p. 7*a*: Shih Ssu-ming issued two coinages, the first called *Te-i yüan-pao*, the second called *Shun-t'ien yüan-pao*. Examples are illustrated in the numismatic collections mentioned in note 21 to p. 69 above.

107 See *HTS*, 54, p. 7*b*.

108 The shortage of copper persisted throughout the dynasty (see below, note 129 to p. 78 for production figures).

109 *HTS*, 54, p. 10*b*, quotes a contemporary opinion dating from the period 760–3 that 'copper is dear and coin cheap, and there are people who cast coin into implements. Before another decade is out, money will be so far exhausted that there will not be sufficient for the needs of the time.'

110 See *HTS*, 54, p. 10*b*. A similar policy had already been introduced in 729 (see *TTCLC*, 112, p. 582). The production of coin had already been stepped up by expansion of the two mints at Fen-t'ang and T'ung-yüan at Chiang-chou in Ho-tung under Ti-wu Ch'i in 769 (see *CTS*, 48, p. 10*b*; *TFYK*, 501, p. 11*a–b*).

111 See chapter 11. Not all taxes were fixed in terms of money rates and money quotas, but only the household levy which replaced the old *tsu-yung-tiao* taxes. The land levy continued to be collected in grain. In most cases, even the household levy was paid in commodities, not in actual cash.

112 See Li Ao's memorial on reforming the tax system, *Li Wen-kung chi*, 9, p. 71*a*. Referring to 780 he says that a length of silk cost 4000 cash, and a *tou* of hulled grain 200 cash (cf. *CTW*, 634, p. 13*a*).

113 *TCTC*, 231, p. 7429, gives the price as 500 cash per *tou* in 784. *CTS*, 12, p. 19*a*; *HTS*, 35, p. 3*b*; *HTS*, 53, p. 3*b*, give the price as 1000 cash in 785.

114 *Li Wen-kung chi, loc. cit. HTS*, 52, p. 2*b*, gives the price as 3200 cash. *Han Chang-li chi*, 40, p. 9*a*, gives it as 3000 cash.

PAGE 78

115 See *TCTC*, 233, p. 7508.

116 *Ibid.*

117 *Li Wen-kung chi*, 9, *loc. cit.* reads: 'Today (i.e. 820) the tax rate is the same as it was previously, but grain and silk grow cheaper daily, while money becomes daily more expensive. The price of a length of silk is no more than 800 cash, and of a *tou* of hulled grain no more than 50 cash.' *Ibid.* 3, pp. 14*a* ff., also confirms that the price of silk fell to 800 cash per length.

118 Kanei, 'Tō no tsūka-mondai'.

119 See the edict requesting the counsellors' opinions on the plan to allow free coinage (note 91 to p. 76 above). *THY*, 89, p. 1625: 'Hemp and silk cloth cannot be exchanged by the foot or the inch, nor can grain be used in the smallest quantities in exchange between those who have and those who have not.'

120 See *TT*, 9, p. 53*c*; *TFYK*, 501, p. 8*a*.

121 See *HTS*, 54, p. 8*a*.

122 See *HTS*, 52, p. 7*a*; *TCTC*, 242, p. 7799.

123 See *HTS*, 54, p. 9*a*. Kanei, 'Tō no tsūka-mondai', quotes from the *T'ang-shu chih-pi hsin-li* a figure of 184,231 strings relating to the *Ta-chung* period (847–59). This larger figure may have been the result of continued operation of some of the mints (*ch'ien-fang*) established in 845.

124 The figure of 100,000 strings is given in *HTS*, 54, p. 7*b*. That of 45,000 is cited in Han Hui's memorial of 780 (see *CTS*, 48, p. 10*a–b*; *THY*, 89, pp. 1627–8; *TFYK*, 501, pp. 11*b–*12*a*).

125 See *CTS*, 48; *THY*, 89; *TFYK*, 501, *locc. cit.*

126 A memorial of Chang P'ang, quoted in *CTS*, 48, p. 11*a*; *THY*, 89, p. 1628; *TFYK*, 501, p. 12*b*, blames the shortage of coin in the Yangtze valley upon the breaking up of coin to manufacture bronze utensils, but there can be no doubt that the suspension of the southern mints was a further factor.

127 In 808 Li Sun requested the re-establishment of two hearths at the former Kuei-yang mint in Ch'en-chou. But these were expected to produce only 7000 strings annually (see *CTS*, 48, p. 11*a*; *THY*, 89, p. 1629; *TFYK*, 501, p. 14*a–b*). The account in *HTS*, 54, p. 8*a*, says that their daily production was to be 200,000 cash—just ten times as much. Perhaps *shih* has fallen out of the text in *CTS*, *THY*, *TFYK*, all three of which derive from a common source, or *shih* has been interpolated in *HTS*. I prefer the latter supposition.

128 See *CTS*, 48, p. 12*a*; *THY*, 89, p. 1620, and a fuller version in *TFYK*, 501, pp. 15*b–*16*a*. Some information on the results achieved is given in *HTS*, 54, p. 8*b*: 'Wang O, military governor of Ho-tung, set up hearths and cleared out the Chü-ma river's waters, and cast coin, the labour and expense being greatly reduced. He made the prefect Li T'ing commissioner, and cast coin using five hearths, each of which produced 300,000 cash per month. From this time onwards the lead and tin coinage in Ho-tung was done away with.' However, this improvement was only temporary. In 834

HTS, 54, p. 9*a*, reads: 'Lead and tin coinage again began to arise in Ho-tung. Wang Yai, the commissioner for salt and iron, established the Fei-hu minting establishment (*Fei-hu chu-ch'ien yüan*) at Yü-chou. The annual output of coin in the empire did not exceed 100,000 strings.' This Fei-hu mint was again not new, but only re-established, for in 811 the San-ho copper foundry was said to be only 20 *li* from the former Fei-hu mint (see *HTS*, 54, p. 8*b*).

129 See *HTS*, 54, p. 4*b*.

130 *Ibid.* There were said to be fifty copper mines in the empire during this reign.

131 See *Sung Shih*, 185.

PAGE 79

132 The whole problem of official control of mining operations and of taxes levied upon them is very obscure, as the sources are extremely meagre. Before 780 loose general control seems to have been exercised by the prefectures. In that year, following a memorial from Han Hui, Te-tsung issued an edict by which 'the profits from the mountains and marshes of the empire ought to revert to the state, and should be controlled by the commissioners for salt and iron' (see *CTS*, 49, p. 4*a*; *TFYK*, 494, p. 2*a*; *HTS*, 179, p. 6*b*; *HTS*, 54, p. 4*b*). The Salt and Iron Commission retained nominal responsibility until 836, when the control was returned to the prefectures (see *TFYK*, 494, pp. 2*a*–4*a*). During the reign of Hsüan-tsung (847–60) the commissioners regained control, following a memorial from P'ei Hsiu. Even during the periods when the commissioners were in charge, however, the collection of taxes on mines seems to have been inefficient. During the *T'ai-ho* period (827–36) Wang Yai complained that the provincial governors were misappropriating such taxes to the extent of a million (strings?) annually (see *HTS*, 179, p. 6*b*). This in spite of the fact that there were special officers responsible for iron and copper smelting in three provinces and twelve prefectures. The system by which tax was levied is not clear, but in the case of gold and silver it seems to have been a 10 or 20 per cent levy on output.

133 See *CTS*, 48, p. 11*b*; *THY*, 89, p. 1629; *TFYK*, 501, pp. 14*b*–15*a*; *HTS*, 54, p. 8*a*. The responsibility for the enforcement of this ban was laid on the local officials.

134 See *CTS*, 48, p. 11*b*; *THY*, 89, p. 1630, and a fuller version of the same edict in *TFYK*, 501, p. 14*a*–*b*.

135 See *CTS*, 48, p. 11*a*; *THY*, 89, p. 1628. The longer version of this memorial in *TFYK*, 501, p. 12*b*, cites as precedent two previous edicts forbidding the manufacture of copper utensils, one dated 772 (see note 110 to p. 77), the other 780.

136   See *THY*, 89, p. 1628; *TFYK*, 501, p. 13*a–b*. Yet another ban on the manufacture of copper utensils was imposed in 806, see *TFYK*, 501, p. 13*b*.

137   See the memorial of the 8th month 820 cited in *CTS*, 48, p. 13*a*; *THY*, 89, pp. 1631–2. This was actually part of the same memorial requesting the collection of the *liang-shui* tax in commodities rather than in cash. See the full document in *TFYK*, 501, pp. 18*a–19b*, *Yüan-shih Ch'ang-ch'ing chi*, 36, pp. 3*a–4b*.

138   *THY*, 89, p. 1632, cites an edict of the 8th month 825 threatening that those who melt down coin to make Buddhist statues should be treated as if they were counterfeiters. This 'edict', however, is in fact an extract from a memorial submitted by Wang Ch'i in the 10th month, following the edict, the actual text of which is in *TFYK*, 501, p. 20*a–b*. Wang Ch'i's memorial is in *HTS*, 54, p. 9*a*, and suggested a specific penalty in place of the vague 'heavy penalties' mentioned in the edict.

139   See *HTS*, 54, p. 9*a*. This edict further ordered that Buddhist statues should be made from tin or lead, wood or stone, in place of copper.

140   According to *HTS*, 54, p. 9*a*, although the manufacture of utensils from copper was forbidden, they were still sold in the shops in the Yangtze and Huai region and in Ling-nan.

141   See Reinaud, *Rélation des voyages*, 1, pp. 72–3. See also Kuwabara Jitsuzō, 'On P'u Shou-keng', *Memoirs of the Research Department of the Tōyō bunko*, 2, p. 27, note 23. For an example of the scale of such exports, see the passage from *Tō Daiwajō Tōseidan* cited in note 92 to p. 76 above.

142   *TCTC*, 242, p. 7799, Memorial of Yang Yü-ling, president of the Board of Finance, says that 'now (821) there are only ten or more hearths which produce annually 150,000 (strings of cash), and besides money is hoarded in the houses of the merchants, and even flows abroad among the four barbarians....'

143   *TCTC*, 242, *loc. cit.* This also informs us that in Ho-pei and Shantung lead and iron coin had been used during the *Ta-li* period and before.

144   See the edict of 809, 6th month in *THY*, 89; *CTS*, 48; *TFYK*, 501 (see note 134 to p. 79), which forbade the transport of cash from southern China across the ranges into Ling-nan. Presumably the government had in mind not only the drain of currency from central China, but the possibility of its being sent abroad, by foreign merchants.

145 See *CTS*, 48, p. 12*a*; *THY*, 89, p. 1630; *TFYK*, 501, p. 16*b*.

146 According to the versions in *THY* and *TFYK* this money was issued through the price-regulating authorities in the markets, whose function it was to attempt to keep prices at a reasonable level. It gives a clear idea of the level of deflation at this period, that in spite of the fact that 811 and 814 were years of serious crop failure, when large issues of grain had to be made from public stocks for relief, grain prices still remained low.

147 See *CTS*, 48, p. 12*a*; *THY*, 89, pp. 1630–1; *TFYK*, 501, pp. 16*b*–17*a*.

148 Kanei, 'Tō no tsūka-mondai', considers that a passage in *HTS*, 54, p. 9*a*, referring to an edict issued by Wen-tsung to provincial governors authorising them to allow exchanges of money and grain, refers to similar issues of government money in exchange for commodities, but I am inclined to think that it was another exhortation to use cash and commodities together in official transactions.

149 See *CTS*, 48, p. 11*b*; *THY*, 89, p. 1629; *TFYK*, 501, pp. 14*b*–15*a*.

150 See *CTS*, 48, p. 12*a*; *THY*, 89, p. 1630; *TFYK*, 501, p. 16*a*–*b*.

151 See *CTS*, 48, p. 12*a*–*b*; *THY*, 89, p. 1631; *TFYK*, 501, p. 17*a*–*b*.

152 See *CTS*, 48, p. 12*b*; *THY*, 89, p. 1631; *TFYK*, 501, p. 17*b*. 'At that time much of the money which was accumulated in the stores and shops of the capital was money belonging to the provincial governors. Of such persons as Wang O, Han Hung, and Li Wei-chien, those with the least had not less than 500,000 strings, and they thereupon strove with one another to buy up dwellings and houses to change their cash into property. Those with the greatest amounts bought up whole streets and wards, hiring carts to carry the price for them.... But the administrations and counties were unable thoroughly to investigate their wealth, and in the end the law was not enforced.'

153 See the passage cited in the previous note and *HTS*, 54, p. 8*b*. It seems that the great merchants had also been speculating with funds provided by the Shen-ts'e armies. The latter were the chief military force under the eunuchs, and the civil authorities dared not question their affairs too closely for fear of reprisals.

154 See *CTS*, 48, pp. 13*b*–14*a*; *THY*, 89, pp. 1632–3; *TFYK*, 501, p. 21*a*–*b*.

155 See *CTS*, 48, p. 6*a*–*b*; *THY*, 84, p. 1541; *TFYK*, 501, pp. 18*a*–19*a*.

156 See *THY*, 89, p. 1627; *TFYK*, 501, p. 7*a*. 'In the 10th month (734) an edict was promulgated saying " The use of commodities and coin together will be advantageous; cloth is the root and money is the branch. To hold cheap the root, and highly esteem the branch would be a deep evil, and there should be a reform of the laws and doctrines. From this time onwards in all transactions involving estates slaves, horses, etc., silk cloth, hemp cloth, fine silk, gauze, silk thread, silk floss, etc., should be employed as previously. In other sales, where the price reaches 1000, money and cloth should be employed together. Offenders will be punished." ' cf. *CTW*, 35.

157 See *HTS*, 54, p. 8*a*.

158 See *CTS*, 48, p. 12*a*; *THY*, 89, p. 1630, and a fuller version of this in *TFYK*, 501, p. 15*a*–*b*.

159 See *HTS*, 54, p. 9*a*.

160 See memorial of Pao Chi cited in *THY*, 89, p. 1628; *TFYK*, 501, p. 12*a*.

161 See the memorial of Wang O cited in *CTS*, 48, p. 12*a*; *THY*, 89, p. 1620; *TFYK*, 501, p. 15*b*, as a result of which the mint at Yü-chou was expanded in 811 (or 812 according to *YHCHC*, 14, p. 437). A memorial supporting the expansion of minting in Ho-tung submitted by Li Chi-fu is preserved in *YHCHC*, *loc. cit.* The edict authorising the issue of money to pay the capital costs of the new hearths is in *TFYK*, 501, p. 15*a*.

162 *THY*, 89, p. 1628–9; *TFYK*, 501, p. 14*a*.

163 *HTS*, 54, p. 8*a*: 'In 809 those persons in the capital using less than 1000 cash for a string or possessing coins of lead or tin, were arrested.' The edict which covered this is certainly that of 809 cited in *CTS*, 48, p. 11*b*; *THY*, 89, pp. 1629–30, but these versions have been cut, and deal only with the question of 'short strings'. However, the edict of 829, *TFYK*, 501, pp. 20*b*–21*b*, cites the precedent of this edict of 809, including a passage covering lead and tin coin at some length.

164 *CTS*, 48, pp. 12*b*–13*a*; *THY*, 89, p. 1631; *TFYK*, 501, p. 18*a*. This dealt specifically with offences by underlings attached to the armies or provincial governors, who had been defying the law.

165 See *CTS*, 48, pp. 13*b*–14*a*; *THY*, 89, pp. 1632–3; *TFYK*, 501, pp. 20*b*–21*b*.

166 See *CTS*, 48, p. 14*a*; *THY*, 89, p. 1633; *TFYK*, 501, pp. 22*b*–23*a*: 'All offenders shall be punished as if they had possessed lead or tin coin.'

167 Katō, *Tō-Sō-jidai ni okeru kingin no kenkyū*, 2, p. 476.

168 See *CTS*, 48, p. 4*a*; *THY*, 66, p. 1154. Since this edict is concerned with standards of size and weight it seems most reasonable to take *ch'u-mai-ch'ien* here as a reference to the standard short string. However, Chü Ch'ing-yüan took this as a reference to the use of the same term as a percentage tax on merchants' transactions. His grounds for this are that the tax imposed under this name in 783 had the same rate—20 cash per string—as mentioned in the edict of 750. However, this is undoubtedly a mere coincidence, for the tax imposed in 783 was only a temporary expedient, which was dropped in the next year as impracticable. Katō, *Ku Tōjo shokkashi*, p. 37, note 117, also takes it as referring to short strings, as I have done.

169 See *TFYK*, 501, p. 13*a*.

PAGE 82

170 See *CTS*, 48, p. 11*b*; *THY*, 89, p. 1629; *HTS*, 54, p. 8*a*.

171 See *CTS*, 48, pp. 12*b*–13*a*; *THY*, 89, p. 1631; *TFYK*, 501, p. 18*a*.

172 See *CTS*, 48, p. 13*a*; *THY*, 89, p. 1632; *TFYK*, 501, p. 20*a*.

173 See *THY*, 89, pp. 1633–4; *TFYK*, 501, p. 23*a*. *HTS*, 54, p. 9*b*, gives the date as 904 instead of 905.

174 See the edict of 846 in *CTS*, 48, p. 14*a*; *THY*, 89, p. 1633; *TFYK*, 501, pp. 22*b*–23*a*. Shih Ssu-ming had also used Buddhist images as a source of copper for his coinage.

175 *Ibid.* This rule was operative from the 3rd month 846.

176 *Ibid.*

177 *HTS*, 54, p. 9*b*: 'When Hsüan-tsung came to the throne (847) the policies of the *Hui-ch'ang* period were completely dispensed with, and the new coins which could be distinguished by the characters for the mints were recast into images.'

PAGE 83

178 See appendix IV, 2.

179 See *Wu-tai hui-yao*, 27, pp. 332–5; Miyazaki, *Godai Sōsho no tsūka mondai*.

CHAPTER V

PAGE 84

1 Shan-chou was the present place of the same name on the Huang-ho in north-western Ho-nan.

2 On the costs of this stage of the journey see *HTS*, 53, p. 1*a*: 'The land haulage to Shan-chou is only 300 *li*, but for every two *hu* the cost of transport is 1000 cash.'

PAGE 85

3 On the militia system (*fu-ping*) see des Rotours, *Traité des fonctionnaires et traité de l'armée*, introduction, and the various specialist works on this subject by Lo Chen-yü and Ku Chi-kuang reprinted in the *Erh-shih-wu shih pu-pien*, vol. 5. See also the general survey of the topic in Pulleyblank, *The background of the rebellion of An Lu-shan*; on p. 140, note 1, the author gives a succinct account of the literature. Since the publication of this work a new general survey, Ts'en Chung-mien, *Fu-ping chih-tu yen-chiu*, has appeared.

4 See Pulleyblank, *The background of the rebellion of An Lu-shan*, map 1, for a picture of the distribution of the militia units. According to the monograph on the army in *HTS*, 50 (see des Rotours, *Traité des fonctionnaires et traité de l'armée*, introduction p. xxxii, text p. 761), in T'ai-tsung's reign 271 of a total of 630 militias (i.e. 43 per cent) were concentrated in Kuan-nei, which province contained only 10 per cent of the total population.

PAGE 86

5 On the decay of the militia system, see Hamaguchi, 'Fuhei-seido yori shinhei-sei e', *Shigaku zasshi*, 41, XI, pp. 1255–95; XII, pp. 1430–1507. The connection between the decay of the militia system and the growth in the importance of the transport system was already noted by the Sung historian Lü Tsu-ch'ien (1137–81) in his *Li-tai chih-tu hsiang-shuo*, 2. He says that until 650 only some 100,000 *shih* of grain were transported annually. This compares with a figure of 200,000 *shih* given in *HTS*, 53, p. 1*a*. Lü also stresses the fact that the increase of expenditure on the armies was a much greater factor than the extravagance of the imperial house in the growth of state expenditure. By *K'ai-yüan* times, army expenditures had reached such a point that the Department of Public Revenues had to appoint special officers (*chih-tu shih*) to keep a check on the armies' expenditure.

6 The numbers of officials expanded considerably under the empress Wu and during the reigns of Chung-tsung and Jui-tsung, when great numbers of

supplementary officials without established posts were appointed (see *TT*, 15, p. 83*b*; *TCTC*, 209, p. 6623, and the memorial of Li Chiao in *CTW*, 247, p. 2*b*).

7 Even in 749 the proportion of the revenue which went to pay official salaries was very high (see appendix II, 4, p. 155). When the fact that military expenditure before the reign of Hsüan-tsung was only a fraction of what it later became is taken into account, this proportion must have been even higher in the early days of the dynasty, for the growth of the bureaucracy was by no means as marked.

8 Ch'u Lang's plan is mentioned in *THY*, 87, p. 1595, and in *HTS*, 53, p. 1*a*, which reads: 'In 656 Ch'u Lang, the director of the Western Park, gave counsel to cut through the San-men mountain and to build bridges so that land traffic could get through. Thereupon 6000 soldiers were despatched to dig out the channel, but the work was never completed.' Recent archaeological surveys conducted during the construction work on the great barrage being built at San-men has revealed extensive traces of the early T'ang tracking paths along the gorges, and also of the new channel excavated by Li Ch'i-wu in 741. The results of these investigations have appeared in a splendid report *San-men shan ts'ao-yün i-chi*, Chung-kuo t'ien-ye K'ao-ku pao-kao, series *ting* no. 8 (Peking, 1959).

9 Yang Wu-lien's opening up of a towing-path along the cliff face is described in *HTS*, 53, p. 1*a*, and in far greater detail in Chang Tsu's *Ch'ao-ye ch'ien-tsai*, 2, pp. 19–20, but in neither source is a date given.

10 See *TT*, 10, p. 56*c*; *TFYK*, 497, p. 8*a*; *TFYK*, 498, p. 15*b*.

11 See Ch'üan Han-sheng, *T'ang Sung ti-kuo yü yün-ho*, pp. 20–8.

12 For an example of this, see *TCTC*, 203, p. 6407, which gives an account of the circumstances under which Kao-tsung made his last progress in 682. Many of the imperial cortège died of hunger, and the danger from bandits was so great that a notable brigand chieftain had to be employed to keep his rivals at bay.

PAGE 87

13 A large proportion of the tax remissions collected in *TFYK*, 490, relating to this period are local Acts of Grace issued to give relief to places through which the imperial cortège had passed.

14 See the memorials of Li Chiao, 'Pai-kuan ch'ing pu-ts'ung pi-chia piao in *CTW*, 245, pp. 13*b*–14*b*; *WYYH*, 600, pp. 8*a*–9*a*; and of Sung Chih-wen, 'Tung tu seng teng ch'ing liu chia' in *CTW*, 240, pp. 10*b*–11*b*; *WYYH*, 605, pp. 10*a*–11*a*.

15 The empress Wei was a native of Ch'ang-an as we know from her biography in *CTS*, 51. Cf. *TCTC*, 209, p. 6639: 'This year (707) there was a famine in Kuan-chung and grain reached the price of 100 cash per *tou*. Grain was transported from east of the mountains (i.e. Ho-nan and Ho-pei) and from the Yangtze and Huai regions, and paid in at the capital. Of the oxen employed in haulage eight or nine out of ten died. Many of the officials requested that the court should return to Lo-yang. But the empress Wei's family originated in Tu-ling and she did not like to live in the east. She therefore made the *sramana* P'eng Chün-ch'ing and others tell the emperor that in this year it would not be advantageous to travel to the east. Afterwards somebody again raised the matter. The emperor got angry and said "How can you have an emperor who chases around after rations!" and he then stayed in Ch'ang-an.'

16 The edict is in *TFYK*, 113, pp. 18*a*–20*a*, and *TTCLC*, 79, p. 451.

17 See *THY*, 87, p. 1601. His title of commissioner is not mentioned in his biography, *CTS*, 100. He was first appointed in 713 while he was prefect of Shan-chou, and retained the title of commissioner when he was promoted governor of Lo-yang at the beginning of the following year.

18 This is described in *TT*, 10, p. 57*c*: 'At the beginning of the *K'ai-yüan* period (713) Li Chieh, governor of Lo-yang, was made commissioner for land transport. Between the Han-chia granary at Lo-yang, and the T'ai-yüan granary at Shan-chou he established stage-stations at intervals of 40 *li* [earlier in the dynasty the recognised day's stage for transport carts had been 30 *li*—see *THY*, 87, p. 1595, and note 27 to p. 88 below]. Transportation was begun at the beginning of winter each year. At first 800,000 *shih* were transported, and later the amount reached 1,000,000.'

19 Aoyama Sadao, 'Tō-Sō jidai no tenunshi to hatsuunshi ni tsuite', *Shigaku zasshi*, 43, VII (1933), pp. 1105–29, considers that the powers of the post of commissioner granted to Li Chieh were limited to the stretch of the route between Lo-yang and Ch'ang-an. However, since he memorialised the throne on this matter (see *CTS*, 49, p. 1*a*; *THY*, 87, p. 1596; *TFYK*, 497, p. 8*b*; *CTS*, 100, p. 2*a*) his terms of reference were probably rather wider, even if he had no direct authority over traffic on the canal.

20 Hsüan-tsung's visits to Lo-yang were made in 717–18 (*CTS*, 96, p. 3*b*), 722–3 (*TTCLC*, 79, p. 453; *TFYK*, 113, p. 23*b*), 724–7, 731–2 (*TFYK*, 113, p. 24*a*) and 734–6 (*CTS*, 98, p. 6*a*; *TFYK*, 113, p. 27*b*). Ch'üan Han-sheng, *T'ang Sung ti-kuo yü yün-ho*, has found mention of specific economic reasons underlying the move in each case apart from the move of 724–7.

21 The first memorial had been presented when P'ei Yao-ch'ing was a delegate to court (*ch'ao-chi shih*) in 730. It is preserved in *CTS*, 49, pp. 1*b*–2*a*;

TFYK, 498, pp. 16*a*–17*a*; *TT*, 10, pp. 56*c*–57*a*; *YHCHC*, 5, p. 144. At this time the emperor did not pay heed to his advice. The second memorial is in *TT*, 10, p. 57*a*–*b*; *THY*, 87, p. 1596; *TFYK*, 498, pp. 17*a*–18*b*; *CTS*, 98, p. 11*b*. Both memorials are translated with notes by Pulleyblank, *The background of the rebellion of An Lu-shan*, appendix IV, pp. 183–91.

PAGE 88

22 Since in 744 an edict was issued ordering the preparation of extra copies of all census documents in order to reduce the cost of journeys between the two capitals by keeping copies on file in each (see *CTS*, 48, p. 3*b*) we know that, although in fact such a transfer of the administration was never made again, the government still reckoned on its happening and made preparations in accordance.

23 On the laws governing the despatch of taxes, see appendix I, 1, *Land Statutes*, art. 2. On the despatch of taxes from Ling-nan, see also Twitchett, 'The fragment of the ordinances of the Department of Waterways discovered at Tun-huang', *Asia Major*, 6, 1, pp. 23–79, art. 22 (pp. 55–6): 'The coin cast in the two administrations of Kuei-chou and Kuang-chou, together with the cloth from the *yung* and *tiao* and goods acquired by "harmonious purchase" and as substitute goods for the tax in grain (*che-tsu*) from the prefectures of Ling-nan, will be transported (by the prefectures) only as far as Yang-chou. The authorities at Yang-chou should appoint transport units (*kang-pu*) to take charge of its transport on to the capital. The necessary costs of transportation should be provided out of the goods which are to be conveyed.'

24 See Chü Ch'ing-yüan, *T'ang-tai tsai-cheng shih*, p. 155. The costs of transport were specifically laid down in the *Statutes* (see *TLT*, 3, p. 45 *a*–*b*). After 737 these costs, which had previously been assessed annually by the Department of Public Revenue, were covered by the newly compiled *Permanently Applicable Orders* of Li Lin-fu drawn up in the previous year. The passage in *TLT*, 3, reads:

'For all the transportation in the empire, by land or water, ship or cart, transportation costs (*chüeh-chih*) are to be assessed. A rule was made in accordance with whether the commodities conveyed are heavy or light, valuable or cheap, and whether the journey is flat and easy or mountainous and difficult.

(*Commentary*—probably taken from the *Ordinances:*) Regarding the transport of the *tsu* and *yung* taxes and miscellaneous commodities from the four provinces of Ho-nan, Ho-pei, Ho-tung and Kuan-nei, a load will consist of 100 *chin*. For every 100 *li* the cost of transport will be 100 cash, or 120 cash in mountainous places. A cart-load will consist of 1000 *chin*, and the cost will be 900 cash. On the Huang-ho and the Lo-shui* for transport upstream 16 cash (per load per 100 *li*), downstream 6 cash. On other waterways, upstream 15 cash, downstream, 5 cash, and from the prefectures such as Li-chou, Ching-chou, etc., as far as Yang-chou, 4 cash. In mountainous places which are dangerous and where there are few donkeys, the cost must not exceed 150 cash. In flat and easy places it must not fall below 80 cash. In areas where human porterage is employed, a load will be divided between two men. In places where small boats are used, and where goods are transported towards Po-chou and Ch'ien-chou, etc., together with places on the sea coast, the prefectural authorities concerned may estimate and fix the rates of payment.'

* I follow the reading of *Lo-shui ho* in the Sung print in preference to Konoe's suggestion of *yü shui ho*, 'other rivers', and to the Kuang-ya shu-chü edition's *Chiang shui ho*.

This transport charge (*chüeh-chih*) was levied on the taxpayers as a surcharge on their general taxes. It is probable that in the early years of the dynasty this surcharge was a universal one. Later it was assigned only to families in the higher categories as a *ch'ai-k'o*.

25   See *Code*, 15, XXIII: 'No directing or supervising official (i.e. chief of a local administration) may hire transport for tax goods within the area under his personal jurisdiction. Offenders will be liable as if they were guilty of misappropriation to the extent of the profits which they have made' (see also *Sung hsing-t'ung*, 19, p. 14*a–b*). The previous article of the T'ang *Code* rules that responsibility of the prefectural and county authorities for their tax goods ended when once the *kang-tien* had been sent off.

26   See *TFYK*, 487, p. 17*a*. Edict of *K'ai-yüan*, 9, X (721): 'It has come to our notice that the transport units carrying the taxes from the prefectures of the empire receive the correct amounts of goods when they set out, but that when they arrive at the capital, the amounts do not correspond and there are deficiencies. Sometimes the persons conveying the goods themselves stop *en route* and because of this allow loss or damage, or even exchange the goods on their own authority. They then often wrongfully raise loans to make good the deficiencies, and when they return to their prefecture improperly levy the amount of the loan from the common people. At other times they pretend to be persons of authority, and cause trouble in the shops and stores. Such offences are particularly flagrant in the Yangtze–Huai region. . . .'

27   The specified distances, presumably deriving from an article in the *Statutes*, are laid down in *THY*, 87, p. 1595, and *TLT*, 3, p. 44*a–b*. 'Stages for land transport: by horse 70 *li* per day; by donkey or on foot 50 *li*; by

cart 30 *li*; stages for water transport: laden vessels going upstream; on the Huang-ho 30 *li*, on the Yangtze 40 *li*, other waterways 45 *li*. Empty vessels going upstream, respectively 40, 50, and 60 *li*. Vessels travelling with the current: both laden and unladen vessels have the same stages; on the Huang-ho 150 *li*, on the Yangtze 100 *li*, and on other waterways 70 *li*.
(*Commentary:*) Such places as the Ti-chu (i.e. San-men) rapids shall not come within the scope of this rule. Should the boats encounter contrary winds, or should the water be too shallow for them to proceed, the matter should be notified to the nearest authorities....'

28   See the memorial of Ch'en Tzu-ang, 'Shang chün-kuo chi-yao shih', collected in *Ch'en-Po-yü chi*, 8, p. 13*a*. This memorial is undated but was probably written shortly before his death in 695. 'Some thousands of tax boats from the prefectures of Chiang-nan and Huai-nan have already arrived at Kung-hsien and Lo-yang, bringing in all a million or more *hu* of grain. The authorities have then forced them to go on to Yu-chou to deliver the grain to provide rations for the armies. Many of the seamen are vagrants and vagabonds and different sorts of people who have lost their livelihood and have nothing upon which to depend. When they leave their families to go on the journey they take on provisions only for the stretch to the capital (i.e. Lo-yang). Yet now when they arrive at the capital they have been forced to go on to Yu-chou. Yu-chou is more than 2000 *li* away from here, and the return journey is 2000 *li* more. They suffer from cold and freezing, and are entirely without provisions. The state will show no pity to them, but forces them to go on to the very limit. We hear that the men are all mourning and lamenting....'

PAGE 89

29   See P'ei Yao-ch'ing's memorials (see above, note 21 to p. 87), also Ch'üan Han-sheng, *T'ang Sung ti-kuo yü yün-ho*; Hamaguchi, 'Tō no Gensōchō ni okeru Kōwai jōkyō bei to chizei to no kankei', *Shigaku zasshi*, 45, I (1934), pp. 78–97; 45, II, pp. 221–54.

30   According to *TT*, 10, p. 57*c*; *TFYK*, 498, p. 17*b*; *HTS*, 53, p. 1*b*, the road was cut along the northern side of the rapids. The San-men granary is referred to in *CTS*, 49, p. 2*b*, and *HTS*, 53, p. 1*b*, as the Yen granary. Hamaguchi, 'Tō no Gensōchō ni okeru Kōwai jōkyō bei to chizei to no kankei', p. 86, note 16, suggests that this is a name deriving from the later period when it had become a store for salt from the nearby pools of P'u-chou. The recent archaeological investigations have revealed traces both of the granaries and of the road itself. See *San-men shan ts'ao-yün i-chi* (cf. note 7 to p. 86 above), pp. 38–40 and plates 37–40.

31   These figures come from *CTS*, 49, p. 2 *b*. It is possible that the saving in transport costs should be corrected to the 300,000 strings given by all other sources. See *TT*, 10, p. 57 *c*; *TFYK*, 498, p. 18 *b*; *THY*, 87, p. 1597; *CTS*, 98, p. 12 *a*.

32   On the stoppage of transport and of harmonious purchases in 737, see *TCTC*, 214, p. 6830. The edict relating to this is in *TFYK*, 502, p. 5 *b*.

33   See the edict ordering this in *CTS*, 48, p. 4 *a*–*b*; *TFYK*, 487, pp. 18 *b*–19 *a*; *THY*, 83, p. 1533, and *TT*, 6, p. 33 *b*. It is also referred to in the commentary to the section of *TLT*, 3, p. 7 *a*, dealing with the taxes of Kuan-nei. The full version is in *TTCLC*, 111, pp. 578–9.

34   *CTS*, 9, p. 1 *a*, dates the suspension of transport in the 2nd month of 737. I follow the view of Hamaguchi, 'Tō no Gensōchō ni okeru Kōwai jōkyō bei to chizei to no kankei', that the date should in fact be the 6th month in accordance with the entry in *THY*, 87, p. 1602. The edict would thus have followed that of the 3rd month ordering the payments of taxes to be made in grain. It appears from *THY* that the amount to be transported in that year had already been cut down from 1,800,000 *shih* to 1,000,000 *shih*, and that transport was suspended because the Great Granary was full.

35   On Li Ch'i-wu see *CTS*, 49, p. 2 *b*; *TFYK*, 497, p. 10 *a*; *TT*, 10, p. 57 *b*–*c*; *THY*, 87, p. 1597; *HTS*, 53, p. 2 *a*. The last of these accounts is the fullest: 'In the 29th year (*K'ai-yüan*) (741) Li Ch'i-wu, prefect of Shan-chou, cut an opening through the Ti-chu (i.e. San-men) to allow water traffic through. He opened up a towing-path along the cliff, heating the rocks and then wetting them with vinegar to split them. But the rocks fell into the stream, making the fierce current still more torrential, and ships could not enter the new opening. They had to wait for floodwater, and were then hauled through by manpower. The emperor felt misgivings about the whole affair, and sent a eunuch to investigate. But Li Ch'i-wu bribed the eunuch heavily, and he returned to court and reported that the scheme was advantageous.'

The *San-men shan ts'ao-yün i-chi* records many traces of Li Ch'i-wu's new channel. Its position is shown on the map, *ibid.* p. 2, and there is a detailed plan of the channel, pp. 33–7. A competent discussion of the historical sources on San-men in T'ang times is given on pp. 66–71.

36   See *HTS*, 53, p. 3 *a*: Ts'ui Hsi-i had been one of his two assistant commissioners (*fu-shih*). The other was Hsiao Chiung.

37   See Toyama, 'Tōdai no Sōun', *Shirin*, 22 (1937), pp. 264–304.

38 The passage in *TT*, 10, p. 57*c*, commentary, reads: 'In the 9th month of the 9th year of *T'ien-pao* (750), P'ei Hsiang, the governor of Lo-yang, considering that transit was onerous, and fearing injury to the oxen, replaced the stage stations (*ti-ch'ang*) to change-over stations (*chiao-ch'ang*), making two stages instead of one. The places nearest the river were chosen for rest stations.' Officials were told off to control these stations and to guard them against robbery. Both Ch'üan Han-sheng, *T'ang Sung ti-kuo yü yün-ho*, and Hamaguchi, 'Tō no Gensō ni okeru Kōwai bei to chizei to no kankei', consider that under P'ei Hsiang the eight-stage system of Li Chieh was replaced by a series of resting places along the banks of the Huang-ho, between which boat transport was employed as far as possible. But this is unlikely for two reasons. First, the passage in *TT*, 10, p. 57*c*, specifically states that injury to the *oxen* was feared, and it thus obviously refers to an overland route. Secondly, to go from Lo-yang to Shan-chou *via* the Huang-ho would entail a detour *via* Kung-hsien, a matter of some 80 miles. The actual route was undoubtedly that employed previously under Li Chieh, and by the modern railway, up the valley of the Ku-shui. This journey is little over 80 miles in all, and less than half the distance *via* the Huang-ho. The resting places were placed near the water (i.e. the Ku-shui) for convenience in watering the oxen drawing the waggons. *HTS*, 53, p. 2*b*, gives P'ei Hsiang's name as P'ei Hui.

39 See *CTS*, 190B, p. 16*a*ff.; *THY*, 87, p. 1597. See Andō Kōsei, *Ganjin Daiwajō den no kenkyū*, pp. 184–5, 372–4, for detailed notes on the canals at Yang-chou.

39*a* See *THY*, 87, p. 1602: 'After this (713) the prefect of Shan-chou always held the concurrent title of commissioner for land and water transport.'

40 In the seventh century the transport boats had been provided with a dock in the 'old city'—that is, the Han-time capital which lay north-west of Ch'ang-an (see *TT*, 10, p. 56*c*; *TFYK*, 497, p. 8*a*, relating to 672). We also know, from the fragment of the *Ordinances of the Department of Waterways*, that the transport boats passed through the imperial park (see Twitchett, *Asia Major*, 6, I, p. 49, note 50). On the construction of the new pool, see *CTS*, 49, p. 2*b*; *HTS*, 53, p. 2*a*–*b*; *TT*, 10, p. 57*c*, and the biographies of Wei Chien in *CTS*, 105, pp. 4*a*ff., and *HTS*, 134, p. 2*a*–*b*.

41 See *CTS*, 105, p. 4*a*; *TT*, 10, p. 57*c*; *TFYK*, 498, p. 19*b*; *HTS*, 53, p. 2*b*.

42 See the preface to *CTS*, 48, p. 1*b*: 'He requested that the grain tax (*tsu*) should be collected in grain in the Chiang-huai region, and that the grain from the relief granaries (*i-ts'ang*) should be exchanged for light commodities of high value.' Thus the proceeds of the conversion of the stocks of the relief granaries into tax revenue no longer reached the capital as grain, but in the form of miscellaneous commodities of high value.

43   Wei Chien's biography in *CTS*, 105, pp. 4 *a*–5 *a*, gives a detailed description of this exhibition, which is summarised by Balázs, 'Beiträge', *MSOS*, 35, p. 44.

44   See note 22 to p. 88 above. The decline of Lo-yang after the An Lu-shan rebellion is described in Waley, *The life and times of Po Chü-i*, pp. 158–9.

PAGE 91

45   *TT*, 12, pp. 71 *c*–72 *b*, and the table in appendix v, 2.

46   The increase in power of the local governors is dealt with in chapter VI below. The best general account of the problem is that in Hino, *Shina chūsei no gumbatsu* (1942).

47   On the exorbitant demands of the Uighurs in 769, see *TCTC*, 224, p. 7208; *HTS*, 217, p. 1 *b*; *HTS*, 51, p. 5 *b*. The standard price demanded for each horse was 40 lengths of silk, even though many of the beasts proved useless. However, the continued assistance of the Uighurs was so vital at this point that the emperor continued to pay this form of blackmail.

48   The canal was cut from the time of An Lu-shan's first invasion of Ho-nan, and remained blocked because of fighting even after Lo-yang was finally recovered from the forces of Shih Ch'ao-i in 762.

49   See *HTS*, 53, p. 2 *b*: 'In the last year of Su-tsung's reign (763) Shih Ch'ao-i's forces cut off Sung-chou, and interrupted transport from the Huai valley.'

50   See *CTS*, 49, p. 3 *a*; *HTS*, 53, p. 2 *b*; *THY*, 87, p. 1588; *CTS*, 155, p. 1 *b*.

51   See *TCTC*, 219, pp. 7001–2: 'In the 10th month of *Chih-te*, 1 (756), Ti-wu Ch'i had an audience with the emperor at P'eng-yüan. He requested that light commodities be purchased with the taxes from the Huai and Yangtze regions, and sent up the Yangtze and the Han river to Yang-chou. Wang Yü-shan was ordered to transport the goods up the Han river to Fu-feng, to relieve the plight of the armies. The emperor followed this advice.'

52 See *CTS*, 10, pp. 11*b*–12*a*. The rebels led by Chang Chia-yen reached as far as Chiang-ling, and thus cut transport both on the Yangtze and on the Han river.

53 See Mu Ning's biography in *CTS*, 155, p. 1*b*; also see *CTS*, 49, p. 3*a*; *THY*, 87, p. 1588.

54 On the plague of locusts in 758 and 759 see *CTS*, 37, p. 12*a*: 'In 758 during the autumn there was a great plague of locusts in Kuan-pu, which ate up entirely the crops in the fields. . . . In the summer of the succeeding year, the locusts were even worse. From the sea westward to Ho-lung (i.e. Kansu) their flying swarms blotted out the sky, and this continued without cease for a whole month. Where they had passed, there was not a scrap left on the trees or plants, and even the hair of domestic animals had been consumed.' See also *CTS*, 10, p. 12*b*, and *THY*, 44, p. 789, which record a severe drought at the same period.

55 On Ti-wu Ch'i's attempt to debase the coinage in 758, and its failure, see chapter IV above. Also see *CTS*, 48, p. 10*a*–*b*; *TFYK*, 501, pp. 8*b*–10*a*; *TT*, 9, p. 53*b*.

56 On the crop failures of 763 see *CTS*, 37, p. 5*a*; *HTS*, 35, p. 3*b*. According to *CTS*, 11, p. 8*b*; *HTS*, 35, *loc. cit.*, and *TCTC*, 223, p. 7164, both 764 and 765 too were bad years of famine, and the price of a *tou* of rice in the Kuan-chung area rose to 1000 cash.

57 Liu Yen's letter is preserved in *THY*, 87, pp. 1588–90; *TFYK*, 498, pp. 20*a*–22*b*; *CTW*, 370, pp. 14*a*–16*a*, and *CTS*, 123, pp. 1*b*–2*b*. The version in *THY* is slightly abbreviated.

58 Speaking of the depopulation of Ho-nan, Liu Yen's letter says: 'The eastern capital has been sacked, and not one in a hundred remain there. . . . From I-yang and Hsiung-erh as far as Wu-lao and Cheng-kao, a distance of 500 *li*, there are only just over 1000 households left on the registers. Houses are left without so much as a foot of rafter, the people are without cooking fires. All is desolate and melancholy and wild beasts roam about howling like demons. . . .' The biography of Kuo Tzu-i in *CTS*, 120, p. 6*a*–*b*, paints an even more dismal picture.

59 According to *TCTC*, 223, p. 7164: 'The emperor ordered Liu Yen, together with the military governors of the provinces, to make a fair allocation of taxes and *corvée* labour allowing them to act as convenient. . . . Liu Yen thereupon dredged out the Pien canal.' In *THY*, 87, p. 1590; *CTS*, 49, p. 3*b*, he is said to have consulted about the plan for the canal with the vice-generalissimo of Ho-nan.

NOTES

60 See *CTS*, 49, p. 3*a*; *THY*, 87, p. 1590; *HTS*, 53, p. 3*a*.

61 See *CTS*, 49, p. 3*a*; *THY*, 87, p. 1589. 'He did not mobilise men, and did not cause any trouble to the prefectural and county authorities.'

PAGE 93

62 The edict establishing defences along the Pien canal is preserved in *CTW*, 46, p. 23*a*: 'We have heard that in the prefectures and counties along the canal from the eastern capital to the Huai and Ssu rivers, the people have declined in numbers since the outbreak of trouble from rebels. The land is broad but the people few, and there are many brigands and bandits. The merchants and transports do not escape hardship and mishaps. Wang Chin ought therefore to be deputed to consult with the military governors of the provinces concerned, and to establish defence detachments of 300 men at every second relay station on the banks of the canal. They should be granted good and fertile lands nearby, and made to cultivate them.' The people of Ho-nan seem to have remained notorious, for in 845 the Japanese pilgrim Ennin travelled down the Pien canal and wrote: 'The people along the banks of the Pien-ho are evil at heart and not good. One might liken them to the swift and turbulent waters of the Pien-ho which they drink' (see Reischauer, *Ennin's Diary*, 4, p. 371).

63 On the organisation of the units for transport see *TCTC*, 226, pp. 7286–7: 'Ten boats form a flotilla (*kang*), and army officers are placed in charge of them. After ten journeys without mishap, such officers became *yu-lao kuan*.' *HTS*, 53, p. 3*a*, reads: 'Ten boats formed a flotilla, and each carried 300 men and 50 polers (*kao-kung*).' *T'ang yü-lin*, 1, p. 23, has an account which confirms these details.

64 See *TCTC*, 226, p. 7286: 'Liu Yen considered that the currents of the Yangtze, the Pien canal, the Huang-ho and the Wei-ho were not equally strong, and so constructed ships in accordance with what was suitable for each section, and instructed crews (*ts'ao-tsui*) for them. The Yangtze ships went as far as Yang-chou. The Pien canal boats went as far as Ho-yin. The Huang-ho boats went as far as the mouth of the Wei-ho, and the Wei-ho boats went as far as the Great Granary (*t'ai-ts'ang*).'

That the Yangtze ships in fact must have gone to Ch'u-chou is shown by Hu San-hsing's commentary to this passage: 'The Yangtze ships went to Yang-chou, and entered the Huai. The Pien canal boats went from Ch'ing-k'ou to Ho-yin. Between these points granaries were established along the waterway, and goods were transmitted from one to the next of them.'

HTS, 53, p. 3*a*, bears out this picture of several independent sections: 'From Yang-chou to Ho-yin, the cost of transporting 1 *tou* of hulled grain

323

had been 120 cash. Yen built 2000 *hsieh-huang chih-chiang ch'uan* boats, each with a cargo capacity of 1000 *hu*, and ten of these boats formed a flotilla (*kang*). Each flotilla had a crew of 300 men and 50 polers. Officers were despatched from Yang-chou to take them as far as Ho-yin. The boats which ascended the rapids at San-men were known as *shang-men tien-chüeh ch'uan*. The cost of transporting each *tou* of grain was cut by 90 cash. Hemp and rattan were levied in Szechuan and the Han valley, and used to make tow-ropes for the boats. The old rotten ropes and decayed timbers were used instead of firewood; nothing was thrown away. Before ten years had elapsed, all the personnel were accustomed to the perils of the waterways. The ships from the Yangtze did not enter the Pien canal, the Pien canal boats did not enter the Huang-ho, the Huang-ho boats did not enter the Wei-ho. The goods transported from the Yangtze region were accumulated at Yang-chou, those transported up the Pien canal were piled up at Ho-yin, those transported on the Huang-ho were piled up at Wei-k'ou, and the goods transported by the boats on the Wei-ho were paid into the great granary.'

65 See *TCTC*, 226, *loc. cit.*

66 See *TCTC*, 226, p. 7287: 'For each vessel 1000 strings of cash were provided. Some said that what was actually spent did not amount to a half of this sum, and that most of it was wasted. Yen said, "This is not so. Those who discuss grand policies cannot worry about petty waste. This whole scheme looks a long way ahead. At the moment we are establishing ship-yards. The first thing to be done is to ensure that the interests of private individuals are not affected. Thus official goods will be made secure. If we were to grant only trifling amounts, and take exact account of the smallest quantities, how should we be able to practise the system for a long period? At some future time there would be a disaster. Now what I grant them is a great deal. If I were to cut it down to half, it would still be possible. But if it were cut down still further it would be impracticable."' It seems from this that boats were being built for the Transport Commission by private ship-builders working to a contract.

67 See note 64 above. These were called *hsieh-huang chih-chiang ch'uan*.

68 These were the *shang-men tien-chüeh ch'uan*. Lu Ssu-mien, in his selection of extracts from *HTS*, mispunctuates this passage (p. 55).

69 *HTS*, 53, p. 3 *a*, reads as follows: 'Previously cargoes were transported from Jun-chou to Yang-tzu county by land-haulage. This cost 19 cash per *tou* of hulled grain. Yen ordered the grain to be bagged and carried by boat, thus reducing the cost by 15 cash. From Yang-chou to Ho-yin the cost of transporting 1 *tou* was previously 120 cash....90 cash was saved on each *tou*. ... On light commodities taken from Yang-tzu to Pien-chou, the cost of transporting each pack-load (100 *chin*) had been 2200 cash. This was reduced by 900 cash. The annual saving was more than 100,000 strings of cash.'

70 *CTS*, 49, p. 4*a*; *THY*, 87, p. 1590; *TCTC*, 223, p. 7164, say first: 'When Liu Yen was in control of policy...the amount of grain which came in each year was several hundred thousand *hu*...', and then later (see *CTS*, 49, p. 6*b*; *THY*, 87, p. 1592): 'Under the former system, 500,000 *hu* of hulled grain from the Huai–Yangtze region was transported annually to Ho-yin. Of this 100,000 *hu* was retained there, and 400,000 *hu* sent on to the granaries on the Wei....' These accounts are substantiated by *CTS*, 123, p. 2*b*, and *TFYK*, 498, p. 12*b*.

71 The high figure of 1,000,000 or 1,100,000 given in *HTS*, 53, p. 3*a*, and *TCTC*, 226, p. 7287, is corroborated by a memorial of Lu Chih, 'Ch'ing chien ching-tung shui-yün shou-chüeh-chia yü yen-pien chou-chên chu-ch'u chün-liang', *Lu Hsüan-kung Han-yüan chi*, 18, pp. 4*b*–17*a* (at 12*b*). 'Recently the rice transported annually from the provinces of Chiang-hsi, Hunan, Che-tung, Che-hsi and Huai-nan and arriving at Ho-yin has totalled 1,100,000 *shih*. 400,000 *shih* of this has been taken away and stored in the granary at Ho-yin, and the remaining 700,000 sent on to Shan-chou. Here again 300,000 *shih* has been taken away and stored in the T'ai-yüan granary, and only the remaining 400,000 *shih* has been taken as far as the bridge on the Wei and paid in (at the great granary).' This passage clearly provides the link between the two accounts, and shows that the 400,000 *shih* refers only to that part of the total which actually reached the capital. *HTS*, 149, p. 2*a*, again bears this out: 'Each year 400,000 *hu* arrived (in the capital). From this time on, even though there were floods and droughts in Kuan-chung, the prices of grain never rose excessively high.' The discrepancy between Lu Chih's memorial and the second account in *CTS* and *THY*, however, cannot be explained away.

72 See Ch'üan Han-sheng, 'T'ang-tai wu-chia ti pien-tung', *CYYY*, 11 (1947), pp. 101–48. From 765 to 780 prices of from 800 to 1000 cash per *tou* of grain are quoted. Like nearly all the price data cited by Ch'üan, these are famine prices restricted to the vicinity of the capital, but they show that prices were relatively very high at the time.

PAGE 94

73 Chou Chih-kuang was military governor of T'ung and Hua prefectures, and defence commissioner for the T'ung-kuan pass, the eastern gateway to Kuan-chung (see *CTS*, 114, p. 6*a*, and *TCTC*, 224, pp. 7192ff.). We are told that 'he retained on his own authority 200,000 *hu* of rice which was being transported to Kuan-chung. He frequently stole the tribute offerings which were sent in by the provincial governors, murdering the envoys accompanying them.'

74 On Li Ling-yao, see *TCTC*, 225, pp. 7237–9; *CTS*, 134, pp. 2*b* ff. Ling-yao was a subordinate military officer of the military governor of Pien and Sung prefectures. He rebelled and usurped power in this vital region, cutting communications on the canal in the 5th month 777. His rising received the backing of T'ien Ch'eng-ssu, a powerful military governor in Ho-pei. After initial successes the rebels were defeated by powerful forces under Ma Tsui and Li Chung-ch'en, reinforcements sent by T'ien Ch'eng-ssu arriving too late. The revolt was cleared up by the 10th month 777.

75 Transport was cut in 781 by Li Cheng-i, who captured two vital centres in Ho-nan. See *TCTC*, 227, p. 7302: 'Li Cheng-i sent out troops to hold Hsü-chou, Yung-ch'iao, and Wo-k'ou (all on the Pien canal), while Liang Ch'ung-i obstructed the troops at Hsiang-yang (on the Han valley route). The transport routes were cut off, and the people quaked with fear. A thousand and more boats carrying tribute from the Yangtze and Huai regions anchored below Hua-k'ou, not daring to proceed further....' Later in the same year transport was resumed following the defeat of the rebel forces at Hsü-chou.

76 See *TCTC*, 227, p. 7336–7; *HTS*, 225, p. 1 *a–b*.

77 On Han Huang's convoys sent to assist Li Sheng, see *TCTC*, 231, pp. 7428–9: 'Han Huang also sent a hundred boats of grain to supply Li Sheng. He himself carried sacks of grain and put them into the boats, and his generals and officers fought to pick them up, so that in a short while the job was finished. On each boat he posted five archers for defence. If any bandits appeared, they banged on the bulwarks to warn one another, and five hundred archers would together draw their bows. Thus the convoy arrived at the Wei bridge and the bandits did not dare to go near them. At that time Kuan-chung had been laid waste by the troops, and a *tou* of grain cost 500 cash. When Huang's grain arrived this price was reduced by four-fifths.' Some of the legends current in late T'ang times about Han Huang's activities are recorded in *T'ang kuo-shih pu*, A, pp. 26–7.

During the period when the canal route was blocked for normal traffic, Tu Yu, who had been appointed commissioner for land and water transport from the Yangtze and Huai regions in 780, advocated the revival of the old canal route, north of the Pien canal, which had been used under the Han, but abandoned after the construction of the Pien canal under Sui Yang-ti (see *HTS*, 53, p. 3*b*). Apparently the rebellion was over before anything was done to implement the proposal.

78 *CTS*, 12, p. 19 *a*, reports a famine east of the passes in 785, 4th month, and a severe drought and plague of locusts in Kuan-chung in the 7th month of the same year. At the beginning of 786 an edict ordered the reduction of the expenses of imperial banquets, and a reduction of the salaries paid in grain to officials in the capital. Later in 786 a great many people are said to have died from over-eating of the new wheat crop after long suffering from starvation.

79 See *Chu Lu Hsüan-kung tsou-i*, 9, pp. 1 *a*–9 *a* (Shih-wan ch'üan lou ts'ung-shu edition). This memorial suggested that of the 1,100,000 *shih* despatched annually from the south, no less than 800,000 *shih* should be suspended. This grain was to be sold off at an estimated price, well below its market value, of 640,000 strings of cash, so as to relieve the victims of the severe floods which had ravaged Ho-nan and Huai-nan earlier in the year. The saving on transporting 800,000 *shih*, and the further reduction of transport onwards from Ho-yin to the capital, was estimated to save 690,000 strings.

80 *TCTC*, 234, p. 7536, records the beginning of large-scale local procurements in the north-west, but is silent as to whether transport from the south was reduced.

81 *CTS*, 13, p. 16*a*–*b*, records that in 799 no less than 2,000,000 *shih* should have been despatched from the south, but that the amount actually shipped each year was never more than 400,000 *shih*.

PAGE 95

82 Hu San-hsing's commentary to *TCTC*, 235, pp. 7586 ff., says that the garrison at Pien-chou rebelled in 792, 794, 796, 797 (?), and 798 (the latter is corrected to 799 by Ch'üan Han-sheng, *T'ang Sung ti-kuo yü yün-ho*, p. 75, note 54). *THY*, 87, p. 1598, records that the rising of 799 resulted in a request to the throne to move the branch (*hsün-yüan*) of the transportation commissioners from Pien-chou to Ho-yin, because of the repeated disorders at the former place. *THY*, 85, pp. 1565–6, preserves a memorial from the prefect of Yüeh-chou dated 796, complaining that the rising at Pien-chou in 794 had resulted in the loss of 1700 lengths of silk from Yüeh-chou which were on their way to the capital.

83 In the 8th month 799 Han Hung was appointed prefect of Pien-chou and military governor of the Hsüan-wu army. He remained in this office for more than twenty years (see Wu Yen-hsieh, *T'ang fang-chen nien-piao k'ao-cheng*, Erh-shih-wu shih pu-pien edition, vol. 6, p. 36). *TCTC*, 235, p. 7586, gives a graphic account of the way in which he brought his mutinous forces to order: 'Since the death of Liu Hsüan-tso, the Hsüan-wu army had mutinied five times. The men became increasingly rebellious and would not obey their commanders. After Han Hung had looked at the situation for a few months he knew all the names of the ringleaders. There was one colonel Liu O who was always a ringleader. In the 3rd month of 800, Hung drew up his forces at the yamen, summoned out Liu O and 300 of his henchmen, enumerated all their preparations for mutiny and had them all beheaded, so that their blood formed a red stream. From this time until his recall to court (at the end of 819), there was not one of his troops who dared to cause trouble in the city.'

84 See Hino, *Shina chūsei no gumbatsu*, for a general discussion of this period.

85 See *CTS*, 13, p. 16*a–b*. In 799 Te-tsung ordered 2,000,000 *shih* of grain to be transported annually from Chiang-Huai, but only 400,000 were actually sent.

86 See *HTS*, 53, p. 4*b*, which tells us that the construction works carried out by Tu Ya, and others performed by Li Chih-fu, met with no success. An edict was issued in 799 ordering the transportation from the Yangtze and Huai valleys of 2,000,000 *shih* of grain, but admitted that although this was the theoretical quota, the amount actually transported had not exceeded 400,000 *shih* (see *TFYK*, 498, p. 24*b*). In 806 we are again informed that although 500,000 *shih* was supposed to be transported annually as far as Ho-yin, this quota was never met in practice. *CTS*, 49, p. 5*a*, and *THY*, 87, p. 1592, say that only under Li Sun's reformed administration did the amount transported approach that of Liu Yen's period in control.

87 See *HTS*, 53, p. 4*b*.

88 See *HTS*, 53, pp. 4*b*–5*a*. Huang-fu Po proposed that anyone who lost less than 300 *shih* of a total of 10,000 should be rewarded, while those who lost up to 1700 *shih* should be exiled to the frontiers and those who lost more than this put to death. Anyone who stole 10 *hu* was to be exiled, and those who stole 30 *hu* or more were to be put to death.

89 See *HTS*, 53, p. 5*a*.

90 See *TCTC*, 242, pp. 7818 ff.

91 They looted the depot of the salt and iron commissioners at Yung-ch'iao, and stole a great quantity of tribute goods at Pien-chou (see *TCTC*, *loc. cit.*).

PAGE 96

92 See *CTS*, 177, p. 11*a*, from which this quotation derives. The same number of sinkings is given by *CTS*, 49, p. 6*b*; *THY*, 87, p. 1594.

93   See the long letter from Tu Mu to Li Te-yü (dated probably 844 or early 845), 'Shang Li T'ai-wei lun Chiang-tsei shu', *Fan-ch'uan wen-chi*, 11, pp. 6*a*–10*a*.

94   See *CTS*, 177, p. 11*a*; *HTS*, 182, pp. 8*b*–9*a*; *CTS*, 49, p. 6*a*–*b*. *HTS*, 53, p. 5*a*, confirms these figures.

95   These officers were called *ch'ang-ting kang* (see *HTS*, 53, p. 5*a*). 'At the beginning of the *K'ai-ch'eng* period *ch'ang-ting kang* were created. The prefectures chose honest and powerful officers (for these) to transport their *liang-shui* tax moneys, up to 100,000 strings each. They each selected one officer, and after he had performed these journeys for ten years he was eligible for appointment as a county magistrate. The money coming from the Yangtze and Huai regions was stored up at Ho-yin, and the annual cost of transporting it there was 170,000 strings. Many of the escorting officers met their death from bandits' (see also *TFYK*, 489, p. 26*a*).

96   The rebellion was that of P'ang Hsün, on which see *TCTC*, 251, pp. 8127ff.

97   See *TCTC*, 226, p. 7287: 'In the *Hsien-t'ung* period those in office first reckoned up the expense before making payment, and no longer left a margin for profit. The ships thus became more and more weakly built and more easily destroyed. Transportation thereupon fell into disorder.' According to *T'ang yü-lin*, 1, pp. 23–4: 'Fifty or more years (after Liu Yen's time) it was possible to reckon the excess in the allowance made for building ships and reduce it by 500 cash in every thousand. At this time it was still possible to provide a ship from the money remaining. But at the end of the *Hsien-t'ung* period the censor Tu, officer of the branch of the Transport Commission at Yang-tzu county, instead of building one boat of 1000 *shih* capacity, used the funds provided for this purpose to construct two boats of 500 *shih* capacity, the timber used in their construction being skimpy. Also the *chih-shih* Wu Yao-ch'ing became an officer at Yang-tzu county, and altered the system of the salt and iron commissioners. He ordered merchants to pay as a monopoly tax (*na-chüeh*) all the cloth and grain which was to be despatched. This was reckoned up and converted, and out of the income was provided the amount of planks, nails, ashes, oil and charcoal needed for each ship.'

98   See *THY*, 87, pp. 1594, 1599; *TFYK*, 498, pp. 26*b*–27*a*. Dissatisfaction among the seafaring population of T'ai-chou in Chekiang, and the surrounding region, resulting from these policies, was an important factor in the rising of Chiu Fu at this same period.

99   See *THY*, 87, pp. 1594–5: 'From this time onwards the transport routes from the south were cut off. Those places over which the state had control were just the provinces of Ho-nan, Shan-nan, Chien-nan, and the western part of Ling-nan.... The Three Offices (*san-ssu*) had no source from which to raise taxes.'

100 On these officials see Aoyama, 'Tō-Sōjidai no denunshi to hatsuunshi ni tsuite', *Shigaku zasshi*, 43, VII (1933), pp. 1105–29. On the appointment of the first of them, see *TCTC*, 253, p. 8221.

101 See *CTS*, 20A, p. 21 *b* and p. 28 *b*.

CHAPTER VI

PAGE 98

1 The basic accounts of the various administrative departments discussed below will be found as follows: (*a*) Board of Finance: *TLT*, 3; *CTS*, 43, pp. 6 *b*–9 *a*; *HTS*, 46, pp. 7 *b*–8 *b* (translated in des Rotours, *Traité des fonctionnaires et traité de l'armée*, pp. 71–9). (*b*) Court of Treasury: *TLT*, 20, pp. 4 *b*–22 *a*; *CTS*, 44, pp. 15 *b*–16 *b*; *HTS*, 48, pp. 13 *b*–14 *b* (des Rotours, *ibid.* pp. 434–42). (*c*) Court of Agriculture: *TLT*, 19, pp. 8 *a*–25 *b*; *CTS*, 44, pp. 14 *a*–15 *b*; *HTS*, 48, pp. 12 *a*–13 *b* (des Rotours, *ibid.* pp. 418–34). (*d*) Department of Judicial Control: *TLT*, 6, pp. 44 *a*–46 *b*; *CTS*, 43, p. 16 *a*–*b*; *HTS*, 46, p. 12 *b* (des Rotours, *ibid.* pp. 120–1). (*e*) Censorate: *TLT*, 13; *CTS*, 44, pp. 1 *a*–2 *a*; *HTS*, 48, pp. 1 *a*–4 *a* (des Rotours, *ibid.* pp. 281–314).

Materials relating to the function of these offices are collected in *TT*, *THY*, *WHTK*, *TPYL*, *Yü Hai*, etc., conveniently arranged under the individual offices.

PAGE 99

2 See the passages noted in previous note. Many of these underlings were outside the official hierarchy, and are thus not mentioned in *CTS* and *HTS*.

3 For details of the procedure for registration, see Niida, *Tō-Sō hōritsu bunsho no kenkyū*, pp. 650–67, and the articles from *Tonkō Torohan shakai-kaizai shiryō* (1959) by Nishijima Sadao and Nishimura Genyu.

4 The *Household Statutes* on registration read as follows:

'The household registers (*hu-chi*) are to be compiled every 3rd year. Beginning in the first ten days of the 1st month, the county officials should examine the statements (*shou-shih*) and tax registers (*chi-chang*), and take them to the prefecture. According to the *Ordinances* they should compile a separate scroll for each locality (*hsiang*). All should be made in triplicate, and the joins between the sheets of paper inscribed—prefecture, county, year register. The prefectural seal should be stamped over the name of the prefecture, and the county seal over that of the county. Their presentation should be completed by the 30th of the 3rd month. One copy should always be mounted with a yellow wrapper, and sent to the Department of State. The prefecture and county should each keep one copy. The paper, brushes and yellow binding cloth required should be paid for by charging 1 cash per person included on each given register. Each of the households should already have had its household category fixed before the year of compilation, and this should be entered on the foot of the register. Any new families formed by dividing households or newly to be appended should be added in order after the old households' (see *THY*, 85, p. 1559; *TFYK*, 486, p. 15 *a–b*).

'All the registers due for despatch to the Department of State should be sent together with the cloth for the *yung* and *tiao* taxes from the prefecture concerned. If the *yung* and *tiao* are not paid in to the capital, carriers may be hired (*ku-chüeh*) to transport them, the necessary costs of carriage being provided from official funds' (see *THY*, 85, p. 1559; *TFYK*, 486, p. 14 *a–b*).

'All household registers, statements, and tax registers of prefectures and counties should be preserved until five subsequent ones have been compiled (*wu-pi*). The registers sent to the Department of State should be preserved until nine subsequent ones have been sent in (*chiu-pi*)' (see *THY*, 85, p. 1559).

5 See *CTS*, 48, p. 3 *b*, which cites an edict issued in 744 requesting the copying of a fourth copy of household registers which could be stored in the branch of the Board of Finance in Lo-yang, and thus save the expense of moving the files to and fro.

6 See chapter II above, and Yang Yen's memorial, appendix II, 5, 1.

7 See *TT*, 23, p. 136 *c*: 'In the 1st month of 782, Tu Yu, vice-president of the Board of Finance, memorialised the throne: "In and before the *T'ien-pao* period, the business of the Board of Finance itself was multifarious, and for this reason there were two chief secretaries and under-secretaries to manage the department's business. After the outbreak of the rebellion, the business of the Board itself diminished, while that of the Department of Public Revenue became more complicated. Yet they have only one chief secretary and under-secretary. I request that one of each of these posts [in the Board of Finance] should be abolished. The external decision [i.e. by officials of other departments seconded to special responsibility over Public Revenue] of matters concerning the Department of Public Revenues should be maintained until the end of the present military crisis, and responsibility should then revert to the office itself."'

8 See *TLT*, 3, p. 43 *b*.

9 See Su Mien's note in *THY*, 58, p. 1011, also *THY*, 59, p. 1018.

10 On this reform see *TLT*, 3, p. 43 *b* (the text of the current Kuang-ya shu-chü edition of *TLT* is here very corrupt). Edict of 736: 'As each year there are deficiencies in taxes and the amounts of the various types of contribution are different, we order the Board of Finance to prepare a permanently applicable directive in five chapters. The prefects and magistrates should hand [their copy of] these over to their successors on the day on which they are relieved in their post. The offices of the Department of State need only prepare and present annually a schedule of the amounts of commodities which are to be paid out. This shall be promulgated and sent out by postal relay. The allocation of moneys and the decision of disputes shall accord with the edict. The Department of Treasury shall entirely revise its methods and put this into effect.'

The memorial of Li Lin-fu which preceded this edict gives some idea of the immense amount of paperwork involved under the old system (see *THY*, 59, p. 1020; *TT*, 23, p. 136*c*). On the 6th day of the 3rd month 736 Li Lin-fu, Great Minister and president of the Board of Finance, memorialised the throne: 'The imperial directives (*chih-fu*) concerning taxation (*tsu-yung*), conscription, harmonious purchase, miscellaneous expenditure, spring clothing, and taxation of hay and of various sorts, were, according to the former practice, written up annually. According to the total of the various prefectures and administrations and the different offices involved, they took up more than 500,000 sheets of paper, and the trouble involved in assigning them to various departments for copying was very complicated. The items involved being extremely numerous, it was difficult to complete the calculations, and since there were no fixed quotas (*o*), and payments and levies were not constant, long-standing abuses in the conduct of affairs have arisen. I have now discussed the matter with the provincial inspecting commissioners (*ts'ai-fang shih*) and the prefectural delegates to court (*ch'ao-chi shih*), and feel that wherever there is anything not beneficial to the people or not in accordance with what the locality produces, it should be reformed in the light of the actual circumstances. The authorities should make it their special concern to bring into being a system that is fitting and convenient. Then we may hope that the people will know the fixed regular rules, and the administration will have a regular pattern. These rules should also be compiled in five chapters to provide a permanently applicable directive (*ch'ang-hsing chih-fu*). The department of the ministry will then only need to memorialise annually the amounts due to be paid out, and have this promulgated. This should not amount to more than one or two sheets of paper for each prefecture, which may be entrusted to the postal couriers for delivery.'

11 See *THY*, 59, p. 1018.

12 On this tally system see des Rotours, 'Les insignes en deux parties (fou) sous la dynastie des T'ang', *T'oung Pao*, 41, I–III (1952), pp. 1–148 (at pp. 56–60).

13 See chapter II.

14 See, for material on this system, *TT*, 12; *TFYK*, 502; *THY*, 88; *CTS*, 49. See also Balázs, 'Beiträge', *MSOS*, 35, pp. 66–71.

PAGE 102

15 See note 12 to p. 101 above. See map 6 for the location of the two granaries. The department was also in control of salt production at the salt pools at P'u-chou. See the fragment of the *Ts'ang-pu ko* cited in *TT*, 10, p. 59*b*, and translated note 7 to page 50 above.

16 I have attempted to make such a delineation in the case of the offices concerned with water control, in 'The fragment of the T'ang ordinances of the Department of Waterways', *Asia Major*, 6, 1 (1957), pp. 36–8. It is clear from the small fragments of the *Ordinances* which survive that they defined the areas of responsibility of offices much more closely than do the surviving accounts listed in note 1 to p. 98 above.

17 See *TLT*, 20, pp. 15*b*–19*a*; *HTS*, 48, p. 13*b*.

18 See *CTS*, 48, p. 1*b*; *CTS*, 105, pp. 6*a*–8*a*.

19 See *THY*, 59, p. 1024. In 745 similar commissioners were appointed to supervise the Court of Agriculture, and in 747 to the great granaries of the two capitals. The last such commissioner was Ti-wu Ch'i, who became Commissioner for Income and Expenditure for the Courts of Agriculture and of Treasury at the two capitals (*Liang-ching Ssu-nung T'ai-fu ch'u-na shih*) in 758.

20 See *TLT*, 20; *CTS*, 44; *HTS*, 48, *loc. cit.* (note 1 to p. 98). This must have been an important part of the court's business, for most of the cases in which we know it to have been active involved standards of price, measures, weights, etc. (see *THY*, 66, pp. 1153–5). The office for price-control was established in 658 (*THY*, *loc. cit.*).

PAGE 103

21 See *TLT*, 19, pp. 16*a*–18*b*. The Great Granary was administered by its own controller (*ling*). On the location of the granary, see Twitchett, *Asia Major*, 6, 1, p. 49, note 49.

22 See *CTS*, *HTS*, *TLT*, *locc. cit.* (note 1 to p. 98).

23 See appendix v, 2.

24 See Twitchett, 'Lands under state cultivation in T'ang China', *Journal of Economic and Social History of the Orient*, 2, II (1959), pp. 167–8.

25 See *CTS*, 43, p. 16a (see also *HTS*, 46, p. 12b). Des Rotours's translation of this passage is in some respects unsatisfactory. It should read as follows: 'The chief secretary and under-secretary of the Department of Judicial Control are in charge of accounting for the taxes of the capital and the provinces, for current expenditure, salaries, official buildings and funds, honorific titles and awards, cases of corruption, the payment of money fines, employment of convict labour, the amount of impositions, arrears and commodities owing to the state, the provisioning of the armies, harmonious purchases, and the income from military colonies. They are to make an audit of the granaries and storehouses of the capital every three months. The various services (*chu-ssu*) and commissioners will present their accounts to the Department of State in the capital every quarter. During each quarter, the accounts for the preceding quarter shall be audited. The prefectures shall have a general audit at the end of each year.'

PAGE 104

26 The system generally enforced is best set out in the following memorial presented by the department in 780 (see *THY*, 59, p. 1036): 'The *Regulations* (*ko*) concerning the presentation of account-lists (*kou-chang*) by the prefectures and army administrations of the empire say that the different amounts levied daily should be made up into a detailed account (*kou-hui*) on the basis of the official records by the senior official, managing clerk, or executive office responsible. At the end of the year the total amount and the name of the official responsible for the management of the account are to be reported to the Department of Judicial Control. If the place is less than 1000 *li* from the capital, the report should arrive during the 1st month, if less than 2000 *li*, during the 2nd month. All other reports should arrive during the 3rd month. The office of the ministry will investigate them, and return them to the officers in charge of the prefectures. All this should be completed by the 6th month. Amounts which concern the Department of Public Revenues should be entered among the annual disbursements. After the instruction has been promulgated, all payments should be completed by the 30th day of the 12th month. The revenue commissioners of the various armies shall also accord with these rules....'

For the different system employed in the metropolitan district, see the memorial of Lu Man dated 792, *THY*, 59, p. 1036.

27 See *THY*, 59, p. 1036. A preliminary audit by one of the executive officers (*p'an-kuan*) of the provincial governors had been ordered in an edict dated 777, cited in the memorial of 780 quoted in note 26 to p. 104. But as we know from this same memorial, such preliminary audits had rarely been carried out. After this date the law was reintroduced, and the commissioners sent to the provinces to supervise the assessment of the new *liang-shui* taxes were ordered to make this rule effective.

28 See *THY*, 62, p. 1086.

29 See *HTS*, 48, p. 14*a*. It was most probably after 733, since at that date Yang Shen-chin and Yang Shen-ming were appointed examining censors for this type of duty (see *CTS*, 105, p. 7*a*).

30 See *THY*, 59, p. 1024, and *THY*, 62, p. 1086, for edicts dated 731 and 733 appointing simple censors to the same type of duties.

31 See the memorial of Li Ku-yen, *THY*, 60, pp. 1054–5; and edict, p. 1057.

32 See *TLT*, 13, *loc. cit.* (note 1 to p. 98).

PAGE 105

33 See *TLT*, 30; *HTS*, 49 B, pp. 4*a*–7*b* (des Rotours, *Traité des fonctionnaires et traité de l'armée*, pp. 694–6); *CTS*, 44, pp. 28*b*–31*b*, for a general description of the responsibilities of local officials. An edict of 728 (see *THY*, 83, p. 1533; *TFYK*, 487, p. 17*b*) made quite specific the personal responsibility of prefects and magistrates for taxes and levies in their district. A number of articles of the *Code* also provide for penalties to be imposed on such officials, even for offences of which they were not cognisant.

34 See the sources cited in the last note. Some further idea of the type of business handled by these different services may be gained from the fragmentary registers of correspondence recovered from Turfan by the Stein and Otani expeditions (see Maspero, *Les documents chinois de la troisième expédition de Sir Aurel Stein en Asie Centrale*, pp. 93–5, and Ogasawara Senshu, 'Torohan shutsuto keizai-bunsho no tokushoku', *Ryūkoku Daigaku ronshū*, 349 (1955), pp. 1–15).

35 These officials were first added to prefectural staffs in 709 (*HTS*, 49 B, p. 4*b*; *TT*, 33, p. 189*a*) and abolished either in 710 (*HTS*) or during the *K'ai-yüan* period (*TT*). There is something wrong with the information given by these two sources, however, since we know that such officers still existed in the metropolitan district in 745, when their numbers were reduced (*THY*, 69, p. 1224), and in Shang-chou in 752 when they were suppressed (*ibid.*). They were re-established generally in either 758–9 (*TT*) or 761 (*HTS*).

Even thereafter they were not appointed in every prefecture, since in 798 the military governor of Wei-po (southern Ho-pei) requested that he might confirm the previous system of appointing such officials, in some cases appointing two heads of the service in a single prefecture. It seems to have been not uncommon to double these posts, as an edict of 801 forbids the practice beyond the metropolitan district (*THY*, 69, p. 1226).

PAGE 106

36 See *TT*, 3, p. 23*b*, translated note 104 to p. 11; *TLT*, 30, p. 35*a*.

37 On this whole question of sub-bureaucratic administration see Matsumoto Yoshiumi, 'Rimpo-soshiki wo chūshin toshitaru Tōdai no sonsei', *Shigaku zasshi*, 53, III (1942), pp. 323–71; Naba, 'Tōdai rimpo-seido shakugi', *Haneda Hakase shōju ronsō* (1950); Niida, 'Tōdai no rimpo-seido', *Rekishigaku kenkyū*, 6, X (1936). There is a further study of this problem, which I have been unable to consult: Shida Fudōma, 'Tōdai kyōtōsei no kenkyū', *Shakai-keizai shigaku*, 5, XI (1934).

38 See P. 3560 v°, which is a sort of code of practice in water-distribution drawn up by the local authorities of Tun-huang, and which plainly incorporates customary usage. See Twitchett, 'Some remarks on irrigation under the T'ang', *T'oung Pao*, 48, 1–3 (1961), pp. 175–94, and Naba Toshisada, 'Tōdai no nōden-suiri ni kansuru kitei ni tsukite', *Shigaku zasshi*, 54, I, pp. 49–55.

PAGE 107

39 Some, at least, of these appointments to the censorate were probably quite nominal, and were a device by which the commissioner was given a regularised position of responsibility in the bureaucracy, rather than the titles of commissioner were a device to give a censor special powers.

40 See *CTS*, 48, p. 8*a*; *CTS*, 96, p. 9*a*.

41 See *CTS*, 48, p. 14*b*; *THY*, 88, p. 1603; *TFYK*, 493, p. 14*a–b*; *TT*, 10, p. 59*a–b*.

42 On these titles, and the similar concurrent title of commissioner for military colonies, with which it was frequently combined, see Aoyama, 'Tōdai no tonden to eiden', *Shigaku zasshi*, 63, I (1954), p. 49, notes 34–5.

43 See *THY*, 87, p. 1602.

44 See chapter I, and the works by Pulleyblank and Suzuki cited in note 127 to p. 14.

45 See chapter I; Pulleyblank, *The background of the rebellion of An Lu-shan*, pp. 50 ff., 29 ff.

46 Pulleyblank, *The background of the rebellion of An Lu-shan*. See also the same author's article in *Tōyō gakuhō*, 35 (1952), pp. 102 ff.

47 See *CTS*, 105, pp. 6a–8a; *CTS*, 48, p. 1b; *TCTC*, 213, p. 6804. The Yang family were direct descendants of the Sui imperial house.

48 On Yang Ch'ung-li's retirement through old age in 733 (he was over ninety years of age), his three sons Yang Shen-ch'in, Yang Shen-ming, and Yang Shen-yü were given charge of the Court of Treasury, the Han-chia Granary, and the Great Granary, respectively, the first two becoming also concurrently censors. The family thus controlled the great part of the empire's revenue.

49 See note 19 to p. 102.

50 See chapter V, and the sources cited in note 21 to p. 103.

51 His other deputy commissioner had been Ts'ui Hsi-i. There is strong likelihood that both he and Hsiao Chiung were of aristocratic origin.

52 Wei Chien was also an aristocrat. It is not clear when he was put in charge of transport. The whole system must have been disrupted with the suspension of P'ei Yao-ch'ing's 'northern route' in 737. After he was demoted Hsiao Chiung succeeded him, and we know that Ts'ui Hsi-i also had control of transport at about this time (*HTS*, 53, p. 3a). This must have been in 738, when he became governor of Ho-nan, for he died in that year. Wei Chien's appointment was made in 742. It is not clear whether there was any holder of the office in the preceding years.

53 Wei Chien's elder sister was a concubine of the Hui-hsüan heir apparent, and his younger sister concubine to the heir apparent, while he himself was married to a niece of Li Lin-fu. He and Li Lin-fu, however, had been in opposite groups since the dispute over the appointment of the new heir apparent in 738, in which Li Lin-fu had been defeated.

54 They were Lu Yu and Yüan Wei-tou.

55 See chapter IV, and note 14 to p. 68.

56 See *THY*, 59, p. 1022.

57 See appendix II, 5, I. See also *CTS*, 118, p. 12b; *THY*, 59, pp. 1015–16.

58   See *CTS*, 123, p. 4*b*.

59   See *THY*, 84, p. 1549.

60   See *HTS*, 149, p. 4*a*.

61   See *CTS*, 48, p. 2*a*.

62   *Ibid.*; *HTS*, 51, p. 4*b*.

63   See *CTS*, 48, p. 5*b*; *TFYK*, 487, p. 23*a*; *CTS*, 11, p. 10*b*.

64   See *THY*, 62, p. 1083.

65   On the coinage commissioners see *THY*, 59, p. 1022. Ti-wu Ch'i and Liu Yen succeeded one another as coinage commissioners during the period 758 to 770, at which date the title was abolished, and it is possible that responsibility for coinage passed into the hands of the commissioners for salt and iron. In the early 760's there were also special coinage commissioners for individual provinces (see *THY*, *loc. cit.*).

66   See chapter v. On Mu Ning, see *CTS*, 138, pp. 4*a–b*; *CTS*, 155, p. 1*b*; *CTS*, 49, p. 3*a*; *THY*, 87, p. 1588.

67   These officials were always called *Yen-t'ieh shih*, but this was only a reference to the Han precedent. There was never any government monopoly of iron in T'ang times. On the whole question of these commissioners, see Twitchett, 'The salt commissioners after the rebellion of An Lu-shan', *Asia Major*, 4, 1 (1954), pp. 60–89. This study presents a more detailed account of central financial organisation after 760 than the present chapter, which is largely based thereon.

68   See chapter iii.

69   This is confirmed by all the sources except *HTS*, 54, p. 1*b*, which refers to sales direct from producer to merchant (see chapter iii, note 21 to p. 52). However, this text contradicts itself, for it later tells us that when merchants paid for salt in cloth, the officials made a surcharge, and it is clear that the merchant dealt with the officers of the commission.

70   In 762–3 the annual revenue from salt was only 400,000 strings (*HTS*, 54, p. 1*b*), or 600,000 strings (*CTS*, 49, p. 4*a*; *THY*, 87, p. 1590).

71   See Yen Keng-wang, *T'ang p'u-shang-ch'eng-lang piao*, pp. 766, 788. Yen's collection of source material on the appointments of the commissioners is somewhat fuller than the sources cited in Twitchett, *Asia Major*, 4, 1, pp. 62–80.

72 Liu Yen was appointed in the 5th month 760. See Yen Keng-wang, *T'ang p'u-shang-ch'eng-lang piao*, p. 766.

73 See *CTS*, 118, p. 1*b*; *CTS*, 123, p. 1*a*.

74 He was appointed commissioner in the 6th month 762, and became Great Minister in addition in the 1st month 763. See Twitchett, *Asia Major*, 4, I, p. 64; Yen Keng-wang, *T'ang p'u-shang-ch'eng-lang piao*, p. 788.

75 The date of his reappointment is not clear. See Twitchett, *Asia Major*, 4, I, p. 64; Yen Keng-wang, *T'ang p'u-shang-ch'eng-lang piao*, pp. 789–95, and Chü Ch'ing-yüan, *Liu Yen P'ing-chuan*, pp. 161 ff.

76 See *CTS*, 123, pp. 1*b*–2*b*; *THY*, 87, pp. 1588–90; *TFYK*, 498, pp. 20*a*–22*b*; *CTW*, 370, pp. 14*a*–16*a*.

77 See chapter v above.

PAGE 112

78 Aoyama, 'Tō-Sōjidai no denunshi to hatsuunshi ni tsuite', *Shigaku ṭasshi*, 44, VII (1933), pp. 1105–29, attempts to prove that the branches were not shared by the two organisations. But I find his arguments unconvincing, especially when bearing in mind that the co-ordination of the two enterprises was the basic principle behind Liu Yen's reforms. For an account of the organisation of the commission, see Twitchett, *Asia Major*, 4, I, and Chü Ch'ing-yüan, *Liu Yen P'ing-chuan*, pp. 26–32.

79 See *HTS*, 54, p. 1*b*. See also map 3.

80 See *THY*, 31, p. 576. The status of these subordinate officials must have been very similar to the members of the staff of provincial governors. Like the latter, the members of the Salt Commission seem to have been more closely linked by personal ties than was the case in the regular bureaucracy. On the question of patronage within the commission, see Twitchett, *Asia Major*, 4, I, pp. 87–8.

81 See Twitchett, *Asia Major*, 4, I; Yen Keng-wang, *T'ang p'u-shang-ch'eng-lang piao*, pp. 789–95.

82 This was always the case. The Department of Public Revenue maintained its own salt monopoly commissioners (*chüeh-yen shih*) at the pools, and levied a monopoly tax at a rate different from that in force in the coastal region (see chapter III).

83 See *CTS*, 123, pp. 4*b*–5*a*; *CTS*, 129, p. 1*a–b*.

84 See *CTS*, 129, p. 1*b*. Han Huang had been in trouble since 777 over an attempt to frame the governor of Ch'ang-an on a charge of making a fraudulent report of a crop failure in the hope of gaining exemption from taxation.

85 Yang Yen's enmity was partly due to the disagreements which he and Liu Yen had had when he was the latter's subordinate at the Board of Civil Office (*li pu*). But the most important factor was the fact that Liu Yen had been responsible for the prosecution of Yüan Tsai in 777. Yang Yen had been intimately connected with the latter. Both were from the same district (Feng-hsiang), and Yang Yen's mother was a relative of Yüan Tsai. Yang Yen had been banished when Yüan Tsai was executed.

PAGE 113

86 See *THY*, 59, p. 1016; *CTS*, 118, p. 7*b*.

87 See Yang Yen's memorial, appendix II, 5, 1.

88 This is abundantly clear from Yang Yen's memorial in *THY*, 59, pp. 1015–16: 'Taxation is the principal foundation of the state...and if there is a single error in the calculations the whole empire will be shaken. Yet, under the irregular system of the late reign, the eunuchs controlled these duties. The foundation of the state's prosperity was managed by five foot eunuch lackeys. Even the great ministers were unable to control them...there is no evil so potent as these maggots....' There was certainly factual foundation for such a complaint. Both Ti-wu Ch'i and Liu Yen had been dismissed from office on account of implication with eunuch politics, and when Liu Yen was eventually removed from high office in 780, the charge against him was that he had formerly been implicated with yet another eunuch in a palace plot to replace the future Te-tsung as heir apparent.

89 *THY*, 59, p. 1016.

90 See *CTS*, 12, p. 4*b*; *CTS*, 49, p. 3*b*; *THY*, 87, p. 1590.

91 See *CTS*, 12, p. 4*a*; *CTS*, 49, p. 3*b*; *THY*, 87, p. 1590.

92 See *THY*, 87, p. 1590; *CTS*, 49, pp. 3*b*–4*a*.

93 See *CTS*, 123, p. 5*b*; *HTS*, 126, p. 17*a*, and his *hsing-chuan* in *Ch'üan Tsai-chih wen-chi*, 20, p. 6*a*.

94 See *CTS*, 49, p. 3*b*; *THY*, 87, p. 1590; *CTS*, 147, p. 4*a*; *CTS*, 12, p. 5*a*; *TCTC*, 226, p. 7276. The appointment was designated 'temporary' (*chüan*) so as to save face over the premature abolition of the commission a few weeks earlier.

PAGE 114

95 See chapter II above.

96 See above, note 27 to p. 104.

97 See the Act of Grace of the 1st month 780, appendix II, 5, 2, and the directive of the 2nd month of the same year (*ch'i-ch'ing-t'iao*) which ordered the envoys to report all assessments and detailed arrangements for each province to the same department (see appendix II, 4, 5).

98 See, for instance, the record of the appointment of Pao Chi and Ts'ui Tsung, *CTS*, 49, p. 4*a*; *THY*, 87, p. 1590; *CTS*, 12, p. 10*b*.

99 See Twitchett, *Asia Major*, 4, 1, p. 70; Yen Keng-wang, *T'ang p'u-shang-ch'eng-lang piao*, p. 767. Tu Yu controlled both public revenue and transportation from the 11th month 781 to the 5th month of the next year. During this period he consolidated the predominant position of the Public Revenue Department by reducing the official establishment of the parent Board of Finance (see above, note 7 to p. 100).

100 See Twitchett, *Asia Major*, 4, 1; Yen Keng-wang, *T'ang p'u-shang-ch'eng-lang piao*. He controlled public revenue from the 5th month 782 to the 12th month 783.

101 See Twitchett, *Asia Major*, 4, 1; Yen Keng-wang, *T'ang p'u-shang-ch'eng-lang piao*. P'ei Tien was in charge from the 12th month 783 to the 9th month 784.

102 See Twitchett, *Asia Major*, 4, 1; Yen Keng-wang, *T'ang p'u-shang-ch'eng-lang piao*, pp. 767–8 and pp. 659–60. During his period in office, which lasted from the 9th month 784 to the 12th month 786, the great minister Ts'ui Tsao, probably hoping that administration could revert to normal with the end of the Ho-pei rebellions, attempted to revise the old system by which local authorities had been responsible for transporting their own taxes, and shut down the Transport Commission and the local branches of the Public Revenue Department in the provinces. At the same time responsibility for the business previously handled by the Salt and Iron Commission and the Public Revenue Department was placed under the two vice-presidents of the Board of Finance, Yüan Hsiu and Chi Chung-fou. It is probable that business continued as before, apart from transportation of tax income. But there was undoubtedly an attempt to consolidate all financial administration in the hands of the Board of Finance. Thus Yen Keng-wang's comment that this was a nominal reform only (*T'ang p'u-shang-ch'eng-lang piao*, p. 659) is not altogether apt. On this attempted reform see Twitchett, *op. cit.* p. 72.

103 See Twitchett, *Asia Major*, 4, 1, pp. 71–2; Yen Keng-wang, *T'ang p'u-shang-ch'eng-lang piao*, pp. 768, 797. He was appointed in the 12th month 786, and died in the 2nd month of the following year.

104 Twitchett, *Asia Major*, 4, 1; Yen Keng-wang, *T'ang p'u-shang-ch'eng-lang piao*, pp. 644–6, 696–7, 798.

105 See *CTS*, 123, p. 6*a* ; *TCTC*, 234, p. 7527.

106 They fell from power in the 4th month 792. See *CTS*, 13, p. 7*a*; *TCTC*, 234, p. 7527 ff.

107 These appointments were made in the 3rd month 792. See *CTS*, 123, p. 6*a*; *THY*, 88, p. 1609; Yen Keng-wang, *T'ang p'u-shang-ch'eng-lang piao*, p. 798.

108 See *CTS*, 123, p. 6*a*. Hung's reluctance to hand over control of the salt administration may well have been due to his fear of punishment for corruption. The principal branch of the commission during his tenure had been in charge of Hsü Ts'an, a notoriously corrupt official. See *CTS*, 123, p. 5*b*.

109 This division of authority was made in the 4th month 792, a few days after the new Great Ministers, Lu Chih and Chao Chung, had been appointed. Some account of the discussions leading up to the decision is given in *CTS*, 123, pp. 6*a–b*.

110 See Twitchett, *Asia Major*, 4, 1, pp. 73–5. P'ei Yen-ling's appointment was bitterly opposed by Lu Chih, whose nominee was Li Sun, who had previously been in trouble with Tou Shen.

111 For details of his malpractices, see *CTS*, 135, pp. 5*b*ff., and the memorial of denunciation prepared by Lu Chih, *T'ang Lu Hsüan-kung Han-yüan chi*, 20, pp. 1*a–20a*. See also Tu Yu's memorial of 805 requesting the abolition of the new practices of the Public Revenue Department (see *THY*, 59, p. 1016) and the Act of Grace issued earlier in the same year (see *TFYK*, 89, pp. 16*a–19b*; *Shun-tsung Shih-lu*, 2; *Han Ch'ang-li chi, wai-chi*, 7, pp. 1*a–2a*, translated, Solomon, *The veritable record of the T'ang emperor Shun-tsung*, pp. 15 ff.).

112 See Twitchett, *Asia Major*, 4, 1, p. 74. The doubt there raised (note 1) over the appointment of Li Heng, is resolved by Yen Keng-wang, *T'ang p'u-shang-ch'eng-lang piao*, pp. 698, 798, by the suggestion that Li Heng's authority was limited to Szechuan, Shan-nan, Kuan-chung and Ho-tung— the areas under the Public Revenue Department. He thus had no power over the Salt and Iron Commission itself, but only over similar affairs in western and north-western China. For Wang Wei's appointment, see *CTS*, 146, p. 6*b*; *CTS*, 49, p. 4*b*.

113 See *CTS*, 146, pp. 6*b–7a*. Li Jo-ch'u planned a comprehensive reform of the commission, in which various abuses had arisen under Wang Wei's administration. But unfortunately Li died prematurely after only a few months in office.

114 See Twitchett, *Asia Major*, 4, I, p. 74. Li Ch'i was appointed in the 2nd month of 799 (see *CTS*, 13, p. 16*a*; *THY*, 88, p. 1609; *THY*, 87, p. 1591; *CTS*, 49, p. 4*b*). According to *CTS*, 112, p. 4*b*, he owed his appointment to bribery. His period in office was marked by widespread corruption and maladministration (see *CTS*, 49, pp. 4*b*–5*a*; *THY*, 87, p. 1592; *CTS*, 112, *loc. cit.*; *TCTC*, 235, p. 7582; *CTS*, 174, p. 2*b*).

115 On these provincial chancelleries, see Aoyama, 'Tōdai shinsōin kō', *Katō Hakase kanreki kinen Tōyōshi Shūsetsu*, pp. 21–46.

116 See *Shun-tsung shih-lu*, 1–2; Solomon, *The veritable record of the T'ang emperor Shun-tsung*, pp. 18 ff.; Twitchett, *Asia Major*, 4, I, p. 77.

PAGE 118

117 See *CTS*, 14, p. 8*b*; *CTS*, 147, p. 4*b*. This was in the 4th month 806. The incorrect date given in *CTS*, 49, p. 4*b*; *THY*, 87, p. 1592, derived from a confusion of this event with Tu Yu's complete withdrawal from official service, which took place in the following year (see *CTS*, 14, p. 10*a*; *CTS*, 147, p. 5*b*).

118 See *THY*, 84, pp. 1552–3; *CTS*, 14, pp. 12*b*–13*a*; *TCTC*, 237, pp. 7647–8, and the commentary of Hu San-hsing to the latter.

119 See *CTS*, 49, p. 5*a*; *THY*, 87, p. 1592; *TFYK*, 493, p. 19*a*.

120 See chapter IV above. The probable date of the beginning of administration by the Salt and Iron Commission is 770.

121 They controlled mining from 780 onwards (see chapter IV above). The edict giving them authority is in *CTS*, 49, p. 4*a*; *THY*, 87, p. 1591; *TFYK*, 494, p. 2*a*.

122 Taxation of tea began in 793 with Chang P'ang (see chapter III above). Li Ch'i collected many dues on transported goods, but it is not clear whether he did this by virtue of his post of commissioner for salt and iron, or simply as provincial governor.

123 See *CTS*, 49, p. 5*a–b*; *THY*, 87, p. 1593. However, there is some question about this date. An edict of 810 says that the control of salt in Szechuan reverted to the Public Revenue Department in *that* year, and the report of salt income for 811 in *TFYK*, 493, p. 20*a*, specifically states that Szechuan is not included in the total, which is certainly that of income from the Salt and Iron Commission.

124 See *THY*, 88, pp. 1610–11.

125 See *THY*, 59, p. 1016. See also *Shun-tsung shih-lu*, 2; Solomon, *The veritable record of the T'ang emperor Shun-tsung*, pp. 18–19, for a passage which clearly shows the power of the Public Revenue Department at this period. 'Wang Shu-wen...plotted with his clique as follows, "If we controlled the office of the Department of Public Revenue, the national revenues would be in our hands...".'

126 See *THY*, 59, p. 1016.

127 See *THY*, 59, p. 1020.

128 *Ibid.*

PAGE 119

129 See *CTS*, 49, p. 5 *b*; *THY*, 87, pp. 1592–3.

130 See Twitchett, *Asia Major*, 4, I, pp. 78–81. The Board of Finance recovered prestige during Hsien-tsung's reign largely due to the personal influence of Wang Shao, its president from 811 to 814. The *san-ssu* never became a single organisation, a joint co-ordinating ministry of finance, as it did under the Sung. The first single head of the three offices seems to have been appointed under the Later Liang in 906, and during T'ang times the three offices had no unified control.

PAGE 120

131 The article of des Rotours, 'Les grands fonctionnaires des provinces en Chine sous la dynastie des T'ang', *T'oung Pao*, 25 (1927), pp. 1–114, which remains useful for the earlier half of the dynasty, is completely out of date for the post-An Lu-shan period. On this period see Hino, *Shina chūsei no gumbatsu* (1942), the same author's 'Tōdai hanchin no bakko to chinshō', *Tōyō gakuhō*, 26, IV (1939); 27, I; 27, II; 27, III (1940). Much the best study of the whole problem, although dealing in particular with later developments in the provincial system under the Wu-tai, is Sudō, 'Godai no setsudoshi no shihai taisei', *Shigaku zasshi*, 61 (1952), IV, pp. 1–41; VI, pp. 20–38. The latter deals largely with the institutions developed in northern China, but has some notes on regional differences.

PAGE 121

132 Sudō, 'Godai no setsudoshi no shihai taisei'.

133 For an example, see P. 3155.

134 See Hino, *Shina chūsei no gumbatsu*, pp. 71 ff.; Sudō, 'Godai no setsudoshi no shihai taisei'.

NOTES

PAGE 122

135 See Hino, *Shina chūsei no gumbatsu,* and *Tōdai hanchin no bakko to chinshō.*

136 There is no adequate study of these developments, apart from a somewhat sketchy outline in Hino, *Shina chūsei no gumbatsu,* pp. 167–76.

APPENDIX I

PAGE 136

1 *Li Chi,* 3 (*Record of Rites*). The second part of the quotation is Chêng Hsüan's Commentary to the *Li Chi* text.

APPENDIX II

PAGE 141

1 *ting* 丁 is written *ting-chiang* 'adult artisan' in *TT.* But this agrees neither with the other sources for this article (nor with the *Code,* 13, art. 10, which gives *ting-i erh-shih jih*) nor with the bulk of historical examples which show that the *corvée* exemption tax was levied on adults in general—not on artisans.

2 Niida's reconstruction of the first clause 若 留 役 者 conflates two versions of this sentence in differing grammatical forms: (i) 若 留 役 則 in *CTS, TFYK, THY, TLT,* and (ii) 留 役 者 in *TT,* 6. Presumably the basis of his reconstruction is the clause in *RGG,* 3, p. 117; *RSG,* 13, p. 390, 若 須 收 庸 者. But I prefer to retain the form found in *CTS, THY, TLT, TFYK.*

3 Here again the text of *TT,* which Niida follows in his reconstruction, as being closest to the Japanese statutes, differs from the version in *CTS, TFYK, THY, TLT,* which reads 'If there is some business, so that additional labour service is imposed, after one *hsün* and five days, the tax in kind should be remitted, after three *hsün* both tax in kind and grain tax is to be remitted'. The sense is, of course, identical.

4 This note is included as commentary in *TT,* 6. In the Japanese statutes it is also included as commentary in small type, and presumably appeared in this form in the *Statutes* both of 651 and 737. The Japanese statutes, however, include the character 計 before 見 役 日, which gives a smoother reading and should, I think, be retained.

5 This clause about *pu-ch'ü* is missing in all the Chinese sources, being retained only in the *RSG,* 13, commentary, p. 392, where it is cited by the

Shaku as from the T'ang *Statutes*. Some texts of *RSG* read not *pu-ch'ü* but 部 與 曲, but the text of the Kanazawa Bunko MS. which omits 與 is undoubtedly correct. The *RSG* quotation of the 'T'ang *Statute*' omits 聽 之, but this is supplied from the parallel in the Japanese statute. The *Shaku's* author gives his opinion that in T'ang China it was also permissible to send one's slaves as substitutes. The Japanese statutes also permitted the hiring (*ku*) of substitutes from the same *kuni* or *gun*, and in the case of artisans specified that hired substitutes must be men of the same trade.

PAGE 142

6 *TLT*, 3, p. 36*b*, reads 銀 錢. The other texts read simply *ch'ien shih wen* 錢 十 文, which would be an impossibly small amount. Silver coin was in common use on the northern frontiers and in Central Asia. Niida is probably in error in omitting 銀 in his text.

7 This passage, which is commentary in *TLT*, 3, pp. 36*b*–37*a*, is probably not part of the *Statute*, but a passage from the relevant *Ordinance* (*pieh-shih*).

8 半 輸 輕 稅 according to *TLT*, 3, p. 37*a*. *Ch'ing shui* is omitted by other sources. *THY*, 83, reads 半 稅 *han shui*.

9 This ruling is quoted only by *TLT*, *loc. cit.*

PAGE 143

10 A fief of maintenance in T'ang times was not a territorial entity, but simply a number of households whose taxes went to the ennobled person. See Niida, *Tōhō Gakuhō* (Tokyo), 10, 1 (1939), pp. 1–64.

PAGE 144

11 *Kuo* and *i* are simply two grades of fief.

12 Following the reading *ting* in *TLT*, 3, rather than *hsia* as in *THY*, 90, which gives no sense in the context.

13 The corresponding Japanese statute is in *RSG*, 13, pp. 395–6, and is much simpler. Under that system half the grain tax only went to the holder of the fief, and half to the state.

14 Only *PSLT*, 23, retains 諸 田 at beginning.

15 The clause about the local authorities making a report is preserved only in *PSLT*, 23.

16 This clause is preserved only by *TLT*, 3; *Code*, 13, and *PSLT*, 23.

17 This clause is preserved only by *TLT*, 3.

18 From 'After two years . . .' to the end is preserved only by the quotation in *PSLT*, 23. The last sentence is probably corrupt.

PAGE 145

19 Simple 附 in *TT*, 6, and *RSG*, 13, is glossed by *TLT*, 3, with 新 附 于 籍 帳 者 'Newly entered in the registers'.

20 This clause is commentary in *TLT*, 3, and with the following may come from the *Ordinances*.

21 This clause is only found in *TT*, 6.

22 *WHTK* has confused 沒 *mei*, at the beginning, with the *tou* 投 of the last clause, giving a nonsensical reading.

PAGE 146

23 In the Japanese statutes arts. 16–18 here form a single article. The text of this section mistakenly writes 奴 被 for 奴 婢. Nakada Kaoru has suggested that 被 is in fact the correct reading, but is certainly in error. In the commentary *Koki* on this passage the text is quoted as reading 家 人 奴 婢 被 放 附 戶 貫 者 復 三 年, which is probably correct.

24 See appendix III, art. 5 a, for relevant *Ordinances*.

25 This last passage is only found in *TLT*, 3—and does not appear in the quotation in the *Ordinance*. But it is paralleled in *RSG*, 13, pp. 414–15.

26 This is certainly incomplete. *TLT*, 3, adds to the list 及 諸 色 雜 有 職 常 人 'and all sorts of persons holding various minor offices'. *WHTK*, 13, adds 'the fathers and sons of serving officials of the third rank and above and barons of counties...'.

27 *Wei hsü*: when an official was struck off, he could, after the lapse of 6 years, be reinstated at a very much inferior rank: this was called *hsü*.

PAGE 147

28 Both cite this as T'ang *Statute*, but it is difficult to see where these passages fit in.

29 See Niida Noboru, 'Tonkō hakken Tō Suibushiki no kenkyū', *Hattori sensei koki shukuga kinen rombun-shū* (1936), pp. 761–88; Twitchett, 'The fragment of the T'ang *Ordinances of the Department of Waterways* discovered at Tun-huang', *Asia Major*, (n.s.) 6, 1 (1957), pp. 23 ff.

PAGE 148

30 *TLT*, 3, pp. 5 b–26 b.

31 See *Wamyō ruiju-shō*, 3, p. 95 b; 96 b; *ibid.* 5, p. 90 a.

32 See Niida Noboru, 'Tō Gumbōryō to hōsui-seido', *Hōseishi kenkyū*, 4 (1953), pp. 201–4.

33 The term *ts'ung-fu* or *ch'ung-fu* means to perform the miscellaneous local labour services known as *tsa-yao*.

34 Miyazaki, *loc. cit.* at p. 6, suggests the restoration of '*corvée*' (*i*) to the text here. A word has clearly fallen out, and the only possible words are *i* (*corvée*), or *yung* (*corvée* exemption tax).

35 The second part of the clause (from 'when adolescent males...') is omitted by Miyazaki. Land levy at its first occurrence is written *ti-tsu* but this is certainly an error, as adolescents did not pay *tsu*. It is probably an error for *ti-shui* as at second occurrence.

36 *PSLT* writes 謂 *wei*, which is clearly a misprint for *chu* 諸.

37 Niida quotes *PSLT* as giving a defective reading 11 for 21, but the facsimile Sung print reads 21 quite plainly.

PAGE 149

38 See appendix I, art. 19.

39 See appendix III, art. D, for a connected clause from the *Regulations* (*ko*).

40 See appendix I, art. 13.

41 See appendix I, art. 14.

42 These were various types of special labour service performed on behalf of the local authorities.

PAGE 150

43 I am not sure of the meaning of the first clause.

44 There is an illegible character here in the facsimile Sung print.

PAGE 151

45 In the case of the surviving MS. of the *Regulations of the Board of Justice* (P. 3078 + S. 4673), the *Regulations* of the four sub-departments of a Board seem to have been promulgated in a single document. See the text printed in Takigawa Masajirō, *Shina hōseishi kenkyū*, pp. 465 ff.

46 The text of the document is printed by Niida, 'Tō no ritsuryō oyobi kaku no shin shiryō; Stein Tonkō bunken', *Tōyōbunka kenkyūjo kiyō*, 13 (1957), pp. 109–48. His identification of the MS. as a fragment of the K'ai-yüan *Regulations* rests on a close parallel with fragment D below, p. 152.

47 I have been unable to discover any other occurrence of the term *tse-hu*. It must refer to some type of household subordinate to a military government.

PAGE 152

48 The *Regulations* were essentially a codification of amendments to the law originally promulgated as edicts.

49 These were all situated in the mountainous borderlands of Szechuan.

PAGE 157

50 The date of the memorial cannot be the 8th month 780, as by that time the measures advocated had already been enforced for six months. It is most likely that the memorial was submitted in the 8th month of the preceding year, directly after Yang Yen's recall from the provinces and appointment as Great Minister. (This is dated 7th day 8th month 779 in *TCTC*, 226.) This same error is also made in the memorial quoted in *THY*, 59 [*Tu-chih-shih*], which was obviously submitted at the same time. This is also paralleled in *CTS*, 118, but not specified as a memorial.

51 *p'ai* [敗] is omitted in the *CTS*, 118, version.

PAGE 158

52 The *chu-shih* here refer to the provincial governors, *chieh-tu-shih* and *kuan-ch'a-shih*.

53 This sentence is omitted in the *T'ang hui-yao* version, but occurs in identical form in *CTS*, 118, and *TFYK*, 488.

54 The foregoing is historical description in *CTS*, 118, version, and commentary in *TFYK*, 488. The various link-phrases and introductions for the following passages are translated in the comment.

55 This is the opposite of the traditional Confucian economic dictum 'Regulate expenditure by measuring revenue' [*liang ju erh wei ch'u*]. (*Li Chi*, 5, *Wang chih*.)

PAGE 159

56 *Sheng* [省] is translated 'abolish' rather than 'reduce', since it is glossed in *Ts'e-fu yüan-kuei* and *Chiu T'ang-shu*, 48, with *pa*. The latter texts also read, in place of 'The *tsu* and *yung* taxes and minor *corvées*...', 'Other taxes and impositions...'. The reading *cheng* [征] in *CTS*, 48, is probably an error for the *cheng* [徵] in *TFYK*, 488.

57 *Ting-o* is the local quota of adult male taxpayers. Here it is very probably a reference to the liability for labour services rather than taxes as such. This sense is borne out by a quotation in *P'ei wen yün fu* (p. 3957/3) from the Yüan poet Kung Shih-t'ai's *Ho shang ch'eng-an-i shih*: 'Already they have made weak women pay money to the officials. Now they send youths to supplement the labour of grown men.'

58 This sentence is inserted from *TFYK*, 488, and *CTS*, 48, which certainly derive from a common original.

59 The *she-wen* which figure so largely among imperial acts were not criminal amnesties alone, as they are often mistakenly translated, but usually granted measures of tax relief and remissions of labour dues. There were many grades; the *ta-she* such as the present were general acts of grace embracing the whole empire. *Ch'ang-she* were partial amnesties. *Ch'ü-she* were local acts of grace, such as those granted after the imperial cortège had passed through a district to compensate the local population for the expenses involved.

60 The 'troubles' refers to the An Lu-shan rising.

61 This reassessment of household grades is mentioned in the *T'ang hui-yao* passages. The translation is based on the reading 計百姓及客戶約丁 產 ... in *THY*, 83 (first passage). *Ting*, however, is glossed with *jen* [人] in the second passage of *THY*, 83, and replaced by *tzu-ch'an* [資產], which reads more smoothly, in *THY*, 78.

62 On the implications of this see *Code* 11, art. 6, and more particularly 13, art. 10. The *Code* itself provided the death penalty (by strangulation) for severe offences of this kind, but the *Statutes* contained a ruling incorporated into the Commentary *Shu-i* to the *Code*, which allowed the remission of the death penalty and the imposition of banishment with additional hard labour (*chia-i-liu*).

63 I have been unable to find such an edict, but it is interesting to see that the document was promulgated on the very day of Yang Yen's appointment as Great Minister. It is clear from this that his regime was reformist from the beginning.

64 I am unable to identify this office.

65 *THY*, 78, writes his name Wei Chen 楨 instead of Chen 貞.

66 Shan-tung is an abbreviation for or corruption of Shan-nan tung-tao. It occurs in many documents of this period.

67 Wu Ching-lun is mentioned as Hung Ching-lun in *Kao-i*, 17, p. 9*a*. *TCTC*, 226, pp. 7276–7.

68 Although Li Ch'eng was certainly the commissioner sent to Huai-hsi and Huai-nan, for we possess a memorial submitted in that capacity in 780 (see *TFYK*, 503, p. 22*b*), there is some doubt about the appointment. Han Hui's Account of Conduct (*hsing-chuang*) 'T'ang ku Ta-chung ta-fu shou Kuo-tzu chi-chiu Ying-ch'uan hsien k'ai-kuo nan ssu tzu-chin yü-tai tsêng Hu-pu shang-shu Han kung hsing chuang', *Ch'üan Tsai-chih wen chi*, 20, pp. 4*a*–9*a*, informs us, however (at p. 6*a*), that he received the appointment. Possibly Han Hui, who had been in disgrace with his relative Han Huang, was first recalled to this post, but owing to his financial experience was immediately transferred (on the 28th day of the 3rd month according to *CTS*, 12, p. 5*a*, and other authorities cited by Yen Keng-wang, *T'ang p'u-shang-ch'eng-lang piao*, p. 694) to the post of vice-president of the Board of Finance, which was then being restored to full financial authority. Li Ch'eng must have been the replacement appointed at the time of Han Hui's transfer.

69 See *TFYK*, 162.

PAGE 162

70 See *TCTC*, 226, pp. 7276–7.

71 Or perhaps 'according to the established system'. The text reads *chih* 制.

72 The quota of adults was retained presumably for purposes of labour services, which still continued under the new system.

PAGE 163

73 The Department of Judicial Control carried out the annual audit of local accounts.

APPENDIX III

PAGE 165

1 On Chang P'ing-shu, see Yen Keng-wang, *T'ang p'u-shang-ch'eng-lang piao*, 12, pp. 708–9.

APPENDIX IV

PAGE 180

1 *CTS*, 48, p. 6*b*; *THY*, 89, p. 1623; *TPYL*, 836, p. 2*a*; *HTS*, 54, p. 5*a*.

2 *TLT*, 22, p. 29*a*; *TT*, 9, p. 53*b*; *CTS*, 44, p. 19*a*; *HTS*, 54, p. 6*b*.

3 *CTS*, 48, p. 7*a*; *THY*, 89, p. 1623.

4 *TLT*, 22, p. 29*a*; *TT*, 9, p. 53*b*; *CTS*, 44, p. 19*a*; *HTS*, 54, p. 6*b*. For the increase in the number of hearths in 769, see *CTS*, 48, p. 10*b*. The names of the two mints are given as listed in *TFYK*, 501, p. 11*a–b*. *CTS*, 48, p. 10*b*, writes Fen-t'ang chien (*t'ang* 湯 may be a graphic error for *yang* 陽). *HTS*, 38, p. 12*a*, records the establishment of a copper smeltery at Wen-hsi county in 618.

5 As note 2 to p. 180. *HTS*, 41, p. 1a, records that there were two coinage offices for the Tan-yang chien and Kuang-ling chien mints. The entry of Yang-chou in *YHCHC*, which might have added further information, is unfortunately missing.

6 As note 2 to p. 180. Established in 738 according to *HTS*, 54, p. 6b; *THY*, 89, p. 1627. According to *HTS*, 41, p. 8b; *YHCHC*, 28, p. 756, the two mints were in Nan-ling county. *YHCHC*, *loc. cit.*, gives their combined annual output as 50,000 strings of cash.

7 See *TT*, 9, p. 53b; *TLT*, 22, p. 29a. Established in 738 according to *HTS*, 54, p. 6b; *THY*, 89, p. 1627.

8 As note 2 to p. 180. The Feng-shan mint is mentioned by *HTS*, 41, p. 9a.

9 As note 2 to p. 180. The increase in hearths in 811 is mentioned by *CTS*, 48, p. 12a; *THY*, 89, p. 1630; *TFYK*, 501, p. 15b; *TPYL*, 836, p. 2b. *YHCHC*, 14, p. 437, however, gives the date 812. This source quotes a memorial of Li Chi-fu requesting the resumption of minting in that year. It says that the previous number of mints had been forty. The rebuilding began in the 6th month 812, and five hearths were ready by the 10th month, having an annual output of 18,000 strings. Since Li Chi-fu was himself the compiler of *YHCHC*, we may rely upon the date he gives to his own memorial. According to *HTS*, 54, p. 9a, the Fei-hu chou-ch'ien yüan mint was established in 834 by Wang Yai. There had been a Fei-hu mint previous to 811. See *HTS*, 54, p. 8b. The San-ho mint and its coinage office were in Fei-hu county. See *HTS*, 39, p. 8b.

10 See *TT*, 9, p. 53b; *CTS*, 44, p. 19a; *HTS*, 54, p. 6b.

11 As note 2 to p. 180. The Kuang-ya shu-chü edition of *TLT* gives Liu-chou for Ch'en-chou, but the correct writing is preserved in the Sung print and the Konoe edition. The Kuei-yang chien mint is listed in *HTS*, 41, p. 11a; *YHCHC*, 29, p. 789. The latter says that it was inside the prefectural city of Ch'en-chou, and that its annual output was 50,000 strings of cash. The mint went out of operation at some time prior to 808 when it was revived. See *CTS*, 48, p. 11a; *THY*, 89, p. 1629; *TFYK*, 501, p. 14a.

12 As note 2 to p. 180. The Kuang-ya shu-chü edition of *TLT* writes 楊 instead of 洋 for Yang-chou.

13 As note 2 to p. 180.

14 See *HTS*, 41, p. 9b; *YHCHC*, 28, p. 745.

15 Re-established in 780 after long disuse. See *CTS*, 48, p. 10a; *THY*, 89, p. 1627; *TFYK*, 501, p. 11b.

PAGE 181

1 The mark '*ch'ang*' has been taken by some authors as referring to the *nien-hao* of the period in which the *ch'ien-fang* were established (*Hui-ch'ang*). But as all the others refer to the place of minting I prefer to accept it as the place Ch'ang-chou.

APPENDIX V

PAGE 192

1 The *Pei-ts'ang* (northern granary) is not otherwise known. Since it contained a very large quantity of grain, it seems possible that it was a metropolitan granary at Ch'ang-an, like the T'ai-ts'ang. Another possibility is that it was the great granary in southern Ho-pei, a central reserve for the north-eastern armies. Two such centres of strategic stores are known. One was at Ta-ming hsien, in Wei-chou (see *T'ai-p'ing huan-yü chi*, 54, p. 5*b*). The other, slightly further north, was at Ch'ing-ho hsien in Pei-chou. Both were supplied by the Yung-chi ch'ü canal. Pei-chou is slightly more likely, since we know that it was currently described, at the time of An Lu-shan's rebellion, as the *Pei-k'u* (northern storehouse) (see *HTS*, 153, p. 5*b*). It had been used as a storage depot for supplies from the south from the time of Wu-hou or earlier (see Ch'en Yin-k'o, *Sui-T'ang chih-tu yüan-yüan lüeh-lun k'ao*, pp. 155–6). *CTW*, 514, p. 14*a-b*, gives this account of Pei-chou in 756: 'According to the former system, the cloth paid as commutation for the *tsu* tax from the Chiang-Huai region was stored at Ch'ing-ho to provision the northern armies. This has continued for many years. Common tradition calls it the "Northern storehouse" (*Pei-k'u*) of the empire. At present there are in store there more than 3,000,000 lengths of hemp cloth from Chiang-tung, more than 700,000 lengths of silk from the taxes of Ho-pei, more than 100,000 lengths of coloured patterned damask from Pei-chou itself, more than 300,000 strings of cash representing several years' accumulation of the household levy, and 300,000 *shih* of grain in the granaries. The arms and armour used in chastising Mo-cho (in Kao-tsung's reign) are also stored in the arsenals, to the number of 500,000 or more . . . ' See also *TCTC*, 217, p. 6957.

BIBLIOGRAPHY

A. THE CLASSICS

The memorials and edicts quoted in the notes make wide use of the Confucian canonical writings as authorities. These are cited for the most part after Legge's *Chinese Classics*. The works most frequently mentioned in the notes are

(1) *Shu ching*, 'The Book of Documents', a collection of early state documents, speeches of rulers, etc., dating from the early Chou period (before 700 B.C.).

(2) *Shih ching*, 'The Book of Odes', a collection of early poetry dating from the same period. T'ang scholars interpreted these poems in a highly moralistic way.

(3) *Ch'un-ch'iu*, 'The Spring and Autumn Annals', an early chronicle of the state of Lu covering the period 722–484 B.C., the compilation of which was attributed to Confucius.

All the above were believed to have been edited by Confucius. Much of the *Shu ching* as currently circulating in T'ang times was however spurious.

(4) *Lun yü*, 'The Analects of Confucius', a collection of *logia* attributed to Confucius.

(5) *Meng tzu*, 'Mencius', a philosophical text by a later disciple of Confucius. Although now a canonical work, in T'ang times *Meng-tzu*, although widely quoted, did not have canonical status.

(6) *Li chi*, 'The Record of Rites', a collection of early texts compiled in the early Han period, loosely connected with 'ritual' in the broadest sense.

(7) *Chou li*, 'The Ritual of Chou', a highly idealised account of the institutions of the Chou dynasty, probably compiled during the early Han period as a sort of political Utopia.

There is no version of (7) by Legge. The only European version is E. Biot, *Le Tcheou-Li ou rites des Tcheou* (Paris, 1851). For (2) and (4) there are good modern translations by A. Waley, *The book of songs* (London, 1937) and the *Analects of Confucius* (London, 1938). Legge's version of (6) does not form part of his *Chinese Classics*, but forms part 3 of his *Texts of Confucianism* (*The Li Ki*, Oxford, 1885).

354

B. ORIGINAL SOURCE MATERIAL

The following does not list all sources employed in the preparation of this book, but only those to which constant reference is made, together with the abbreviations employed in the notes and the editions to which page references refer. In almost all cases other editions have been used for collation purposes, and where textual variants are important these are mentioned in notes.

In the case of works not listed below, unless otherwise stated, page references are to the Po-na edition of the standard histories, the Ssu-pu ts'ung-k'an edition for collected works of individual authors, and the Taishō Tripiṭaka for Buddhist works.

Chapter numbers refer to the *chüan* of the original edition. Where these are not numbered but designated *shang, chung, hsia*, etc., they are referred to as A, B, C, etc.

Page references *a, b* refer to *recto* and *verso* of traditionally bound books. In the case of works cited from the Shih-t'ung edition and from the Taishō Tripiṭaka, *a, b, c* refer to the horizontal frames into which the pages are divided.

Standard histories

Chiu T'ang-shu 舊唐書. Po-na edition (*CTS*).

Hsin T'ang-shu 新唐書. Po-na edition (*HTS*).

Tzu-chih t'ung-chien 資治通鑑. Ku-chi ch'u-pan she edition (Peking, 1956) (*TCTC*).

Contemporary legal compilations

Ku T'ang-lü shu-i 故唐律議. Tai-nan-ko ts'ung-shu edition (*Code*).

T'ang liu-tien 唐六典. Edition of Konoe Iehiro (1724), together with Tamai Zehaku's complete collation with the fragmentary Sung print, in his *Shina shakai-keizai-shi kenkyū* (1942) (*TLT*).

Administrative geography

Yüan-ho chün-hsien t'u-chih 元和郡縣圖志. Wan-yu wen-k'u edition (1937) including the *K'ao-cheng* of Chao Chü-chien (*YHCHC*).

Administrative encylopaedias, collections of official documents

(a) T'ang period

T'ung-tien 通典. Shih T'ung edition (Shanghai, 1936) (*TT*).

Po-shih liu-t'ieh shih-lei chi 白氏六帖事類集. Edition of Chang Ch'in-po, facsimile of Sung edition (1933) (*PSLT*).

(*b*) Sung and Yüan periods

T'ang hui-yao 唐會要. Kuo-hsüeh chi-pen ts'ung-shu edition (1935) (*THY*).

Ts'e-fu yüan-kuei 冊府元龜. Edition of Li Ssu-ching (1642) (*TFYK*).

T'ai-p'ing yü-lan 太平御覽. Ssu-pu ts'ung-k'an edition (*TPYL*).

T'ang ta chao-ling chi 唐大詔令集. Shang-wu yin-shu kuan edition (Shanghai, 1959) (*TTCLC*).

Wen-hsien t'ung-k'ao 文獻通考. Shih T'ung edition (Shanghai, 1936) (*WHTK*).

Shan-T'ang chün-shu k'ao-suo 山堂群書考索. Ming edition in Seikado Bunko (*STCSKS*).

Yü-hai 玉海. Edition of 1806.

Literary encyclopaedias, anthologies

Wen-yüan ying-hua 文苑英華. Edition of 1567 with prefaces of T'u Tse-min and Hu Wei-hsin, with Ming MS. in the collection of the University Library, Cambridge (*WYYH*).

T'ai-p'ing kuang chi 太平廣記. Chung-hua shu-chü edition (Peking, 1959) (*TPKC*).

T'ang-wen ts'ui 唐文粹. Wan-yu wen-k'u edition (1937).

Ch'üan T'ang-wen 全唐文. Kuang-ya shu-chü edition (1901) (*CTW*).

Unofficial histories, collections of anecdotes

T'ang yü-lin 唐語林. Chung-kuo wen-hsueh ts'an-k'ao tzu-liao ts'ung-shu edition (Shanghai, 1956–7).

T'ang kuo-shih pu 唐國史補. Chung-kuo wen-hsueh ts'an-k'ao tzu-kiao ts'ung-shu edition (Shanghai, 1956–7).

Ta T'ang hsin-yü 大唐新語. Chung-kuo wen-hsueh ts'an-k'ao tzu-liao ts'ung-shu edition (Shanghai, 1956–7).

Sui-T'ang chia-hua 隋唐嘉話. Chung-kuo wen-hsueh ts'an-k'ao tzu-liao ts'ung-shu edition (Shanghai, 1956–7).

Contemporary Japanese sources

Ryō-no-gige 令義解. Zōtei Kokushi taikei edition (Tokyo, 1953) (*RGG*).

Ryō-no-shūge 令集解. Zōtei Kokushi taikei edition (Tokyo, 1953–4) (*RSG*).

Nittō guhō junrei gyōki 入唐求法巡禮行記. Facsimile of the Tōji MS., Tōyō bunko (Tokyo, 1926) (*Ennin's Diary*).

Tō Daiwajō Tōseiden 唐大和上東征傳. Dai Nihon Bukkyō Zensho, vol. 113 (Tokyo, 1915).

Wamyō ruiju-shō 和名類聚抄. Facsimile of Kariya Ekisai's edition of 1883 (Osaka, 1943–4).

The non-sinologist reader wishing for information about the above-mentioned sources may refer to the bibliographical sections of Robert des Rotours, *Le traité des examens* (Paris, 1932), and *Traité des fonctionnaires et traité de l'armée* (Leiden, 1947).

C. SECONDARY STUDIES

The following selective bibliography attempts neither to be a full bibliography of all that has been written on T'ang finance and related topics, nor to list every article consulted during the preparation of this book. The volume of writing on the T'ang produced during the past four decades has been formidable, and any reader who wishes to go further into this literature may easily consult the following specialised bibliographies.

(1) *Tōdai shi kenkyū bunken ruimoku* 唐代史研究文獻類目. Compiled by Nakatani Hideo (中谷英雄) (Wakayama shi, 1956).

(2) *Tochi-mondai wo chūshin toshita Chūgoku keizaishi kenkyū bunken mokuroku* 土地問題を中心とした中國經濟史研究文獻目錄. Chūgoku tochi seido ōkenkyūkai (Tokyo, 1954).

(3) *Tonkō bunken kenkyū rombun mokuroku* 敦煌文獻研究論文目錄. Tōyō bunko (Tokyo, 1959).

Of these, only the last, which deals only with material on the discoveries at Tun-huang, is at all reliable. Many further items will be found listed in the annual bibliography:

Tōyōshi kenkyū bunken ruimoku 東洋史研究文獻類目. Prepared by the Jimbun kagaku kenkyūjo, Kyōto (before 1946 the Tōhō-bunka Gakuin, Kyōto kenkyūjo).

This covers the years from 1934 onwards, and includes material in Japanese, Chinese and western languages. For periodical articles in Japanese published during the pre-war period there are two volumes in the Harvard–Yenching Sinological Index Series:

Supplement 6. Yü Shih-yü 于式玉: *A bibliography of orientological contributions in thirty-eight Japanese periodicals* (1933) 日本期刊三十八種中東方學論文篇目附引得;

Supplement 13. Yü Shih-yü and Liu Hsüan-min 劉選民: *A bibliography of orientological contributions in one hundred and seventy-five Japanese periodicals* (1940) 一百七十五種日本期刊中東方學論文篇目附引得;

while for Chinese articles published before 1937, there is a very good recent bibliography:

Chung-kuo shih-hsüeh lun-wen so-yin 中國史學論文索引. Compiled by the Chung-kuo k'o-hsüeh-yüan, li-shih yen-chiu so, and Pei-ching Ta-hsüeh, li-shih hsi, 2 vols. (Peking, 1957).

In addition to these, specialist bibliographies are included in the volume *Tonkō Torohan shakai-keizai shiryō*, and in the Japanese translations of Chü Ch'ing-yüan's *T'ang Sung kuan ssu kung-ye* and *T'ang-tai ching-chi shih* (listed below). The last of these is far from dependable.

I have excluded from the list all articles of very inferior quality, studies superseded by more recent work, purely controversial articles dealing with problems irrelevant to my argument, such as feudalism, periodisation, etc., and works on purely textual matters.

There are comparatively few Chinese articles listed. Collections of Chinese periodicals (particularly from the pre-war period) in British libraries are extremely meagre, and when preparing the first draft of this book I feared that I had overlooked many important studies. However, subsequent inspection of the excellent collections in Japanese and American libraries has yielded very little of prime importance. In the case of the many articles produced by the school which flourished in the 1930's under T'ao Hsi-sheng and published in the journal *Shih-huo* 食貨, most of the material was superseded by the three excellent books of Chü Ch'ing-yüan (see below). But on the whole, especially in the legal and administrative connections of finance, with which I am most concerned, there can be no doubt that the Japanese contributions have been far more important.

Both in the notes and in the following list I have avoided the use of abbreviations for periodical titles, with the exception of the following, whose full names are unusually unwieldly.

BSOAS = Bulletin of the School of Oriental and African Studies.
CYYY = Kuo-li chung-yang yen-chiu yüan Li-shih yü-yen yen-chiu so chi-k'an *(Bulletin of the Institute of History and Philology, Academia Sinica).*
MSOS = Mitteilungen des Seminars für Orientalische Sprachen zu Berlin.

ANDŌ, KŌSEI 安藤更生
    Ganjin Daiwajō den no kenkyū 鑒眞大和上傳之研究 (Tokyo, 1960).
AOYAMA, SADAO 青山定雄 (定男)
    'To-Sōjidai no tenunshi to hatsuunshi ni tsuite' 唐宋時代の轉運使と發運使に就いて. *Shigaku zasshi*, 44, IX (1933), pp. 1105–29.
    'Tō-Sō Benga kō' 唐宋汴河考. *Tōhō gakuhō* (Tokyo), 2 (1931), pp. 1–49.
    'Tōdai shinsōin kō' 唐代進奏院考. *Katō Hakase kankreki kinen Tōyōshi Shūsetsu* (1940), pp. 21–46.
    'Tōdai no chisui-suiri kōji ni tsuite' 唐代の治水水利工事について. *Tōhō gakuhō* (Tokyo), 15, I (1944), pp. 1–44; 15, II (1944), pp. 35–70. •
    'Tōdai no tonden to eiden' 唐代の屯田と營田. *Shigaku zasshi*, 63, I (1954), pp. 17–57.

BALÁZS, STEFAN (ÉTIENNE)

'Beiträge zur Wirtschaftsgeschichte der T'ang-Zeit' (abbreviated in the notes as 'Beiträge'). *MSOS*, 34 (1931), pp. 1–92; 35 (1932), pp. 1–73 36 (1933), pp. 1–62.

'Le traité économique du Souei-chou.' *T'oung Pao*, 42, III–IV (1953) pp. 113–329. (Also issued as a separate work.)

CH'EN TENG-YÜAN 陳登原

Chung-kuo t'ien-fu shih 中國田賦史 (Shanghai, 1931).

CH'EN YIN-K'O (YIN-CH'ÜEH) 陳寅恪

Sui-T'ang chih-tu yüan-yüan lüeh-lun kao 隋唐制度淵源略論稿 (Chungking, 1944; reissued Shanghai, 1946; Peking, 1954).

CHÜ CH'ING-YÜAN 鞠清遠

T'ang-tai ching-chi shih (with T'ao Hsi-sheng) 唐代經濟史 (Shanghai, 1936). [Japanese translation by Mutsuhana Kenya 六花謙哉 and Okamoto Goichi 岡本午一 *Tōdai keizaishi* 唐代經濟史 (Tokyo, 1942). Contains a great many important additional notes and references, together with a rather unsatisfactory bibliography.]

T'ang-tai tsai-cheng shih 唐代財政史 (Changsha, 1943). [Japanese translation by Nakajima Satoshi 中島敏, *Tōdai zaiseishi* 唐代財政史 (Tokyo, 1944). No additional notes.]

T'ang Sung kuan ssu kung-ye 唐宋官私工業 (Shanghai, 1934). [Japanese translation by Fukuzawa Sokichi 福澤宗吉, *Tō-Sō kōgyōshi* 唐宋工業史 (Tokyo, 1955). Contains a bibliography and index, and a bibliography of Chü Ch'ing-yüan's writings.]

Liu Yen p'ing-chuan 劉晏評傳 (Shanghai, 1937).

CH'ÜAN HAN-SHENG 全漢昇

T'ang Sung ti-kuo yü yün-ho 唐宋帝國與運河 (Chungking, 1944; Academia Sinica monograph, reissued Shanghai, 1946).

'T'ang Sung shih-tai Yang-chou ching-chi ching-k'uang ti fan-jung yü shuai-lo' 唐宋時代揚州經濟景況的繁榮與衰落. *CYYY*, 11 (1947), pp. 149–76.

'T'ang-tai wu-chia ti pien-tung' 唐代物價的變動. *CYYY*, 11 (1947), pp. 101–48.

GERNET, JACQUES

Les aspects économiques du Bouddhisme dans la société chinoise du ve au xe siècle (Hanoi, 1956).

'La vente en Chine d'après les contrats de Touen-houang.' *T'oung Pao*, 45, IV–V (1957), pp. 295–391.

HAMAGUCHI SHIGEKUNI 濱口重國

'Fuhei-seido yori shinhei-sei e' 府兵制度より新兵制へ. *Shigaku zasshi*, 41, XI (1930), pp. 1255–95; 41, XII (1930), pp. 1430–1507.

'Tō no chizei ni tsuite' 唐 の 地税 に 就 いて. *Tōyō gakuhō*, 20, I (1932), pp. 138–48.

'Tō ni okeru ryōzeihō-izen no yōeki rōdō' 唐 に 於 ける 兩税法以前 の 徭役勞働. *Tōyō gakuhō*, 20, IV (1933), pp. 567–88; 21, I (1933), pp. 66–90.

'Tō no Gensōchō ni okeru Kōwai jōkyō bei to chizei to no kankei' 唐 の 玄宗朝 に 於 ける 江淮上供米 と 地税 と の 關係. *Shigaku ʒasshi*, 45, I (1934), pp. 78–97; 45, II (1934), pp. 221–54.

'Tō ni okeru zatsuyō no kaishi nenrei' 唐 に 於 ける 雜徭 の 開 始 年齡. *Tōyō gakuhō*, 23, I (1935), pp. 65–74.

'Tō ni okeru zatsuyō no gimu nengen' 唐 に 於 ける 雜徭 の 義 務年限. *Rekishigaku kenkyū*, 8, V (1938), pp. 2–13.

HAN KUO-P'AN 韓國磐

'T'ang-tai ti chün-t'ien-chih yü tsu-yung-tiao' 唐代的均田制與租 庸調. *Li-shih yen-chiu*, V (1955), pp. 79–90.

Sui-T'ang ti chün-t'ien chih-tu 隋唐的均田制度 (Shanghai, 1957).

HINO KAISABURŌ 日野開三郎

'Tōdai hanchin no bakko to chinshō' 唐代藩鎮 の 跋扈 と 鎮將. *Tōyō gakuhō*, 26, IV (1939), pp. 503–39; 27, I (1939), pp. 1–62; 27, II (1940), pp. 153–212; 27, III (1940), pp. 311–50.

Shina chūsei no gumbatsu 支那中世 の 軍閥 (Tokyo, 1942).

'Yō En no ryōzeihō ni okeru zeigaku no mondai' 楊炎 の 兩税法 に 於 ける 税額 の 問題. *Tōyō gakuhō*, 38, IV (1956), pp. 370–410.

'Ryōzeihō to bukka' 兩税法 と 物價. *Tōyō shigaku*, 12 (1955), pp. 1–54; 13 (1955), pp. 1–60.

'Hanchin-jidai no shuzei sambunsei ni tsuite' 藩鎮時代 の 州税三 分制 に 就 いて. *Shigaku ʒasshi*, 65, VII (1956), pp. 646–66.

'Hanchin taisei ka ni okeru Tōchō no shinkō to ryōzei jōkyō' 藩鎮体制 下 に 於 ける 唐朝 の 新興 と 兩税上供 *Tōyō gakuhō*, 40, II (1957), pp. 223–61.

'Tōdai ryōzei no bunshūsei' 唐代兩税法 の 分收制. *Tōyō shigaku*, 16 (1956), pp. 37–52; 17 (1957), pp. 1–31.

'Yō En no ryōzeihō jisshi to doko kakuko' 楊炎 の 兩税法實施 と 土 戶客戶. *Takikawa Hakase kanreki kinen rombunshū*, I (Tokyo, 1957), pp. 27–50.

'Gensō-jidai wo chūshin toshite mitaru Tōdai Hokushi kaden chiiki no hachi-kyū-tō ko ni tsuite' 玄宗時代 を 中心 と して 見たる 唐 代北支禾田地域 の 八九等戶 に 就 いて. *Shakai keizai shigaku*, 21, V–VI (1957), pp. 441–68.

'Tōdai katei no yōchō menjo to soyō menjo' 唐代課丁 の 庸調免除 と 租庸免除. *Hōseishi kenkyū*, 8 (1957), pp. 226–36.

'Tempō-izen ni okeru Tō no kokō-tōkei ni tsuite' 天寶以前に於ける唐の戶口統計に就いて. *Shigematsu sensei koki kinen Kyūshū daigaku Tōyōshi ronsō* (Fukuoka, 1957), pp. 229–72.

'Ryōzeihō-izen ni okeru seibyōsen chitōsen ni tsuite no shiken' 兩稅法以前に於ける青苗錢地頭錢に就いての試見. *Tōyō shigaku*, 20 (1958), pp. 1–18; 21 (1959), pp. 1–15.

HO CH'ANG-CHÜN 賀昌群

Han T'ang chien feng-chien ti kuo-yu t'u-ti-chih yü chün-t'ien-chih 漢唐間封建的國有土地制與均田制 (Shanghai, 1958).

HSIANG TA 向達

T'ang-tai Ch'ang-an yü hsi-yü wen-ming 唐代長安與西域文明. *Yenching Journal of Chinese Studies*, Monograph Series 2 (Peking, 1933); reissued, in volume of the same title, containing a number of other studies on related topics (Peking, 1957).

HU JU-LEI 胡如雷

'Lun Wu-Chou she-hui ti-ch'u' 論武周的社會基礎. *Li-shih yen-chiu*, 1 (1955), pp. 85–96.

HUANG WEN-PI 黃文弼

T'u-lu-fan k'ao-ku chi 土魯番考古記 (Peking, 1954).

IKEDA ON 池田溫

'Tonkō hakken Tō Taireki-yonnen shujitsu zankan ni tsuite' 敦煌發見唐大曆四年手實殘卷に就いて. *Tōyō gakuhō*, 40, II (1957), pp. 151–93; 40, III (1957), pp. 262–85.

ISHIDA MIKINOSUKE 石田幹之助

'Tempō-jūsai no teiseki ni miyuru Tonkō chihō no seiiki jūmin ni tsuite' 天寶十載の丁籍に貝ゆる敦煌地方の西域住民に就いて. *Katō Hakase Kanreki-kinen Tōyōshi shūsetsu* (Tokyo, 1941), pp. 83–91.

KANEI YUKITADA 金井之忠

'Tōdai no senka mondai' 唐代の錢貨問題. *Bunka*, 4, III (1937), pp. 39–59.

'Tō no empō' 唐の鹽法. *Bunka*, 5, V (1938), pp. 491–529.

'Tō no chahō' 唐の茶法. *Bunka*, 5, VIII (1938), pp. 35–53.

KATŌ SHIGESHI (SHIGERU) 加藤繁

Tō-Sō-jidai ni okeru kingin no kenkyū 唐宋時代に於ける金銀の研究. 2 vols. (Tokyo, 1924).

Ku Tōjo shokkashi, Ku Godaishi shokkashi 舊唐書食貨志：舊五代史食貨志. Iwanami Zensho (Tokyo, 1948).

Shina keizai shi kōshō 支那經濟史考證. 2 vols. (vol. I, Tokyo, 1952; vol. II, Tokyo, 1954). [All articles by the author are cited from this collection of reprints, which often contain additions and corrections.]

'On the "Hang" or association of merchants in China, with special reference to the institution in the T'ang and Sung periods.' *Memoirs of the Research Department of the Tōyō Bunko*, 9 (1936), pp. 45–83.

KOGA NOBORU 古賀登
'Tōdai ryōzeihō no chiiki sei' 唐代兩税法の地域性. *Tōhōgaku*, 17 (1958), pp. 63–81.
'Tōdai kinden-seido no chiiki sei' 唐代均田制度の地域性. *Shikan*, 46 (1956), pp. 42–54.

KUWABARA JITSUZŌ 桑原騭藏
'Zui-Tō-jidai ni Shina ni raijū shita seiikijin ni tsuite' 隋唐時代に支那に來住した西域人に就いて. *Naitō Hakase kanreki shukuga Shinagaku ronsō* (Tokyo, 1926), pp. 565–660.
'Tō-Sō-jidai no dōsen' 唐宋時代の銅錢. *Rekishi to chiri*, 13, I (1924), pp. 1–8.
'On P'u Shou-keng.' *Memoirs of the Research Department of the Tōyō Bunko*, 2 (1928), pp. 1–79; 7 (1935), pp. 1–104. [See also Chinese translation of this, with additional notes by Ch'en Yü-ching 陳裕菁, *P'u Shou-keng k'ao* 蒲壽庚考 (Peking, 1954).]

LIU, JAMES T. C.
Reform in Sung China (Cambridge, Mass., 1959).

MASPERO, HENRI
Les documents chinois de la troisième expédition de Sir Aurel Stein en Asie Centrale (London, 1953).
Mélanges postumes sur les religions et l'histoire de la Chine. 3 vols. (Paris, 1950).
'Les régimes fonciers en Chine, des origines aux temps modernes.' *Recueil de la Société Jean Bodin*, tome II (Brussels, 1937), pp. 265–314. Reprinted in the foregoing, vol. 3, pp. 149–92.

MATSUMOTO YOSHIMI 松本善海
'Rimpo-soshiki wo chūshin toshitaru Tōdai no sonsei' 鄉保組織を中心としたる唐代の村政. *Shigaku zasshi*, 53, III (1942), pp. 323–71.

MATSUNAGA MASAO 松永雅生
'Tōdai saeki kō' 唐代差役考. *Tōyō shigaku*, 15 (1956), pp. 17–41.
'Ryōzeihō-izen ni okeru Tōdai no saka' 兩税法以前に於ける唐代の差科. Pt. I: *Shigematsu sensei koki kinen Kyūshū Daigaku Tōyō-shi ronsō* (Fukuoka, 1957), pp. 295–315; pt. II: *Tōyō Shigaku*, 18 (1957), pp. 1–41.
'Kindensei ka ni okeru Tōdai kotō no igi' 均田制下に於ける唐代戸等の意義. *Tōyō shigaku*, 12 (1956), pp. 81–112.
'Tōdai no "ka" ni tsuite' 唐代の課について. *Shien* (Kyūshū), 55 (1953), pp. 71–96.

MICHIHATA YOSHIHIDE 道端良秀

Tōdai Bukkyōshi no kenkyū 唐代佛教史の研究 (Kyōto, 1957).

MIYAZAKI ICHISADA 宮崎市定

Godai Sōsho no tsūka mondai 五代宋初の通貨問題 (Kyōto, 1943).

'Tōdai fueki-seido shinkō' 唐代賦役制度新考. *Tōyōshi kenkyū*, 14, IV (1955), pp. 1–24.

MORIYA MITSUO 守屋美都雄

Rikuchō mombatsu no ichi kōsatsu 六朝門閥の一考察 (Tokyo, 1951).

NABA TOSHISADA 那波利貞

'Seishi ni kisai saretaru Dai Tō Tempō-jidai no kosū to kōsū to no kankei ni tsukite' 正史に記載せられたる大唐天寶時代の戸數と口數との關係に就きて. *Rekishi to chiri*, 33, I (1934), pp. 47–82; 33, II (1934), pp. 10–40; 33, III (1934), pp. 16–50; 33, IV (1934), pp. 25–57.

'Ryōko kō' 梁戸攷. *Shina Bukkyō shigaku*, 2, I (1938), pp. 1–40; 2, II (1938), pp. 27–68; 2, IV (1938), pp. 30–82.

'Tōdai no nōden-suiri ni kansuru kitei ni tsukite' 唐代の農田水利に關する規定に就きて. *Shigaku zasshi*, 54, I (1943), pp. 18–56; 54, II (1943), pp. 48–80; 54, III (1943), pp. 43–84.

'Tōdai rimpo-seido shakugi' 唐代鄰保制度釋疑. *Haneda Hakase shōju ronsō* (Tokyo, 1950), pp. 711–78.

NIIDA NOBORU 仁井田陞

Tōryō shūi 唐令拾遺 (Tokyo, 1933).

Tō-Sō hōritsu monjo no kenkyū 唐宋法律文書の研究 (Tokyo, 1937).

Shina mibunhō shi 支那身分法史 (Tokyo, 1942).

'Tonkō hakken Tō Suibushiki no kenkyū' 敦煌發見唐水部式の研究. *Hattori sensei koki shukuga kinen rombun-shū* (Tokyo, 1936), pp. 761–88.

'Tō-Sō-jidai no kazoku kyōsan to yuigon hō' 唐宋時代の家族共產と遺言法. *Ichimura Hakase koki kinen Tōyōshi ronsō* (Tokyo, 1933), pp. 885–929.

'Torohan hakken Tōdai no yōchōfu to sofu ni tsuite' 吐魯番發見唐代の庸調布と租布に就いて. *Tōhō gakuhō* (Tokyo), 11, I (1939), pp. 243–59.

'Tōdai no hōshaku oyobi shokuhō-sei' 唐代の封爵及び食封制. *Tōhō gakuhō* (Tokyo), 10, I (1939), pp. 1–64.

'Tōdai rimpo seido' 唐代鄰保制度. *Rekishigaku kenkyū*, 6, X (1936), pp. 81–92.

'Tō no ritsuryō oyobi kaku no shin shiryō: Stein Tonkō bunken' 唐の律令及び格の新資料—スタイン敦煌文獻. *Tōyō-bunka kenkyūjo kiyō*, 13 (1957), pp. 109–48.

'Tō Gumbōryō to hōsui-seido' 唐軍防令と燧燧制度. *Hōseishi kenkyū*, 4 (1953), pp. 197–213.

'Tōmatsu Godai no Tonkō jiin-denko kankei monjo' 唐末五代の敦煌寺院佃戸關係文書. *Tonkō Torohan shakai-keizai shiryō*, I (Kyōto, 1959), pp. 69–90.

NISHIJIMA SADAO 西島定生

'Torohan shutsudo monjo yori mitaru kindensei no sekō jōtai' 吐魯番出土文書より見たる均田制の施行狀態. *Tonkō Torohan shakai-keizai shiryō*, I (Kyōto, 1959), pp. 151–292; *Tonkō Torohan shakai-keizai shiryō*, II (Kyōto, 1960), pp. 469–80.

'Tengai no kanata' 碾磴-の彼方. *Rekishigaku kenkyū*, 125 (1947), pp. 38–46.

NISHIKAWA MASAO 西川正夫

'Tonkō hakken no Tōdai koseki-zankan ni arawareta "jiden" ni tsuite' 敦煌發見の唐代戸籍殘簡に現れた自田について. *Shigaku zasshi*, 64, X (1955), pp. 38–60.

NISHIMURA GENYU 西村元佑

'Tōdai Torohan ni okeru kindensei no igi' 唐代吐魯番における均田制の意義. *Tonkō Torohan shakai-keizai shiryō*, I (Kyōto, 1959), pp. 293–366.

'Tōdai Tonkō sa-ka-bo no kenkyū' 唐代敦煌差科簿の研究. *Tonkō Torohan shakai-keizai shiryō*, II (Kyōto, 1960), pp. 377–464.

OGASAWARA SENSHU 小笠原宣秀

'Torohan shutsudo keizai-monjo no tokushoku' 吐魯番出土唐代經濟文書の特色. *Ryūkoku Daigaku ronshū*, 349 (1955), pp. 1–15.

OKAZAKI FUMIO 岡崎文夫

'Ubun Yū no kakko-seisaku ni tsuite' 宇文融の括戸政策に就いて. *Shinagaku*, 2, V (1939), pp. 42–51.

OKUTAIRA MASAHIRO 奥平昌洪

Tōa senshi 東亞錢志 (Tokyo, 1938).

ONO KATSUTOSHI 小野勝年

'Tōdai ni okeru ichi kinrei no kaishaku ni tsuite' 唐代に於ける一禁令の解釋に就いて. *Shirin*, 22, I (1937), pp. 87–110.

OSAKI SHŌJI 大崎正次

'Tōdai kyōkan shikiden kō' 唐代京官職田攷. *Shichō*, 12, III–IV (1943), pp. 121–38.

PULLEYBLANK, EDWIN G.

The background of the rebellion of An Lu-shan (London, 1955).

'The origins and nature of chattel slavery in China', *Journal of Economic and Social History of the Orient*, I, II (1958), pp. 185–220.

REISCHAUER, EDWIN O.
  Ennin's Diary (New York, 1955).
  Ennin's travels in T'ang China (New York, 1955).
DES ROTOURS, ROBERT
  'Les grands fonctionnaires des provinces en Chine sous la dynastie des
    T'ang.' *T'oung Pao*, 25 (1927), pp. 1–114.
  Traité des fonctionnaires et traité de l'armée. 2 vols. (Leiden, 1947). (Biblio-
    thèque de l'Institut des hautes études chinoises, vol. VI.)
  'Les insignes en deux parties (fou) sous la dynastie des T'ang.' *T'oung
    Pao*, 41, I–III (1952), pp. 1–148.
SAIIKI BUNKA KENKYŪ KAI 西域文化研究會
  Tonkō Torohan shakai-keizai shiryō 敦煌吐魯番社會經濟資料
    (vol. 1, Kyōto, 1959; vol. 2, Kyōto, 1960). [Forming vols. 2 and 3 of
    Saiiki bunka kenkyū, English title *Monumenta Serindica*.]
SHIH SHENG-HAN 石聲漢
  A preliminary survey of the work 'Ch'i-min yao-shu' (Peking, 1958).
SOGABE SHIZUO 曾我部靜雄
  Kinden-hō to sono zeieki-seido 均田法とその稅役制度 (Tokyo,
    1953).
  'Sono go no kaeki no kaishaku mondai' その後の課役の解釋問題.
    Shirin, 38 (1955), pp. 288–303.
  'Hoku-Gi Tō-Gi Hoku-Sei Zui jidai no kakō to fukakō' 北魏東魏北
    齊隋時代の課口と不課口. *Tōhōgaku*, 11 (1955), pp. 59–70.
  'Tō no kozei to chitōsen to seibyōsen no honshitsu' 唐の戶稅と地
    頭錢と青苗錢の本質. *Bunka*, 19 (1955), pp. 91–102.
SOLOMON, BERNARD
  The veritable record of the T'ang emperor Shun-tsung (Cambridge, Mass.,
    1956).
SUDŌ YOSHIYUKI 周藤吉之
  'Godai no setsudoshi no shihai taisei' 五代の節度使の支配体制.
    Shigaku zasshi, 61, IV (1952), pp. 1–41; 61, VI (1952), pp. 20–38.
  Chūgoku tochi-seido shi kenkyū 中國土地制度史研究 (Tokyo, 1955).
  'Tōmatsu Godai no shōen-sei' 唐末五代の莊園制. *Tōyō bunka*, 12
    (1953), pp. 1–41. Reprinted in the foregoing, pp. 8–64.
  'Dennin monjo no kenkyū' 佃人文書の研究. *Tonkō Torohan
    shakai-keizai shiryō*, I (Kyōto, 1959), pp. 91–150.
  'Tōdai chūki ni okeru kozei no kenkyū' 唐代中期における戶稅
    の研究. *Tonkō Torohan shakai-keizai shiryō*, II (Kyōto, 1960),
    pp. 227–41.
SUZUKI SHUN 鈴木俊
  'Tōdai teichū-sei no kenkyū' 唐代丁中制の研究. *Shigaku zasshi*,
    46, XI (1935), pp. 82–106.

'Tonkō hakken Tōdai koseki to kinden-hō' 敦煌發見唐代戶籍と
均田法. *Shigaku ʒasshi*, 47, VII (1936), pp. 1–61.

'Tō no kozei to seibyōsen to no kankei ni tsuite' 唐の戶稅と青苗
錢との關係に就いて. *Ikeuchi Hakase kanreki kinen Tōyōshi
ronsō* (Tokyo, 1940), pp. 375–96.

'Tō no kazei, shuzei ni tsuite' 唐の夏稅秋稅について. *Katō
Hakase kanreki kinen Tōyōshi shūsetsu* (Tokyo, 1941), pp. 435–45.

'Ubun Yū no kakko ni tsuite' 宇文融の括戶について. *Wada
Hakase kanreki kinen Tōyōshi ronsō* (Tokyo, 1951), pp. 329–44.

'Tōdai kindenhō sekō no igi ni tsuite' 唐代均田法施行の意義
について. *Shien* (Kyūshū), 50 (1951), pp. 117–26.

'Koseki sakusei no nenji to Tōryō' 戶籍作成の年次と唐令.
Chūō Daigaku bungakubu kiyō, 9 (1957), pp. 81–9.

TAKIGAWA MASAJIRŌ 瀧川政次郎
Shina hōseishi kenkyū 支那法制史研究 (Tokyo, 1940).

TAMAI ZEHAKU 玉井是博
Shina shakai-keizai shi kenkyū 支那社會經濟史研究 (Tokyo, 1942).
[All articles by the author are cited from this volume which reprints
his complete writings, many of which were first published in journals
published in Korea which are not generally available.]

T'AO HSI-SHENG 陶希聖
See under Chü Ch'ing-yüan, above.

TENG KUANG-MING 鄧廣銘
'T'ang-tai tsu-yung-tiao-fa yen-chiu' 唐代租庸調法研究. *Li-shih
yen-chiu*, IV (1954), pp. 65–86.

TING FU-PAO 丁福保
Ku-ch'ien ta-tʒu-tien 古錢大辭典 (Shanghai, 1938).

TOYAMA GUNJI 外山軍治
'Sōun ni kansuru shokenkyū' 漕運に關する諸研究. *Tōyōshi
kenkyū*, 3, II (1937), pp. 54–67.

'Tōdai no Sōun' 唐代の漕運. *Shirin*, 22 (1937), pp. 264–304.

TS'EN CHUNG-MIEN 岑仲勉
'Tsu-yung-tiao yü chün-t'ien yu wu kuan-hsi?' 租庸調與均田有無
關係. *Li-shih yen-chiu*, V (1955), pp. 65–78.

Fu-ping chih-tu yen-chiu 府兵制度研究 (Peking, 1957).

Sui-T'ang shih 隋唐史 (Peking, 1957).

Huang-ho pien-ch'ien shih 黃河變遷史 (Peking, 1957).

TWITCHETT, DENIS
'The salt commissioners after the rebellion of An Lu-shan.' *Asia Major*,
(n.s.) 4, I (1954), pp. 60–89.

'Monastic estates in T'ang China.' *Asia Major*, (n.s.) 5, II (1956), pp. 123–
146.

'The government of T'ang in the early eighth century.' *BSOAS*, 18, II (1956), pp. 322–30.

'The monasteries and China's economy in medieval times.' *BSOAS*, 19, III (1957), pp. 526–49.

'The fragment of the T'ang Ordinances of the Department of Waterways discovered at Tun-huang.' *Asia Major* (n.s.) 6, 1 (1957), pp. 23–79.

'Lands under state cultivation during the T'ang dynasty.' *Journal of Economic and Social History of the Orient*, 2, II (1959), pp. 162–203, and 2, III (1959), pp. 335–6.

'Some remarks on irrigation under the T'ang', *T'oung pao*, 48, 1–3 (1961), pp. 175–94.

WADA SEI 和田清 (ed.)

Shina chihō-jichi hattatsu shi 支那地方自治發達史 (Tokyo, 1939).

WALEY, ARTHUR

The life and times of Po Chü-i (London, 1949).

The real Tripiṭaka (London, 1952).

WANG YI-T'ONG

'Slaves and other comparable social groups during the northern dynasties.' *Harvard Journal of Asiatic Studies*, 16, III–IV (1953), pp. 293–364.

WANG YUNG-HSING 王永興

'Tun-huang T'ang-tai ch'ai-k'o-pu k'ao-shih' 敦煌唐代差科簿考釋. *Li-shih yen-chiu*, 1957, XII, pp. 71–100.

YAMAMOTO TATSURŌ 山本達郎

'Tonkō hakken keichō-yō monjo zankan' 敦煌發見計帳樣文書殘簡. *Tōyō gakuhō*, 37, II (1954), pp. 1–60; 37, III (1954), pp. 83–98.

'Tonkō hakken kosei densei kankei monjo jūgo shu' 敦煌發見戶制田制關係文書十五種. *Tōyōbunka kenkyūjo kiyō*, 10 (1956), pp. 179–228, plates I–V.

YANG LIEN-SHENG 楊聯陞

Money and credit in China (Cambridge, Mass., 1952).

'Numbers and units in Chinese economic history.' *Harvard Journal of Asiatic Studies*, 12 (1949), pp. 216–25.

'Buddhist monasteries and four money-raising institutions in Chinese history.' *Harvard Journal of Asiatic Studies*, 13 (1950), pp. 174–91.

'Notes on the economic history of the Chin dynasty.' *Harvard Journal of Asiatic Studies*, 9 (1946), pp. 107–85.

'Chung-T'ang i-hou shui-chih yü nan-ch'ao shui-chih chih kuanhsi' 中唐以後稅制與南朝稅制之關係. *Ching-hua hsüeh-pao*, 12, III (1937), pp. 613–18.

YEN KENG-WANG 嚴耕望

T'ang p'u-shang-ch'eng-lang piao 唐僕尚丞郎表. 4 vols. (T'ai-pei, 1956). (Academia Sinica Monograph no. 36.)

GLOSSARY-INDEX

377

SUBJECT-INDEX